DECODING GENESIS 1-11

Decoding Genesis 1-11

Paul Nadim Tarazi

OCABS PRESS
ST PAUL, MINNESOTA 55124
2020

For the members of OCABS

who work tirelessly to hear the scriptural text
and
teach others to do so

DECODING GENESIS 1-11

ISBN 1-60191-052-5

PRINTED IN THE UNITED STATES OF AMERICA

Other Books by the Author

I Thessalonians: A Commentary

Galatians: A Commentary

The Old Testament: An Introduction

Volume 1: Historical Traditions, revised edition

Volume 2: Prophetic Traditions

Volume 3: Psalms and Wisdom

The New Testament: An Introduction

Volume 1: Paul and Mark

Volume 2: Luke and Acts

Volume 3: Johannine Writings

Volume 4: Matthew and the Canon

The Chrysostom Bible

Genesis: A Commentary

Philippians: A Commentary

Romans: A Commentary

Colossians & Philemon: A Commentary

1 Corinthians: A Commentary

Ezekiel: A Commentary

Joshua: A Commentary

2 Corinthians: A Commentary

Isaiah: A Commentary

Jeremiah: A Commentary

Hebrews: A Commentary

The Pastorals: A Commentary

Ephesians & 2 Thessalonians: A Commentary

Land and Covenant

The Rise of Scripture

Decoding Genesis 1-11

ISBN 1-60191-052-5

Published by OCABS Press, St. Paul, Minnesota.
Printed in the United States of America.

Books are available through OCABS Press at special discounts for bulk purchases in the United States by academic institutions, churches, and other organizations. For more information please email OCABS Press at press@ocabs.org.

Abbreviations

Books by the Author

1 Thess	*I Thessalonians: A Commentary*, Crestwood, NY: St. Vladimir's Seminary Press, 1982
Gal	*Galatians: A Commentary*, Crestwood, NY: St. Vladimir's Seminary Press, 1994
OTI_1	*The Old Testament: An Introduction, Volume 1: Historical Traditions,* revised edition, Crestwood, NY: St. Vladimir's Seminary Press, 2003
OTI_2	*The Old Testament: An Introduction, Volume 2: Prophetic Traditions,* Crestwood, NY: St. Vladimir's Seminary Press, 1994
OTI_3	*The Old Testament: An Introduction, Volume 3: Psalms and Wisdom,* Crestwood, NY: St. Vladimir's Seminary Press, 1996
NTI_1	*The New Testament: An Introduction, Volume 1: Paul and Mark,* Crestwood, NY: St. Vladimir's Seminary Press, 1999
NTI_2	*The New Testament: An Introduction, Volume 2: Luke and Acts,* Crestwood, NY: St. Vladimir's Seminary Press, 2001
NTI_3	*The New Testament: An Introduction, Volume 3: Johannine Writings,* Crestwood, NY: St. Vladimir's Seminary Press, 2004
NTI_4	*The New Testament: An Introduction, Volume 4: Matthew and the Canon,* St. Paul, MN: OCABS Press, 2009
LAC	*Land and Covenant,* St. Paul, MN: OCABS Press, 2009
C-Gen	*Genesis: A Commentary.* The Chrysostom Bible. St. Paul, MN: OCABS Press, 2009

C-Phil *Philippians: A Commentary*. The Chrysostom Bible. St. Paul, MN: OCABS Press, 2009

C-Rom *Romans: A Commentary*. The Chrysostom Bible. St. Paul, MN: OCABS Press, 2010

C-Col *Colossians & Philemon: A Commentary*. The Chrysostom Bible. St. Paul, MN: OCABS Press, 2010

C-1Cor *1 Corinthians: A Commentary*. The Chrysostom Bible. St. Paul, MN: OCABS Press, 2011

C-Ezek *Ezekiel: A Commentary*. The Chrysostom Bible. St. Paul, MN: OCABS Press, 2012

C-Josh *Joshua: A Commentary*. The Chrysostom Bible. St. Paul, MN: OCABS Press, 2013

C-2Cor *2 Corinthians: A Commentary*. The Chrysostom Bible. St. Paul, MN: OCABS Press, 2013

C-Is *Isaiah: A Commentary*. The Chrysostom Bible. St. Paul, MN: OCABS Press, 2013

C-Jer *Jeremiah: A Commentary*. The Chrysostom Bible. St. Paul, MN: OCABS Press, 2013

C-Heb *Hebrews: A Commentary*. The Chrysostom Bible. St. Paul, MN: OCABS Press, 2014

C-Pas *The Pastorals: A Commentary*. The Chrysostom Bible. St. Paul, MN: OCABS Press, 2016

ROS *The Rise of Scripture*, St. Paul, MN: OCABS Press, 2017

C-Eph *Ephesians & 2 Thessalonians: A Commentary*. The Chrysostom Bible. St. Paul, MN: OCABS Press, 2019

Abbreviations

*Books of the Old Testament**

Gen	Genesis	Job	Job	Hab	Habakkuk
Ex	Exodus	Ps	Psalms	Zeph	Zephaniah
Lev	Leviticus	Prov	Proverbs	Hag	Haggai
Num	Numbers	Eccl	Ecclesiastes	Zech	Zechariah
Deut	Deuteronomy	Song	Song of Solomon	Mal	Malachi
Josh	Joshua	Is	Isaiah	Tob	Tobit
Judg	Judges	Jer	Jeremiah	Jdt	Judith
Ruth	Ruth	Lam	Lamentations	Wis	Wisdom
1 Sam	1 Samuel	Ezek	Ezekiel	Sir	Sirach
2 Sam	2 Samuel	Dan	Daniel	Eccl	Ecclesiasticus
1 Kg	1 Kings	Hos	Hosea	Bar	Baruch
2 Kg	2 Kings	Joel	Joel	1 Esd	1 Esdras
1 Chr	1 Chronicles	Am	Amos	2 Esd	2 Esdras
2 Chr	2 Chronicles	Ob	Obadiah	1 Macc	1 Maccabees
Ezra	Ezra	Jon	Jonah	2 Macc	2 Maccabees
Neh	Nehemiah	Mic	Micah	3 Macc	3 Maccabees
Esth	Esther	Nah	Nahum	4 Macc	4 Maccabees

Books of the New Testament

Mt	Matthew	Eph	Ephesians	Heb	Hebrews
Mk	Mark	Phil	Philippians	Jas	James
Lk	Luke	Col	Colossians	1 Pet	1 Peter
Jn	John	1 Thess	1 Thessalonians	2 Pet	2 Peter
Acts	Acts	2 Thess	2 Thessalonians	1 Jn	1 John
Rom	Romans	1 Tim	1 Timothy	2 Jn	2 John
1 Cor	1 Corinthians	2 Tim	2 Timothy	3 Jn	3 John
2 Cor	2 Corinthians	Titus	Titus	Jude	Jude
Gal	Galatians	Philem	Philemon	Rev	Revelation

**Following the larger canon known as the Septuagint.*

Contents

Foreword

When Christians first undertake to read the Bible, they generally have to come to understand the Old and New Testaments not as a single book, or even two, but as libraries. The name Bible, in fact, is *tà biblía*, "the books," plural. Thus, David's reign is presented in 1 and 2 Samuel, and again in 1 and 2 Chronicles. Jesus preaches, dies, and rises in Matthew and "again" in John. Genres, too, must be read differently: the symbolism of the metaphors in Psalms cannot be read literally like the prose narratives of Ezra or Nehemiah.

On the other hand, Christians receive the Scriptures as a whole, as a "canon." In Luke 24, when the risen Jesus meets disciples on the road to Emmaus, "Beginning with Moses and all the Prophets, he explained to them what was said in all the Scriptures concerning himself.... He said to them, 'This is what I told you while I was still with you: Everything must be fulfilled that is written about me in the Law of Moses, the Prophets and the Psalms.'" This suggests one, continuous whole.

For the past two centuries, these two reading requirements have sometimes been set at odds. One could argue that biblical scholarship has contributed to the discord by its own proper insistence on reading texts for their plain sense, in their historical and generic contexts. Scholarship amplified the discourse by further dividing what had hitherto been seen as single texts. So, not one book of Isaiah, but three; not one creation account, but two.

Now, on the one hand, such subdivision often clarified texts that were nearly impossible to read as units: Exodus 24 makes little sense unless it is seen as a cut-and-pasting of multiple versions. And on the other hand, biblical scholarship joined as much as it divided: instead of Ezra and Nehemiah, scholars studied Ezra-Nehemiah; instead of Joshua, Judges, Samuel, and Kings, scholars spoke of the Deuteronomistic History.

Nevertheless, the problem remains: how to read a library as a single canon.

A burgeoning trend in biblical scholarship, however, has begun to turn attention back to the unity of Scripture. This volume by Fr. Paul Nadim Tarazi is a tour de force in just that way of reading. Tarazi elucidates how all of the Old Testament is encoded in Genesis 1 (or, properly, Gen 1:1-2:4). The vocabulary of nouns and verbs, idiomatic phrases, and themes of the so-called first creation account inform the entire Old Testament—Leviticus, Isaiah, Ezekiel, Jonah, the Psalms. At the same time, the rest of the Old Testament informs the correct understanding of Genesis 1, which "cannot be fully grasped by hearers until they have listened to the entire Scriptures."

Tarazi does not weigh this study down with references to secondary scholarship, but it is important to point out that scholars are increasingly aware of precisely the kind of canon-wide continuity that he notes. In the pages that follow, Tarazi actually presents both Genesis 1 and 2 as the touchstone for the rest of Scripture. Thus, it is not only the *reshit* "beginning," *bara* "to create," *hibdil* "to divide," and *śadeh* "field" of Genesis 1 that will appear again and again through the Old Testament, but also the *'aphar*, the "wet clod" from which man is made in Genesis 2, resurfacing in the name of Ephron the Hittite of Genesis 23, and from there to the Hittites of Joshua, Judges, and Kings. This is not a novel nostrum: scholars like Joseph Blenkinsopp have noted (really following on what is said in the apocryphal books of 2 Baruch 4:1-6 and Jubilees 4:26; 8:19) that a) Genesis 1-3 must be read as a unit—e.g., God does not name in chapter 1 what man will name in chapter 2, "God saw that it was good" is countered by the improper "Eve saw it was good [for food]"; and b) that Genesis 1-3 tells the story of Joshua-2 Kings. Adam is placed in a Promised Land and exiled to the

East for sin, a sin dependent on women's complicity (1 Kgs 11:1-8), sacred trees (2 Kgs 18:4), and serpents (2 Kgs 18:4).[1]

The grand, unified narrative that Tarazi sees running through the remainder of the so-called Primary History, through the end of 2 Kings, has become known in scholarly jargon as the Enneateuch ("nine books"). David Noel Freedman discussed this grand narrative, showing how each of the Ten Commandments was broken, in order, one commandment per book, from Sinai to the Exile.[2]

For Tarazi, this masterpiece is the work of the "Ezekiel School," an Ezekiel figure he calls the "Father of Scripture," who is associated with a 6th-century prophet but is really a 4th-century anti-Hellenistic propagandist, trying to undercut the philosophy-ridden master narratives of the Greek overlords and their Jewish collaborators. Freedman argued the same thing for the Primary History: an indispensable role for a Judean prophet of the Babylonian Exile who was both Ezekiel and the so-called Priestly Writer, and a conscious design of countering Hellenistic literature, specifically Herodotus.[3]

Blenkinsopp and Freedman were not, however, looking also into the Prophets and Psalms, as Tarazi is. Tarazi will speak of an "intentional link between Genesis 10 and Isaiah…the author is looking ahead to Isaiah." Tarazi does not explore in detail what was written first, what was written at the same time, or the specifics of these links, but many scholars are beginning to take note of what Randall Heskett calls, following his teacher Gerald Sheppard, "canon-conscious editing." In this concept, Heskett moves beyond Sheppard's teacher Brevard Childs, the founder of so-called Canonical Criticism, who would have argued of

---

1 Joseph Blenkinsopp, *Treasures Old and New: Essays in the Theology of the Pentateuch* (Grand Rapids, MI: William B. Eerdmans, 2004), 109.

2 David Noel Freedman, *The Nine Commandments: Uncovering a Hidden Pattern of Crime and Punishment in the Hebrew Bible* (New York: Doubleday, 2000).

3 Freedman, *Nine Commandments*; Sara Mandell and David Noel Freedman, *The Relationship between Herodotus' History and Primary History*, South Florida Studies in the History of Judaism 60 (Atlanta: Scholars Press, 1993).

Isaiah, for example, that we must read Isaiah 7 in the light of the entire book, including chapters 60-61, simply because we have a canonical book of Isaiah that has come down to us. Rather, Heskett shows that canon-conscious editing has taken place in the construction of the book of Isaiah itself, so that Isaiah 9 is already in its written form responding to Isaiah 60-61—Isaiah 11 responding to Isaiah 40 and 65—and understands itself as a part of an emerging Hebrew Bible.[4]

By no means does Tarazi simply build on these scholars. Tarazi's scholarship is entirely original, building instead on a life's work most recently coalesced in his 2017 *Rise of Scripture.* And while he opens this present volume speaking of the relationship of Genesis 1-2 to the rest of the Old Testament, the New Testament is here, as well. Matthew plays the same role for the New Testament that Genesis 1-2 plays for the Old, and the links that stretch from Genesis to Jonah lead directly to Matthew, as you will see.

It is important to note, however, that all this discussion of *reading* misses the point entirely if we ignore Tarazi's insistence that the Scriptures were and are to be *heard.* He speaks repeatedly of "hearers": "One is to hear Scripture in sequence," not "read Scripture." As I have argued elsewhere, even ancient Israelite audiences who knew how to read still preferred and even expected to experience their literature orally.[5] The Bible is *Miqra*, that which is read aloud (Neh 8:8), even when it is *Katub*, written (Ezra 3:4; Neh 8:15). Tarazi elsewhere speaks of "A scroll that is to be read aloud to the hearers, whomever they might be [so that] the hearers are 'sucked into' the story."[6] Something happens when the Scriptures are read aloud, which for most Christians means in the liturgy. Tarazi is well aware, as readers will be after this present volume, that English translations can be abysmal, that they can so lose the plays on

4 Randall Heskett, *Messianism within the Scriptural Scrolls of Isaiah*, Library of the Hebrew Bible/Old Testament Studies 456 (London: T & T Clark, 2007), 83, 94, 98-131.
5 Robert D. Miller II, *Oral Tradition in Ancient Israel*, Biblical Performance Criticism 4 (Eugene, OR: Cascade Books, 2011).
6 Paul Nadim Tarazi, *The Rise of Scripture* (St. Paul: OCABS Press, 2017), 455.

consonantal roots and on sound that their listeners are not hearing Scripture at all. Barring every Christian learning to read Hebrew, the thoroughgoing commentary of this present volume will have to supply what the translations have taken from us.

There is a great deal more in this volume that cannot and should not be summarized in advance. Tarazi has no patience for "theology," for instance, when it is the arrogant mental machinations of human prelates undertaken without regard for the Bible. In this, he is an authentic son of his (only?) favorite Church Father, John Chrysostom, who was the likely originator of a quote later ascribed to several others: "The floor of hell is paved with the skulls of bishops." This volume, on the other hand, is paved with amazing insights and challenging questions.

Robert D. Miller II, OFS
The Catholic University of America
Washington, DC
October, 2020

1

Hearing the Original

In my book *The Rise of Scripture*, and thereafter in my "Tarazi Tuesdays" podcast series, I contend that Genesis 1-4 reflects the entire scriptural message in a nutshell, and that Genesis 1-11 is the "expanded" compact version of the entire scripture. The rest of scripture, i.e., the extended story of the descendants of Abram the Hebrew, functions merely as a "coin flipping" example of one of the totality of nations already covered in Genesis 10. The authors' intent is to show that scriptural Israel is not so much a special nation per se. It is singled out as an example to show that any nation would have behaved similarly, that is, not abiding by God's will for it. This can be determined by the authors' blatant omission of referencing Abram's story as a *toledot* (as was done with Adam, Noah, and his three sons). Terah, Abram's father, is the concluder of the *toledot* of Shem, one of Noah's sons. Abram's story is a sad (*teraḥ*) episode in the story of the nations—the interest of which is the avowedly sole purview of scripture: "Now these are the descendants (*toledot*) of Terah (*teraḥ*). Terah was the father of Abram, Nahor, and Haran; and Haran was the father of Lot." (Gen 11:27). The omission of the story of Abram as his *toledot* will be shown to be even more blatant when we hear of the successive *toledot* of Isaac and of Jacob and even of Ishmael and Esau. In other words, Abram's progeny is a stand-in for any and all nations mentioned in Genesis 10 as is implied in the promise of blessing of Genesis 12:2 that harks back to Genesis 9-10:

> And I will make of you a great nation (*goy*),[1] and I will bless[2] you, and make your name (*šem*)[3] great, so that you will be a blessing. I will bless those who bless you, and him who curses you I will

---

1 See Genesis 10:5 (twice), 20, 31, 32.
2 See Genesis 1:28; 5:2; 9:1.
3 See Genesis 9:26.

curse; and by you all the families (*mišpaḥot*)[4] of the earth (*'adamah*; ground)[5] shall bless themselves (shall be blessed). (Gen 12:2-3)

From these the coastland peoples spread. These are the sons of Japheth in their lands, each with his own language, by their families (*mišpaḥot*), in their nations (*goyim*). (Gen 10:5)

These are the sons of Ham, by their families (*mišpaḥot*), their languages, their lands, and their nations (*goyim*). (Gen 10:20)

These are the sons of Shem, by their families (*mišpaḥot*), their languages, their lands, and their nations (*goyim*). These are the families (*mišpaḥot*) of the sons of Noah, according to their genealogies, in their nations (*goyim*); and from these the nations (*goyim*) spread abroad on the earth after the flood. (Gen 10:31-32)

He also said, "Blessed by the Lord my God be Shem; and let Canaan be his slave. God enlarge Japheth, and let him dwell in the tents of Shem; and let Canaan be his slave." (Gen 9:26-27)

This function of representativeness can be clearly gathered from the Law and the Prophets:

Do not say in your heart, after the Lord your God has thrust them out before you, "It is because of my righteousness that the Lord has brought me in to possess this land"; whereas it is because of the wickedness of these nations that the Lord is driving them out before you. Not because of your righteousness or the uprightness of your heart are you going in to possess their land; but because of the wickedness of these nations the Lord your God is driving them out from before you, and that he may confirm the word which the Lord swore to your fathers, to Abraham, to Isaac, and to Jacob. (Deut 9:4-5)

For you are a people holy to the Lord your God; the Lord your God has chosen you to be a people for his own possession, out of all the peoples that are on the face of the earth. It was not because you were more in number than any other people that the Lord set his love upon you and chose you, for you were the fewest of all peoples; but it is because the Lord loves you, and is keeping the oath which he swore to your fathers, that the Lord has

4 See Genesis 10:5, 18, 20, 31, 32.
5 See Genesis 1-9 passim.

> brought you out with a mighty hand, and redeemed you from the house of bondage, from the hand of Pharaoh king of Egypt. (Deut 7:6-8)

Whenever Israel is punished, it is an example to be heeded by all nations:

> And you shall perish among the nations, and the land of your enemies shall eat you up. (Lev 26:38)

> Beware lest you say in your heart, "My power and the might of my hand have gotten me this wealth." You shall remember the Lord your God, for it is he who gives you power to get wealth; that he may confirm his covenant which he swore to your fathers, as at this day. And if you forget the Lord your God and go after other gods and serve them and worship them, I solemnly warn you this day that you shall surely perish. Like the nations that the Lord makes to perish before you, so shall you perish, because you would not obey the voice of the Lord your God. (Deut 8:17-20)

Most importantly, in Ezekiel—when it comes to revolting against God—Israel is literally equated with the nations strikingly in the plural:

> And he said to me, "Son of man, I send you to the people of Israel, to a nation (*goyim* [nations] in the original) of rebels, who have rebelled against me; they and their fathers have transgressed against me to this very day. The people also are impudent and stubborn: I send you to them; and you shall say to them, 'Thus says the Lord God.'" (Ezek 2:3-4)

The thesis I came to endorse through an in-depth study of the scriptural text is that the entire message of the scriptural story is imbedded/encoded in the first creation account of Genesis 1:1-2:4. In order for me to defend this proposition, I shall go over these verses in detail to show how the vocabulary and phraseology chosen by the authors look ahead to the entire scriptural narrative by informing it in its three parts (Law, Prophets, and Ketubim). I shall show how the nouns and verbs used in Genesis 1:1-2:4 and their interrelationship inform—even control—the way the hearers are to perceive them when they appear again and again in the course of the scriptural literature and the scriptural story. In other words, the terminology of Genesis 1:1-2:4 acts as building blocks for the construction and thus structure of the rest of scripture. In order to convince my readers that such approach is a device or methodology intended by the authors, I shall cover words central to the scriptural narrative which occur in Genesis 1-11, but are not found in Genesis 1:1-2:4, and I will show how they too are chosen to inform the rest of scripture. And if scripture is informed and shaped by Genesis 1-11, it ought to be heard on its ground, so to speak, as an authoritative dictating text and not as an open ended text whose meaning is to be determined by each and every reader after the latest fad of the reader-response approach. The scriptural text, by the assessment of scripture itself, is not alive in the sense that it is brought to life and its meaning determined by each reader. Rather the scriptural text presents itself as life-giving in the sense that it bestows the life it—the text—is defining. Put otherwise, the scriptural text *imposes* its understanding of life over every hearer. Thus, it should be hearkened unto and obeyed. The hearers may accept such a proposition or refuse it; however, they are forbidden by the text itself to rephrase it, let alone redefine or redetermine its proposition. At the end of the scriptural canon, Paul will capture the intent of scripture by referring to it as the gospel of *hypakoē*, which should be translated as *submission* rather than *obedience* (Rom 1:5; 5:19; 6:16; 15:18; 16:19, 26).

The literary divisions of the Book of Genesis are determined by the term *toledot*. This plural noun meaning "birthings" stands at the beginning of the section it is introducing, much as a chapter title would do. Genesis 1-4 is an exception in that the phrase "the *toledot*/birthings of the heavens and the earth" is found not in Genesis 1:1, but in Genesis 2:4. One might ask, "Is the precise location of this title at Genesis 2:4 intended to function merely as a straddle that links the two creation narratives and thus invite the hearers to regard Genesis 1-4 as an entire chapter that precedes the chapter of the *toledot* of Adam in Genesis 5:1-6:8? Or is it there to separate the two creation narratives and make of them sub-sections of the same chapter?" In other words, "Is Genesis 1:1-2:4 intended to be heard as a totality on its own?" From the structure as well as the vocabulary of that passage, I am convinced that this is the case. Genesis 1:1-2:4 is intended to be a unit and function as an overarching introduction to the entire scripture. To defend this position, let me start with what would be the closing of that section (2:4) which is viewed by many as a straddle between the two creation narratives, Genesis 1:1-2:4, on the one hand, and the rest of chapter 2, on the other hand. This view is reflected in the translations that divide Genesis 2:4-5 into two parts using a period after "created" in the middle of v.4 and a comma at the end of that verse, thus making of it an introduction to v.5. Consequently, vv.4-5 are read in the following way:

> [4]These are the generations of the heavens and the earth when they were created. In the day that the Lord God made the earth and the heavens, [5]when no plant of the field was yet in the earth and no herb of the field had yet sprung up—for the Lord God had not caused it to rain upon the earth, and there was no man to till the ground. (Gen 2:4-5)

This punctuation is found in French, German, Italian, and Spanish translations, as well. Although KJV uses a comma in the middle of v.4, it still uses a comma at the end of the verse thus linking vv.4-5 into one statement. There is no punctuation in the Hebrew, the Greek LXX, and the Latin Vulgate texts.

An analysis of the Hebrew text will reveal the following features:

- The phrase *'elleh toledot* of so and so (these are the *toledot* of so and so) in scripture is systematically self-standing as a complete sentence: 5:1; 6:9; 10:1; 11:10, 27; 25:12, 19; 36:1, 9; 37:2.[6] It stands to reason to treat Genesis 2:4 as a no exception to the rule.

---

6 See also Ruth 4:18.

- As to the addition of a referential time frame, "These are the generations of the heavens and the earth when they were created, in the day (*beyom*) that the Lord God made the earth and the heavens" (2:4), we have a parallel instance in Numbers 3:1: "These are the generations of Aaron and Moses at the time (*beyom*; in the day) when the Lord spoke with Moses on Mount Sinai." The original Hebrew reflects better the full parallelism: Genesis—"on the day of the Lord's making/having made (*beyom 'aśot yahweh)*; Numbers—"on the day of the Lord's speaking/having spoken (*beyom dabber yahweh*).[7]

- The heavens as a repeated subject matter in Genesis 1 and 2 does not occur again until Genesis 14: "And he [Melchizedek] blessed him and said, 'Blessed be Abram by God Most High, maker of heaven[8] and earth.'" (v.19) In between, we hear of the heavens only as an appendage, a complement to another noun and thus functioning as an adjective would.[9] This makes sense since we hear in Genesis 2:1: "Thus the heavens and the earth were finished (completed/fulfilled), and all the host of them."

- To use the phrase "the *toledot* of so and so" as an introduction to an enumeration of names, as it is used in the rest of Genesis, would not have made

---

7 The Masoretic Text is misleading in that it punctuated the more natural infinitive construct *dabber* in Numbers as the perfect *dibber*, in spite of the fact that it endorsed the punctuation of *beyom* as a construct state (on the day of) as opposed to the absolute state *bayyom* (on the day). The construct state requires, according to the grammatical rules of the Masoretes themselves, that it be followed by an infinitive construct.

8 The Hebrew does not differentiate between "heavens" and "heaven." It uses the same plural—or more accurately dual—noun *šamayim* throughout.

9 For instance, in our "silver platter" (platter of silver) that corresponds to "golden platter" (platter of gold). See notably the phrase "birds of the air" which is RSV's translation of *'oph haššamayim* (fowl of the heavens; 1:26, 28, 30; 2:19, 20; 6:7; 7:3, 23; 9:2).

sense in 2:4 for several reasons. First, it would have had to be positioned at Genesis 1:1 and followed by the enumeration of "all the host" of the heavens and the earth. However, this would have sounded odd, to say the least. The verbal root of *toledot* literally means "give birth" as a female mammal would, which obviously does not apply to either the earthly vegetation or the sun, moon, and stars of the heavens. Secondly, and more importantly, Genesis 1 would then have sounded as though the heavens and the earth were the progenitors or the originators of all that is. The scriptural authors intentionally avoided speaking of God as "giving birth" and phrased Genesis 1 in a way that presents the heavens and the earth as instruments in the hands of God, who alone is the originator of everything that is. The authors purposely relegated "the *toledot* of the heavens and the earth" as a conclusion to the description of the origins, while reminding the hearers that the statement is linked to the preceding by adding, "when they were *created*, in the day that the Lord God *made* the earth and the heavens." This forces on the hearers' ears the two basic verbs that described God's activity in Genesis 1: *bara'* (create) and *'aśah* (made). The result is that "these are the *toledot*" in 2:4 functions as a recapitulation of, rather than an introduction to, the chapter.

- Genesis 2:4a constitutes a perfect literary *inclusio* with 1:1: "In the beginning God created the heavens and the earth" (1:1); "These are the generations of the heavens and the earth when they were created" (2:4).

Genesis 1:1 and 2:4 form a diptych whereby the first side of that diptych functions as the official title of the entirety of scripture, while the second side has the function of describing Genesis 1-4 as the first scriptural section dealing with the entirety of creation. The man (*ha'adam*) is viewed as a denizen, i.e., a member of the host of the heavens and earth, and the entire creation is posited as the backdrop of the individual forefather Adam (*'adam*) and his *toledot* starting at Genesis 5:1. That the authors intended a clear delineation between Genesis 1-4 and Genesis 5:1-6:8 is evident in that they singled out Adam's *toledot* as a "book" ("This is the book of the generations of Adam" [5:1]) in order to draw to the hearers' attention that the authors are moving to another "chapter" in their presentation of the same story line. This is ensured, at the outset, through the use of the phraseology of the previous literary chapter describing the *toledot* of the heavens and the earth in the new literary chapter describing the *toledot* of Adam: "When God created man, he made him in the likeness of God. Male and female he created them, and he blessed them and named them Man when they were created." (5:1-2) Put otherwise, *toledot* functions as trigger to indicate that the author is dealing with another chapter of his basic and interrelated story line. This is ingenious indeed.

Note that the features of Genesis 1:1-2:4 ensure its oneness to the hearers' ears and thus as a totality with a beginning and an end:

- A most compelling feature is the ubiquitous jussive command where the recipient of the command is not addressed directly as in the case of the verbal imperative mood. Jussive,[10] in grammar, is used to speak of a command that is to be relayed to an absentee or third person. In English it is usually rendered through the phrase

10 While "imperative" is from the Latin verb *imperare* whose meaning is "to give an order," "jussive" is from another Latin verb *jubere* whose meaning is also "to give an order."

"let him, her, them do so and so" or "let it be done." This way of speaking is encountered in 1:3, 6 (twice), 9, 11, 14 (twice), 15, 20 (twice), 22, 24, 26 (twice).

- The frequency feature also applies to the verbs denoting making (*'aśah*), used six times, and creating/making functional (*bara'*), used five times, in Genesis 1. In the passage Genesis 2:1-4, *'aśah* occurs 4 times and *bara'* twice. Thus, we have a total of 10 times for *'aśah* and of 7 times for *bara'*. This is overbearing, to say the least. It is mainly God who is the subject of both verbs, the exception being Genesis 1:11-12 where *'aśah* twice applies to fruit trees making fruits, the first time within the divine command, and the second time their action being the result of the divine command: "And God said, 'Let the earth put forth vegetation, plants yielding seed, and fruit trees bearing (making, *'aśah)* fruit in which is their seed, each according to its kind, upon the earth.' And it was so. The earth brought forth vegetation, plants yielding seed according to their own kinds, and trees bearing (making, *'aśah*) fruit in which is their seed, each according to its kind." The intention is obviously to stress the vegetation's activity as being independent of the sun and rather the immediate result of the divine command. It is worth noting the parallelism in connotation between *'aśah* (make) and *bara'* (make functional), which is reflected in the LXX that translates both into the same verb *poiein* (make, do, [whence *poiētēs* "poet" who produces a literary product without any artifact, unlike an artisan]). *poiētēn*[11] (*maker*) is precisely the term

11 *poiētēn* is the accusative (noun complement) form of *poiētēs*.

used of God in the Nicene creed. This interconnection between *'aśah* and *bara'* can be heard in the original Hebrew in Gen 2:3-4:

> וַיְבָרֶךְ אֱלֹהִים אֶת־יוֹם הַשְּׁבִיעִי וַיְקַדֵּשׁ אֹתוֹ כִּי בוֹ שָׁבַת מִכָּל־מְלַאכְתּוֹ אֲשֶׁר־בָּרָא אֱלֹהִים לַעֲשׂוֹת׃ אֵלֶּה תוֹלְדוֹת הַשָּׁמַיִם וְהָאָרֶץ בְּהִבָּרְאָם בְּיוֹם עֲשׂוֹת יְהוָה אֱלֹהִים אֶרֶץ וְשָׁמָיִם׃
>
> *waybarek 'elohim 'et-yom haššebi'y wayqaddeš 'oto ki bo šabat mikkol mela'keto 'ašer bara' 'elohim la'aśot (created in order to do it). 'elleh toledot haššamayim weha'areṣ behibbare'am beyom 'aśot yahweh 'elohim 'ereṣ wešamayim.*
>
> So God blessed the seventh day and hallowed it, because on it God rested from all his work which he had done in creation.[12] These are the generations of the heavens and the earth when they were created, in the day that the Lord God made the earth and the heavens.

Underscoring the superiority of *bara'* over *'aśah* by pointing out that the first means "create" while the second means simply "do/make" is problematic since it would demean the human being made in the image of God that God had planned to make (Gen 1:26; 5:1).

- The totality of the divine world and its oneness is stressed through the high incidence of "all" (every; *kol*) which is used 17 times in 14 verses between Genesis 1:21 and 2:3. Further, one hears the verb *kalah* (to finish/to complete/to fulfil; from the same root as *kol*) twice in a row to describe God's fulfilling all (every; *kol*) his work (*mela'kah*): "Thus the heavens and the earth were finished, and all the host of them. And on the seventh day God finished his work which he had done, and he rested on the seventh day from all

12 In Hebrew it sounds as "created in order to do it."

his work which he had done. So God blessed the seventh day and hallowed it, because on it God rested from all his work which he had done in creation." (Gen 2:1-3)

- Finally, in order to confirm that everything—the whole, the all—is accomplished, at least on God's part, the authors conclude their narration of God's activity with the statement "And God saw everything (*kol*) that he had made, and behold, it was very good. And there was evening and there was morning, a sixth day." (1:31) One hears about all (*kol*) that God made (*'aśah*), and that God saw, and it was "very good" and not just "good" as in the case of the previous days. That is, what was done by God cannot be topped or added to; God is fully satisfied with what he did and thus nothing can be added. His task is finished/completed/fulfilled (Gen 2:1) and God "rests" (*šabat*) from all his work (vv.2 and 3[13]). The rest (*not* do/make/*'aśah* anything) on the seventh day parallels Exodus 20, which picks up the same terminology: "Six days you shall labor, and do all your work; but the seventh day is a sabbath to the Lord your God; in it you shall not do any work, you, or your son, or your daughter, your manservant, or your maidservant, or your cattle, or the sojourner who is within your gates; for in six days the Lord made heaven and earth, the sea, and all that is in them, and rested the seventh day; therefore the Lord blessed the sabbath day and hallowed it." (vv. 9-11)

---

13 Notice the stress on "rest" that is used twice.

This analysis of Genesis 1:1-2:4 shows that almost certainly it was conceived formally as a literary unit within the larger literary chapter of scripture Genesis 1-4. In the following I shall discuss materially Genesis 1:1-2:4 in detail to show that both its vocabulary and the phraseology are expressly chosen and woven in a way that clearly militates for the thesis I endorsed earlier, that is, this passage functions as an opening statement by the authors which sums up the entire message of scripture. In other words, the authors are saying, to the educated and commoner alike, that there is no need to continue if you do not accept the following:

1. That the authors devised an original language[14] to write this book;
2. That the premise proposed must be accepted/endorsed as it stands;
3. That from the beginning (*bere'šit*), the scriptural *'elohim* found what he created *very good* for "all" (everything, *kol*), i.e., for the humans and the animals and the vegetation that ensures the livelihood of both;
4. That God fully and completely rested his case way before *ha'adam* uttered a single word, including his philosophical and assumedly scientific jargon;[15] in fact, *ha'adam* does not say anything until Genesis 2:19 when he starts naming his companions, the animals.

Consequently, there is nothing new under the sun. The non-ending repetitiveness of this 'elohim book after book will literally bore you to death. The unmerry-go-round of repetitiveness culminates with your being taken under the boot of Cyrus I, the hero and idol of Alexander of Macedon. You imagine that you are going forward or at least somewhere of your choosing. In

---

14 See *ROS* 61-72.

15 I insist on qualifying it as jargon since scientific as well as philosophical statements and even assertions keep changing over time.

reality, you are being tossed back and forth between Jerusalem and Babel enjoying your delusions around a temple in Jerusalem and a tower in Babel, which are your handicraft according to Isaiah 66 and Genesis 11, respectively. You never enter God's rest in the scriptural heavenly Zion, which is nothing else than the oasis Tadmor that has been lying and still lies before your eyes at the heart of the Syrian wilderness.

> Now in the first year of Cyrus king of Persia, that the word of the Lord by the mouth of Jeremiah might be accomplished, the Lord stirred up the spirit of Cyrus king of Persia so that he made a proclamation throughout all his kingdom and also put it in writing: "Thus says Cyrus king of Persia, 'The Lord, the God of heaven, has given me all the kingdoms of the earth, and he has charged me to build him a house at Jerusalem, which is in Judah. Whoever is among you of all his people, may the Lord his God be with him. Let him go up.'" (2 Chr 36:22-23)

> In the first year of Cyrus king of Persia, that the word of the Lord by the mouth of Jeremiah might be accomplished, the Lord stirred up the spirit of Cyrus king of Persia so that he made a proclamation throughout all his kingdom and also put it in writing: "Thus says Cyrus king of Persia: 'The Lord, the God of heaven, has given me all the kingdoms of the earth, and he has charged me to build him a house at Jerusalem, which is in Judah. Whoever is among you of all his people, may his God be with him, and let him go up to Jerusalem, which is in Judah, and rebuild the house of the Lord, the God of Israel—he is the God who is in Jerusalem.'" (Ezra 1:1-3)

> What has been is what will be, and what has been done is what will be done; and there is nothing new under the sun. Is there a thing of which it is said, "See, this is new"? It has been already, in the ages before us. There is no remembrance of former things, nor will there be any remembrance of later things yet to happen among those who come after. (Eccl 1:9-11)

> O come, let us sing to the Lord; let us make a joyful noise to the rock of our salvation! Let us come into his presence with thanksgiving; let us make a joyful noise to him with songs of praise! For the Lord is a great God, and a great King above all

gods. In his hand are the depths of the earth; the heights of the mountains are his also. The sea (*yam*) is his, for he made (*'aśah*) it; for his hands formed (*yaṣar*)[16] the dry land (*yabbešet*).[17] O come, let us worship and bow down, let us kneel before the Lord, our Maker (*'ośenu*; from *'aśah*)! For he is our God, and we are the people of his pasture, and the sheep of his hand. O that today you would hearken to his voice! Harden not your hearts, as at Meribah, as on the day at Massah in the wilderness, when your fathers tested me, and put me to the proof, though they had seen my work. For forty years I loathed that generation and said, "They are a people who err in heart, and they do not regard my ways." Therefore I swore in my anger that they should not enter my rest (*menuḥah*)[18]. (Ps 95)

---

16 The verb used in Genesis 2:7-8 and 19.

17 The noun used in Genesis 1:9 and 10.

18 From the same root as the verb used to speak of the man's enjoyment of his stay in the garden (Gen 2:15). KJV, RSV, and NRSV have the insipid "put him." The English NJB has the more nuanced "settled him," following the French JB that has "established him." None of these translations captures the connotation of the Hebrew *heniaḥ* (provide rest) from the same root as *noaḥ* (Noah): "and (Lamech) called his name Noah, saying, 'Out of the ground which the Lord has cursed this one shall *bring us relief* (*yenaḥamenu*) from our work and from the toil (*'iṣṣabon*) of our hands.'" (Gen 5:29) This is intended to be the reversal of Genesis 3:17: "cursed is the ground because of you; in toil (*'iṣṣabon*) you shall eat of it all the days of your life," which is the opposite of Genesis 2:15.

2

A Short Lexicon of Genesis 1:1-2:4

A detailed analysis of some of the vocabulary of the magisterial introduction (Gen 1:1-2:4) will demonstrate that it sums up the entirety of scripture. Let us begin with *re'šit* (beginning), which occurs only three times in Genesis:

> In the *beginning* (*re'šit*) God created the heavens and the earth. (1:1)

> Cush became the father of Nimrod; he was the first on earth to be a mighty man. He was a mighty hunter before the Lord; therefore it is said, "Like Nimrod a mighty hunter before the Lord." The *beginning* (*re'šit*) of his kingdom was Babel, Erech, and Accad, all of them in the land of Shinar. From that land he went into Assyria, and built Nineveh, Rehobothir, Calah, and Resen between Nineveh and Calah; that is the great city. (10:8-12)

> Then Jacob called his sons, and said, "Gather yourselves together, that I may tell you what shall befall you in days to come. Assemble and hear, O sons of Jacob, and hearken to Israel your father. Reuben, you are my first-born, my might, and the *first fruits* (*re'šit*) of my strength, pre-eminent in pride and pre-eminent in power. Unstable as water, you shall not have pre-eminence because you went up to your father's bed; then you defiled it—you went up to my couch!" (49:1-4)

The three *re'šit* are not functionally equal, let alone identical, in meaning. Only the first is positively linked to "God created" (*bara' 'elohim*). The latter two cases reflect the abuse of power. This is clear in the case of Reuben, and will become clear for Genesis 10 when one hears the story of the tower of Babel (Genesis 11) where the connection is detectable in that Babel is in the land of Shinar (10:10 and 11:2, 9). Shinar occurs in 14:1, 9 (Amraphel, king of Shinar, is mentioned in conjunction with the five kings of Mesopotamia whom Abram fought), and later in Joshua 7:21. Thus, *re'šit* is used to intentionally underscore the abuse of the divine *re'šit* by humans—Gentiles as well as Israelites.

The importance of the positive-negative aspect of a word, which of the two aspects is to be determined from the context, can be gathered from looking at another related noun, *ro'š*, whose literal meaning is "head." It is beneficial when it relates to a divine action: the four heads/sources (*ra'šim*, plural of *ro'š*) of the great rivers that originate from the river in the garden the Lord God planted (2:10), or at the end of the punishing flood: the sight of the tops (*ra'šim*; heads) of the mountains (8:5) and the full drying out of the waters off the earth on the first day of the first (*ri'šon*–reminiscent of *re'šit*) month (8:13). It reflects arrogance and thus is detrimental when it is linked to an earthly being or earthly endeavor (Gen 3:15, the head [*ro'š*] of the serpent, and 11:4, the top/head [*ro'š*] of the tower reaching the heavens).

Hearing the original, one can notice the interplay between all the words from the same root in the context of Genesis 1-11. This cannot be happenstance, especially in the case of the four rivers referred to as four "heads" (*ra'šim*, plural of *ro'š*) (1:10) coming from the one river. The LXX kept the original connotation by translating heads here as *arkhas,* the plural of *arkhē*, used for "beginning" in 1:1 and in 10:10 (the beginning [*arkhē*] of Nimrod's kingdom). In 2:10 KJV keeps "heads;" JB has "arms," branches of a river. The English word "head" when applied to a river means its source, which is not the case of the four rivers. All in all, no translation can keep the link between all the Hebrew words whose root is *r'š.*

The corollary is no translation can possibly render the more important aspect of the matter at hand, that is, the possibility of opposite meanings of the same word, depending on its function in the context where it appears. Beginning can be bad and is not readily good. An example is the Arabic for New Year, *Ra's as-sanat,* head of the year, corresponding to the Hebrew *Rosh Hashshanah* (*ro'š haššanah*). We all know from experience that a beginning does not necessarily end up as "good news." Another example is the word *ge'ut* whose meaning is majesty, grandeur, height, arrogance. This is good when it applies to God, but is evil when it applies to man, buildings, mountains, waves, etc. In scripture only God looks good in his arrogance. Everybody and everything else, when arrogant, are setting themselves up for being leveled or brought down by the overbearing scriptural deity.

Let us look at *bara'* (create, with God as the subject) and *tohu wabohu* (waste [formless] and void). I combined these words since they are found one verse apart and in a clear relationship. What makes them special is that *bara'* is used profusely (9 times) up to Genesis 6:7 and then disappears until Numbers 16:30 where *bara'* introduces a negative action on God's part. As for the couple *tohu wabohu*, they are found only twice more in parallel in Isaiah 34:11 but separated, and in Jeremiah 4:23 where they are combined as *tohu wabohu* just as in Genesis 1:2. The use of *bohu* is restricted to these three instances. On the other hand, *tohu* occurs many more times, however, its first appearance outside of Genesis is not until Deuteronomy 32:10. A window to understanding this conundrum is offered to us in Isaiah 40-66. There we encounter the highest incidence in scripture of both the verb *bara'* (nineteen times plus one time in Isaiah 4:5, compared to twenty eight in the rest of scripture out of which 11 of those times occur in Genesis 1-6), and the noun *tohu* (eight times in Isaiah 40-59 plus three times in Isaiah 1-39 compared to only eight times in the rest of scripture outside Genesis 1:2). It is then advisable to look for help in the matters of *bara'* and *tohu* in Isaiah 40-66.

Let us begin with *tohu wabohu* as it appears in Isaiah and in Jeremiah.

> For the Lord has a day of vengeance, a year of recompense for the cause of Zion. And the streams of Edom shall be turned into pitch, and her soil into brimstone; her land shall become burning pitch. Night and day it shall not be quenched; its smoke shall go up for ever. From generation to generation it shall lie waste; none

shall pass through it for ever and ever. But the hawk and the porcupine shall possess it, the owl and the raven shall dwell in it. He shall stretch the line of confusion (*tohu*) over it, and the plummet of chaos (*bohu*) over its nobles. They shall name it No Kingdom There, and all its princes shall be nothing. Thorns shall grow over its strongholds, nettles and thistles in its fortresses. It shall be the haunt of jackals, an abode for ostriches. And wild beasts shall meet with hyenas, the satyr shall cry to his fellow; yea, there shall the night hag alight, and find for herself a resting place. There shall the owl nest and lay and hatch and gather her young in her shadow; yea, there shall the kites be gathered, each one with her mate. (Is 34:8-15)

Disaster follows hard on disaster, the whole land is laid waste. Suddenly my tents are destroyed, my curtains in a moment. How long must I see the standard, and hear the sound of the trumpet? "For my people are foolish, they know me not; they are stupid children, they have no understanding. They are skilled in doing evil, but how to do good they know not." I looked on the earth, and lo, it was waste and void (*tohu wabohu*); and to the heavens, and they had no light. I looked on the mountains, and lo, they were quaking, and all the hills moved to and fro. I looked, and lo, there was no man, and all the birds of the air had fled. I looked, and lo, the fruitful land was a desert, and all its cities were laid in ruins before the Lord, before his fierce anger. For thus says the Lord, "The whole land shall be a desolation; yet I will not make a full end. For this the earth shall mourn, and the heavens above be black; for I have spoken, I have purposed; I have not relented nor will I turn back." At the noise of horseman and archer every city takes to flight; they enter thickets; they climb among rocks; all the cities are forsaken, and no man dwells in them. (Jer 4:20-29)

The conclusion is unmistakable: *tohu wabohu* describes a desolation, a ruin and more precisely its outcome, the rubble. In other words, the rubble contains stones, but they are not functional. Dilapidated stones do not equal a house or a city. Thus was the earth (and not the heavens) in Genesis 1:2. Consequently, the verb *bara'* cannot logically mean "create" the way it has come to be understood in philosophy and theology, that is, create out of nothing, ex nihilo. For how can one possibly speak of nothing, let alone posit nothing? That is why the Ancient Greeks—before philosophy—spoke of a chaos out of which the gods made a *kosmos*, that is, they cosmeticized it and made it functional.[1] The LXX got it right when it introduced the term *kosmos* in Genesis 2:1 to render "their hosts":

> Thus the heavens and the earth were finished, and all the host of them (*ṣeba'am*, their host). (2:1)
>
> καὶ συνετελέσθησαν ὁ οὐρανὸς καὶ ἡ γῆ καὶ πᾶς ὁ κόσμος (cosmos) αὐτῶν (2:1 LXX)

Kosmos does not occur again until Exodus 33:5-6 to speak of the ornaments (cosmetics) for which Israel was criticized. Otherwise LXX translates the singular *ṣeba'* three times into *dynamis* (power) according to its original meaning of "army" (Gen 21:22, 32; 26:26). Theology, which is essentially religious philosophy, disliked that the so-called chaos was there next to God, so it asserted that God created the chaos and then he cosmeticized it.[2]

The most logical way—according to the inner logics of scripture—is to render *bara'* as "functionalize." The Arabic counterpart of the root *bara'* has the connotation of healing or empowering functionally, as in the healing of the withered hand of a man in Matthew 12: "Then he said to the man, 'Stretch out your hand.' And the man stretched it out, and it was restored (*apokatestathē*)[3], whole like the other." (v. 13) It then makes sense that *bara'* pervades Isaiah 40-66, the so-called Second Isaiah, that is dedicated to the restoration of the scriptural Israel at the end of the Babylonian exile. By the same token, one can understand why the same book profusely uses *tohu* to reflect the

---

1 Whence our term "cosmetics" that is functionally used to render someone or something presentable.

2 Thank God the scriptural authors were already dead when theology was conceived in Alexandria, the philosophical Rome of the times. My guess is that they did rollover in their graves, but I cannot prove it.

3 Whence the theological term "apokatastasis" that refers to the ultimate restoration of everything to its original state.

rubble of the destroyed Jerusalem and Judah, and also uses the same *tohu* to make fun of God's enemies as well as their gods by referring to them as vain, empty, and non-functional, thus rendering them powerless against God and the people he is about to wrench out of their claws:

> All the nations are as nothing before him, they are accounted by him as *tohu.* (Is 40:17)
>
> It is he who sits above the circle of the earth, and its inhabitants are like grasshoppers; who stretches out the heavens like a curtain, and spreads them like a tent to dwell in; who brings princes to nought, and makes the rulers of the earth *tohu.* (Is 40:22-23)
>
> Behold, they are all a delusion; their works are nothing; their molten images are *tohu.* (Is 41:29)
>
> All who make idols are *tohu*, and the things they delight in do not profit; their witnesses neither see nor know, that they may be put to shame. (Is 44:9).
>
> For thus says the Lord, who created (*bara'*) the heavens (he is God!), who formed the earth and made (*'aśah*) it—he established it; he did not create (*bara'*) it a *tohu*, he formed it to be inhabited!—: "I am the Lord, and there is no other. I did not speak in secret, in a land of darkness; I did not say to the offspring of Jacob, 'Seek me *tohu*'. I the Lord speak the truth, I declare what is right." (Is 45:18-19)
>
> That they may know from the rising of the sun, and from the west, that there is none beside me. I am the Lord, and there is none else. I form (*yaṣar*) the light, and create (*bara'*) darkness: I make (*'aśah*) peace, and create (*bara'*) evil: I the Lord do (*'aśah*) all these things. (Is 45:6-7)

In scripture *bara'* occurs only with God as subject, which makes the case of Isaiah 45:7 more compelling. Three verbs of Genesis 1-2— *yaṣar*, *bara'*, *'aśah* —occur in Isaiah 45:7 in conjunction with nouns also found in Genesis 1-2. The verb *yaṣar* (form as out of clay) is used in Genesis 2. The verb *'aśah*, the other common verb in Genesis 1, is used twice, once with the positive "peace" and the other time introducing "all things."

What is definitely striking, however, is that the verb *bara'*, eminently positive in theological circles that link it to the creativity of God, is repeated twice, and in both cases it introduces a negative outcome: "darkness" and "evil." This confirms that the best understanding of *bara'* is to "make functional," "render something real," "bring something into reality" in the original sense of the Latin *realis*, which is the adjective corresponding to the Latin noun *res* whose meaning is "the matter at hand, the matter under discussion." The original Latin that gave our nondescript "republic" is *res publica* referring to the public "reality" (issue, matter, concern) that had to be *discussed* and *debated*, and not so much an *established* reality that, once there, remains there as our "republic" is viewed.

From all this, we can conclude that the phraseology of Genesis 1:1-2 cannot be fully grasped by the hearers until they have listened to the entire scripture. Most often, theologians and lay people alike do not hear scripture, let alone listen to it, by submitting to the entire story, to the entire treks of its vocabulary, until all the parts are brought together. Rather, they seek to find a philosophical solution to every passage within its parameters. They imagine that they can understand Genesis upon having finished it, forgetting that it is part of a whole. Genesis, after all, is a prelude to Exodus in the same way as Deuteronomy is a prelude to Joshua and Judges, which are a prelude to Samuel that, in its turn, is a prelude to Kings. In the Hebrew canon Joshua, Judges, (1 and 2) Samuel and (1 and 2) Kings are part of a larger whole referred to as "the Prophets," the second part of scripture. They are not "historical" books. From the beginning, this scriptural literature was conceived as an integrated whole, just as the human body is.[4] The uniqueness

4 In medical school acing the course of anatomy is of no practical value unless the student has mastered the course of physiology, which in turn prepares for the study of the symptoms of malfunction of the physiological functions of the organs in interrelation with one another. In order to realize not only the importance but also the necessity of this process, one has to read the endless labels on the drugs that cover contraindications and side effects.

of this scriptural literature is that it is the first of its kind to cover the entire story of life on earth from its start in Genesis 1 to its conclusion in Daniel 12, or conversely in Revelation 22. Any literary product that gives the impression it is doing the same is after scripture and draws on it.

Another reason–if not the main reason—for this scripture's encompassing view of a beginning and an end is the result of an essential premise[5] within its purview. The premise in scripture, conceived by the scriptural writers, is that the primary and ultimate function of the *'elohim* of scripture is the judgment of all people in all nations covering the inhabited scriptural world, that is, the Syro-Arabian wilderness of Genesis 2-3 and, by extension, the entire world subsumed in the phrase "the heavens and the earth" of Genesis 1:1-2:4. Thus the end judgment informs the entire scripture. That is why the rubble (*tohu wabohu*) of divine judgment in scripture is placed at the beginning (*bere'šit*), in the face—or rather in the ear—of the hearers, and functions as the framework for *'elohim*'s intervention to make this rubble functional. In order to fully comprehend the matter, one has to wait until the Book of Ezekiel when the restoration of Israel is presented in chapter 37 in a terminology reminiscent of Genesis 2:

> then the Lord God formed man of dust from the ground, and *breathed* (*naphaḥ*) into his nostrils the *breath* (*nešamah*) of *life* (*ḥayyim*); and man became a living (*ḥayyah*) being (*nepheš*) ... So the Lord God caused a deep sleep to fall upon the man, and while he slept took one of his *ribs* and closed up its place with flesh (*baśar*); and the *rib* which the Lord God had taken from the man he made into a woman and brought her to the man. Then the man said, "This at last is *bone* of my *bones* and *flesh* of my *flesh*; she shall be called Woman, because she was taken out of Man." (Gen 2:7, 21-23)

> The hand of the Lord was upon me, and he brought me out by the Spirit of the Lord, and set me down in the midst of the valley; it was full of *bones* ... Thus says the Lord God to these bones:

---

5 I use the word "premise" because it cannot be proven from the outside as classical theology has tried to do in vain.

> "Behold, I will cause *breath* (*ruaḥ*) to enter you, and you *shall live* (*ḥeyitem*). And I will lay sinews upon you, and will cause *flesh* (*baśar*) to come upon you, and cover you with skin, and put *breath* (*ruaḥ*) in you, and you *shall live* (*ḥeyitem*); and you shall know that I am the Lord." … Then he said to me, "Prophesy to the breath, prophesy, son of man, and say to the breath, Thus says the Lord God: Come from the four *winds* (*ruḥot*), O *breath* (*ruaḥ*), and breathe (*naphaḥ*) upon these slain, that they *may live* (*yiḥyu*)." So I prophesied as he commanded me, and the *breath* (*ruaḥ*) came into them, and they lived (*yiḥyu*), and stood upon their feet, an exceedingly great host … "And I will put my Spirit (*ruaḥ*) within you, and you shall live (*ḥeyitem*), and I will place you in your own land; then you shall know that I, the Lord, have spoken, and I have done it, says the Lord." (Ezek 37:1, 5-6, 9-10, 14)[6]

A study of the rest of the vocabulary of Genesis 1-11 will show how Ezekiel, more than any other book, informs those chapters in Genesis. A very striking and immediately noticeable feature of Ezekiel is that it is the only prophetic book that opens up with a reference to *'elohim*[7]:

> In the thirtieth year, in the fourth month, on the fifth day of the month, as I was among the exiles by the river Chebar, the heavens were opened, and I saw visions of God (*'elohim*). (Ezek 1:1)

yahweh is introduced only later in v.3 in the phrase "the word of the Lord": "the word of the Lord (*debar yahweh*) came to Ezekiel the priest, the son of Buzi."

---

6 Later I shall discuss in detail the interconnection between "spirit," breath," "breathe," and *nepheš*.

7 The mention of God after "oracle of" in Habakkuk 1:1 is an addition not found in the original that just has "oracle." KJV does not have it; it translates literally the original *maśśah* (oracle) into "burden," which is, by the way, its technical meaning: something that is lifted, and thus carried.

3

The Heavens and the Earth

In the opening statement of scripture, "the heavens and the earth" are the object complement of the verb *bara'*. The immediately following v.2, however, deals specifically with the earth, whereas the mention of the heavens does not occur until v.9. Earlier I showed the close relationship between *tohu wabohu* that describes the earth in v.2 and the verb *bara'* in v.1. The place of priority, if not of eminence, given the earth over the heavens is readily explainable and stands to reason: it is the domain of the human beings who are the addressees and thus the hearers of the scriptural message. This is obvious in Genesis 2-3 where it is the man and his woman who are the main characters, followed by their son Cain in chapter 4. This trend will continue in chapter 5 with the story of *bene 'adam*, the sons of Adam, the children of man.

The mention of the heavens first in 1:1 is literarily functional since, with the exception of 1:2 that is a parenthetical statement parallel to 1:1, in the following verses that describe God's action or activity, so to speak, the heavens are referred to twice in vv.8 and 9 before the mention of earth in v.10. God makes the heavens (v.7) and names them (v.9) before prompting the earth to appear as dry land (v.10) and naming it earth in v.11.

Although the heavens are not, in fact, where human beings reside, they are an integral part of the human domain. They are mentioned independently of the earth no less than five times in conjunction with the second, third, fourth and fifth days of creation (in vv.8, 9, 14, 15, 17, 20 [in conjunction with the birds]). Actually, the third instance of the "earth" after vv.1 and 2 occurs in v.10, that is, after the reference to the heavens (*šamayim)* twice in vv.8 and 9.

The importance of the couple "heavens and earth" is reflected in that (1) it appears at the outset of scripture in Genesis 1:1, and (2) it brackets the first creation narrative Genesis 1:1-2:4 at the conclusion of which it occurs no less than 3 times.

> Thus the heavens and the earth were finished, and all the host of them. And on the seventh day God finished his work which he had done, and he rested on the seventh day from all his work which he had done. So God blessed the seventh day and hallowed it, because on it God rested from all his work which he had done in creation. These are the generations of the heavens and the earth when they were created. In the day that the Lord God made the earth and the heavens (Gen 2:1-4)

Notice the authors' ingenuity. The first mention of "heavens and earth" in 2:4 is just as it is in 1:1 and 2:1, however, this order is reversed at the end of the same 2:4 into "earth and heavens," which introduces the starting point of the authors' specific interest in the earth of the human domain. Heavens will recede out of the scriptural horizon until 7:11. In between Genesis 2:4 and 7:11, the earth unequivocally has the lion's share—21 times on its own. The value of the couple "heavens and earth" lies in that it expresses totality[1], and it is *'elohim* and only he that *bara'*, that is, renders everything in the humans' domain functional.

Therefore, the view of the scriptural world as a totality has nothing to do with science or philosophy. It is a literary construct/concoction out of the mind of the authors who have a specific and intentional perspective and program. In today's jargon, their narrative is not only their take on the so-called creation, but creation itself is their own "creation." Later in the second creation narrative they will point out to the hearers the geography of the human realm as being the Syro-Arabian wilderness encompassed within the boundaries of Arabia (Havilah; 2:11-12) and Egypt-Sudan (Kush; v.13) in the south, and the rivers Tigris and Euphrates (v.14) in the north. It is within those boundaries that the scriptural *ha'adam* was located by the scriptural Lord God himself (v.15).

---

1 See my comments on parallel as well as opposing literary "couples" reflecting an encompassing reality in *C-Gen* 57.

In the Syro-Arabian wilderness, the scriptural world, i.e., the world in which the concocted scriptural story evolves, develops, progresses and even ends—as per Ezekiel 48 and Daniel chapters 11-12—is a geographical setting where the reality "heavens and earth" is a total oneness. The heavens are an integral part of the earth's and its denizens' daily life, were it not for anything else than the heavens are the source of the rain showers that secure the filling of the oases, as well as the underground waters and the rivers, with life-giving water:

> These are the generations of the heavens and the earth when they were created. In the day that the Lord God made the earth and the heavens, when no plant of the field was yet in the earth and no herb of the field had yet sprung up—for the Lord God had not caused it to rain upon the earth, and there was no man to till the ground, but a mist went up from the earth and watered the whole face of the ground. (Gen 2:4-6)

This organic—and not emotionally poetic— oneness of the heavens and the earth in the authors' purview can be heard in the literary structure of the introduction to the entire scripture:

> In the beginning God created the heavens and the earth. The earth was without form and void, and darkness was upon the face of the deep; and the Spirit of God was moving over the face of the waters. (1:1-2)

It is a subtle literary *inclusio* ABB'A'. An outright *inclusio* would have been heavens-earth-earth-heavens. Here we hear heavens-earth-earth-darkness/waters. A knowledgeable person might have immediately detected that the couple darkness/waters is linked to heavens. However, such knowledge is not necessary since the authors themselves will soon flesh out this connection, and any patient hearer would end up capturing textually the *inclusio* structure of Genesis 1:1-2. As a matter of fact, "darkness" and "waters" in v.2 clearly look ahead to their immediately following instances in the description of God's first actions or activities:

> And God said, "Let there be light"; and there was light. And God saw that the light was good; and God separated the light from the darkness. God called the light Day, and the darkness he called Night. And there was evening and there was morning, one day. And God said, "Let there be a firmament in the midst of the waters, and let it separate the waters from the waters." And God made the firmament and separated the waters which were under the firmament from the waters which were above the firmament. And it was so. And God called the firmament Heaven/s [same word in Hebrew]. And there was evening and there was morning, a second day. (Gen 1:3-8)

It is interesting to add at this junction that the Hebrew תְּהֹום (*tehom* Gen 1:2), translated as "deep," resurfaces twice in 7:11 and 8:2 and is not to be found again in the Pentateuch except in Genesis 49:25 and Deuteronomy 33:13. What is striking is that in both Genesis 7:11 and 8:2 תְּהֹום (*tehom*) is heard in the same setting as הַשָּׁמַיִם (the heavens):

> And after seven days the waters of the flood came upon the earth. In the six hundredth year of Noah's life, in the second month, on the seventeenth day of the month, on that day all the fountains of the great *deep* burst forth, and the windows of the heavens were opened. (Gen 7:10-11)

> But God remembered Noah and all the beasts and all the cattle that were with him in the ark. And God made a wind blow over the earth, and the waters subsided; the fountains of the *deep* and the windows of the heavens were closed, the rain from the heavens was restrained, and the waters receded from the earth continually. At the end of a hundred and fifty days the waters had abated. (Gen 8:1-3)

The tight relation between the deep and its parallel the waters (and darkness was upon the face of the deep; and the Spirit of God was moving over the face of the waters; Gen 1:2), on the one hand, and the heavens, on the other hand, is soon corroborated in the primary function of the heavens described over the length of the second day of creation, which is the separation between waters and waters:

> And God said, "Let there be a firmament in the midst of the waters, and let it separate the waters from the waters." And God made the firmament and separated the waters which were under the firmament from the waters which were above the firmament. And it was so. And God called the firmament Heaven[s]. And there was evening and there was morning, a second day. (Gen 1:6-8)

As usual in scripture, especially in Genesis 1-11, there is always something more than what meets the ear the first time around. So, it would be worthwhile to go into more detail so that my readers could appreciate the forcefulness of the original phraseology as well as the vocabulary and could delight in the scriptural text as though they were the original addressees. This can be easily done by comparing the accounts of day one and day two with the account describing the fourth day of creation. The hearers will immediately notice that activity in all three days revolves around the verb *hibdil*, that is translated as "separated," which is encountered only in these instances and not to be found again until Exodus 26:33. It is this verb that holds together the three accounts in that it defines the functionality of the heavens in conjunction with the earth, the domain of the human beings, the addressees of the scriptural message. Notice that any mention of *hibdil* is skipped on the third day, which specifically deals with the earth (Gen 1:9-13) although it could have been used in vv.9-10 to point out the separation between land and sea:

> And God said, "Let the waters under the heavens be gathered together into one place, and let the dry land appear." And it was so. God called the dry land Earth, and the waters that were gathered together he called Seas. And God saw that it was good. (Gen 1:9-10)

So the omission seems to be and is, in fact, intentional. Life on earth would not have been possible without the function of the heavens and their denizens (sun, moon, and stars) that are the instruments of God to do his work of dividing between darkness/night and light/day. The aim of this first action of

God is to establish the basic cyclical unit, the twenty-four-hour period. Interestingly, God establishes this unit as "one day" (and not "the first day"). The ordinal numbering starts with the second day (v.8) that is patterned after the day God has already made (vv.3-5).

The only plausible way to account for the absence of *hibdil*, "separate," on the third day is to force the hearers to realize that the different actions of days one through four are to be taken together as dealing with one topic that was introduced at the outset of v.2: the earth. So, the impression is first and foremost auditory. At the end of the third day the hearers are prone to assume that their earth—as the ground on which they live (notice the later connection between *'adam* and *'adamah* in chapter 2)—was not only completed with the essential daily cycle already established (1:3-5), but it was also fully functional with all its vegetation in place to feed them: "And God said, 'Behold, I have given you every plant yielding seed which is upon the face of all the earth, and every tree with seed in its fruit; you shall have them for food.'" (1:29) However, the same *hibdil*, which controlled day one and the second day, reappearing on day four, after its omission on day three, brackets the activity of day four (vv.14-18) through its use at the beginning in v.14 and at the end in v.18 as an *inclusio*.[2] The hearers are forced to recollect the activities of days one and two. Actually, the hearers do not need to recollect since the entire phraseology of vv.14-18 is reminiscent of that of days one and two. On the one hand, the unnamed sun and moon are introduced as *me'orot* (luminaries/enlighteners) from the same root as *'or* (light) that God made on day one. On the other hand, the authors' insistence (thrice in vv.14, 15, and 17) on referring to the sky as "firmament of the heavens" and not just "heavens" cannot be explained except as an intended pointer to day two where the "heavens" are the name God gave to the firmament

2 And God said, "Let there be lights in the firmament of the heavens to *separate* (*lehabdil*) the day from the night..." (v.14) ... and *to separate* (*lehabdil*) the light from the darkness... (v.18)

(*ruqia'*) whose function is to separate (*hibdil*) between the waters above it and the waters below it. Since the waters below have been dealt with and named "seas" in the first part of day two (vv.9-10), the thrice use of "firmament of the heavens" on day three is to bring into the picture the waters above and by association the rain which is essential for the production and growth of the vegetation that is the main topic of day three (vv.10-12).

The astute literary device of skipping on day three *hibdil*, an essential element of the entire picture of days one through four, in order to underscore not exclusion but rather commonness is not a figment of my imagination. The same authors will use this technique again in dealing with day six to impress upon the hearers the basic commonness of nature between land mammals and human beings. It is strange and unexpected, to say the least, that the procreation among land animals is not directly linked to a divine blessing while the procreation of the fish and the fowl of the air, on the one hand, and that of humans, on the other hand, are expressly associated with a blessing, if not the subject of the blessing. The hearers have no possible choice but to "hear" that the land animals, and especially the mammals who "beget" just as humans do, are subsumed under the one blessing of day six that overarches humans and animals alike. Let us look in more detail at the interconnection between and the oneness of the divine actions or the one divine activity of days one through four to show how the vocabulary looks not only to Genesis 1-11, but also to the entirety of scripture.

The making of the human domain, where the human action or activity takes place, is the basic cyclical unit of the twenty-four-hour period. More specifically, the activities of humans take place during daytime, i.e., when there is light. Night/darkness is the time when humans rest or sleep, that is, they are inactive except for clandestine activities that are viewed negatively:

> But as to the times and the seasons, brethren, you have no need to have anything written to you. For you yourselves know well that the day of the Lord will come like a thief in the night. When people say, "There is peace and security," then sudden destruction will come upon them as travail comes upon a woman with child, and there will be no escape. But you are not in darkness, brethren, for that day to surprise you like a thief. For you are all sons of light and sons of the day; we are not of the night or of darkness. So then let us not sleep, as others do, but let us keep awake and be sober. For those who sleep sleep at night, and those who get drunk are drunk at night. (1 Thess 5:1-7)

Notice that in Genesis 1:2 darkness and the waters are already there as an expression of the *tohu wabohu*, whose function is negative, and thus are not made by God, at least in the context of Genesis 1 where the result of God's activity is always qualified as "good," a refrain that is repeated at the closure of each twenty-four-hour period. God made the light, but not the darkness, yet he controls both, just as he does the waters that he has not made according to Genesis 1. It is God who makes the light functional and thus defines the day:

> And God saw that the light was good; and God separated (*hibdil*) the light from the darkness. God called the light Day, and the darkness he called Night. And there was evening and there was morning, one day. (vv.4-5)

Let us hear how the text prepares for day four where the sun and moon are introduced as merely instruments made by God, in the same way as light is, in order to help the human beings differentiate between days, and years, and seasons:

> The earth was without form and void, and darkness was upon the face of the deep; and the Spirit of God was moving over the face of the waters. And God said, "Let there be light"; and there was light. And God saw that the light was good; and God *separated* the light from the darkness. (vv. 2-4)

The two luminaries, the sun and the moon, are later introduced as just *me'orot* (lights or luminaries; v.14). *me'orot* is the plural of *ma'or*, the verbal noun from the verb *'or* whose meaning is "shine." The same triliteral *'or* is also a noun meaning "light."

Thus, *ma'or* means something that shines or gives light. As such, then, their definition or role—separation between light and darkness—has been established earlier and consequently they are just *one* expression—and not *the* expression—of the "light" (*'or*) that was *already* there since it came about at God's command (v.3) and which God separated from the darkness (v.4). In other words, the luminaries are just the medium through which God, the ultimate agent, separates between day and night. Or, in the words of scripture, it is God who *defines* the "day" as a twenty-four-hour period, whereas the luminaries just "rule" over its two constituents, daylight and night:

> And God said, "Let there be lights in the firmament of the heavens to *separate* the day from the night; and let them be for signs and for seasons and for days and years, and let them be lights in the firmament of the heavens to give light upon the earth." And it was so. And God made the two great lights, the greater light to *rule* the day, and the lesser light to *rule* the night; he made the stars also. And God set them in the firmament of the heavens to give light upon the earth, to *rule* over the day and over the night, and to *separate* the light from the darkness. And God saw that it was good. And there was evening and there was morning, a fourth day. (1:14-19)

What God produces (creates; makes; makes functional) by a sheer command is first a reality, namely, *'or* (v.3), that is both noun (light) and verb (shine) in the *qal* (basic) form, at the same time. On the other hand, the verbal noun *ma'or* functions only in the fifth verbal form, the causative *hiphil*, and thus corresponds consonantally to the active participle *me'ir* of that verbal form, which means "enlightener," as one gathers from the following passage in Isaiah:

> For the fortified city is solitary, a habitation deserted and forsaken, like the wilderness; there the calf grazes, there he lies down, and strips its branches. When its boughs are dry, they are

> broken; women come and *make a fire of* (*me'irot*)[3] them. For this is a people without discernment; therefore he who made them will not have compassion on them, he that formed them will show them no favor. (Is 27:10-11)

The Centrality of **hibdil** *in Scripture*

If Genesis 1 insists that it is God himself, and not the sun and moon, who is the originator of the "separation," it is in view of how *hibdil* will become central in the Mosaic Law where it will be used to indicate the total opposition between two domains with the intention of testing the actions of the human beings. The topic of testing the human resolve is definitely on the authors' mind since they soon will be tackling the matter in Genesis 2-3 and, no less, on the basis of a command issued by the Lord God in the same kind of phraseology encountered endlessly in the Law: "And the Lord commanded the man" (Gen 2:16); "as the Lord commanded Moses."[4] Still the verb *hibdil* will prove to be so essential that it will be encountered often not only in the Law but also in the Prophets:

> You are to distinguish (*lehabdil*) between the holy and the common, and between the unclean and the clean. (Lev 10:10)

> Every swarming thing that swarms upon the earth is an abomination; it shall not be eaten. Whatever goes on its belly, and whatever goes on all fours, or whatever has many feet, all the swarming things that swarm upon the earth, you shall not eat; for they are an abomination. You shall not make yourselves abominable with any swarming thing that swarms; and you shall not defile yourselves with them, lest you become unclean. For I am the Lord your God; consecrate yourselves therefore, and be holy, for I am holy. You shall not defile yourselves with any swarming thing that crawls upon the earth. For I am the Lord who brought you up out of the land of Egypt, to be your God;

---

3 Feminine plural active participle *hiphil*: the "women" turn the dry boughs into fire or light. In the writers' times there was no electricity and thus fire was light, and light was fire. Actually, in scriptural Hebrew, the two terms *'or* (light) and *'ur* (fire, flame) are identical consonantally: אֹור and אֻור respectively.

4 Lev 8:9, 13, 17, 21, 29; 9:10; 24:23; Numbers passim.

you shall therefore be holy, for I am holy." This is the law pertaining to beast and bird and every living creature that moves through the waters and every creature that swarms upon the earth, to make a distinction (*lehabdil*) between the unclean and the clean and between the living creature that may be eaten and the living creature that may not be eaten. (Lev 11:41-47)[5]

But I have said to you, "You shall inherit their land, and I will give it to you to possess, a land flowing with milk and honey." I am the Lord your God, who have separated (*hibdalti*) you from the peoples. You shall therefore make a distinction (*hibdaltem*) between the clean beast and the unclean, and between the unclean bird and the clean; you shall not make yourselves abominable by beast or by bird or by anything with which the ground teems, which I have set apart for you to hold unclean. You shall be holy to me; for I the Lord am holy, and have separated (*'abdel*) you from the peoples, that you should be mine. (Lev 20:24-26)

Thus says the Lord: "Keep justice, and do righteousness, for soon my salvation will come, and my deliverance be revealed. Blessed is the man who does this, and the son of man who holds it fast, who keeps the sabbath, not profaning it, and keeps his hand from doing any evil." Let not the foreigner who has joined himself to the Lord say, "The Lord will *surely separate me* (*habdel yabdilani*) from his people"; and let not the eunuch say, "Behold, I am a dry tree." For thus says the Lord: "To the eunuchs who keep my sabbaths, who choose the things that please me and hold fast my covenant, I will give in my house and within my walls a monument and a name better than sons and daughters; I will give them an everlasting name which shall not be cut off. (Is 56:1-5)

Behold, the Lord's hand is not shortened, that it cannot save, or his ear dull, that it cannot hear; but your iniquities have made a separation (*mabdilim*) between you and your God, and your sins have hid his face from you so that he does not hear. For your hands are defiled with blood and your fingers with iniquity; your

5 Notice how this thought pertaining to the clean and unclean among animals is already encountered in the story of the flood (Gen 7:2, 8; 8:20). This again shows how the authors were looking ahead to the entirety of scripture already throughout Genesis 1-11.

> lips have spoken lies, your tongue mutters wickedness. No one enters suit justly, no one goes to law honestly; they rely on empty pleas, they speak lies, they conceive mischief and bring forth iniquity. (Is 59:1-4)

> Her priests have done violence to my law and have profaned my holy things; they have made no distinction (*hibdilu*) between the holy and the common, neither have they taught the difference between the unclean and the clean, and they have disregarded my sabbaths, so that I am profaned among them. (Ezek 22:26)

> Now when he had finished measuring the interior of the temple area, he led me out by the gate which faced east, and measured the temple area round about. He measured the east side with the measuring reed, five hundred cubits by the measuring reed. Then he turned and measured the north side, five hundred cubits by the measuring reed. Then he turned and measured the south side, five hundred cubits by the measuring reed. Then he turned to the west side and measured, five hundred cubits by the measuring reed. He measured it on the four sides. It had a wall around it, five hundred cubits long and five hundred cubits broad, to make a separation (*lehabdil*) between the holy and the common. (Ezek 42:15-20)

It is this looking forward to the Law and its dictates that in turn explains why in Genesis 1 the authors subordinated the sun and the moon to God in the matter of separation between, and ruling over, day and night. The reason for this is straightforward: sun and moon are not functional deities; in Genesis they are not even named. In the Law we shall hear repeatedly:

> And beware lest you lift up your eyes to heaven, and when you see the sun and the moon and *the stars, all the host of heaven*, you be drawn away and worship them and serve them, things which the Lord your God has allotted to all the peoples under the whole heaven. (Deut 4:19)

> If there is found among you, within any of your towns which the Lord your God gives you, a man or woman who does what is evil in the sight of the Lord your God, in transgressing his covenant, and has gone and served other gods and worshiped them, or the

> sun or the moon or *any of the host of heaven*, which I have forbidden… (Deut 17:2-3)[6]

After having used the verb *hibdil*, especially in conjunction with two opposites (light and darkness, day and night) as well as with the same element in two different locations (waters above the firmament and waters below the firmament), it is definitely strange that the authors refrained from using *hibdil* in dealing with the earth versus seas on the third day (Gen 1:9-13). The opposition between the two is underscored in their referring to the earth specifically as "dry land" or more accurately as "the (feminine grammatically)[7] dry one" (*hayyabbaśah*).[8] As for the aspect of location, it is specifically stressed in the way the text is phrased: "And God said, 'Let the waters under the heavens be gathered together into one place, and let the dry land appear.' And it was so." (1:9) Thus the omission must be intentional and, consequently, functional in the authors' purview. Let us examine in detail the vocabulary and phraseology of Genesis 1:9-13 related to the third day.

> And God said, "Let the waters under the heavens be gathered together into one place, and let the dry land appear." And it was so. God called the dry land Earth, and the waters that were gathered together he called Seas. And God saw that it was good. And God said, "Let the earth put forth vegetation, plants yielding seed, and fruit trees bearing fruit in which is their seed, each according to its kind, upon the earth." And it was so. The earth brought forth vegetation, plants yielding seed according to their own kinds, and trees bearing fruit in which is their seed, each according to its kind. And God saw that it was good. And there was evening and there was morning, a third day.

---

6 Notice the parallelism with Genesis 1-2 through the mention of "the host of heaven" in both instances (compare with Gen 2:1) and the addition of "stars" in Deuteronomy 4:19 (compare with Gen 1:16).

7 Since the Hebrew *'ereṣ* (earth) is a feminine noun.

8 This usage is common in Semitic languages. It is encountered commonly in scripture when the referent is the "right hand." The classic example is Psalm 110:1 (Sit at my right hand) where the Hebrew has simply *yemini* (my right) while the English supplies "hand."

To put it simply, the heavenly waters and the earthly waters are one element that had to be separated into two functional entities as is clear from Genesis 2:5-6: "when no plant of the field was yet in the earth and no herb of the field had yet sprung up—for the Lord God *had not caused it to rain* (*himṭir* from the root *mṭr*) upon the earth, and there was no man to till the ground; but a mist went up from the earth and watered the whole face of the ground." The same applies to the flood story. In spite of the fact that only rain is referred to in the divine decision at the beginning (For in seven days I *will send rain* [*mamṭir* from the same root *mṭr*] upon the earth forty days and forty nights; and every living thing that I have made I will blot out from the face of the ground; 7:4), however, in the actual description of the flood we hear of the two sources of waters:

> In the six hundredth year of Noah's life, in the second month, on the seventeenth day of the month, on that day all the fountains of the great deep burst forth, and the windows of the heavens were opened. And rain fell/was upon the earth forty days and forty nights. (Gen 7:11-12)

> But God remembered Noah and all the beasts and all the cattle that were with him in the ark. And God made a wind blow over the earth, and the waters subsided; the fountains of the deep and the windows of the heavens were closed, the rain from the heavens was restrained, and the waters receded from the earth continually. At the end of a hundred and fifty days the waters had abated. (Gen 8:1-3)

Both waters have the same effect—positive or negative, depending on the circumstances—and work in unison. Notice that while two different verbs are used in conjunction with the start of the flood (the fountains of the great deep burst forth, and the windows of the heavens were opened; 7:11), at the close of the flood we have the same verb used for both: the fountains of the deep and the windows of the heavens were closed (8:2).

Although different in nature, when it comes to the waters below and the earth (wet versus dry), the wet always threatens the dry and not vice versa. Still they relate to each other symbiotically. There is no livable earth without the waters of the sea and rivers, and the subterranean waters. In other words, the earth is never "separated" from the waters—these are just pushed aside, as it were, to be "gathered together (*yiqqawu* from the verb *qawah*) into one place (*miqweh* [verbal noun from the verb *qawah*])" to allow the earth to appear or, more in tune with the original, to be seen (*tera'eh*; the *niphal* [passive] form of the verb *ra'ah* [see]; 1:9). Hence the use of "gather" to describe the waters that are called by God "sea/seas." (v.10). Just as in the case of light and darkness it is the naming of the second in line that gives it functional priority over the earlier:

> And God said, "Let there be light"; and there was light. And God saw that the light was good; and God separated the light from the darkness. God called the light Day, and the darkness he called Night. And there was evening and there was morning, one day. (Gen 1:3-5)

> And God said, "Let the waters under the heavens be gathered together into one place, and let the dry land appear." And it was so. God called the dry land Earth, and the waters that were gathered together he called Seas. And God saw that it was good. (Gen 1:9-10)

So the phraseology of Genesis 1:9-13 concerning the earth's "emergence" (being brought about in order to be seen) is intelligent in that it reflects the factuality as well as the actuality of the matter: the symbiosis between dry land and seas which parallel the symbiosis between darkness and light, night and day. Night and day, two opposites, are conjoined to form a totality that is referred to as "day" (night + day = day), however, the upper hand is given to the light/day that God has established as opposite of the darkness/night that already was there. So also is the dry land/earth that emerged by a decision of God, whereas the waters were already there: "darkness was upon the face of the deep; and the Spirit of God was moving over the face of the waters." (v.2) Only the naming of the darkness as night (v.5) and the naming of the waters as sea/seas (v.10) is God's bidding. The two verbs that reflect making or manufacturing (*bara'*/create and *'aśah* /make) are not found in the description of days one and three related to the institution of the daily cycle and the emergence of the dry land. They abound, however, in the description of days two, four, five and six. Thus, this omission must be intentional. It is as though the two basic components of human and animal life as we know and experience it –the daily cycle of night and day (time)[9] and the human, animal, and vegetation space as a symbiosis between earth and sea—were not made/created by God; rather they were already there, yet it is God who rendered them functional for the human, animal, and vegetation.

That the naming or calling is to be understood as rendering something functional according to the connotation of the given name is evident throughout Genesis 1-3:

> So out of the ground the Lord God formed every beast of the field and every bird of the air, and brought them to the man to see what he would call them; and whatever the man called every living creature, that was its name. (2:19)
>
> Then the man said, "This at last is bone of my bones and flesh of my flesh; she shall be called Woman, because she was taken out of Man." (2:23)
>
> The man called his wife's name Eve, because she was the mother of all living. (3:20)

In this regard, it is important to notice that the naming heard in days one and three in Genesis 1 occurs only once more in conjunction with the heavens that God made:

> And God made (*'aśah*) the firmament and separated the waters which were under the firmament from the waters which were above the firmament. And it was so. And God called (*qara'*) the firmament Heaven. And there was evening and there was morning, a second day. (v.7-8)

This finding corroborates that *functionally* the heavens are regarded, by the author, from the perspective of their relation

9 See later God's promise at the end of the flood: "While the earth remains, seedtime and harvest, cold and heat, summer and winter, *day and night, shall not cease.*" (8:22)

to the earth/dry land in that the heavens are the source of life-giving rain that is "the pouring down of the waters above through the windows of the firmament":

> In the six hundredth year of Noah's life, in the second month, on the seventeenth day of the month, on that day all the fountains of the great deep burst forth, and the windows of the heavens were opened ... the fountains of the deep and the windows of the heavens were closed, the rain from the heavens was restrained. (Gen 7:11; 8:2)

This primary function of the heavens as being in the purview of the earth and life on it is evident in the description of day four:

> And God said, "Let there be lights in the firmament of the heavens to separate the day from the night; and let them be for signs and for seasons and for days and years, and let them be lights in the firmament of the heavens to give light upon the earth." And it was so. And Go made the two great lights, the greater light to rule the day, and the lesser light to rule the night; he made the stars also. And God set them in the firmament of the heavens to give light upon the earth, *to rule over the day and over the night, and to separate the light from the darkness.* And God saw that it was good. And there was evening and there was morning, a fourth day. (Gen 1:14-19)

4

Vegetation

> And God said, "Let the earth put forth (*tadše'*) vegetation (*deše'*; same root), plants yielding seed, and fruit trees bearing fruit in which is their seed, each according to its kind, upon the earth." And it was so. The earth brought forth (*hoṣi'*; causative hiphil of *yaṣa'* [go out]) vegetation, plants yielding seed according to their own kinds, and trees bearing fruit in which is their seed, each according to its kind. And God saw that it was good. (Gen 1:11-12)

Although the vegetation, together with animal and human life, will be included into one organic whole, the author introduces the vegetation on day three, and animal and human life on days five and six. Separating them is day four, dedicated to the inanimate denizens of the heavens. Three main reasons are behind the decision to separate vegetation from animal and human life.

First, the vegetation is organically part of the earth in that it does not move on its own like the animals and humans, those who have an *anima*, *nepheš*/breathing [hence animals]. Vegetation, from this perspective, is part and parcel of the earth. Notice that vegetation alone is food for animals and humans.

> And God said, "Behold, I have given you every plant yielding seed which is upon the face of all the earth, and every tree with seed in its fruit; you shall have them for food. And to every beast of the earth, and to every bird of the air, and to everything that creeps on the earth, everything that has the breath of life, I have given every green plant for food." And it was so. (Gen 1:29-30)

The consumption of meat is introduced only later in Genesis 9 as a concession after the flood:

> Every moving thing that lives shall be food for you; and as I gave you the green plants, I give you everything. Only you shall not eat flesh with its life, that is, its blood. For your lifeblood I will

> surely require a reckoning; of every beast I will require it and of man; of every man's brother I will require the life of man. (Gen 9:3-5)

Still, that, in itself, is not reason enough to isolate vegetation from the animal kingdom as the author does in Genesis 1. A more important reason lies in the fact that the act of life, growth, and multiplication of vegetation on earth is intimately linked to the cycles of "seasons and days and years" (v.14) that are controlled by sun and moon (vv.14-18). Given that these were universal and thus ubiquitous deities in all religions of the author's times[1], they were blatantly demeaned and disparaged through the simple connotation of "luminaries" and not identified by their own names.[2] The first mention of sun is relegated to Genesis 15 and that of the moon to Genesis 37. Moreover, they are presented as instruments to continue the work of the scriptural God that was already described in days one and two. In other words, they are merely instrumental subalterns to the one God of scripture. Notice in this regard the use of the same jussive form "let it/they" to refer to those luminaries, as well as to light, firmament, waters, and earth:

> And God said, "Let there be light"; and there was light. (Gen 1:3)

> And God said, "Let there be a firmament in the midst of the waters." (Gen 1:6)

> And God said, "Let the waters under the heavens be gathered together into one place, and let the dry land appear." (Gen 1:9)

> And God said, "Let the earth put forth vegetation, plants yielding seed, and fruit trees bearing fruit in which is their seed." (Gen 1:11)

> And God said, "Let there be lights in the firmament of the heavens to separate the day from the night; and let them be for signs and for seasons and for days and years, and let them be lights in the firmament of the heavens to give light upon the earth." (Gen 1:14-15)

---

1 Deuteronomy 4:19; 17:2-3.

2 See earlier pp. 52-53.

> And God said, "Let the waters bring forth swarms of living creatures, and let birds fly above the earth across the firmament of the heavens." (Gen 1:20)

> And God said, "Let the earth bring forth living creatures according to their kinds: cattle and creeping things and beasts of the earth according to their kinds." (Gen 1:24).

In other words, just as God did not need the sun and moon to make light/daylight/day, he did not need them to have vegetation grow and produce its fruits to feed the animal and human kingdoms. Actually, the sun and the moon, together with the stars, are simply fixtures in the heavens (Gen 1:6-8) that God already made on the second day:

> And God made the two great lights, the greater light to rule the day, and the lesser light to rule the night; he made the stars also. And God *set them* in the firmament of the *heavens*. (Gen1:16-17)

The terminology the author uses to speak of the vegetation on day three not only asserts to its independence from the sun and the moon, but also belittles them. The activity of the earth producing plants and trees is described in a way that twice ascribes to the trees the same verb *'aśah* (made) that is otherwise used only of God and no one or nothing else in Genesis 1:1-2:4. That is remarkable given that the repetition was not necessary and is thus definitely intended. Usually the author is either satisfied with the jussive "let" followed by "and it was so," or writes that it is God who actually made (*'aśah*) or created (*bara'*) what he had commanded:

> And God said, "Let there be light"; and there was light. (Gen 1:3)

> And God said, "Let there be a firmament in the midst of the waters, and let it separate the waters from the waters." And God made the firmament and separated the waters which were under the firmament from the waters which were above the firmament. And it was so. (Gen 1:6-7)

> And God said, "Let the waters under the heavens be gathered together into one place, and let the dry land appear." And it was so. (Gen 1:9)

> And God said, "Let there be lights in the firmament of the heavens to separate the day from the night; and let them be for signs and for seasons and for days and years, and let them be lights in the firmament of the heavens to give light upon the earth." And it was so. And God made the two great lights, the greater light to rule the day, and the lesser light to rule the night; he made the stars also. (Gen 1:14-16)

> And God said, "Let the waters bring forth swarms of living creatures, and let birds fly above the earth across the firmament of the heavens." So God created the great sea monsters and every living creature that moves, with which the waters swarm, according to their kinds, and every winged bird according to its kind. (Gen 1:20-21)

> And God said, "Let the earth bring forth living creatures according to their kinds: cattle and creeping things and beasts of the earth according to their kinds." And it was so. And God made the beasts of the earth according to their kinds and the cattle according to their kinds, and everything that creeps upon the ground according to its kind. (Gen 1:24-25)

The only exception occurs in vv.11-12 where we hear that not only is vegetation the recipient of the command that does God's bidding, but also one of its produce, the trees, are said to be *'aśah*/making their own fruit:

> And God said, "Let the earth put forth vegetation, plants yielding seed, and fruit trees bearing (*'aśah* /making) fruit in which is their seed, each according to its kind, upon the earth." And it was so. The earth brought forth vegetation, plants yielding seed according to their own kinds, and trees bearing (*'aśah* /making) fruit in which is their seed, each according to its kind. And God saw that it was good. (Gen 1:11-12)

This short study on vegetation in the author's purview in Genesis would not have been possible without knowing the original Hebrew. Let me single out the two venerable translations, the LXX and the Vulgate, as a case in point.

LXX

> [11]καὶ εἶπεν ὁ θεός *βλαστησάτω ἡ γῆ βοτάνην* χόρτου σπεῖρον σπέρμα κατὰ γένος καὶ καθ᾽ ὁμοιότητα καὶ ξύλον κάρπιμον ποιοῦν καρπόν οὗ τὸ σπέρμα αὐτοῦ ἐν αὐτῷ κατὰ γένος ἐπὶ τῆς γῆς καὶ ἐγένετο οὕτως [12]καὶ *ἐξήνεγκεν ἡ γῆ βοτάνην* χόρτου σπεῖρον σπέρμα κατὰ γένος καὶ καθ᾽ ὁμοιότητα καὶ ξύλον κάρπιμον ποιοῦν καρπόν οὗ τὸ σπέρμα αὐτοῦ ἐν αὐτῷ κατὰ γένος ἐπὶ τῆς γῆς καὶ εἶδεν ὁ θεὸς ὅτι καλόν

Vulgate

> [11]et ait *germinet terra herbam* virentem et facientem semen et lignum pomiferum faciens fructum iuxta genus suum cuius semen in semet ipso sit super terram et factum est ita [12]et *protulit terra herbam* virentem et adferentem semen iuxta genus suum lignumque faciens fructum et habens unumquodque sementem secundum speciem suam et vidit Deus quod esset bonum

At the start of v.11 neither βλαστησάτω ἡ γῆ βοτάνην nor *germinet terra herbam* captures the play in the original Hebrew whereby both the verb *tadšeh* and the noun *dešeh* share the same root and thus sounding "let the earth vegetate vegetation." This feature prepares for the following verse where another verb is used and thus one hears "the earth brought forth (*toṣeʾ*) vegetation (*dešeh*)." The LXX captures the play of the original in rendering *mazriaʿ zeraʿ* (seeding [sowing] seed; English yielding seed) into σπεῖρον σπέρμα (from the same root *speirō*, sow), whereas the Vulgate has *facientem semen* (making seed) in v.11 and switches to *adferentem semen* (producing seed) in v.12, completely missing the wordplay.

Both translations keep close to the original *'ośeh peri* (making fruit)[3] when referring to the "fruit trees" in both verses. The LXX has ποιοῦν καρπόν and the Vulgate has *faciens fructum*. Still, as I mentioned earlier, the LXX throughout Genesis 1:1-2:4 botches the differentiation between *bara'* (create, render functional) and *'aśah* (make, do) by translating both into the Greek *poiein* (make), while the Vulgate has *creare* for *bara'* and *facere* for *'aśah*. This will allow the Vulgate to reflect the play in the original on the use of the combination of *bara'* and *'aśah* in the same phrase twice in a row in Genesis 2:3-4 whereas the LXX is forced to resort to two completely different verbs to render *bara'*, ἤρξατο (started, began) in v.3 and ἐγένετο (happened, were) in verse 4:

> So God blessed the seventh day and hallowed it, because on it God rested from all his work which he had done (*'aśot*) in creation (*bara'*). These are the generations of the heavens and the earth when they were created (*hibbare'*). In the day that the Lord God made (*'aśot*) the earth and the heavens

> καὶ ηὐλόγησεν ὁ θεὸς τὴν ἡμέραν τὴν ἑβδόμην καὶ ἡγίασεν αὐτήν ὅτι ἐν αὐτῇ κατέπαυσεν ἀπὸ πάντων τῶν ἔργων αὐτοῦ ὧν ἤρξατο ὁ θεὸς ποιῆσαι αὕτη ἡ βίβλος γενέσεως οὐρανοῦ καὶ γῆς ὅτε ἐγένετο ᾗ ἡμέρᾳ ἐποίησεν ὁ θεὸς τὸν οὐρανὸν καὶ τὴν γῆν

> et benedixit diei septimo et sanctificavit illum quia in ipso cessaverat ab omni opere suo quod creavit Deus ut faceret istae generationes caeli et terrae quando creatae sunt in die quo fecit Dominus Deus caelum et terram

---

3 RSV has "yielding fruit."

5

Sun and Moon

> And God said, "Let there be lights in the firmament of the heavens to separate the day from the night; and let them be for signs and for seasons and for days and years, and let them be lights in the firmament of the heavens to give light upon the earth." And it was so. And God made the two great lights, the greater light to rule the day, and the lesser light to rule the night; he made the stars also. And God set them in the firmament of the heavens to give light upon the earth, to rule over the day and over the night, and to separate the light from the darkness. And God saw that it was good. And there was evening and there was morning, a fourth day. (Gen 1:14-19)

At first impression these verses sound like a repeat of day one in thought as well as phraseology:

> And God saw that the light was good; and God separated the light from the darkness. God called the light Day, and the darkness he called Night. And there was evening and there was morning, one day. (Gen 1:4-5)

So a detailed analysis of Genesis 1:14-18 dealing with the sun and moon on the fourth day is definitely worthwhile to show that it has in its purview the rest of Genesis, the following four books of the Law, i.e., the entire Pentateuch, and indeed the entire scriptural canon.

"Separation" (*hibdil*) of day and night, light and darkness is in view of the teaching of the Law where light is associated with the correctness of knowledge and more so of behavior according to the dictates of the Law. Darkness is associated with disregard of the Law on all levels, knowledge and, more so, behavior.

> Yea, thou dost light my lamp; the Lord my God lightens my darkness. (Ps 18:28)

> The Lord is my light and my salvation. (Ps 27:1)

> Oh send out thy light and thy truth; let them lead me, let them bring me to thy holy hill and to thy dwelling! (Ps 43:3)
>
> For thou hast delivered my soul from death, yea, my feet from falling, that I may walk before God in the light of life. (Ps 56:13)
>
> Thy word is a lamp to my feet and a light to my path. (Ps 119:105)
>
> The unfolding of thy words gives light; it imparts understanding to the simple. (Ps 119:130)
>
> O house of Jacob, come, let us walk in the light of the Lord. (Is 2:5)
>
> But if you call yourself a Jew and rely upon the law and boast of your relation to God and know his will and approve what is excellent, because you are instructed in the law, and if you are sure that you are a guide to the blind, a light to those who are in darkness ... (Rom 2:17-19)
>
> Let us then cast off the works of darkness and put on the armor of light; let us conduct ourselves becomingly as in the day, not in reveling and drunkenness, not in debauchery and licentiousness, not in quarreling and jealousy. (Rom 13:12-13)
>
> For you are all sons of light and sons of the day; we are not of the night or of darkness. So then let us not sleep, as others do, but let us keep awake and be sober. For those who sleep sleep at night, and those who get drunk are drunk at night. But, since we belong to the day, let us be sober, and put on the breastplate of faith and love, and for a helmet the hope of salvation. (1 Thess 5:5-8)

In the account of day four, the author describes the function of the luminaries as separating day and night at the beginning of Genesis 1:14, and concludes with "And God set them ... to separate the light from the darkness" just before "God saw that it was good" (v.17, 18.) The intended link between the two separation statements is that they bracket the fourth day as *inclusio*. In other words, the ultimate goal of the separation between day and night, light and darkness, that establishes the basic unit of time in order for the human beings to regulate their lives, is not done so that human beings can do their own bidding during the day. From the purview of scripture, the separation between day and night is a foretaste of the good and the evil, that is, the way of life and the way of death according to God's will expressed in his law. This is corroborated in that the function assigned by God to the scriptural sun and moon, which are his handicraft and not self-standing entities, is to be luminaries (*me'orot,*[1] enlightened enlighteners; v.16). That is precisely why "God set them in the firmament of the heavens to give light (*ha'ir*) upon the earth" (v.17). Thus, their essential function is related to light and not darkness. Even the nightly luminary, the moon, is assigned to give light at night. The moon is as much *ma'or* as is the sun. The moon rules with its light over the night just as the sun rules with its light over the day: "And God made the two great lights, the greater light to rule the day, and the lesser light to rule the night." (v.16) Let us rehear Paul in this context:

> So then let us not sleep, as others do, but let us keep awake and be sober. For those who sleep sleep at night, and those who get drunk are drunk at night. But, since we belong to the day, let us be sober, and put on the breastplate of faith and love, and for a helmet the hope of salvation. (1 Thess 5:6-8)

The author's use of the verb *mašal* to speak of ruling (Gen 1:16) is clearly intentional in that it looks ahead to the rest of scripture. The noun *mašal* means parable or example, and thus the verb *mašal* means rule as a teacher would through teaching and educating. In order for the hearers to perceive the meaning and function of that verb they will have to wait for scripture to reveal this connotation. The English "rule" is used to translate two Hebrew verbs (1) *malak* (to own, to be king over)[2] and (2) *mašal.*[3] The sin of Israel in 1 Samuel 8 is that the people wanted a human king to rule over them and thus for them to be "like the

---

1 *Me'orot* is the plural of *ma'or* the nominalized verb *'or; me'irot* is the active participle plural of the verb *ha'ir* (enlighten).

2 Remember the citizens of a kingdom are the "subjects" of the monarch; in scripture they are the *'abadim*, slaves.

3 For *mašal* as "rule" see Joshua 12:2, 5 and 1 Kings 5:1.

nations," consequently forgetting that their sole *melek*/owner/proprietor is the Lord:

> Then all the elders of Israel gathered together and came to Samuel at Ramah, and said to him, "Behold, you are old and your sons do not walk in your ways; now appoint for us a king to govern us like all the nations." But the thing displeased Samuel when they said, "Give us a king to govern us." And Samuel prayed to the Lord. And the Lord said to Samuel, "Hearken to the voice of the people in all that they say to you; for they have not rejected you, but they have rejected me from *being king* (the Hebrew verb *malak*) over them." (1 Sam 8:4-7)[4]

The sun and the moon are posited as *mošelim* (rulers/ruling) by God and thus act according to his will:

> Then spoke Joshua to the Lord in the day when the Lord gave the Amorites over to the men of Israel; and he said in the sight of Israel, "Sun, stand thou still at Gibeon, and thou Moon in the valley of Aijalon."And the sun stood still, and the moon stayed, until the nation took vengeance on their enemies. Is this not written in the Book of Jashar? The sun stayed in the midst of heaven, and did not hasten to go down for about a whole day. (Josh 10:12-13)

> O give thanks to the Lord of lords, for his steadfast love endures for ever; to him who alone does great wonders, for his steadfast love endures for ever; to him who by understanding made the heavens, for his steadfast love endures for ever; to him who spread out the earth upon the waters, for his steadfast love endures for ever; to him who made the great lights, for his steadfast love endures for ever; the sun to rule over the day, for his steadfast love endures for ever; the moon and stars to rule over the night, for his steadfast love endures for ever. (Ps 136:3-9)

---

4 By their using of the verb "govern" (*šapat*; judge) to speak of the king they are asking for, they thought they would win the argument. Until then their leaders appointed by the Lord, the sole King of Israel, were the "judges" (*šopetim*)—in the Book that bear their name "Judges"—of whom Samuel was the last (And Samuel judged the people of Israel at Mizpah; 1 Sam 7:6). So, by asking for a king that would only judge and not *malak*, the Lord's kingship will be maintained. However, the Lord foils the people's subterfuge to Samuel: "they have rejected me from *being king* (the Hebrew verb *malak*) over them."

> Praise him, all his angels (*mal'akim*), praise him, all his host! Praise him, sun and moon, praise him, all you shining stars! (Ps 148:2-3)[5]

As such the sun and moon are given as examples to be followed by the king. They submit, just as the angels submit, and do God's bidding:

> The Lord has established his throne in the heavens, and his kingdom (*malkut* from the root *malak*) rules (*mašal*) over all. Bless the Lord, O you his angels, you mighty ones who do (*'aśah*) his word, hearkening to the voice of his word! Bless the Lord, all his hosts,[6] his ministers that do his will! Bless the Lord, all his works,[7] in all places of his dominion (*memšalah*). Bless the Lord, O my soul! (Ps 103:19-22)

> A Psalm of Solomon. Give the king thy justice, O God, and thy righteousness to the royal son! May he judge thy people with righteousness, and thy poor with justice! Let the mountains bear prosperity for the people, and the hills, in righteousness! May he defend the cause of the poor of the people, give deliverance to the needy, and crush the oppressor! May he live while the sun endures, and as long as the moon, throughout all generations! (Ps 72:1-5)

> *May* his name endure for ever, *his fame continue as long as the sun*! May men bless themselves by him, all nations call him blessed![8] Blessed be the Lord, the God of Israel, who alone does wondrous things. Blessed be his glorious name for ever; may his glory fill the

---

5 See later my comments on the relation between *mal'akim* (angels, messengers) and *mel'akah* (work; Gen 2:2-3).

6 This is the plural of "host" found in Genesis 2:1: "Thus the heavens and the earth were finished, and all the host of them."

7 From the verb *'aśah* (do, make, work).

8 This phraseology clearly harks back to Genesis 12:2-3: "And I will make of you a great nation, and I will bless you, and make your name great, so that you will be a blessing … and by you all the families of the earth shall bless themselves." The link between Abram/Abraham and the king of Judah is further hinted at a few chapters later in a passage whose phraseology recollects that of Genesis 12:2-3: "No longer shall your name be Abram, but your name shall be Abraham; for I have made you the father of a multitude of nations. I will make you exceedingly fruitful; and I will make nations of you, and *kings* shall come forth from you." (Gen 17:5-6).

> whole earth! Amen and Amen! The prayers of David, the son of Jesse, are ended. (Ps 72:17-20)

I should like to deal in more detail with a striking oddity that will hopefully convince my readers of my thesis that the authors had in mind the entire scripture while penning Genesis 1. The start of the divine declaration in the passage concerning day four (vv.14-19) sounds thus: "Let there be lights in the firmament of the heavens to separate the day from the night; and let them be for signs and for seasons and for days and years." (v.14) Any hearer listening to scripture *as literature*—which it is through and through—cannot help but be struck by three words—signs, seasons, years—that have absolutely no function in the setting of this chapter, especially since they are thrown in together with "days," the plural of "day," a constitutional noun of Genesis 1:1-2:5 where it appears in the singular no less than 13 times and starting as early as v.5. Add to this the statement "and let them be for signs and for seasons and for days and years" (1:14b) that clearly sounds as an appendage to "Let there be lights in the firmament of the heavens to separate the day from the night" (v.14a). And an appendage it is since it interrupts the flow of thought covering day four:

> And God said, "Let there be lights in the firmament of the heavens to separate the day from the night; ~~and let them be for signs and for seasons and for days and years~~, and let them be lights in the firmament of the heavens to give light upon the earth." And it was so. And God made the two great lights, the greater light to rule the day, and the lesser light to rule the night; he made the stars also. And God set them in the firmament of the heavens to give light upon the earth, to rule over the day and over the night, and to separate the light from the darkness. And God saw that it was good. And there was evening and there was morning, a fourth day. (Gen 1:14-19)

It is immediately noticeable that the entire passage is dealing specifically with the luminaries' ruling over the twenty-four-hour period known as "day." So, the question is, "What are the three other elements doing in this context, especially that two of them are mentioned at the outset, *before* days." The reaction of an impartial hearer might be to ask in tandem: "Why do I suddenly hear of 'signs' and 'seasons' that appear here out of the blue sky? What do these words mean? Why are they followed by the plural 'days' when the entire Genesis 1:1-2:4 is concerned with 'day' in the singular? Why are 'years' added after 'days'? And above all, why did the author squeeze this out of place statement right at the beginning of the entire passage (vv.14-19)?"

Let me begin with "years", the easiest to account for since it is coupled with "days" after the one preposition "for": "and let them be *for* signs and *for* seasons and *for* days and years." Just as day, year is a well-established time unit, unlike week and month that are time units devised by humans.[9] That is why year is assumed as a recognizable time unit in Adam's *toledot* to render the patriarchs' lifespan (Gen 5). On the other hand, both *'otot* (signs) and *mo'adim* (seasons) refer to elements whose meaning and value are assigned to them by a deliberate decision. They are far from being "natural" or "given" as days and years are.

The earliest following instance of *'ot* (sign) occurs in Genesis 4:15: "Then the Lord said to him, 'Not so! If any one slays Cain, vengeance shall be taken on him sevenfold.' And the Lord put a mark (*'ot)* on Cain, lest any who came upon him should kill him." Thereafter, we hear it three more times in a row in reference to the rainbow:

> And God said, "This is the *sign* of the covenant which I make between me and you and every living creature that is with you, for all future generations: I set my bow in the cloud, and it shall be a *sign* of the covenant between me and the earth" … God said to Noah, "This is the *sign* of the covenant which I have established between me and all flesh that is upon the earth." (Gen 9:12-13, 17)

---

9 Yet, even the "year" is omitted, let alone "week" and "month" in the divine post-diluvial statement: "While the earth remains, seedtime and harvest, cold and heat, summer and winter, day and night, shall not cease." (Gen 8:22)

It is very clear from the above two examples that *'ot* refers to the meaning of something that may be either natural, as the rainbow is, or artificial, as the "mark" inscribed by God on Cain, or as a scar or a tattoo would be. Accordingly, a scriptural "sign" does not necessarily need to be extraordinary or miraculous. However, the speaker can make an extraordinary event, such as an eclipse or an earthquake or a volcanic eruption, into a "sign" for the addressee. Later the text will differentiate between "signs" (*'otot*) and "wonders" or "extraordinary phenomena" (*mophetim*):

> But I will harden Pharaoh's heart, and though I multiply my signs (*'otot*) and wonders (*mophetim*) in the land of Egypt. (Ex 7:3)

> Or has any god ever attempted to go and take a nation for himself from the midst of another nation, by trials, by signs (*'otot*), by wonders (*mophetim*), and by war, by a mighty hand and an outstretched arm, and by great terrors, according to all that the Lord your God did for you in Egypt before your eyes? (Deut 4:34)

Consequently, in Genesis 1:14 the authors would have already had in mind the "sign" of the rainbow, which is extremely important for two reasons. It is the sign of the first scriptural covenant, which deals with the entire creation (between me and the earth; Gen 9:13) rather than with a set of human beings. The other more important reason is that this sign is totally under God's control and thus beyond the human reach and involvement as will be the case with circumcision and the Mosaic Law:

> *I set my bow* in the cloud, and it shall be a sign of the covenant between me and the earth. When *I bring clouds over the earth* and the bow is seen in the clouds, *I will remember* my covenant which is between me and you and every living creature of all flesh; and the waters shall never again become a flood to destroy all flesh. When the bow is in the clouds, *I will look upon it and remember* the everlasting covenant between God and every living creature of all flesh that is upon the earth. (Gen 9:13-16)

It makes sense then that this sign is in the divine domain, the heavens. Although heavens, per se, are not named, both "cloud" and, more specifically, "rain" associated with it, are "heavenly" phenomena.[10] This will find corroboration in the first and last verse of Ezekiel's opening chapter:

> In the thirtieth year, in the fourth month, on the fifth day of the month, as I was among the exiles by the river Chebar, the *heavens* were opened, and I saw visions of God ... Like the appearance of the *bow* that is in the *cloud* on the day of *rain*, so was the appearance of the brightness round about. Such was the appearance of the likeness of the glory of the Lord. And when I saw it, I fell upon my face, and I heard the voice of one speaking. (Ezek 1:1, 28)

At any rate, "the waters shall never again become a flood to destroy all flesh" (Gen 9:15) is a clear pointer to the opening statement of the flood episode:

> And after seven days the waters of the flood came upon the earth. In the six hundredth year of Noah's life, in the second month, on the seventeenth day of the month, on that day all the fountains of the great deep burst forth, and *the windows of the heavens were opened*. And *rain fell upon the earth* forty days and forty nights." (Gen 7:10-12).

The intentionality and aim of the unexpected "seasons" (*mo'adim*) in Genesis 1:14 is unmissable in that the three following instances of the singular *mo'ed* occur in conjunction with God's promise to Sarah that she would conceive and bear Isaac:

> But I will establish my covenant with Isaac, whom Sarah shall bear to you at this season (*mo'ed*) next year. (Gen 17:21) ... Is anything too hard for the Lord? At the appointed time (*mo'ed*) I will return to you, in the spring, and Sarah shall have a son.

---

10 My readers are reminded that scriptural Hebrew has no word for our "sky" or "air." Hence "the birds of the air" render the Hebrew *'oph haššamayim* (fowl of the heavens) as I indicated earlier. The two instances of "sky" in RSV's Old Testament translate the original *šamayim* (heavens; Ps 85:11; Prov 30:19).

> (18:14) … And Sarah conceived, and bore Abraham a son in his old age at the time (*mo'ed*) of which God had spoken to him. (21:2)

Even those of my readers who do not know Hebrew will have figured out the connotation of *mo'ed* through these three different renderings. Still they all converge around the understanding of a set time by decision.[11] This is confirmed in the following instance of that noun found in Exodus 9:5: "And the Lord set (*wayyaśem* from the verb *śim*)[12] a time (*mo'ed*), saying, 'Tomorrow the Lord will do this thing in the land.'"

Ultimately, Genesis 1:14 is preparing its hearers for the most important use of *mo'ed* in conjunction with the scriptural God who is first and foremost a shepherd:

> Give ear, O Shepherd of Israel, thou who leadest Joseph like a flock! Thou who art enthroned upon the cherubim, shine forth before Ephraim and Benjamin and Manasseh! Stir up thy might, and come to save us! (Ps 80:1-2)

And, since a shepherd's residence is a tent, the scriptural God meets the priests of his people in the tent that is "the tent (*'ohel*) of meeting (*mo'ed*)" and, thus more accurately, the tent where he gives them a "date" for them to meet with him! My understanding is supported by the following interesting statement by God:

> … and you shall beat some of it very small, and put part of it before the testimony in the tent of meeting (*mo'ed*) where I shall meet (*'iwwa'ed*) with you (*leka*; to you). (Ex 30:36)

The verbal *niphal* form *'iwwa'ed* is from the verb *ya'ad*, whence the verbal noun *mo'ed* originates, and its technical meaning is "I shall be bound by my promise to keep a date with," "I shall hold myself committed to an appointment," "I shall be beholden to a meeting," since it is followed by *leka* whose technical meaning

---

11 Those cognizant of Arabic will have guessed that the corresponding Arabic noun with the same consonants is *maw'ed* which means a "set time" or a "set date," as in our English "date" or "appointment."

12 The verb *śim* is very versatile, which explains its ubiquity in the Hebrew Old Testament. Its meaning is "set, posit, deposit, appoint, lay down, fix, define, etc…" which reflects intention on the part of the subject agent.

is "to/toward you." In other words, the original verb reflects a promise made by God "to you." RSV translation gives the impression that the tent is a tent of meeting, that is, a tent where God meets someone else, whereas the original stresses the aspect of a (*promised*) *established date* to which God commits himself toward the recipient of that promise. In other words, it is God who sets the "dates" of his "dates" with the leaders of his people through assigned "days" and "years."

With this mind one can see why the authors mentioned *mo'adim* before "days and years" in Genesis 1:14. They invited the hearers to perceive the latter two as also set times in view of their handling within the purview of the Law where certain set days and certain set years have a function: "You shall therefore keep this ordinance at its appointed time (*mo'ed*) from year to year." (Ex 13:10) Let me just mention here as an example the three yearly major feasts that take place on set dates:

> Three times in the year you shall keep a feast to me. You shall keep the feast of unleavened bread; as I commanded you, you shall eat unleavened bread for seven days at *the appointed time* (*mo'ed*) in the month of Abib, for in it you came out of Egypt. None shall appear before me empty-handed. You shall keep the feast of harvest, of the first fruits of your labor, of what you sow in the field. You shall keep the feast of ingathering at the end of the year, when you gather in from the field the fruit of your labor. (Ex 23:14-16)

That the authors had such purview in mind is confirmed by the ingenious singling out of the seventh day as a day of rest: "And on the seventh day God finished his work which he had done, and he rested (*wayyišbot* from the verb *šabat*) on the seventh day from all his work which he had done. So God blessed the seventh day and hallowed it, because on it God rested (*šabat*) from all his work which he had done in creation." (Gen 2:2-3) Although the verb *šabat* is repeated in conjunction with "the seventh day" that is also repeated, the authors ingeniously refrained from using the noun *šabbat* (sabbath) out of deference to the fact that the seventh day will be *instituted* as sabbath by God himself later after the exodus from Egypt:

> On the sixth day they gathered twice as much bread, two omers apiece; and when all the leaders of the congregation came and told Moses, he said to them, "This is what *the Lord has commanded*: 'Tomorrow is a day of solemn rest (*šabbaton*), a holy sabbath (*šabbat qodeš*; sabbath of holiness) to the Lord; bake what you will bake and boil what you will boil, and all that is left over lay by to be kept till the morning.'" So they laid it by till the morning, as Moses bade them; and it did not become foul, and there were no worms in it. Moses said, "Eat it today, for today is a sabbath to the Lord (*šabbat leyahweh*); today you will not find it in the field. Six days you shall gather it; but *on the seventh day,* which is a sabbath (*šabbat*), there will be none." On the seventh day some of the people went out to gather, and they found none. And the Lord said to Moses, "How long do you *refuse to keep my commandments and my laws*? See! The Lord *has given you* the sabbath (*šabbat*), therefore on the sixth day he gives you bread for two days; remain every man of you in his place, let no man go out of his place on the seventh day." So the people *rested on the seventh day*. (Ex 16:22-30)

Still, and perhaps more importantly, regarding the years as set times are the sabbatical year, set every seventh year, as rest for the land, and the jubilee year, set every fifty years, when everybody is set free and even the earth itself is set free from their subjugation by the human being (Lev 25). The "ground" (*'adamah*) that has been cursed due to the disobedience of Adam (*'adam*) (Gen 3:17) will be rehabilitated together with all those who live on and out of it (Gen 1:29-30).

6

The Sea Animals and the Seas

[20]And God said, "Let the waters bring forth swarms of living
creatures (*nepheš ḥayyah*), and let birds (*'oph*) fly above the earth
across the firmament of the heavens." [21] So God created the great
sea monsters and every living creature (*nepheš ḥayyah*) that moves,
with which the waters swarm, according to their kinds, and every
winged bird (*'oph*) according to its kind. [22] And God saw that it
was good. And God blessed them (*'otam*), saying, "Be fruitful and
multiply and fill the waters in the seas, and let birds multiply on
the earth." [23] And there was evening and there was morning, a
fifth day. (Gen 1:20-23)

The sea animals are given the first place among the "living creatures" (*nepheš ḥayyah*), including the human beings (Gen 2:7) and even a place of honor when one considers that they were the first to be "created" by God well before the human beings were (1:27). Just as will be the case with the land animals, the sea animals are under God's hold, and he will use them throughout scripture to threaten or tame the human beings. The author ingeniously planted the seed of this magisterial plan by specifically, and at face value unwarrantedly, singling out the "great sea monsters" (*hattanninim haggedolim*) from among the sea animals created by God. The strangeness of the singling out of the sea monsters (*tanninim*) is evident in the way the author handled the fifth day of creation in the original Hebrew.

When hearing this passage as it stands, without any preconception, one is struck by the following features:

1. The blessing of v.22 specifically aimed at the sea animals is "Be fruitful and multiply and fill the waters in the seas." The birds are summoned to simply multiply through a bland jussive form (imperative to a third person) "let birds multiply" similar to what we heard earlier in v.20 (let the waters ... let birds ...)

2. When comparing vv.20 and 21 in the original Hebrew one notices a parallelism in the use of *nepheš ḥayyah* (living creature; generic singular noun) and *'oph* (bird; generic singular noun) except for the additional *hattanninim haggedolim* (the great [sea] monsters; v.21) which is (1) in the plural; (2) preceded by the definite article *ha(l)* (the) compared to the singular *nepheš ḥayyah* and *'oph* each preceded by *kol* (every); (3) further defined by the adjective *haggedolim* (the great), a unique instance in scripture since *tannin* ([sea] monster) already reflects a huge size as is clear in that most translations follow the LXX in rendering it later as "dragon" (Greek *drakōn*).

3. The importance of this specificity contrasts with the generic singular noun *dagat* (fish) used twice in a row a few verses later to speak of the sea animals: "let them have dominion over the fish of the sea (*degat hayyam*), and over the birds of the air" (v.26); "and have dominion over the fish of the sea (*degat hayyam*) and over the birds of the air" (v.28)

4. My fourth point is aimed especially at those cognizant of scriptural Hebrew. Although the masculine plural accusative (direct complement) *'otam* (them) in v.22 could apply to both the sea monsters and the living creatures of the sea, technically speaking—to the ear—it is aimed more specifically at *hattanninim* that is masculine plural. And if so, then the "sea monsters" are not only "created" (v.21) well before the human beings will be (v.27), but also they are specifically "blessed" (v.22) as the human beings will be (v.28)—and, to boot, with the same words (Be fruitful, multiply, and fill)—, a blessing that

> neither the birds nor the land animals were expressly graced with.

Thus, attentive hearers of the original Hebrew cannot help but being curious, to say the least. However, such curiosity will not be satisfied until Exodus 7 when their patience will have either been eroded or completely disappeared. Even then, they will be perplexed to hear, no less than three times in a row, that the *tanninim* are "land creatures." Although the LXX uses *drakōn* (plural *drakontes*), most translations opt for "serpent/s" or "snake/s" and understandably so since the Hebrew itself switches to *naḥaš* (serpent, snake; Gen 3:1, 2, 4, 13, 14), a *ḥayyat haśśadeh* (creature [animal] of the field; v.1), and thus a land animal, to refer to the same *tannin*:

> And the Lord said to Moses and Aaron, "When Pharaoh says to you, 'Prove yourselves by working a miracle,' then you shall say to Aaron, 'Take your rod and cast it down before Pharaoh, that it may become a serpent (*tannin*).'" So Moses and Aaron went to Pharaoh and did as the Lord commanded; Aaron cast down his rod before Pharaoh and his servants, and it became a serpent (*tannin*). Then Pharaoh summoned the wise men and the sorcerers; and they also, the magicians of Egypt, did the same by their secret arts. For every man cast down his rod, and they became serpents (*tanninim*). But Aaron's rod swallowed up their rods. Still Pharaoh's heart was hardened, and he would not listen to them; as the Lord had said. Then the Lord said to Moses, "Pharaoh's heart is hardened, he refuses to let the people go. Go to Pharaoh in the morning, as he is going out to the water; wait for him by the river's brink, and take in your hand the rod which was turned into a serpent (*naḥaš*)."[1] (Ex 7:8-15)

This interconnection between *tannin* and *naḥaš* in scripture is sealed in Isaiah where both are intertwined in a synonymic parallelism:

> In that day the Lord with his hard and great and strong sword will punish Leviathan the fleeing serpent (*naḥaš bariaḥ*), Leviathan

1 Here the LXX has *ophis* the same noun as throughout Genesis 3.

> the twisting serpent (*naḥaš*), and he will slay the dragon (*tannin*) that is in the sea. (Is 27:1)[2]

The following passages reflect a similar parallelism between the "dragon/serpent" and another mythical figure, Rahab, the meaning of the original being "terror":[3]

> Awake, awake, put on strength, O arm of the Lord; awake, as in days of old, the generations of long ago. Was it not thou that didst cut Rahab in pieces, that didst pierce the dragon (*tannin*)? (Is 51:9)

> By his power he stilled the sea; by his understanding he smote Rahab. By his wind the heavens were made fair; his hand pierced the fleeing serpent (*naḥaš bariaḥ*). (Job 26:12-13)

Notice how both Leviathan and Rahab (1) are likened to the fleeing serpent as well as to the *tannin*, and (2) are intimately linked to the sea. These features are encountered again in the following passages:

> Am I the sea, or a sea monster (*tannin*), that thou settest a guard over me? (Job 7:12)

> Can you draw out Leviathan with a fishhook, or press down his tongue with a cord? (41:1)

> Yet God my King is from of old, working salvation in the midst of the earth. Thou didst divide the sea by thy might; thou didst break the heads of the dragons (*tanninim*) on the waters. Thou didst crush the heads of Leviathan, thou didst give him as food for the creatures of the wilderness. (Ps 74:12-14)

> Yonder is the sea, great and wide, which teems with things innumerable, living things both small and great. There go the

---

2 The LXX renders Leviathan into "dragon" both times. The hearer is bombarded with *drakonta* three times.

3 My English speaking readers should beware of the mix in the European translations, including the LXX and the Vulgate, between the equalization of the harlot Rahab (*raḥab*) of Jericho and Rahab (*rahab*) due to their languages' non-differentiation between two different consonants in the Semitic languages, the *ḥ* and the *h*. Sometimes the *ḥ* is rendered as "ch" as in *raḥel* (Rachel). Yet that is not the case with *'aḥ'ab* ([King] Ahab).

> ships, and Leviathan which thou didst form (*yaṣar*) to sport in it. (Ps 104:25-26)

The last passage is also interesting in that it confirms the intimate relation between the "great seas monsters" and the human beings in Genesis 1 through the use of the verb *yaṣar* (form, as a potter does out of clay) that describes the formation of the land animals and birds (Gen 2:19) as well as the human being (Gen 2:7). The distinct impression is that the *tannin*, though a sea creature, is also active on dry land where it is likened to a serpent as in Exodus 7. Also note the following instances where *tannin* occurs in parallel with land animals:

> For their vine comes from the vine of Sodom, and from the fields of Gomorrah; their grapes are grapes of poison, their clusters are bitter; their wine is the poison of serpents (*tanninim*), and the cruel venom of asps. (Deut 32:32-33)

> You will tread on the lion and the adder, the young lion and the serpent (*tannin*) you will trample under foot. (Ps 91:13)

All the preceding militates for the importance of the great sea monsters and the phraseology surrounding them in Genesis 1. In Exodus 7, Deuteronomy 32, and Psalm 71, the *tannin* goes hand in hand with land animals, especially the *naḥaš* (serpent, snake; Ex 7) that was instrumental in the human being's early disobedience (Gen 3). When one considers that most of the quotations concerning those *tanninim* are clustered mainly in the Ketubim, the last part of the Old Testament which was conceived to pressure the children of the scriptural Israel into sharing the teachings of the Law and the Prophets with the Japhethites,[4] then one understands why suddenly in these writings we hear of God challenging the mighty seas and their denizens that pose a continual threat to the isle nations (10:5) as well as to the nations around the Syrian wilderness. Suffice it

---

4 I have covered this view of the function of the Ketubim in detail elsewhere. See *OTI*3 157-9.

here to point out the "statement of purpose" found in the Prologue to Sirach written specifically in Greek:

> Many great teachings have been given to us through the Law and the Prophets and the others that followed them, and for these we should praise Israel for instruction and wisdom. Now, those who read the scriptures must not only themselves understand them, but must also as lovers of learning be able through the spoken and written word to help (*khrēsimous*; be useful, beneficial to) the outsiders (*tois ektos*; those [who are, stand] outside). So my grandfather Jesus, who had devoted himself especially to the reading of the Law and the Prophets and the other books of our ancestors, and had acquired considerable proficiency in them, was himself also led to write something pertaining to instruction and wisdom, so that by becoming familiar also with his book those who love learning might make even greater progress in living according to the law.
>
> You are invited therefore to read it with goodwill and attention, and to be indulgent in cases where, despite our diligent labor in translating, we may seem to have rendered some phrases imperfectly. For what was originally expressed in Hebrew does not have exactly the same sense when translated into another language. Not only this book, but even the Law itself, the Prophecies, and the rest of the books differ not a little when read in the original.
>
> When I came to Egypt in the thirty-eighth year of the reign of Euergetes and stayed for some time, I found opportunity for no little instruction. It seemed highly necessary that I should myself devote some diligence and labor to the translation of this book. During that time I have applied my skill day and night to complete and publish the book for those living abroad (*tois en tē paroikia*) who wished to gain learning and are disposed to live according to the law. (NRSV)

The adverb *ektos* (outside) is self-explanatory, referring to the members of the nations who do not stand "inside" the synagogue gatherings. It is the noun *paroikia*, however, that is of interest because, clearly from the context, it refers to the hearers of the Law who are residing particularly in Egypt and thus as "strangers" (*paroikoi*) there, outside the "earth of Canaan." This is exactly and repeatedly how the "children of Jacob/Israel" are described in Genesis while in Egypt, through the rendering of the Hebrew root *gur/ger* translated as "soujourn/ing" in English:

> So Abram went down to Egypt to sojourn (Greek *paroikēsai*; Hebrew *gur*) there, for the famine was severe in the land. (Gen 12:10)

> Then the Lord said to Abram, "Know of a surety that your descendants (Greek *sperma*; Hebrew *zera'*) will be sojourners (Greek *paroikon*; Hebrew *ger*)[5] in a land that is not theirs, and will be slaves there, and they will be oppressed for four hundred years." (Gen 15:13)

> They said to Pharaoh, "We have come to sojourn (Greek *paroikein*; Hebrew *gur*) in the land; for there is no pasture for your servants' flocks, for the famine is severe in the land of Canaan; and now, we pray you, let your servants dwell in the land of Goshen." (Gen 47:4)

It is worthwhile noting that the noun *paroikia* occurs a few verses earlier in the LXX, in the Wisdom of Solomon 19:10,[6] in conjunction with the sojourn in Egypt. This understanding is sealed in Acts 13:17: "The God of this people Israel chose our fathers and made the people great during their stay (*paroikia*) in the land of Egypt, and with uplifted arm he led them out of it."[7] However, what is more important for our discussion is that Genesis refers even more often to the Patriarchs' stay in the earth of Canaan with the same term "sojourning-sojourner," a usage that also overflows into the New Testament:

---

5 Both the Greek *sperma* (seed) and the Hebrew *zera'* (seed) are singular nouns, which explains the singular *paroikon, ger* respectively while RSV has "sojourners" corresponding to "descendants" for the original "seed."

6 In the LXX canon the Wisdom of Solomon immediately precedes the Wisdom of Sirach and has nineteen chapters, the last composed of twenty verses.

7 See also "And God spoke to this effect, that his posterity (*sperma*) would be aliens (*paroikon*) in a land belonging to others, who would enslave them and ill-treat them four hundred years" (Acts 7:6).

And I will give to you, and to your descendants after you, the land of your sojournings (*paroikeis*), all the land of Canaan, for an everlasting possession; and I will be their God." (Gen 17:8)

And Abraham rose up from before his dead, and said to the Hittites, "I am a stranger (*paroikos*) and a sojourner (*parepidēmos*) among you; give me property among you for a burying place, that I may bury my dead out of my sight." (Gen 23:3-4)

My master made me swear, saying, "You shall not take a wife for my son from the daughters of the Canaanites, in whose land I dwell (*paroikō*); but you shall go to my father's house and to my kindred, and take a wife for my son." (Gen 24:37-38)

And the Lord appeared to him (Isaac), and said, "Do not go down to Egypt; dwell in the land of which I shall tell you. Sojourn (*paroikei*) in this land, and I will be with you, and will bless you; for to you and to your descendants I will give all these lands, and I will fulfil the oath which I swore to Abraham your father." (Gen 26:2-3)

(Isaac speaking to Jacob) God Almighty bless you and make you fruitful and multiply you, that you may become a company of peoples. May he give the blessing of Abraham to you and to your descendants with you, that you may take possession of the land of your sojournings (*paroikēseōs*) which God gave to Abraham!" (Gen 28:3-4)

Then Esau took his wives, his sons, his daughters, and all the members of his household, his cattle, all his beasts, and all his property which he had acquired in the land of Canaan; and he went into a land away from his brother Jacob. For their possessions were too great for them to dwell together; the land of their sojournings (*paroikēseōs*) could not support them because of their cattle. So Esau dwelt in the hill country of Seir; Esau is Edom. (Gen 36:6-8)

Then one of them, named Cleopas, answered him, "*Are you* the only *visitor* (*paroikeis*) to Jerusalem who does not know the things that have happened there in these days?" (Lk 24:18)

And God spoke to this effect, that his posterity would be aliens (*paroikon*) in a land belonging to others, who would enslave them and ill-treat them four hundred years. (Acts 7:6)

> At this retort Moses fled, and became an exile (*paroikos*) in the land of Midian, where he became the father of two sons. (Acts 7:29)

> So then you are no longer strangers and sojourners (*paroikoi*), but you are fellow citizens with the saints and members of the household of God (Eph 2:19)

> And if you invoke as Father him who judges each one impartially according to his deeds, conduct yourselves with fear throughout the time of your exile (*paroikias*). (1 Pet 1:17)

> Beloved, I beseech you as aliens (*paroikous*) and exiles (*parepidēmous*) to abstain from the passions of the flesh that wage war against your soul. (1 Pet 2:11)[8]

In other words, the addressees of scripture, the scriptural Israel, are always posited as living on the earth (*'ereṣ*) as *'adamah*, the dry land of every and any *'adam* (human being), which they share with the *toledot* of the three sons of Noah at the same time (Gen 10:1). Everywhere the children of Israel are is their *paroikia*, their earth of "sojourn," however, this is experienced or felt more so when they are living together with or within the nations as in Egypt or Assyria or Babylonia, or when the Macedonians or Romans are ruling the area around the Syrian wilderness, that is to say in scriptural terms, when the Japhethites are "enlarged" with God's blessing in order to "dwell in the tents of Shem" (Gen 9:27) and share in the "blessing of Shem by that same God" (v.26). This, in turn, explains why the only two instances of the overcoming of the *tannin* by God outside the Ketubim are found in Isaiah in contexts that reflect the togetherness of Israel and the nations. Isaiah 27:1 occurs toward the end of what is referred to as "the Little Apocalypse of Isaiah" (chapters 24-27), whose literary context is God's ultimate judgment of and victory over his entire creation:

> Behold, the Lord will lay waste the earth and make it desolate, and he will twist its surface and scatter its inhabitants. (Is 24:1)

---

8 Compare with Genesis 23:4.

> The earth is utterly broken, the earth is rent asunder, the earth is violently shaken. The earth staggers like a drunken man, it sways like a hut; its transgression lies heavy upon it, and it falls, and will not rise again. On that day the Lord will punish the host of heaven, in heaven, and the kings of the earth, on the earth. They will be gathered together as prisoners in a pit; they will be shut up in a prison, and after many days they will be punished. Then the moon will be confounded, and the sun ashamed; for the Lord of hosts will reign on Mount Zion and in Jerusalem and before his elders he will manifest his glory. (Is 24:19-23)

> For behold, the Lord is coming forth out of his place to punish the inhabitants of the earth for their iniquity, and the earth will disclose the blood shed upon her, and will no more cover her slain. In that day the Lord with his hard and great and strong sword will punish Leviathan the fleeing serpent, Leviathan the twisting serpent, and he will slay the dragon (*tannin*) that is in the sea. (Is 26:21-27:1)

The second instance in Isaiah (Awake, awake, put on strength, O arm of the Lord; awake, as in days of old, the generations of long ago. Was it not thou that didst cut Rahab in pieces, that didst pierce the dragon [*tannin*]? 51:9) follows the passage concerning the Servant of the Lord (50:4-11) whose mission was depicted twice earlier as inclusive of both the nations and the remnant of Israel scattered among them:

> Behold my servant, whom I uphold, my chosen, in whom my soul delights; I have put my Spirit upon him, he will bring forth justice to the nations. He will not cry or lift up his voice, or make it heard in the street; a bruised reed he will not break, and a dimly burning wick he will not quench; he will faithfully bring forth justice. He will not fail or be discouraged till he has established justice in the earth; and the coastlands (*'iyyim*; isles) wait for his law. Thus says God, the Lord, who created (*bara'*) the heavens and stretched them out, who spread forth the earth and what comes from it, who gives breath to the people upon it and spirit to those who walk in it: "I am the Lord, I have called you in righteousness, I have taken you by the hand and kept you; I have given you as a covenant to the people, a light to the nations, to open the eyes that are blind, to bring out the prisoners from the dungeon, from the prison those who sit in darkness." (Is 42:1-7)

> Listen to me, O coastlands (*'iyyim*; isles), and hearken, you peoples from afar. The Lord called me from the womb, from the body of my mother he named my name. He made my mouth like a sharp sword, in the shadow of his hand he hid me; he made me a polished arrow, in his quiver he hid me away. And he said to me, "You are my servant, Israel, in whom I will be glorified." But I said, "I have labored in vain, I have spent my strength for nothing and vanity; yet surely my right is with the Lord, and my recompense with my God." And now the Lord says, who formed me from the womb to be his servant, to bring Jacob back to him, and that Israel might be gathered to him, for I am honored in the eyes of the Lord, and my God has become my strength—he says: "It is too light a thing that you should be my servant to raise up the tribes of Jacob and to restore the preserved of Israel; I will give you as a light to the nations, that my salvation may reach to the end of the earth." (Is 49:1-6)

Earth versus Sea

In choosing the Syrian wilderness as their scriptural "world" the authors were bound by the socio-polity of shepherdism where animals, especially sheep, shared the human world as equals and even defined the meaning of family for both.[9] This was the world of the Shemites who were basically shepherds (Gen 11:10-26).[10] By the same token, by linking the Japhethites with the isles of the seas, the authors were intentionally identifying the maritime animal kingdom as a full-fledged partner in the "world" of the Japhethites. More importantly for the authors, in both cases, the scriptural premise is that God is in control of both "worlds" in their entirety and uses them at will to convey his instruction to the Japhethites as well as to the Shemites.

In the case of the Shemites, this message is already clear in Genesis 10 where Shem and Ham share the same territory as two sides of the same coin. In that world, the people are blessed,

---

9 See later my discussion of this matter, p. 118.

10 See my comments in *ROS* 275-6.

as Shem is, if they follow the dictates of God, or they are cursed, that is, under the ire (*ḥam;* heat) of that same God, as their progeny Canaan was, when they do not follow God's dictates. The double-sidedness of their world can be seen in its following features:

1. God can use the sun as beneficent light or as scorching heat.[11]
2. The wind could function as life-giving breeze or breath, on the one hand, or as destructive storm, on the other hand.
3. The animals, co-citizens of the humans to the extent that they were included among the remnant of the ark, can sustain the humans with their milk and meat as well as with their skin, or some of those animals can become, in God's hand, a medium for his punishment:

> And David said, "The Lord who delivered me from the paw of the lion and from the paw of the bear, will deliver me from the hand of this Philistine." And Saul said to David, "Go, and the Lord be with you!" (1 Sam 17:37)
>
> Set the trumpet to your lips, for a vulture is over the house of the Lord, because they have broken my covenant, and transgressed my law. (Hos 8:1)
>
> Herds shall lie down in the midst of her, all the beasts of the field; the vulture and the hedgehog shall lodge in her capitals; the owl shall hoot in the window, the raven croak on the threshold; for her cedar work will be laid bare. (Zeph 2:14)

---

11 See e.g. "Do not gaze at me because I am swarthy, because the sun has scorched me" (Song 1:6); "but when the sun rose they were scorched; and since they had no root they withered away" (Mt 13:6); "For the sun rises with its scorching heat and withers the grass" (Jas 1:11); "They shall hunger no more, neither thirst any more; the sun shall not strike them, nor any scorching heat." (Rev 7:16)

> The eye that mocks a father and scorns to obey a mother will be picked out by the ravens of the valley and eaten by the vultures. (Prov 30:17)
>
> Our pursuers were swifter than the vultures in the heavens; they chased us on the mountains, they lay in wait for us in the wilderness. (Lam 4:19)

On the other hand, since the fate of the Japhethites is linked to the seas and their waters, it stands to reason that the sea animals play a role in the scriptural story when it comes to the nations whose territory are the isles. And this is precisely what we find in scripture, strange as it may seem for us heirs of "theological" thinking. But before embarking on our study I need to set the record straight for my readers.

The difference between fiction and historical fiction is clearly not the historical—since how can fiction be history?—but rather the geographical as well as socio-political setting of the story. For a fictional love story in India or Nepal to be engaging for the readers, the author will resort, for example, to setting it against the Himalayas to make them feel as though they are sharing with the heroes the reality of the story. What makes the scriptural narrative "historical" and not simply "fictional" is precisely, as is the case with all historical fictions, that it is anchored within a real geographical area although this may not be the case for each individual location, since such individual location could be made up.[12] This applies even when the major event of the story is presented as universal. A pertinent example that applies to the year 2020 would be that someone in North America decides to write a fictional story about a dedicated and brave health provider during the Covid-19 pandemic. The most interesting or compelling choice for such a story understandably would be Metropolitan New York City due the extremely high number of cases and deaths in that area compared to other

12 This explains the frequency of instances in scripture where the name of a "locality" is explained as to its meaning, just as individual names of persons are.

regions, at least at the start of the pandemic.[13] This choice would help the author impress on the readers that the characters as well as the protagonist, whose "world" in the story is the New York metropolis, are facing a catastrophe of major, if not universal, proportions.

This is how we are supposed to hear the story of the flood and not go on asides debating whether the flood indeed covered the entire earth or was confined to the region delineated by the authors. Such a debate is already skewed because both sides, even unwittingly, are loading the scriptural noun "earth" with a meaning that it acquired only later when humans discovered that their "world" was a spherical planet. However, that was not the original meaning of the scriptural earth that referred to the "dry mass of land" on which animals and humans fared and lived, regardless of the size of that mass. The earth (*'ereṣ*) is always the dry land of the protagonists, which explains the plural "earths" (*'araṣot*) encountered often in scripture, which those who translate into English have no choice but render into "lands"[14] or "countries"[15] or "districts."[16] However, such translations rob the text of its original intent whereby, within the parameters of the scriptural story, the "earth" has an encompassing—total, universal—function for the people living on and from it, as it was so willed by God in scripture:

> And God said, "Behold, I have given you every plant yielding seed which is upon the face of all the earth (*'ereṣ*), and every tree with seed in its fruit; you shall have them for food. And to every beast of the earth (*'ereṣ*), and to every bird of the air, and to everything that creeps on the earth (*'ereṣ*), everything that has the breath of life, I have given every green plant for food." And it was so. And God saw everything that he had made, and behold, it was very good. And there was evening and there was morning, a sixth day. (Gen 1:29-31)

---

13 Another author may choose the states of Florida, Texas, or Arizona as a backdrop.
14 E.g., Gen 41:54.
15 E.g., 2 Kg 18:35.
16 E.g., 2 Chr 11:23.

Still, although historicity or factuality is an authorial production or projection and, thus, concoction, the geographical setting and time period of the story may not be. Take, for instance, the author's choice of Egypt as the "land of slaves" from which the "children of Israel" were brought out after a sojourn of four hundred thirty years (Ex 12:40-41). It is important to realize that Egypt was not a "utopian,"[17] though far away, location since it was already depicted as being within the range of the author's scriptural earth or world:

> A river flowed out of Eden to water the garden, and there it divided and became four rivers. The name of the first is Pishon; it is the one which flows around the whole land of Havilah, where there is gold; and the gold of that land is good; bdellium and onyx stone are there. The name of the second river is Gihon; it is the one which flows around the whole land of Cush. And the name of the third river is Tigris, which flows east of Assyria. And the fourth river is the Euphrates. (Gen 2:10-14)

The closeness between Cush and Egypt will soon be established in Genesis 10: "The sons of Ham: Cush, Egypt, Put, and Canaan." (10:6) Unfortunately, an English reader who is not cognizant of Hebrew will miss the frequent mention of Cush in scripture since the original Hebrew *kuš* is usually rendered as Ethiopia. However, the historical as well as geographical closeness of the latter to Egypt is well known. Consider the following scriptural instances:

> In that day the Lord will extend his hand yet a second time to recover the remnant which is left of his people, from Assyria, from Egypt, from Pathros, from Ethiopia (*kuš*), from Elam, from Shinar, from Hamath, and from the coastlands of the sea. (Is 11:11)

> Ah, land of whirring wings which is beyond the rivers of Ethiopia (*kuš*); which sends ambassadors by the Nile, in vessels of papyrus upon the waters! (Is 18:1-2)

---

17 I have argued plentifully in *ROS* for the non-utopian character of the scriptural epic, pp. 284-5.

> The Lord said, "As my servant Isaiah has walked naked and barefoot for three years as a sign and a portent against Egypt and Ethiopia (*kuš*), so shall the king of Assyria lead away the Egyptians captives and the Ethiopians exiles, both the young and the old, naked and barefoot, with buttocks uncovered, to the shame of Egypt. Then they shall be dismayed and confounded because of Ethiopia (*kuš*) their hope and of Egypt their boast. (Is 20:3-5)

> For I am the Lord your God, the Holy One of Israel, your Savior. I give Egypt as your ransom, Ethiopia (*kuš*) and Seba in exchange for you. (Is 43:3)

> Thus says the Lord: "The wealth of Egypt and the merchandise of Ethiopia (*kuš*), and the Sabeans, men of stature, shall come over to you and be yours, they shall follow you." (Is 45:14)

> Therefore, behold, I am against you, and against your streams, and I will make the land of Egypt an utter waste and desolation, from Migdol to Syene, as far as the border of Ethiopia (*kuš*). (Ezek 29:10)

> A sword shall come upon Egypt, and anguish shall be in Ethiopia (*kuš*), when the slain fall in Egypt, and her wealth is carried away, and her foundations are torn down. (Ezek 30:4)

> Ethiopia (*kuš*) was her strength, Egypt too, and that without limit; Put and the Libyans were her helpers. (Nah 3:9)

> Let bronze be brought from Egypt; let Ethiopia (*kuš*) hasten to stretch out her hands to God. (Ps 68:31)

Just as the exodus story was located in the southern part of the Syro-Arabian wilderness—the author's world, the flood story was specifically located in the author's immediate neighborhood due to the centrality of Babel and the region of the Two Rivers throughout the scriptural story. Thus, that location has the lion's share at the beginning of that story:

> A river flowed out of Eden to water the garden, and there it divided and became four rivers. … And the name of the third river is Tigris, which flows east of Assyria. And the fourth river is the Euphrates. (Gen 2:10, 14)

> Cush[18] became the father of Nimrod; he was the first on earth to be a mighty man. He was a mighty hunter before the Lord; therefore it is said, "Like Nimrod a mighty hunter before the Lord." The beginning of his kingdom was Babel, Erech, and Accad, all of them in the land of Shinar. (Gen 10:8-10)
>
> Now the whole earth had one language and few words. And as men migrated from the east, they found a plain in the land of Shinar and settled there. And they said to one another, "Come, let us make bricks, and burn them thoroughly." And they had brick for stone, and bitumen for mortar. Then they said, "Come, let us build ourselves a city, and a tower with its top in the heavens, and let us make a name for ourselves, lest we be scattered abroad upon the face of the whole earth." … Therefore its name was called Babel, because there the Lord confused the language of all the earth; and from there the Lord scattered them abroad over the face of all the earth. (Gen 11:1-4, 9)
>
> Now these are the descendants of Terah. Terah was the father of Abram, Nahor, and Haran; and Haran was the father of Lot. Haran died before his father Terah in the land of his birth, in Ur of the Chaldeans. … Terah took Abram his son and Lot the son of Haran, his grandson, and Sarai his daughter-in-law, his son Abram's wife, and they went forth together from Ur of the Chaldeans to go into the land of Canaan; but when they came to Haran, they settled there. The days of Terah were two hundred and five years; and Terah died in Haran. (Gen 11:27-28, 31-32)
>
> In the days of Amraphel king of Shinar, Arioch king of Ellasar, Chedorlaomer king of Elam, and Tidal king of Goiim, these kings made war with Bera king of Sodom, Birsha king of Gomorrah, Shinab king of Admah, Shemeber king of Zeboiim, and the king of Bela (that is, Zoar). (Gen 14:1-2)

The authors' interest in that region is sealed through the unwarranted mention of "the mountains of Ararat" as the precise location of Noah's ark's landing (Gen 8:4). The use of the plural "mountains" (*harim*) denotes that either the authors were aware of the two peaks of Ararat or they were referring to

18 Notice how Cush is already posited in close link with Babel.

the “land (*ʾereṣ*; earth) of Ararat” (2 Kg 19:37; Is 37:38) or the “kingdom of Ararat” (Jer 51:27). At any rate, they knew the geographical proximity of Ararat to the Northern Syrian wilderness, and that the two main rivers, the Euphrates and the Tigris, have their sources in that mountainous area. The conclusion imposes itself: the scriptural flood was universal in that it covered the authors’ entire world as described in Genesis 2:10-14.

A more valid—though only seemingly so—question is: “If Japheth was in his father’s ark together with his brothers, how did his progeny end up residing in the isles of the Mediterranean Sea while the progenies of his brothers remained within the boundaries of the Syro-Arabian wilderness?” Essentially, this kind of questioning goes hand in hand with that concerning Cain’s wife: Where did she come from? In both cases the answer lies in the authors’ overall primary and fundamental interest: all human beings, whatever their differentiating features, originate in the one *haʾadam* (the human being). Had the author maintained this oneness of humankind by presenting the post-diluvial humans as originating in the one Noah, his post-diluvial story would have sounded as a new creation, which would have contradicted his premise in Genesis 1-4 where God’s creative activity was finished, fulfilled, and brought to completion by the seventh day. This, in turn, explains why we do not hear about the origin of Cain’s wife. In order to underscore this reality the authors ingeniously brought under the one umbrella, so to speak, the post-diluvial humanity as originating at the same time in the three brothers rather than in the one Noah, which would have made him another “Adam” and would have contradicted the authors’ earlier handling of the *toledot* of Adam where Noah is no more and no less than the linear descendant of Adam. This matter was on the author’s mind when the original pattern of the birth of the first son being the separating moment of “before” and “after” in the life of the patriarch is suddenly broken and replaced with a new one:

> When Lamech had lived a hundred and eighty-two years, he became the father of a son, and called his name Noah, saying, "Out of the ground which the Lord has cursed this one shall bring us relief from our work and from the toil of our hands." Lamech lived after the birth of Noah five hundred and ninety-five years, and had other sons and daughters. Thus all the days of Lamech were seven hundred and seventy-seven years; and he died. After Noah was five hundred years old, Noah became the father of Shem, Ham, and Japheth. (Gen 5:28-32)

What is striking about this new pattern is threefold. To ensure the oneness of the post-diluvial humanity with the pre-diluvial one, the author introduced this new pattern within the *toledot* of Adam that starts in Genesis 5:1 and extends to 6:8 where it ends with the statement: "But Noah found favor in the eyes of the Lord." It is only at this point that the *toledot* are announced in these terms: "These are the generations of Noah. Noah was a righteous man, blameless in his generation; Noah walked with God. And Noah had three sons, Shem, Ham, and Japheth." (vv.9-10)

Notice how the author ingeniously interlocks the pre-diluvial and post-diluvial stories in a way that preserves the oneness of humanity. Both *toledot* are interlocked through the repetition of the same words at the end of Adam's and the beginning of Noah's, an essential feature that is masked in both RSV and NRSV that change the terminology, whereas KJV preserves the identity in phraseology:

> And Noah was five hundred years old: and Noah *begat* (*wayyoled* from *holid*) Shem, Ham, and Japheth ... And Noah *begat* (*wayyoled* from *holid*) three sons, Shem, Ham, and Japheth. (Gen 5:32; 6:10 KJV)

> After Noah was five hundred years old, Noah *became the father of* Shem, Ham, and Japheth ... And Noah *had* three sons, Shem, Ham, and Japheth. (Gen 5:32; 6:10 RSV and NRSV)

The other aspect of the new pattern lies in that, at a certain age (500 years), Noah gives birth to or begets not only three sons instead of one, but as a "triplet" in that the names of all three appear together. The importance of this aspect of "oneness" of the three can be seen in that it is revisited at the start of chapter 10 in this quite strange phraseology: "These are the generations (*toledot*) of the sons of Noah, Shem, Ham, and Japheth; sons were born to them after the flood." (Gen 10:1) Elsewhere in scripture we hear of the *toledot* of one person at a time. Notice further that the *toledot* are not said to be "of Shem, Ham, and Japheth" but rather "of the sons of Noah," namely, "Shem, Ham, and Japheth." In other words, the stress is on the oneness of all three progenies. Only later in Genesis 11:10 will Shem be singled out in his *toledot*.

Finally, the last aspect of the new pattern is that the life of Noah is not divided between the birth of his sons and his death, but rather between the range of years before and after the flood: "After the flood Noah lived three hundred and fifty years. All the days of Noah were nine hundred and fifty years; and he died." (Gen 9:28-29) The importance of this matter for the author will be sealed in how he links the *toledot* of Shem, Noah's son, also with the flood: "These are the descendants of Shem. When Shem was a hundred years old, he became the father of Arpachshad two years *after the flood*." (Gen 11:10)

It is precisely this primary concern with the oneness of humanity wherever it has developed and diversified—of which diversification they are aware, witness thereof is the detailed Genesis 10—that led the authors to universalize the flood to the effect that they locked Japheth, the father of the "isles"—and thus "seas"—nations (Gen 10:5) together with his "brothers," not so much in Shem's and Ham's Syrian wilderness, but rather in the ark that floated over the waters while that wilderness was swamped under them. Consequently, Japhethite hearers listening to scripture will not be allowed to look down on a Shemite since, as hearers and thus addressees, they have already been told that their isles can sustain them as dry land only because "God said: 'Let the waters under the heavens be gathered together into one place, and let the dry land appear.'

And it was so," (Gen 1:9) well before any vegetation (vv.11-12), sun and moon (vv.14-18), fish and fowl (vv.20-22), land animals and humans (vv.24-28) were made. That is to say, Japheth will always be on a straddle between dry land and sea waters. Consequently, the waters will always remain as much a threat to him as they are to his brother Shem, as witnessed in the flood story. Both needed the ark to be able to survive and receive the good news of the covenant of blessing whose sign is the rainbow.

But if this is so, what then is the functional difference in scripture between Japhethite and Shemite? Why is it that scripture suddenly zeroes in on the *toledot* of Shem (Gen 11:10) and its overarching story deals with the descendants of Abram the Hebrew, the quintessential Shemite? Why is it that, after having given the priority to Japheth in Genesis 10,[19] his descendants disappear from scripture's horizon only to re-emerge in force at the end of Isaiah and Ezekiel?

The obvious reason is that the immediate and primary addressees of scripture are the authors' co-citizens in the region of the two rivers. It is they that are under the boot of the Macedonians and are invited to accept the offer of the scriptural God to be freed from that yoke of slavery and willingly accept to be his slaves (Lev 25:55).[20] The Macedonians and the Greeks—the Japhethites—are secondarily the addressees through the Greek translation, the LXX, made by the authors themselves with the caveat:

> You are urged therefore to read with good will and attention, and to be indulgent in cases where, despite our diligent labor in translating, we may seem to have rendered some phrases imperfectly. For what was originally expressed in Hebrew does not have exactly the same sense when translated into another language. Not only this work, but even the law itself, the prophecies, and the rest of the books differ not a little as originally

19 See my comments later in the chapter "Families," pp. 213-219.

20 RSV translates *'abadim* (slaves) here as "servants."

> expressed. (Prologue to the Wisdom of Sirach, originally in Greek.)

The Functionality of the Mediterranean Sea

Early on, the waters, the "seas," are intimately and symbiotically linked with the earth, the "dry land":

> God called the dry land Earth, and the waters that were gathered together he called Seas. And God saw that it was good. (Gen 1:10)

> And God blessed them, saying, "Be fruitful and multiply and fill the waters in the seas, and let birds multiply on the earth." (Gen 1:22)

For the authors, the most important among the scriptural seas is clearly the Mediterranean that is referred to as "the Great Sea" or "the Western Sea":

> For the western boundary, you shall have the Great Sea and its coast; this shall be your western boundary. This shall be your northern boundary: from the Great Sea you shall mark out your line to Mount Hor. (Num 34:6-7)

> Every place on which the sole of your foot treads shall be yours; your territory shall be from the wilderness and Lebanon and from the River, the river Euphrates, to the western sea. (Deut 11:24)

> ... all Naphtali, the land of Ephraim and Manasseh, all the land of Judah as far as the Western Sea. (Deut 34:2)

> From the wilderness and this Lebanon as far as the great river, the river Euphrates, all the land of the Hittites to the Great Sea toward the going down of the sun shall be your territory. (Josh 1:4)

> When all the kings who were beyond the Jordan in the hill country and in the lowland all along the coast of the Great Sea toward Lebanon, the Hittites, the Amorites, the Canaanites, the Perizzites, the Hivites, and the Jebusites, heard of this... (Josh 9:1)

> And the west boundary was the Great Sea with its coast-line. This is the boundary round about the people of Judah according to their families. (Josh 15:12)

> Ashdod, its towns and its villages; Gaza, its towns and its villages; to the Brook of Egypt, and the Great Sea with its coast-line. (Josh 15:47)

> Behold, I have allotted to you as an inheritance for your tribes those nations that remain, along with all the nations that I have already cut off, from the Jordan to the Great Sea in the west. (Josh 23:4)

Clearly, the Great Sea is the sea of the "isles" of the Japhethites and, more specifically, the Javanites, the Greeks, since it is closely connected with Tyre and Sidon, the jewel cities of the East Mediterranean, and "all the regions of Philistia":

> What are you to me, O Tyre and Sidon, and all the regions of Philistia? Are you paying me back for something? If you are paying me back, I will requite your deed upon your own head swiftly and speedily. For you have taken my silver and my gold, and have carried my rich treasures into your temples. You have sold the people of Judah and Jerusalem to the Greeks (*yewanim*; Javanites, plural of *yawan* [Javan]), removing them far from their own border. (Joel 4:4-6)

Add to this the three-chapter harsh invective against Tyre in Ezekiel 26-28 where the nouns "sea" (*yam*) and "seas" (*yammim*) occur 18 times and the noun "waters" (*mayim*) four times. In conjunction with this I should like to remind my readers of the thesis I presented in *The Rise of Scripture*, namely, that the scriptural *pelištim* (Philistines), constructed after the verb *palaš* (whose meaning is spread out), function as a stand-in for Alexander's Macedonians who "spread out" throughout all the Syrian wilderness, and that the full-armored Goliath the Philistine is a stand-in for Alexander of Macedon himself. Interestingly, the LXX supports this thesis in how it renders the original *pelištim* into *tous Hellēnas* (the Hellenes) in Isaiah 9:11 (RSV v.12):

> The Lord has sent a word against Jacob, and it will light upon Israel; and all the people will know, Ephraim and the inhabitants of Samaria, who say in pride and in arrogance of heart: "The bricks have fallen, but we will build with dressed stones; the

> sycamores have been cut down, but we will put cedars in their place." So the Lord raises adversaries against them, and stirs up their enemies. Syria (Syrian; *'aram*) on the east and the Greeks (*tous Hellēnas*; *pelištim*) on the west devour Israel with open mouth. For all this his anger is not turned away and his hand is stretched out still. The people did not turn to him who smote them, nor seek the Lord of hosts. (9:8-13)

Notice how the Greeks or Philistines are linked to the west, corresponding to the "Western Sea."[21]

The Interest of the Scriptural Authors

I have repeatedly stressed that scripture is primarily and primordially interested in the outside aggressor rather than in the ethnic socio-polity of the authors.[22] This stands to reason when one considers that the socio-polity of the authors and their addressees was under such an aggressor's boot. The scriptural story just depicts the sad story of the scriptural Israel while blaming it, not on the aggressor's overwhelming power, but rather on Israel's recalcitrant disobedience to the scriptural God generation after generation.[23] The reason behind this is obvious: Israel should not gloat when ultimately the scriptural God will bring to naught the aggressor's might. The real showdown is with Israel through the medium of the nations. After all it is God himself who stirred foreign power after foreign power to bring down his people whom he previously saved from Egypt, another foreign power, in order to "educate" his people

---

21 A facet of my thesis concerning the production of scripture is that the LXX translators and the authors of the Hebrew original are one and the same. Nevertheless, assuming a different authorship will bolster even more my reading regarding the Philistines and the Greeks since, one wonders, How is it that the translators were aware that the scriptural Philistines function as a stand-in for Alexander's Macedonians when the Philistines were introduced as descendants of Egypt (Gen 10:13-14) who in turn is a son of Ham (v.6) and not Japheth?

22 This goes against the grain of Judeo-Christian theology, which in my view has distorted the scriptural message under the influence of Philo of Alexandria and Josephus Flavius on the Jewish side, and under the Christian Alexandrian school of thought—the "mother" of all Christian theologies—on the Christian side.

23 See especially Isaiah 1:2-4; Jeremiah 2; Ezekiel 2:3; 3:4-7.

who, at every turn of divine intervention on their behalf, grew into even greater self-lauding righteousness.

I believe it necessary here to inform my readers of scriptural data and terminology that has been misconstrued by Judeo-Christian theology. One of the most calamitous examples is the classic, across the board, misconception regarding people (*'am*) versus nations (*goyim*). Suffice it to mention here how the Jews, who consider themselves, by definition, God's "people," refer to all non-Jews as *goyim*. It is hard to pinpoint historically whether it is the Jews who influenced the Christians in this matter or vice versa. In either case, this is a blatant misconception, if not outright distortion. In the Old Testament God's "flock of sheep," that is, leaders and commoners alike, are always under judgment (Ezek 34). God will make them his "people" when they, through their obedience, behave in a manner that shows to any and every onlooker that he is de facto their God. This will not happen until the end of the scriptural odyssey:

> I will make[24] a covenant of peace with them; it shall be an everlasting covenant with them; and I will bless them and multiply them, and will set my sanctuary in the midst of them for evermore. My dwelling place (*miškan*; as a tent) shall be with (*'al*; over, as a tent would) them; and I will be their God, and they shall be my people. Then the nations will know that I the Lord sanctify Israel, when my sanctuary is in the midst of them for evermore. (Ezek 37:26-28)

The same applies to the New Testament church. In his letter to the Ephesians, Paul presents the church as already in God's eternal plan, yet he ends by stating unequivocally that God's plan is still "in the making" until he perfects it:[25]

> Blessed be the God and Father of our Lord Jesus Christ, who has blessed us in Christ with every spiritual blessing in the heavenly places, even as he chose us in him before the foundation of the

24 "*Waw* consecutive" construction, for those cognizant of scriptural Hebrew.

25 See also in the parallel letter to the Philippians: "And I am sure that he who began a good work in you will bring it to completion at the day of Jesus Christ." (1:6)

> world, that we should be holy and blameless before him. He destined us in love to be his sons through Jesus Christ, according to the purpose of his will, to the praise of his glorious grace which he freely bestowed on us in the Beloved. (Eph 1:3-6)

> So then you are no longer strangers and sojourners, but you are fellow citizens with the saints and members of the household of God, built upon the foundation of the apostles and prophets, Christ Jesus himself being the cornerstone, in whom the whole structure is joined together and grows into a holy temple in the Lord; in whom you also are built into it for a dwelling place of God in the Spirit. (Eph 2:19-22)

Compare with the parallel passage in Colossians, the closest letter to Ephesians in content and terminology:

> He [Jesus Christ] is the head of the body, the church; he is the beginning, the first-born from the dead, that in everything he might be pre-eminent. (Col 1:18)

> Let no one disqualify you, insisting on self-abasement and worship of angels, taking his stand on visions, puffed up without reason by his sensuous mind, and not holding fast to the Head, from whom the whole body, nourished and knit together through its joints and ligaments, grows with a growth that is from God. (Col 2:18-19)

Until then Israel, the descendant of Noah through Shem and his great grandchild Terah, Abram's father, is according to Genesis 10 (see also 12:3) just another "nation" (*goy*) and "family" among the earth's "nations" (*goyim*) and "families." And, as if the scriptural authors intended to drill this reality into the hearers' ears early on, their first use of *'am* occurs at the beginning of the following chapter Genesis 11 in reference to the entire humankind and, no less, on the lips of the Lord himself: "And the Lord said, 'Behold, they are one people (*'am 'eḥad*), and they have all one language (*śaphah* [tongue] *'aḥat*);[26] and this is only the beginning of what they will do; and nothing that they propose to do will now be impossible for them.'" (v.6) This, in turn, explains Ezekiel's equating "the people of Israel"

26 Corresponding to the "one tongue (language)" (*śaphah 'eḥat*) of v.1.

(*beney yiśra'el*; the children of Israel) with "nations (*goyim*) of rebels"[27] instead of "nation (*goy*) of rebels."[28]

So, the real showdown is with the oppressing nations when God will show these as well as his flock that he is always in control. That God has that showdown in mind all along is at its clearest in a passage of Isaiah where, in the midst of an announcement where the foreign nation is said to be used by God to punish, and thus, educate his people, the prophet switches gears in an aside in order to foretell how God will ultimately bring down the aggressor, only to return and proceed with his original concern:

> The Lord spoke to me again: "Because this people have refused the waters of Shiloah that flow gently, and melt in fear before Rezin and the son of Remaliah; therefore, behold, the Lord is bringing up against them the waters of the River, mighty and many, the king of Assyria and all his glory; and it will rise over all its channels and go over all its banks; and it will sweep on into Judah, it will overflow and pass on, reaching even to the neck; and its outspread wings will fill the breadth of your land, O Immanuel (*'immanu 'el*)." Be broken, you peoples, and be dismayed; give ear, all you far countries; gird yourselves and be dismayed; gird yourselves and be dismayed. Take counsel together, but it will come to nought; speak a word, but it will not stand, for God is with us (*'immanu 'el*). For the Lord spoke thus to me with his strong hand upon me, and warned me not to walk in the way of this people, saying: "Do not call conspiracy all that this people call conspiracy, and do not fear what they fear, nor be in dread. But the Lord of hosts, him you shall regard as holy; let him be your fear, and let him be your dread. And he will become a sanctuary, and a stone of offense, and a rock of stumbling to both houses of Israel, a trap and a snare to the inhabitants of Jerusalem. And many shall stumble thereon; they shall fall and be broken; they shall be snared and taken." (Is 8:5-15)

---

27 I have shown repeatedly in this book and *ROS* as well as in my commentaries on Genesis and Ezekiel the literary closeness between Genesis 11 and Ezekiel.

28 Virtually all translations, except for the Vulgate, are aware of the oddity and opt for either the singular "nation" or "rebels" without "nation of."

Notice also how the Lord makes it clear that Isaiah and the people should not dread and fear the Assyrians, but rather dread and fear the Lord himself. A few verses earlier, the prophet took an aside to address the Assyrians as well. Although they were summoned to punish Judah, the land of the recalcitrant *'immanu 'el,* still—Assyrians beware!—it is the fear and dread of the Lord, and not of the Assyrians, that will restore the functionality of *'immanu 'el.*

Still the ultimate showdown that the scriptural God has in mind is with the foreign power, i.e., Alexander's Macedonians and Greeks, that crossed from the far away isles of the Mediterranean to overtake the Syro-Arabian wilderness region—the scriptural world (Gen 2:8-14). Isaiah—whose name means "the Lord will save"—depicts the handling of those same faraway *'iyyim* (isles, coastlands) through the message of salvation of the scriptural *torah* (Is 42:1-7). His colleague Ezekiel—whose name means "God gets hold of, God clutches into submission"—presents it as a showdown where the flock of David the shepherd (Ezek 34:21-24; 37:24-25) will overcome the mighty army of Gog of Magog (chs.38-39), a stand-in for Alexander of Macedon,[29] just as David the shepherd overwhelmed Goliath the Philistine, another stand-in for the same Alexander, with a sling and the five smooth stones in his shepherd's bag, representative of the five books of the *torah* (1 Sam 17:40). The link to Isaiah is secured through the reference to the same *'iyyim* at the beginning of Ezekiel 39: "I will send fire on Magog and on those who dwell securely in the coastlands (*'iyyim*); and they shall know that I am the Lord." (v.6) The Ezekelian *'iyyim* are none other than the isles of the Mediterranean Sea since the only other instances of that noun in Ezekiel occurs in the tirade against Tyre (27:3, 6, 7, 35).

---

29 See my comments on Ezekiel 38-39 in *C-Ezek* 311-26 where I show in detail how the scriptural authors use a series of names of nations from Genesis 10 just as they did in Isaiah 66.

7

The Parity Between Animals and Man

Theological thought that pervaded all Christian denominations has its roots, perspective as well as terminology wise, in ancient Greek philosophy (love of [human] wisdom) which was essentially anthropocentric. Scripture, on the other hand, was conceived and written openly against that philosophy. One need only hear Paul's introductory remarks in his first letter to the Corinthians to be convinced of that. The extensive quotation will show how Paul's scathing assessment of human wisdom is repeated *ad nauseam*:

> For Christ did not send me to baptize but to preach the gospel, and not with eloquent wisdom, lest the cross of Christ be emptied of its power. For the word of the cross is folly to those who are perishing, but to us who are being saved it is the power of God. For it is written, "I will destroy the wisdom of the wise, and the cleverness of the clever I will thwart." Where is the wise man? Where is the scribe? Where is the debater of this age? Has not God made foolish the wisdom of the world? For since, in the wisdom of God, the world did not know God through wisdom, it pleased God through the folly of what we preach to save those who believe. For Jews demand signs and Greeks seek wisdom, but we preach Christ crucified, a stumbling block to Jews and folly to Gentiles, but to those who are called, both Jews and Greeks, Christ the power of God and the wisdom of God. For the foolishness of God is wiser than men, and the weakness of God is stronger than men. For consider your call, brethren; not many of you were wise according to worldly standards, not many were powerful, not many were of noble birth; but God chose what is foolish in the world to shame the wise, God chose what is weak in the world to shame the strong, God chose what is low and

> despised in the world, even things that are not, to bring to nothing things that are, so that no human being might boast in the presence of God. He is the source of your life in Christ Jesus, whom God made our wisdom, our righteousness and sanctification and redemption; therefore, as it is written, "Let him who boasts, boast of the Lord." When I came to you, brethren, I did not come proclaiming to you the testimony of God in lofty words or wisdom. For I decided to know nothing among you except Jesus Christ and him crucified. And I was with you in weakness and in much fear and trembling; and my speech and my message were not in plausible words of wisdom, but in demonstration of the Spirit and of power, that your faith might not rest in the wisdom of men but in the power of God. Yet among the mature we do impart wisdom, although it is not a wisdom of this age or of the rulers of this age, who are doomed to pass away. But we impart a secret and hidden wisdom of God, which God decreed before the ages for our glorification. None of the rulers of this age understood this; for if they had, they would not have crucified the Lord of glory. But, as it is written, "What no eye has seen, nor ear heard, nor the heart of man conceived, what God has prepared for those who love him." (1 Cor 1:17-2:9)

Had Paul been preaching these same words from the pulpit, one would have put up with this rehashing of the same thought. However, his *written text* would have been, no doubt, slashed down by an English composition high school teacher to its bones. That is not how someone *writes*! However, Paul knew what he was doing. He was writing *scripturally*: on the one hand, he was writing *after the manner of* the written Pentateuch and the Prophets, as evident from his repeated "as it is written" (1 Cor 1:31; 2:9); on the other hand, and more importantly, he was writing a letter to be *read aloud* to the congregated house church since there were no copiers at that time that would allow "handouts." The addressees were *always hearers*—and never readers as we all are today—as is evident from the following statement: "Blessed is *he who reads aloud* (*ho anaginōskōn*) the words of the prophecy, and blessed are *those who hear* (*hoi akouontes*), and who keep what is written therein; for the time is near." (Rev 1:3) This being the case, one is prone to accept that the Old

Testament authors had the same approach. In order to preempt the Platonic serpent's argumentation in Genesis 3, they had to underscore that humans were of the same "stuff" out of which the serpent was made: they were both *'adamic*, formed "out of the *'adamah* (ground)," earthly, and in no way "godly" in their pretentious "wisdom." They were both, in Paul's terms, "babes" and "of the flesh," that is "mere men" in the matter of the scriptural message:

> Now we have received not the spirit of the world, but the Spirit which is from God, that we might understand the gifts bestowed on us by God. And we impart this in words not taught by human wisdom but taught by the Spirit, interpreting spiritual truths to those who possess the Spirit. The unspiritual man does not receive the gifts of the Spirit of God, for they are folly to him, and he is not able to understand them because they are spiritually discerned. The spiritual man judges all things, but is himself to be judged by no one. "For who has known the mind of the Lord so as to instruct him?" But we have the mind of Christ. But I, brethren, could not address you as spiritual men, but as men of the flesh, as babes in Christ. I fed you with milk, not solid food; for you were not ready for it; and even yet you are not ready, for you are still of the flesh. For while there is jealousy and strife among you, are you not of the flesh, and behaving like ordinary men? For when one says, "I belong to Paul," and another, "I belong to Apollos," are you not merely men? (1 Cor 2:12-3:4)

If Paul was introducing a mere 29 chapters of his Corinthian correspondence and needed a little over two chapters of rehashing to overwhelm his Greek addressees with his premise that was, for them, against the grain, how ingenious must have been the authors of Genesis 1-2 to be able to compact in two chapters the setting of not only chapter three, but the entire voluminous scripture! Their feat was unmatchable through the ages since their premise etched in two chapters was not only against Greek philosophy and its unabashed anthropocentrism, but also against the Greek polity revolving around cities. In order to dynamite the Hellenism of their time in both its constitutional features—the proverbial killing two birds with one stone—the authors opted for building their scriptural world around the reality of the Syrian wilderness shepherd life and present it as a paradigm for their hearers.[1] I stressed *reality* because both Greek philosophy and Greek polity were constructs and not "givens" as shepherd life is. Notice that, in order to support these human constructs, one must resort to a third construct, which is literature that, in turn, requires another construct, a written alphabet. Shepherd life simply is as it is without need for any of these constructs. And this is precisely the world the authors have described in Genesis 1 and then indicated its actual location in Genesis 2:8-14.

The most striking aspect of this scriptural world is its flagrant anti-anthropocentrism, which is visited twice, once in chapter 1 and then again in chapter 2. Twice we are told that, when compared with land animals, including the birds that must alight at some point or another, the human beings are basically *at one* with them. In Genesis 1 we are told that the human being and the land animals were made the same (sixth) day and share the same blessing (vv.24-28) and both, together with the birds of the air, share the same food, the vegetation (vv.29-30) that was produced on the third day (vv.9-13) before any animal life. So, according to scripture the human being does not "top" the animals. One may argue that, still, the human being is presented as the culmination of God's creation, its end product, as though the rest of creation was set up in order to accommodate its "ruler." However, this sequence is turned around in chapter two where the human being is formed out of the ground (v.9) *before* the land animals and the birds were also formed out of the same ground (v.19). Even, in comparison, the human being is belittled in that he was formed out of "the dust" of the ground (v.7)—clearly in view of 3:19—whereas the animals were formed simply out of the ground (*'adamah*). In other words, whereas the animals are simply *the* reference for the *'adamic* reality, the human being, by contrast, is that

1 I discussed this matter in detail in *ROS* 279-97.

"pulverized" reality since, even at his demise, he will return not to the ground but rather to its dust.

The full parity between humans and land animals, especially mammals, is acceptable as well as understandable for the addressees though they are city dwellers, given that the Syrian wilderness lies next door, and there was obviously social intercourse between shepherds and their next-door neighbors, the city dwellers:

> Cain knew his wife, and she conceived and bore Enoch; and he built a city, and called the name of the city after the name of his son, Enoch. To Enoch was born Irad; and Irad was the father of Mehujael, and Mehujael the father of Methushael, and Methushael the father of Lamech. And Lamech took two wives; the name of the one was Adah, and the name of the other Zillah. Adah bore Jabal; *he was the father of those who dwell in tents and have cattle* (*miqneh;* livestock NRSV). His brother's name was Jubal; *he was the father of all those who play the lyre and pipe.* Zillah bore Tubalcain; *he was the forger of all instruments of bronze and iron.* The sister of Tubalcain as Naamah. (Gen 4:19-22)

We have in scripture an incontrovertible evidence that shepherd life is based on the total parity between humans and land mammals, especially the sheep of the shepherd's flock, and that such a lifestyle was well known to those who lived in royal courts, and more so when their king himself had been a shepherd:

> But that same night the word of the Lord came to Nathan, "Go and tell my servant David, 'Thus says the Lord: Would you build me a house to dwell in? I have not dwelt in a house since the day I brought up the people of Israel from Egypt to this day, but I have been moving about in a tent for my dwelling. In all places where I have moved with all the people of Israel, did I speak a word with any of the judges of Israel, whom I commanded to shepherd my people Israel, saying, 'Why have you not built me a house of cedar?' Now therefore thus you shall say to my servant David, 'Thus says the Lord of hosts, I took you from the pasture, from following the sheep, that you should be prince over my

> people Israel; and I have been with you wherever you went, and have cut off all your enemies from before you; and I will make for you a great name, like the name of the great ones of the earth.'" (2 Sam 7:4-9)

> And the Lord sent Nathan to David. He came to him, and said to him, "There were two men in a certain city, the one rich and the other poor. The rich man had very many flocks and herds; but the poor man had nothing *but one little ewe lamb, which he had bought. And he brought it up, and it grew up with him and with his children; it used to eat of his morsel, and drink from his cup, and lie in his bosom, and it was like a daughter to him.* Now there came a traveler to the rich man, and he was unwilling to take one of his own flock or herd to prepare for the wayfarer who had come to him, but he took the poor man's lamb, and prepared it for the man who had come to him." Then David's anger was greatly kindled against the man; and he said to Nathan, "As the Lord lives, the man who has done this deserves to die; and he shall restore the lamb fourfold, because he did this thing, and because he had no pity." (2 Sam 12:1-6)

In other words, the shepherd's household and the members of the flock were part of the same "family." In this regard, it could not have been a "slip of the pen" that the first instance of "families" in scripture is used to refer to the constituency of the animal kingdom: "So Noah went forth, and his sons and his wife and his sons' wives with him. And every beast, every creeping thing, and every bird, everything that moves upon the earth, went forth by *families* out of the ark." (Gen 8:18-19). It is only later that the progenies of Noah's three sons are introduced as "families" (10:5, 18, 20, 31, 32). Thus the hearers are forced to understand human families as families made of *nepheš ḥayyah* in the same way as the animal families are made of *nepheš ḥayyah* and *in this order* as was already established in Genesis 1 and 2. Although the animals were formed out of the ground as *nepheš ḥayyah* (Gen 2:19) after the manner of the human being (v.7), they were, however, already introduced twice as *nepheš ḥayyah* in the previous chapter:

> And God said, "Let the earth bring forth living creatures (*nepheš ḥayyah*) according to their kinds: cattle and creeping things and

> beasts of the earth according to their kinds." And it was so … "And to every beast of the earth, and to every bird of the air, and to everything that creeps on the earth, everything that has the breath of life (*nepheš ḥayyah*), I have given every green plant for food." And it was so. (Gen 1:24, 30)

Still the authors are not satisfied with this "given" and well-known situation on the ground, so to speak, but actually push on their plan of demeaning the arrogant human beings to an unheard of level by making them equal to the far away sea animals, if not making the latter outright primary in that the human beings are presented in Genesis as following the lead pattern of the sea animals. In other words, at hearing the creation of the human being, the hearers are facing a *dejà vu* (been there, seen that), or rather *dejà ouï* (been there, heard that), situation. Let us follow the divine activity over the last two days of creation as it unfolds to the hearers' ears.

> And God said, "Let the waters bring forth (*šaraṣ*) swarms (*šereṣ*) of living creatures, and let birds (*'oph*) fly (*'opheph*) above the earth across the firmament of the heavens." So God created (*bara'*) the great sea monsters and every living creature that moves (*romeśet*), with which the waters swarm (*šaraṣ*), according to their kinds, and every winged bird according to its kind. And God saw that it was good. And God *blessed* them, saying, "*Be fruitful and multiply and fill the waters* in the seas, and let birds *multiply* on the earth." And there was evening and there was morning, a fifth day. And God said, "Let the earth bring forth (*hoṣe'*; *hiphil* of *yaṣa'* [go out]) living creatures according to their kinds: cattle and creeping things (*remeś*) and beasts of the earth according to their kinds." And it was so. And God made (*'aśah*) the beasts of the earth according to their kinds and the cattle according to their kinds, and everything that creeps (*remeś*) upon the ground according to its kind. And God saw that it was good. Then God said, "Let us make (*'aśah*) man in our image, after our likeness; and let them have dominion over the fish of the sea, and over the birds of the air, and over the cattle, and over all the earth, and over every creeping (*remeś*) thing that creeps (*romeś*) upon the earth." So God created (*bara'*) man in his own image, in the image of God he created (*bara'*) him; male and female he created (*bara'*) them. And God *blessed* them, and

> God said to them, "*Be fruitful and multiply, and fill the earth* and subdue it; and have dominion over the fish of the sea and over the birds of the air and over every living thing that moves (*romeśet*) upon the earth." And God said, "Behold, I have given you every plant yielding seed which is upon the face of all the earth, and every tree with seed in its fruit; you shall have them for food. And to every beast of the earth, and to every bird of the air, and to everything that creeps on the earth, everything that has the breath of life, I have given every green plant for food." And it was so. And God saw everything that he had made, and behold, it was very good. And there was evening and there was morning, a sixth day. (Gen 1:20-31)

My intent is to invite my readers to follow the authors' ingenious plan to entrap their obviously human hearers into realizing that they are, at best, not superior to the sea animals and, at worst, worse than those animals. After all, according to scripture, the sea animals did not disobey God's commandment, humans did. And, as we shall see, the consummate irony is that the sea animals did not need Noah's ark as the other animals did! That is why the authors are "killing two birds with one stone" in Genesis 1 in that they are also aiming at belittling the land animals in comparison with their sea counterparts, an impressive tour de force. The reason is that, later in scripture, God's "people" will be cast as a "flock" and the authors were already preempting the addressees' arrogant propensity to take that opportunity to assume that they, as land animals (*nepheš ḥayyah*), are one up over the sea denizens and, by association, over the birds that were created together with the fish on the fifth day (vv.20-23).

In Genesis 1 the authors resort to a series of literary twists to accomplish their aim. A first careless hearing would allow the hearers to assume that the land *nepheš ḥayyah* (both animal and human) are made on the sixth day while the sea *nepheš ḥayyah* are created on the fifth day. However, at a more attentive hearing one realizes that the birds were also created on the fifth day together with the fish. Although they fly against the firmament, yet, unlike the fish, the birds' home or footing is the dry land as ground (*'adamah*): "So out of the *ground* the Lord God formed every beast of the field *and every bird of the air*, and brought them to the man to see what he would call them." (Gen 2:19) That is why, later, they need to be taken into Noah's ark in order to survive. Thus, they function in a way as a go-between, a bridge between the fish and the land denizens. By the same token, one gets the distinct impression, if not the conviction, that the authors, whose geographical perspective is the Syrian wilderness, are trying to "universalize" this perspective by integrating into Genesis 1 the surrounding bodies of water, the Arabian Sea, the Red Sea, and the Mediterranean Sea referred to, in comparison, as "the Great Sea."[2] The authors' intention will be confirmed in their description of that "world" in the following chapter (2:10-14). I shall revisit this intention in showing that it corresponds to the thesis that I fleshed out and defended in *The Rise of Scripture*, namely, that scripture's concern is first and foremost all "the nations and families" of the earth and not the so-called "chosen people or nation" as matters developed in the thought of self-centered Judaism and Christianity.

Let us look into the authorial handling of days five and sixth to show how it is day five that sets the tone for the pattern that will be followed in both parts of day six. That is to say, it is the land animals and the human beings that are patterned after the supposedly "lesser" living creatures in the scriptural God's world since the fish rarely appear in scripture and thus they are, by all counts, not in the authors' purview, except perhaps in the Book of Jonah.

Sea Animals and Land Animals

Whereas the land animals are said neither to have been "blessed" nor to have been summoned to "be fruitful and multiply and fill the earth," and the birds are said to have been

---

2 Num 34:6, 7; Josh 1:4; 9:1; 23:4.

"blessed" and summoned just to "multiply on the earth," of the fish we are told the following:

> So God created the great sea monsters and every living creature that moves, with which the waters swarm, according to their kinds, and every winged bird according to its kind. And God saw that it was good. And God *blessed* them, saying, "*Be fruitful and multiply and fill the waters* in the seas, and let birds multiply on the earth." (Gen 1:21-22)

Moreover, before hearing of the description of some land animals as being *remeś* (moving, creeping) *on earth*, the hearers have been introduced to this root in conjunction with the waters, that is to say, they were programmed to "perceive" the land animals as similar to the sea animals, and not vice versa. The intentionality is unmissable given that the first instance of the root *remeś* is specifically used with the root *šaraṣ/šereṣ* that is exclusively reserved to the sea animals throughout Genesis 1 and is not linked with land animals until chapters 7 and 8:

> And God said, "Let the waters bring forth (*šaraṣ*) swarms (*šereṣ*) of living creatures" ... So God created the great sea monsters and every living creature that moves (*romeśet*), with which the waters swarm (*šaraṣ*)... (Gen 1:20-21)

> And God said, "Let the earth bring forth living creatures according to their kinds: cattle and creeping things (*remeś*) and beasts of the earth according to their kinds." And it was so. And God made the beasts of the earth according to their kinds and the cattle according to their kinds, and everything that creeps (*remeś*) upon the ground according to its kind. And God saw that it was good. Then God said, "Let us make man in our image, after our likeness; and let them have dominion over the fish of the sea, and over the birds of the air, and over the cattle, and over all the earth, and over every creeping (*remeś*) thing that creeps (*romeś*) upon the earth." So God created man in his own image, in the image of God he created him; male and female he created them. And God blessed them, and God said to them, "Be fruitful and multiply, and fill the earth and subdue it; and have dominion over the fish of the sea and over the birds of the air and over every living thing that moves (*romeśet*) upon the earth." (Gen 1:24-28)

> And all flesh died that moved (*romeś*) upon the earth, birds, cattle, beasts, all swarming creatures (*šereṣ*) that swarm (*šereṣ*) upon the earth,[3] and every man; everything on the dry land in whose nostrils was the breath of life died. (Gen 7:21-22)

> "Bring forth with you every living thing that is with you of all flesh—birds and animals and every creeping thing (*remeś*) that creeps (*romeś*) on the earth—that they may breed abundantly (*šaraṣ*) on the earth, and be fruitful and multiply upon the earth." So Noah went forth, and his sons and his wife and his sons' wives with him. (Gen 8:17-18)

It is as though the land animals needed to wait for the experience of the flood for their "remnant"[4] to realize that their sea counterparts, in their totality, were actually spared from the flood and thus proved in the last instance to be superior, not inferior, to the animals that were made after them, both birds and land animals whose footing is the ground and not the waters: "He blotted out every living thing that was *upon the face of the ground*, man and animals and creeping things and birds of the air; they were blotted out from the earth. Only Noah was left (*wayiššaʼer*),[5] and *those that were with him in the ark.*" (Gen 7:23)[6] This is perhaps why the sea animals were honored in that God *"created"* (*baraʾ*) them (Gen 1:21)—an action reserved later for the human beings—whereas God "made" (*ʿaśah*) the land animals (v.25) as he did the firmament (v.7) and the two great lights and the stars (v.16), all inanimate objects.

---

3 Notice how "all swarming creatures (*šereṣ*) that swarm (*šereṣ*) *upon the earth*" mimics Genesis 1:20-21 where this description relates to the sea animals.

4 See footnote 5, below.

5 The verb *šaʼar* (remain) is from the same root as the noun *šaʼar* that is encountered later in Isaiah to speak of the "remnant" of the exiles in Babylon.

6 See also earlier "I will blot out man whom I have created from the face of the ground, man and beast and creeping things and birds of the air, for I am sorry that I have made them" (Gen 6:7); and "For in seven days I will send rain upon the earth forty days and forty nights; and every living thing that I have made I will blot out from the face of the ground." (Gen 7:4).

Sea Animals and Human Beings

As I mentioned earlier, the creation of the sea animals is the blueprint for the creation of the human beings. That is to say, the human beings were created in the same way as—à la—sea animals. In other words, scripturally speaking, the human beings are like the sea animals, not vice versa. That is, to say the least, demeaning since the verb *yalad* (give birth) and its cognates *yilled* (*piel* form) and *holid* (*hiphil* form) are used exclusively[7] in conjunction with humans and, twice in Genesis 31:8, land mammals.[8] This authorial intention to present the human beings à la fish is further detectable in that they both are "blessed" and summoned to "be fruitful, multiply, and fill the waters, respectively the earth" (Gen 1:22 and 1:28), whereas the land animals are not graced at all with the same.

Human beings that we are, we are quick to point out that, in Gen 1:27, one hears the verb *bara'* there times in a row, "So God created man in his own image, in the image of God he created him; male and female he created them," as if the author was intending to point out the difference between the human being and the sea animals. However, my objection to this interpretation is that the same author one verse earlier coined the introductory statement in these words: "Then God said, 'Let us make (*'asah*) man in our image, after our likeness.'" (Gen 1:26) Three elements of note militate against the assumed essential—and not merely functional—"superiority" of the human beings over the animals, including the fish (vv.26 and 28). Note the following:

1. Whereas, in the case of the sea animals, although God relegates to the waters the action of "bringing forth" those animals (v.20), the author is quick to add that God "created" them.

---

7 With the exception of the *toledot* of the heavens and the earth (Gen 2:4) that I dealt with earlier.

8 If he said, "The spotted shall be your wages," then all the flock bore (*yaledu*) spotted; and if he said, "The striped shall be your wages," then all the flock bore (*yaledu*) striped.

2. In the case of the human beings, God starts with a deliberation on his part (v.26) before actually creating the human beings (v.27). However, strangely enough, this deliberation is cast around the verb *'aśah* rather than *bara'*, "Let us make (*'aśah*) man in our image, after our likeness" (v.26), which is in line with his "making" the land animals that, in the hearers' minds, are obviously more akin to the human beings.
3. Although the divine deliberation is aimed at "making man (*'adam*) in our image, after our likeness" (v.26) God seems to settle for "his image" only, which is repeated to underscore that this was his final decision (v.27). The literary tension is corroborated in the switch from *'adam* in v.26 to *ha'adam* (the man) in v.27.

Put in simpler terms, the text seems to prepare for the authors' view that the real headache[9] for God in scripture will eventually originate with the human beings and will lead to his decision to initiate the flood, a punishment that will not affect the sea animals. Further in scripture one will hear that God enrolls the help of a "great fish" in order to force the recalcitrant Jonah's hand into pursuing the mission he was assigned. It would be worth our while to hear the entire passage for us to realize the parallelism with Genesis given the role played by the waters:

> Now the word of the Lord came to Jonah the son of Amittai, saying, "Arise, go to Nineveh, that great city, and cry against it; for their wickedness has come up before me." But Jonah rose to flee to Tarshish from the presence of the Lord. He went down to Joppa and found a ship going to Tarshish; so he paid the fare, and went on board, to go with them to Tarshish, away from the presence of the Lord. But the Lord hurled a great wind (*ruaḥ*

9 See my comments on *wayyit'aṣṣeb* (Gen 6:6) in *C-Gen* 88.

gedolah)[10] upon the sea (*yam*),[11] and there was a mighty tempest (*sa'ar gadol*) on the sea (*yam*), so that the ship threatened to break up. Then the mariners were afraid, and each cried to his god; and they threw the wares that were in the ship into the sea (*yam*), to lighten it for them. But Jonah had gone down into the inner part of the ship and had lain down, and was fast asleep. So the captain came and said to him, "What do you mean, you sleeper? Arise, call upon your god! Perhaps the god will give a thought to us, that we do not perish." And they said to one another, "Come, let us cast lots, that we may know on whose account this evil has come upon us." So they cast lots, and the lot fell upon Jonah. Then they said to him, "Tell us, on whose account this evil has come upon us? What is your occupation? And whence do you come? What is your country? And of what people are you?" And he said to them, "I am a Hebrew; and I fear the Lord, the God of heaven, who made the sea (*yam*) and the dry land (*yabbašah*)."[12] Then the men were exceedingly afraid, and said to him, "What is this that you have done!" For the men knew that he was fleeing from the presence of the Lord, because he had told them. Then they said to him, "What shall we do to you, that the sea (*yam*) may quiet down for us?" For the sea (*yam*) grew more and more tempestuous (*so'er*). He said to them, "Take me up and throw me into the sea (*yam*); then the sea (*yam*) will quiet down for you; for I know it is because of me that this great tempest (*sa'ar gadol*) has come upon you." Nevertheless the men rowed hard to bring the ship back to land (*yabbašah*), but they could not, for the sea (*yam*) grew more and more tempestuous (*so'er*) against them. Therefore they cried to the Lord, "We beseech thee, O Lord, let us not perish for this man's life, and lay not on us innocent blood; for thou, O Lord, hast done as it pleased thee." So they took up Jonah and threw him into the sea (*yam*); and the sea (*yam*) ceased from its raging. Then the men feared the Lord exceedingly, and they offered a sacrifice to the Lord and made vows. And the Lord appointed a great fish (*dag*)[13] to swallow up Jonah; and Jonah was in the belly of the fish (*dag*) three days and three nights. Then Jonah prayed to the Lord his God from the belly of the fish (*dag*) ... and the

---

10 Compare with Genesis 1:2.

11 Compare with Genesis 1:10 where we have the plural *yammim* (seas).

12 Compare with Genesis 1:9.

13 Compare with Genesis 1:26, 28.

> Lord *spoke* (*wayyo'mer*; said)[14] to the *fish* (*dag*), and it vomited out Jonah upon the dry land (*yabbašah*). (Jon 1:1-2:1; 2:10)

In Genesis, as in Jonah, the medium of the calamity is the waters, but the venue of the calamity in Jonah is the seas, whereas it is the earth as dry land in the story of the flood in Genesis. Consequently, appeal for help by Noah in implementing God's plan could not have been done to sea animals, but to their counterparts, the birds that were created along with them on the fourth day (Gen 1:21). What an authorial ingenuity this is! Moreover, to ensure that the hearers would not miss the message, the birds intervene *three times* in the flood story:

> At the end of forty days Noah opened the window of the ark which he had made, and sent forth a raven; and it went to and fro until the waters were dried up from the earth. Then he sent forth a dove from him, to see if the waters had subsided from the face of the ground; but the dove found no place to set her foot, and she returned to him to the ark, for the waters were still on the face of the whole earth. So he put forth his hand and took her and brought her into the ark with him. He waited another seven days, and again he sent forth the dove out of the ark; and the dove came back to him in the evening, and lo, in her mouth a freshly plucked olive leaf; so Noah knew that the waters had subsided from the earth. Then he waited another seven days, and sent forth the dove; and she did not return to him any more. (Gen 8:6-14)

Still, an attentive hearer need not wait for the Book of Jonah to realize the centrality of the sea animals in God's scriptural plan. A hearer with a keen ear will soon realize that, although the sea animals are not an integral "actor" or "participant" in the flood story, they will prove to be an integral "factor" in the outcome of that story. Here again is revealed the ingenuity of the author *in the original text.*

---

14 Compare with Genesis 1:6, 9, 11, 14, 20, 24, 26, 29.

In Genesis 1 the root *šrṣ* is restricted to the sea animals and its use three times in two verses (vv.20-21), twice as verb (*šaraṣ*) and once as noun (*šereṣ*), confirms the author's intentionality. This, in itself, gives the impression to the hearer that the author is simply meticulous about his nomenclature. The hearer will have to wait until the flood story to learn what the text's intention is really about when the author will use no less than four times the root *šrṣ* in the story of the flood where the sea animals are not even mentioned once. That is definitely a far cry from happenstance when that root is heard once as a noun (*šereṣ*), twice as a conjugated verb (*šareṣu*)—just as in Genesis 1:20-21—with the addition of the active participle (*šoreṣ*). It is as though the authors wanted to top the earlier instances in order to impress upon their hearers that the matter is in no way a slip of the pen on their part:

> And God said, "Let the waters bring forth swarms (*yišreṣu*) of living creatures (*šereṣ*), and let birds fly above the earth across the firmament of the heavens." So God created the great sea monsters and every living creature that moves, with which the waters swarm (*šareṣu*), according to their kinds, and every winged bird according to its kind. And God saw that it was good. (Gen 1:20-21)

> And all flesh died that moved upon the earth, birds, cattle, beasts, all swarming creatures (*šereṣ*) that swarm (*šoreṣ*) upon the earth, and every man; everything on the dry land (*ḥarabah*) in whose nostrils (*aphphayim*) was the breath (*nišmat ruaḥ*; the breeze of the spirit) of life died. (Gen 7:21-22)

> Bring forth (*hoṣe'*; *hiphil* of *yaṣa'* [go out]) with you every living thing that is with you of all flesh—birds and animals (*behemah*) and every creeping thing (*remeś*) that creeps (*romeś*) on the earth –that they may breed abundantly (*šareṣu*) on the earth, and be fruitful and multiply upon the earth. (Gen 8:17)[15]

---

15 Notice the closeness in terminology with Genesis 1:24: "And God said, 'Let the earth bring forth (*hoṣe'*; *hiphil* of *yaṣa'* [go out]) living creatures according to their kinds: cattle (*behemah*) and creeping things (*remeś*) and beasts of the earth according to their kinds.' And it was so."

> And God blessed Noah and his sons, and said to them, "Be fruitful and multiply, and fill the earth … And you, be fruitful and multiply, bring forth abundantly (*širṣu*) on the earth and multiply in it." (Gen 9:1, 7)

My first comment is that it is, by any means, impossible for a hearer of RSV—as well as KJV and NRSV—to even detect the interplay in the original. Simply and straightforwardly put, the English-speaking listeners to these translations are not hearing scripture at all. It is no wonder then that quite a few Protestant denominations are hooked on glossolalia as *the* ultimate sign of God's presence among its members. It beats by far putting in the sweat it takes to learn scriptural Hebrew. This is not to say that the speakers of other languages are better off. The only translation I found that uses throughout the same verb is in German, however, it cannot render the Hebrew cognate noun *šereṣ*.

The handling of the land animals is humorously facetious as well as impressive. After the devastating experience of the flood, which again did not even touch the sea animals, the land animals are invited to emulate the sea animals in their way of living, and not only in creeping (*remeś*) as the sea animals are since this was the case already in Genesis 1 (both kinds of animals are presented as *remeś* in vv.21 and 24); however now, the land animals are invited to also "swarm" (*šaraṣ*; Gen 8:17) as the sea animals did right from the beginning (Gen 1:20-21) and thus were in no need of a reminder. Still the authors cleverly prepared the hearers for that ending by already referring to the land animals that were blotted out by the flood as "swarming" (*šereṣ/šoreṣ*; Gen 7:21-22). A quite unexpected twist! It is as though the authors are reminding the land animals that imitating the sea animals by swarming will not cut it per se since their peers that were left outside the ark were swarming and yet were not able to evade God's decision to blot them out. Those who were not obliterated were saved by Noah's gracious action of bringing them aboard the ark under God's command:

> Then the Lord said to Noah, "Go into the ark, you and all your household, for I have seen that *you are righteous before me in this generation.* Take with you seven pairs of all clean animals, the male and his mate; and a pair of the animals that are not clean, the male and his mate; and seven pairs of the birds of the air also, male and female, *to keep their kind* (*zera'*; seed, progeny) *alive upon the face of all the earth.* For in seven days I will send rain upon the earth forty days and forty nights; and every living thing that I have made I will blot out from the face of the ground." And *Noah did all that the Lord had commanded him.* Noah was six hundred years old when the flood of waters came upon the earth. And Noah and his sons and his wife and his sons' wives with him went into the ark, to escape the waters of the flood. Of clean animals, and of animals that are not clean, and of birds, and of everything that creeps on the ground, two and two, male and female, went into the ark with Noah, *as God had commanded Noah.* (Gen 7:1-9)

Consequently, if the land animals will be preserved after the flood it is not because they will magically change their behavior—how is that even possible?—but rather because God, out of the same goodness, will commit himself through a covenant not to blot out living beings through another flood:

> Then God said to Noah and to his sons with him, "Behold, I establish my covenant with you and your descendants after you, and *with every living creature that is with you, the birds, the cattle, and every beast of the earth with you,* as many as came out of the ark. I establish my covenant with you, that never again shall all flesh be cut off by the waters of a flood, and never again shall there be a flood to destroy the earth." And God said, "This is the sign of the covenant which I make between me and you *and every living creature that is with you,* for all future generations: I set my bow in the cloud, and it shall be a sign of the covenant *between me and the earth.* When I bring clouds over the earth and the bow is seen in the clouds, I will remember my covenant which is between me and you *and every living creature of all flesh*; and the waters shall never again become a flood to destroy all flesh. When the bow is in the clouds, I will look upon it and remember the everlasting covenant between God *and every living creature of all flesh that is upon the earth.*" God said to Noah, "This is the sign of the covenant which I have

established between me and all flesh that is upon the earth." (Gen 9:8-17)

Remains the million-dollar question. Why is the author so interested in the animals when scripture is not a treatise on zoology? The question itself contains the answer; namely, the addressees of scripture are the humans. They are the ones who are hearing what the author is saying *to them about* the animals. Let me refer to an interesting instance in the Book of Judges where one hears a lengthy metaphoric parable, a fable, whose subjects are trees nonetheless, and yet whose addressees are admittedly the humans:

> And all the citizens of Shechem came together, and all Bethmillo, and they went and made Abimelech king, by the oak of the pillar at Shechem. When it was told to Jotham, he went and stood on the top of Mount Gerizim, and cried aloud and *said to them*, "Listen to me, *you men of Shechem, that God may listen to you*. The trees once went forth to anoint a king over them; and they said to the olive tree, 'Reign over us.' But the olive tree said to them, 'Shall I leave my fatness, by which gods and men are honored, and go to sway over the trees?' And the trees said to the fig tree, 'Come you, and reign over us.' But the fig tree said to them, 'Shall I leave my sweetness and my good fruit, and go to sway over the trees?' And the trees said to the vine, 'Come you, and reign over us.' But the vine said to them, 'Shall I leave my wine which cheers gods and men, and go to sway over the trees?' Then all the trees said to the bramble, 'Come you, and reign over us.' And the bramble said to the trees, 'If in good faith you are anointing me king over you, then come and take refuge in my shade; but if not, let fire come out of the bramble and devour the cedars of Lebanon.' Now therefore, *if you acted in good faith* and honor when you made Abimelech king, and if *you have dealt* well with Jerubbaal and his house, and have done to him as his deeds deserved—for my father fought for you, and risked his life, and rescued you from the hand of Midian; and you have risen up against my father's house this day, and have slain his sons, seventy men on one stone, and have made Abimelech, the son of his maidservant, king over the citizens of Shechem, because he is your kinsman—*if you then have acted in good faith and honor* with Jerubbaal and with his house

> this day, then rejoice in Abimelech, and let him also rejoice in you; but if not, let fire come out from Abimelech, and devour the citizens of Shechem, and Bethmillo; and let fire come out from the citizens of Shechem, and from Bethmillo, and devour Abimelech."
> (Judg 9:6-20)

I can already imagine my readers' retort, "But, here, the author's intention is made clear in the text and right from the beginning. We do not see that in Genesis." My answer is precisely that such cannot be "seen" but "heard" since scripture is literature, and good literature more often than not engages its hearers so that they *be attentive to the entire story* and, in so doing, realize what the author is doing and saying. When all is said and done, an engaged hearer is prone to never forget the lesson. That scripture, which is a teaching, was poured into the mold of an engaging literature is sealed in the introduction to Psalm 78 whose content covers the entirety of the scriptural story:

> A Maskil (*maskil*; wise teaching) of Asaph. Give ear, O my people, to my teaching (*torah*; instruction); incline your ears to the words of my mouth! I will open my mouth in a parable (*mašal*); I will utter dark sayings (*ḥidot*; teasing, engaging parables) *from of old*, things that *we have heard* and known, that *our fathers have told us*. We will not hide them from their children, but tell to the coming generation the glorious deeds of the Lord, and his might, and the wonders which he has wrought. He established a testimony in Jacob, and appointed a law (*torah*) in Israel, which he commanded our fathers *to teach* (*make known*) to their children; that the next generation might know them, the children yet unborn, and arise and tell them to their children, so that they should set their hope in God, and not forget the works of God, but keep his commandments; and that they should not be like their fathers, a stubborn and rebellious generation, a generation whose heart was not steadfast, whose spirit was not faithful to God. (vv.1-8)

Notice how it is as parables and enigmas (teasing, engaging parables; *ḥidot*, dark sayings)[16] that the "teaching" addressed to the original recipients is communicated to the following generations yet unborn at the time of the issuance of that teaching.

Keeping this in mind, let us listen again to Genesis. Having established firmly (three times, Gen 7:21[twice]; 8:17) that the land animals and the birds, which were formed out of the ground (2:19) just as the human being was (2:7),[17] share the feature of "swarming" with the sea animals, we are attuned, to some extent, to receiving without much resistance that the author would push further and include the humans—the first consorts of the animals and birds[18]—in his program: "And you, be fruitful and multiply, bring forth abundantly (*širṣu*) on the earth and multiply in it." (9:7) Notice how, the way the statement is phrased, the "swarming" qualifies the human "multiplication" (*rebu*; growth) so that the humans, who were "created" (1:27) and "blessed" to "fill" the earth (1:28), would do so now, after the flood, in the same way as the "swarming" sea animals were "created" (1:21) and "blessed" to "fill" the seas (1:22). So the land animals function, in the text, as a literary device to prepare for the author's ultimate goal, to invite the humans after the experience of the flood to live on earth just as

---

16 As in the case of the parable of the Good Samaritan at the end of which Jesus asks in order to engage his hearers: "Which of these three, do you think, proved neighbor to the man who fell among the robbers?" (Lk 10:36)

17 That the author had Genesis 2 in mind is evident especially in 7:21-22 where he refers to the land animals in a phraseology reminiscent of the description of man, and not the animals, in chapter 2. Compare "then the Lord God formed man of dust from the ground, and breathed *into his nostrils the breath of life*" (2:7) and "And all flesh died that moved upon the earth, birds, cattle, beasts, all swarming creatures that swarm upon the earth, and every man; everything on the dry land *in whose nostrils was the breath of life* died." (7:21-22)

18 Then the Lord God said, "It is not good that the man should be alone; I will make him a helper fit for him." So out of the ground the Lord God formed every beast of the field and every bird of the air, and brought them to the man to see what he would call them; and whatever the man called every living creature, that was its name. (Gen 2:18-19)

the sea animals live in the potentially threatening waters—in Genesis 1:2—unharmed even by their surge into a devastating flood. The Book of Jonah functions as a reminder in this matter in that, in the case of another sea surge, Jonah will be preserved unharmed in the belly of a great fish!

Still the scriptural authors introduced before Genesis 9:7 another ingenious twist to prepare the hearers to perceive the land animals as a bridge toward the author's goal: the text is ultimately addressed to the human beings. Even before the reference to the land animals as "swarming" (Gen 7:21), we hear a furtive hint to those same animals as having a "seed" (*zera'*; 7:3), which is a one-time exception since, in scripture, this term is reserved to the seed/s[19] of vegetation and to the progeny (searing) of the humans. Notice how RSV avoids the dilemma by translating here the original *zera'* into "kind": "Take with you seven pairs of all clean animals, the male and his mate; and a pair of the animals that are not clean, the male and his mate; and seven pairs of the birds of the air also, male and female, to keep their *kind* (*zera'*; seed, progeny) alive upon the face of all the earth."[20] The hearers' perplexity will soon be resolved at hearing 7:21; 8:17; and finally 9:7.

Why would the sea animals be an example for humans to follow?

Before answering this question, I need to remind my readers that everything in scripture is within the boundaries of the scriptural perspective. Not only theology and philosophy are out of order, but also contemporary science and interests, including ecology,[21] are not in the authors' purview. If the

19 In this case it is encountered in both the singular and the plural.

20 The unexpectedness of the original is also avoided in the French JB that has "race" and the English NJB that has "species."

21 I am singling out ecology because my dealing with animals and vegetation gives sometimes the impression that I am advocating the same premise as this branch of contemporary science. Modern-day ecologists—or at least their majority—would most certainly not subscribe to the authors' premise concerning the divinity of the

language, history, and, to a great extent, the geographical nomenclature of scripture is concocted by the authors to help them relay *their* message that goes against the common grain, then how much more is the "way" they handle what they write controlled by them for their own purpose. One does not—or at least should not—ever inquire about the "correctness" and "veracity" of the stories of the Iliad and Odyssey. One takes them or leave them. However, one may not impose on others to take one's stand in the matter. What is written is written or, as Paul puts it, "What is written is written *as it is written.*"[22] So the only valid question is, "What is scripture trying to tell us?"

The immediately following chapter after the flood story is what is commonly referred to as "the table of nations" (Gen 10). An aside is in order here for me to show my readers that the device concerning the intentional choice of words to set up the stage for the next chapter in the story is more common, in the original language, than usually acknowledged even by scholars of scripture who look for things that are fixed in their minds and use scripture to back up their presuppositions. However, listening to scripture as a literary text where the plot develops or, more precisely, unfolds—since the authors already know the plot *they* have conceived—will reveal to us more than meets the ear in the translations. Let us compare two texts I referred to in footnote 17:

---

sun and moon, which is an essential element in Genesis 1. Conversely, the authors would not even begin to fathom what a modern-day ecologist would be talking about.

22 So, all the ado about Paul wanting always to impose his own views on us is made up by theologians who are still as frustrated with him as were their predecessors, the fathers of the church. Their way out of the dilemma is to play the different authors against, or at least independently of, one another, as is common in the Protestant fad of the twentieth century "the different voices in scripture," which is nothing else than the echo of the early Christian tradition that added "according to..." after the name of the assumed author of every Gospel. And thus, they came up with book titles as "the theology of Luke," "the theology of Paul," "the theology of Deuteronomy," and so forth. Many of them even play Jesus and Paul against one another!

> Then the Lord God formed man of dust from the ground, and breathed (*naphaḥ*) into his nostrils the breath (*nešamah*) of life (*ḥayyim*)" (Gen 2:7)
>
> And all flesh died that moved upon the earth, birds, cattle, beasts, all swarming creatures that swarm upon the earth, and every man; everything on the dry land (*ḥarabah*) in whose nostrils was the breath (*nešamah*) ~~*of the spirit (ruaḥ)*~~ of life (*ḥayyim*) died." (Gen 7:21-22)

RSV is way off the mark twice in matters that sound not so important for anyone who does not know the original since the common reaction is, "But the essential meaning is captured and we understand *the thought* that the text is conveying."[23]

First, the use of "dry land" to render *ḥarabah* is misleading on two counts. On the one hand, "dry land" has been used twice to render *yabbašah* (dry) which is literally a nominalized feminine adjective that fits with *'ereṣ* (earth), a feminine noun (Gen 1:9, 10). Since these are the only instances of these two nouns in Genesis, one cannot escape the impression, if not the conviction, that all translators across the board did not know what to do with the "function" of the unexpected *ḥarabah* in 7:22. Clearly, as otherwise all theologians and preachers would, they avoided the dilemma. However if that word is used there, the only viable explanation is that the authors intended to impress the hearers' ears with the root *ḥrb* that was heard earlier in the noun *ḥereb* (sword; 3:24) and therefore would be ready to perceive in its own time that, although *yabbašah* and *ḥarabah* may refer to the same solid ground on which we stand as factuality, still the two words refer to two views of it, the first being positive, land versus sea, the other to the dryness as devastation, which connotation is reflected in the cognate *ḥorbah* (desolation,

23 And, in this case, the other translations in different languages do not fare better, including the LXX and the Vulgate. A case in point is the New Jerusalem Bible (English) that has "the least breath of life" (Gen 7:22). The "spirit" (*ruaḥ*)—translated as "breath"—is suddenly divided into levels! If this is not massacring the original text, what is?

desolate place) that, consonantally, is exactly the same word as *ḥarabah*: *ḥrbh*.

This is more important than it looks for most of my readers who were raised with a language where consonants and vowels are equally letters of the alphabet as in our ABCD. However, before the Masoretes conceived the diacritic marks or vocalic sounds to help the official readers in the different congregations "sound" alike and thus ensure that the members of the different congregations are hearing the same "text"—hence the nomenclature of Masoretic Text (MT)—scripture was consonantal. In other words, *ḥarabah* and *ḥorbah* are both *ḥrbh* and are, in (the) reality (of the text), much closer. In turn, this prepares the hearer to be ready for the twist in direction connected with the authors' back to back use of the verb *ḥareb* one chapter later:

> In the six hundred and first year, in the first month, the first day of the month, the waters were dried (*ḥarebu*) from off the earth; and Noah removed the covering of the ark, and looked, and behold, the face of the ground was dry (*ḥarebu*). In the second month, on the twenty-seventh day of the month, the earth was dry (*yabešah*; became dry, from the verb *yabeš*). (Gen 8:13-14)

Here again a hearer of the English will conclude that the endings of vv.13 and 14 are a repetition: "the face of the ground was dry" and "the earth was dry." But this is not what the original addressees are hearing.

The parallelism in Hebrew is between the two *ḥarebu*, which is incomprehensible for an English speaking hearer since the English "waters" is a plural noun while the English "face (of the ground)" is singular and, consequently, cannot possibly comprehend how the two verbs are both in the plural. For a cognizant of Hebrew the dilemma is non-existent since, in the Hebrew language, both *mayim* (waters) and *panim* (corresponding to the English "face") are plural nouns and thus require the plural *ḥarebu*. Notice the following series of play on terms in the original:

1. Ultimately the earth returns to its primordial state of being, positively speaking, "dry" (*yabešah*); hence the use of the verb *yabešah* whose meaning is "became dry" and not simply "was dry." It is a state that was attained by the earth in v.14. Such was possible because the "face" of the ground dried up (end of v.13) but was still nonfunctional and thus in state of desolate dryness (root *ḥrb*). The reason is to be found in the flow of the story. To be a full-fledged "living" earth, besides the vegetation that allowed the dove not to return any more to Noah,[24] the dry land needed to be populated by the humans and animals that were in the ark: "Then God said to Noah, 'Go forth from the ark, you and your wife, and your sons and your sons' wives with you. Bring forth with you every living thing that is with you of all flesh—birds and animals and every creeping thing that creeps on the earth—that they may breed abundantly on the earth, and be fruitful and multiply upon the earth.' So Noah went forth, and his sons and his wife and his sons' wives with him. And every beast, every creeping thing, and every bird, everything that moves upon the earth, went forth by families out of the ark." (Gen 8:15-19)

2. Still, the same verb *ḥareb* plays, functionally, a positive role in 8:13. That is to say, when applied to the waters it describes how they were dried (*ḥarebu*) *from off* (*me'al*; from above) *the earth*. This is not so strange because this linguistic phenomenon is encountered in languages. Take,

24 He waited another seven days, and again he sent forth the dove out of the ark; and the dove came back to him in the evening, and lo, in her mouth a freshly plucked olive leaf; so Noah knew that the waters had subsided from the earth. Then he waited another seven days, and sent forth the dove; and she did not return to him any more. (Gen 8:10-12)

> for instance our English, and compare the function of the same "am glad" with "went down," on the one hand, and "went up," on the other hand: "I am glad your fever (temperature) has gone down since yesterday"; "I am glad your grades have gone up this semester."

This concern with the demeaning of the human beings given their propensity towards arrogance and haughtiness, which pervades scripture through and through—against the grain of theology, Christian and otherwise, as well as against philosophy, Greek and otherwise—will be brought to a head shortly in Genesis 6:1-8 and again in 11:1-9, that is, after as well as before the flood. It is as though the authors are intent early on—while speaking of the entire humanity and, according to the *toledot* of Shem in Genesis 10, way before the appearance of Abram—to underscore that the human beings did not learn anything from the episode of the flood as punishment for their arrogance, i.e., for their not having heeded the lesson of the punishment of Adam and Cain, the forefathers of all humankind, the first for his having sought to be "like God" and the second for his having imagined that human life was his to take away. This authorial assumption will apply to the descendants of the scriptural Abram/Abraham, the authors' special interest throughout scripture starting with Genesis 12. To quote the three major Prophets:

> The vision of Isaiah the son of Amoz, which he saw concerning Judah and Jerusalem in the days of Uzziah, Jotham, Ahaz, and Hezekiah, kings of Judah. Hear, O heavens, and give ear, O earth; for the Lord has spoken: "Sons have I reared and brought up, but they have rebelled against me. The ox knows its owner, and the ass its master's crib; but Israel does not know, my people does not understand." … Hear the word of the Lord, you rulers of Sodom! Give ear to the teaching of our God, you people of Gomorrah! (Is 1:1-3, 10)

> Therefore I still contend with you, says the Lord, and with your children's children I will contend. For cross to the coasts of

Cyprus and see, or send to Kedar and examine with care; see if there has been such a thing. Has a nation changed its gods, even though they are no gods? But my people have changed their glory for that which does not profit. Be appalled, O heavens, at this, be shocked, be utterly desolate, says the Lord, for my people have committed two evils: they have forsaken me, the fountain of living waters, and hewed out cisterns for themselves, broken cisterns, that can hold no water. (Jer 2:9-13)

And he said to me, "Son of man, I send you to the people of Israel, to a nation (nations) of rebels, who have rebelled against me; they and their fathers have transgressed against me to this very day. The people also are impudent and stubborn: I send you to them; and you shall say to them, 'Thus says the Lord God.' And whether they hear or refuse to hear (for they are a rebellious house) they will know that there has been a prophet among them. And you, son of man, be not afraid of them, nor be afraid of their words, though briers and thorns are with you and you sit upon scorpions; be not afraid of their words, nor be dismayed at their looks, for they are a rebellious house. And you shall speak my words to them, whether they hear or refuse to hear; for they are a rebellious house." (Ezek 2:3-7)

And he said to me, "Son of man, go, get you to the house of Israel, and speak with my words to them. For you are not sent to a people of foreign speech and a hard language, but to the house of Israel—not to many peoples of foreign speech and a hard language, whose words you cannot understand. Surely, if I sent you to such, they would listen to you. But the house of Israel will not listen to you; for they are not willing to listen to me; because all the house of Israel are of a hard forehead and of a stubborn heart. Behold, I have made your face hard against their faces, and your forehead hard against their foreheads. Like adamant harder than flint have I made your forehead; fear them not, nor be dismayed at their looks, for they are a rebellious house." (Ezek 3:4-9)

How do the authors accomplish their strike against their addressees who, as Mesopotamian city dwellers (Gen 11:1-9), considered themselves as *bene' 'elohim* (sons of God) superior to, and thus oppressing to, their kin,[25] the *benot ha'adam* (daughters of man) (Gen 6:1-2), let alone superior to and subjugators of the animals and vegetation unlike their neighbors, the shepherds of the Syrian wilderness? Here again the story of Genesis 5-11—the *toledot* of the individualized Adam and his descendant Noah—is already sketched out in the previous *toledot* of the scriptural heavens and earth (Gen 1-4). There Cain the first human (*ben-'adam*; son of man) outside the oasis Eden whence his father was exiled—and in spite of the fact that the Lord admonished him to dwell in the open earth of "wandering" (Nod from the verb *nad* [wander]) and thus live a life similar to the brother he slew and who was a "shepherd of flock"—decided to build a city which he named Enoch, after his first born son, thereby casting in stone his first born and through him all his progeny. This situation will not be corrected until the "end" according to Ezekiel when God will turn the humans' "hearts of stone" into "hearts of flesh" (36:26).

Let us go a step further. The hearers of scripture, i.e. the actual addressees of the scriptural text starting with Genesis 1:1, are faced in Genesis 1:1-2:4 with a story where *ha'adam* as actualized human being located in a given earthly place, the garden of Genesis 2, and conversant with the Lord God "is" not yet. So, the hearers of scripture are privy to a scriptural pre-story to which the actualized *ha'adam* in Genesis 2-3—let alone the individualized *'adam* in Genesis 5—is not privy. Genesis 1:1-2:4 is a reality for and thus of exclusively the *hearers* of scripture.[26] Thus the hearers—and only they—are faced directly with the authors' premise. What is more important is that such premise was stated in the actual original words of

25 *'iš* (man) and *'iššah* (woman) are linguistically from the same root, which allowed *ha'adam* (the man) to say: "This at last is bone of my bones and flesh of my flesh; she shall be called *'iššah*, because she was taken out of *'iš*." (Gen 2:23)

26 All the theological jargon about the contents of Genesis 1 having been revealed to Moses directly by God—since no human was there at least on days 1-5—is pure mental acrobatics nonsense! Scripture itself never mentions that. It is pure speculation on theology's part.

Genesis 1:1-2:4 and nowhere else. To try to speak of the deep or lofty meaning of the text independently of the original morphology, vocabulary, and phraseology of the original consonantal text is a futile exercise that profits only the seekers of an academic position and in no way the seekers of the intent of the original authors expressed in their actual original wording that extend over their entire unitary product: Law, Prophets and Writings.

Consequently, the hearers *of all ages* are faced with the authors' premise stated and articulated *before* they, the hearers, who—as human beings—become functional in Genesis 2:16-17 at the earliest. However, unfortunately for them, the scene is already set: they are not superior to the sea animals except that—as will become clear in the following verses—unluckily for them, they bear the onus of responsibility for God's full work (Gen 2:1-2) that includes not only the vegetation but also the animals, their peers (Gen 1:28-30).

This scriptural interest in the full parity between sea animals and the human beings finds its most extreme expression at the end of the Gospel of John where the human beings are cast *as* fish. The fish caught by the "fishermen"[27] disciples are *numbered* just as human beings would be, a unique instance in scripture: "So Simon Peter went aboard and hauled the net ashore, full of large fish, a hundred and fifty-three of them; and although there were so many, the net was not torn." (21:11)[28]

---

27 Simon Peter, Thomas called the Twin, Nathanael of Cana in Galilee, the sons of Zebedee, and two others of his disciples were together. Simon Peter said to them, "I am going fishing." They said to him, "We will go with you." They went out and got into the boat; but that night they caught nothing. (Jn 21:2-3)

28 See *NTI3* 261-3 for the symbolic value of the numeral "one hundred fifty-three."

8

ruaḥ, hebel, ḥayyim, nepheš

One of the most calamitous developments in classical theology is dealing with the divine spirit and the divine word as self-standing Platonic eternal entities that can be tossed around according to our own preferences and pleasures. We end up writing tomes and tomes trying to explain to the "lesser" brethren how these entities behave according to the rules of our own theology and brand anyone who does not subscribe to our theology as an "ungodly heretic." Let me forego those unscriptural, if not outright anti-scriptural, developments and invite my readers to delve with me into the original Hebrew nomenclature.

I should like to start with a few terminological examples that will help us ease our way into broaching the noun *ruaḥ*, which is most translated into Spirit, spirit, wind, and breath. These divergences reflect the range of nuances connoted in this original Hebrew noun. There are two common nouns, *dam* (blood) and *reḥem* (womb). Their plurals, *damim* (bloods) and *raḥamim* (wombs), acquire different connotations: "bloodshed" in the first case, and even a totally different meaning, "mercy, compassion" in the second case:

> And the Lord said, "What have you done? The voice of your brother's blood (*damim*) is crying to me from the ground. And now you are cursed from the ground, which has opened its mouth to receive your brother's blood (*damim*) from your hand." (Gen 4:10-11)

> When you spread forth your hands, I will hide my eyes from you; even though you make many prayers, I will not listen; your hands are full of blood (*damim*). (Is 1:15)

> He who walks righteously and speaks uprightly, who despises the gain of oppressions, who shakes his hands, lest they hold a bribe,

> who stops his ears from hearing of bloodshed (*damim*) and shuts his eyes from looking upon evil… (Is 33:15)

> When the Lord saw that Leah was hated, he opened her womb (*reḥem*); but Rachel was barren. (Gen 29:31)

> Then God remembered Rachel, and God hearkened to her and opened her womb (*reḥem*). (Gen 30:22)

> May God Almighty grant you mercy (*raḥamim*) before the man, that he may send back your other brother and Benjamin. If I am bereaved of my children, I am bereaved. (Gen 43:14)

> None of the devoted things shall cleave to your hand; that the Lord may turn from the fierceness of his anger, and show you mercy (*raḥamim*), and have compassion on you, and multiply you, as he swore to your fathers (Deut 13:17)

> Have mercy on me, O God, according to thy steadfast love; according to thy abundant mercy (*raḥamim*) blot out my transgressions. (Ps 51:1)

On the other hand, the plural *ḥayyim* of the adjective *ḥay* (living, alive) can mean, depending on the context, either "living ones" or "life":

> then the Lord God formed man of dust from the ground, and breathed (*naphaḥ*) into his *nostrils* the breath (*nešamah*) of life (*ḥayyim*); and man became *a living being* (*nepheš ḥayyah*)[1]. (Gen 2:7)

> For behold, I will bring a flood of waters upon the earth, to destroy all flesh in which is the breath (*ruaḥ;* spirit) of life (*ḥayyim*) from under heaven; everything that is on the earth shall die. (Gen 6:17)

> They went into the ark with Noah, two and two of all flesh in which there was the breath (*ruaḥ;* spirit) of life (*ḥayyim*). (Gen 7:15)

> everything on the dry land in whose nostrils was the breath (*nešamah*) ***of the spirit (ruaḥ)*** of life (*ḥayyim*) died. (7:22)[2]

---

1 *ḥayyah* is the feminine adjective of *ḥay* since *nepheš* is a feminine noun.
2 RSV took its liberty in eliminating the words in bold that are found in the original Hebrew.

> And he stood between the dead and the living (*ḥayyim*); and the plague was stopped. (Num 16:48)

> … as long as my breath (*nešamah*) is in me, and the spirit (*ruaḥ*) of God is in my *nostrils*; my lips will not speak falsehood, and my tongue will not utter deceit. (Job 27:3-4)

The adjective *ḥay* (living) functions like the adjective *ra'* (evil). In both their grammatical genders, masculine and feminine, these adjectives can function as nouns. In the latter case, the singular masculine and the singular feminine can refer to "evil" as noun:

> And out of the ground the Lord God made to grow every tree that is pleasant to the sight and good for food, the tree of life also in the midst of the garden, and the tree of the knowledge of good and evil (*ra'* [masc] noun). (Gen 2:9)

> The Lord saw that the wickedness (*ra'ah* [fem]; evil [noun]) of man was great in the earth, and that every imagination of the thoughts of his heart was only evil (*ra'* [masc] adjective) continually. (Gen 6:5)

In the case of *ḥay*, the masculine plural *ḥayyim* is nominalized in the sense of "life" whereas it is the adjective feminine singular *ḥayyah*[3] that is nominalized in the sense of "living animal or creature" as in the following instances:

> And God blessed them, and God said to them, "Be fruitful and multiply, and fill the earth and subdue it; and have dominion over the fish of the sea and over the birds of the air and over every *living thing* (*ḥayyah*) that moves upon the earth." (Gen 1:28)

> For your lifeblood I will surely require a reckoning; of every beast (*ḥayyah*) I will require it and of man; of every man's brother I will require the life of man. (Gen 9:5)

As is evident from some of the quotations above, "life" in scripture is intricately connected to "breathing" and, by extension, to any expression or connotation that is related to

---

3 See above *nepheš ḥayyah* (living soul) in Genesis 2:7.

"moving air." My readers are reminded that scriptural Hebrew does not have a word for our "air." So, air per se does not give life and, moreover, it is the sign of life only inasmuch as it is moving. In other words, it is "breath" or, more accurately, "breathing" that is the sign of life to the extent that, in all languages, "stop breathing" connotes "lack or absence of life" and thus "death."[4] It is precisely this basic feature of "animal" life[5] that is reflected in a varied terminology at the outset of scripture:

1. *nepheš* whose meaning is "breath" in the sense of exhalation and thus "breathing (blowing) out." Breathing in or inbreath is not a tangible reality since it is perceived only by the inhaling individual. It is breathing out or outbreath which is an actual reality that is witnessed by all those around. When medics check on someone's breathing, they are actually checking on the breathing out which they can feel and hear. It is then understandable that it is used in conjunction with any "animal" (animated) life—and more specifically with humans, land animals, and birds whose exhaling one can "sense" and witness to—and by extension *nepheš* (breathing out) refers to any such individual. The Latin *anima* is the closest rendering of the original *nepheš* since it keeps the original connotation of the Hebrew. It refers to "current of air, wind,

4 I hope none of my readers would retort, "how about spiritual life?" unless that reader is willing to show me an actual reference to the phrase "spiritual life" (*pnevmatikē zōē*) in scripture. "Spirit of life" is found, but not "spiritual life." In other words, as we shall momentarily see, the scriptural "spirit" gives life, but not "spiritual life." That is why Paul requires us to "walk" (live) "according to the Spirit" (*kata pnevma*) (Rom 8:4).

5 The Latin *anima* refers to a current of air, wind, breath, and thus *animal* refers to a breathing (independently moving) being. Hence our English "animal life." This explains why the scriptural authors, who were obviously not cognizant of our contemporary "botany," did not consider vegetation, though a "living" reality through "seeds" (Gen 1:11-12), as a "breathing" reality.

breath." The Arabic has two vocalizations for the same consonantal *nphs: naphas* for (out)breathing, breath) and *naphs* for the individual human being and thus means "individual" or "person." The plural of the Arabic *naphs* is *'anphus* which means "persons, people." This is a far cry from how the Greek rendering of the Hebrew *nepheš* has come to be understood à la Plato's eternal soul in spite of the fact that the original meaning of *psykhē* is "breath" from the verb *psykhazō* or *psykhaō* (refresh) and the adjective *psykheinos* (fresh, refreshing, and thus cold). It is high time that Plato, Alexandrian theology, and, for that matter, all theological jargon and thought be banned from the study of scripture, that is, the Hebrew consonantal text of scripture. The original meaning of the English "scripture" is, after all, "that which is written" and not "that which is translated," let alone "that which is perceived by the hearers or readers of the translation" after having consulted theological books.

2. *nešamah* means "breeze" and thus connotes softly moving air. That is why we are told that, in order to produce a *nepheš* out of the dust of the ground—just as a potter produces (*yaṣar;* forms) a vessel out of clay—the Lord God had first to *breathe* (*naphaḥ*; blow air) into the nostrils of the newly formed object, and only then did that object become a *nepheš ḥayyah* (living breath) and not simply a *nepheš*. One can tell that the author was no Platonist, by any stretch of the imagination, since the "soul" for a Platonist is by definition an essence, that is, essentially existing and thus living: "then the Lord God formed man

> (*ha'adam*) of dust from the ground (*ha'adamah*), and breathed into his nostrils the breath (*nešamah*) of life; and man became a living being." (Gen 2:7) Notice how the original authors, who were the LXX translators, ridiculed Greek philosophy by rendering *nepheš ḥayyah* into *psykhēn zōsan* (living soul). Why would a "soul" understood à la Plato need life? My readers are prompted to ask theologians—that is, themselves—as to how this would square with the common theological given that a "soul" is by definition "immortal" if not "eternal." Notice that scripture does not say "the Lord took a soul and breathed into it life (*ḥayyim*)" but rather "breathed (blew air) into the nostrils of the vessel just formed out of clay"—*'adam* out of the dust of the *'adamah*—"and, in so doing, made him into a *nepheš ḥayyah.*" The importance of *nešamah* (breath, breathing, breeze) as the first and foremost and, thus, ultimate expression of individual life can be gathered from the fact that it is used on its own to refer to *the human being* in the last Psalm dedicated to praising the Lord by humans: "Let *everything that breathes* (*nešamah*) praise the Lord! Praise the Lord!" (150:6) That humans are intended can be gathered from the reference to musical instruments starting with trumpet blast (*teqa' šophar;* v.3a) that cannot be produced except through "blowing air" unlike the rest of the instruments: lute and harp (v.3b), timbrel (v.4a), strings (4b), and cymbals (v.5); except for the pipe (v.4b).

The ubiquitous scriptural Hebrew noun *ruaḥ* has been massacred in translations and, more so, in theology. Since its treatment is the main concern of my study and discussion in this chapter, let me mention here how its original connotation of "wind" (forceful moving air) is intricately linked to the two previous nouns, *nepheš* and *nešamah*. This is evident in the following passage:

> And as I looked, there were sinews on them, and flesh had come upon them, and skin had covered them; but there was no breath (*ruaḥ;* wind) in them. Then he said to me, "Prophesy to the breath (*ruaḥ;* wind), prophesy, son of man, and say to the breath (*ruaḥ;* wind), Thus says the Lord God: Come from the four winds (*ruḥot;* plural of *ruaḥ*), O breath (*ruaḥ;* wind), and breathe (*naphaḥ*; blow air) upon these slain, that they may live (*ḥayah*; from the same root as *ḥay* [living] and *ḥayyim* [life])." So I prophesied as he commanded me, and the breath (*ruaḥ;* wind) came into them, and they lived (*ḥayah*; from the same root as *ḥay* [living] and *ḥayyim* [life]), and stood upon their feet, an exceedingly great host." (Ezek 37:8-10)

Notice how RSV, throughout this passage, rendered *ruaḥ* as "breath," which it used to translate *nešamah* in Genesis 2:7 in conjunction with the noun *ḥayyim* (life) and the verb *naphaḥ* (breathe, blow air): "then the Lord God formed man (*ha'adam*) of dust from the ground (*ha'adamah*), and breathed (*naphaḥ*; blow air) into his nostrils the breath (*nešamah*) of life (*ḥayyim*); and man became a living being."

At the other end of the spectrum we have *hebel*—the name of Cain's brother, Abel—that connotes "vapor," "steam," "vanishing breath," a passing movement of air that does not leave any trace. The highest incidence of that noun in scripture occurs in the Book of Ecclesiastes where it is translated as "vanity" from the Latin *vanitas* whose meaning is "vainness," "emptiness," "passing nothingness," and thus something that only gives the impression that it is something and yet does not leave any recognizable trace. It is the exact opposite of *ruaḥ* (wind) whose "actuality" is unmissable, as is clear from the repeated phrase in Ecclesiastes: "all is vanity (*hebel*) and a striving after wind (*ruaḥ*)." (1:14, 17; 2:11, 17, 26; 4:4, 16; 6:9)

All these four terms, *nepheš, nešamah, ruaḥ*, and *hebel*, are encountered in Genesis 1-11 and thus function as a "code" for their subsequent occurrences in the rest of scripture. A basic rule that I stressed time and again is that one does not read scripture backwards but forwards. Consequently, all the jargon about reading the Old Testament in the light of the New Testament or in the light of Jesus Christ was conceived by careerist theologians who are interested in promoting their "writings" *as scripture.* All one has to do is to read "theological" books to realize that authors reference one another much more frequently than they reference scripture. And why not since they deal with scripture not as canonized literary story that has a beginning and an end, but rather, following the footsteps of their predecessors, conceive it as a Lego construction whose pieces they feel entitled to dismantle and then reassemble "creatively." They then label their attempts with a catchy phrase like "re-appropriating" earlier theological endeavors, one of which, they say, is scripture itself. It is then no wonder that, in all Christian traditions, the number of apostles far exceed twelve and the apostolic voice is still resounding in our books and sermons, as though Paul *the Apostle* has never dictated that it is *his* letters that are to be read in the church gatherings (Col 4:16). One is to hear scripture in sequence: The Prophets are to be heard in the light of the Law, the Ketubim in the light of the Law and the Prophets, and the New Testament in the light of the Law, the Prophets, and the Ketubim. That is how one better understands the New Testament which, otherwise, would be gibberish without the Old Testament. This is contrary to what is often maintained by Christian theologians who support the notion that the Old Testament would be an opaque literature without the "transparency of the New Testament," especially in what they term "the light of (their theologically conceived) Christ."

Let us therefore delve in more detail into how the four aforementioned Hebrew terms are interlocked by the basic scriptural assumption that "life" (*ḥayyim*)—that is "animal" life[6]—is intimately connected with "inhaling through the

6 Vegetative life is not referred to as "life" in scripture.

nostrils." Let us revisit some of the pertinent former quotations and see how all translations, at one point or another, manipulate the original text to suit the translators' presupposition concerning "life":

> Then the Lord God formed man of dust from the ground, and breathed (*napha*ḥ) into his nostrils the breath (*nešamah*) of life (*ḥayyim*); and man became *a living being* (*nepheš ḥayyah*)[7]. (Gen 2:7)

> For behold, I will bring a flood of waters upon the earth, to destroy all flesh in which is the breath (*ruaḥ;* spirit) of life (*ḥayyim*) from under heaven; everything that is on the earth shall die. (Gen 6:17)

> They went into the ark with Noah, two and two of all flesh in which there was the breath (*ruaḥ;* spirit) of life (*ḥayyim*) (Gen 7:15)

> Everything on the dry land in whose nostrils was the breath (*nešamah*) ***of the spirit*** (*ruaḥ*) of life (*ḥayyim*) died. (Gen 7:22)[8]

The most stunning feature of the original is the functional equation between *nešamah* (breeze; soft breath) and *ruaḥ* (wind). This is most evident in the translations' mishandling of Genesis 7:22 where we have in the original Hebrew a combination of both nouns in conjunction with "life," whereas the same two nouns are used independently with the same "life" in 2:7 (*nešamah*) on the one hand, and in 6:17 and 7:15 (*ruaḥ*), on the other hand. KJV, followed by RSV and NRSV, is the most flagrant example in that it renders both as "breath" and, consequently eliminates outright "of the spirit" in order to avoid rendering *nišmat*[9] *ruaḥ ḥayyim* (7:22) into a ludicrous "the breath of the breath of life." If my readers think this is amusing, they should consider the alternative opted for by the New American Bible's "the *faintest* breath of life" and the New Jerusalem Bible's "the *least* breath of life." Given the lamentable state of theology,

---

7 *ḥayyah* is the feminine adjective of *ḥay* since *nepheš* is a feminine noun.
8 RSV took its liberty in eliminating the words in bold that are found in the original Hebrew.
9 The construct form of *nešamah*.

I shall not be surprised if, when these two translations decide to be published as a "Study Bible," the readers will find an extensive note explaining the difference between "breath of life" and a "fainter or lesser breath of life." Such an observation is valid since both translations rendered earlier both *nišmat ḥayyim* (Gen 2:7) and *ruaḥ ḥayyim* (Gen 6:17; 7:15) as "breath of life." So, a reader is entitled to wonder that, if *nešamah* in 7:22 reflects a faintness of breath,[10] *then* the human the Lord God has formed in 2:7 would have been a "sickling" or, worse, the Lord God's "breathing into the man's nostrils" would have been lacking enough *ruaḥ*, wind, spirit, and possibly Spirit! However, as one of my late colleagues told me once: "But, as you well know, Father Paul, we professors of Patristics and Dogmatics, never allow scripture to constrain us. We cannot afford such constraints given that most of us do not know scriptural Hebrew."

The essentiality of breathing for animal life in the scriptural view—against the Platonic premise of the eternal "soul" that is of the same fabric as the eternal deity, a premise that controlled all theological thought—is reflected in that humans as well as animals are referred to both as *nepheš ḥayyah* (living breath) and as simply either *nepheš* (breath) or *ḥayyah* (living [being]), a feminine adjective functioning as a noun. In all three cases, the singular Hebrew form denotes both a collective and a singular individual. Even once *nepheš* is translated as "life" (Gen 9:5). A few examples from the first passages of scripture will illustrate this matter:

> Let the waters bring forth swarms of *living creatures* (*nepheš ḥayyah*), and let birds fly above the earth across the firmament of the heavens. So God created the great sea monsters and every *living creature* (*nepheš haḥayyah*)[11] that moves, with which the waters swarm, according to their kinds, and every winged bird according to its kind. And God saw that it was good.(Gen 1:20-21)

10 The alternative would be to opt for taking *ruaḥ*—the mighty wind—as the "faintest" and the "least"!

11 The *ha* before *ḥayyah* is the definite article.

> And God said, "Let the earth bring forth *living creatures* (*nepheš ḥayyah*) according to their kinds…" (Gen 1:24)
>
> Be fruitful and multiply, and fill the earth and subdue it; and have dominion over the fish of the sea and over the birds of the air and over every *living thing* (*ḥayyah*) that moves upon the earth. (Gen 1:28)
>
> And to every beast of the earth, and to every bird of the air, and to everything that creeps on the earth, everything that has *the breath of life* (*nepheš ḥayyah*), I have given every green plant for food. (Gen 1:30)
>
> Then the Lord God formed man of dust from the ground, and breathed into his nostrils the breath of life; and man became *a living being* (*nepheš ḥayyah*). (Gen 2:7)
>
> So out of the ground the Lord God formed every *beast* (*ḥayyah*) of the field and every bird of the air, and brought them to the man to see what he would call them; and whatever the man called every *living creature* (*nepheš ḥayyah*), that was its name. (Gen 2:19)
>
> For your lifeblood I will surely require a reckoning; of every *beast* (*ḥayyah*) I will require it and of man; of every man's brother I will require the *life* (*nepheš*) of man. (Gen 9:5)
>
> … and with every *living creature* (*nepheš haḥayyah*) that is with you, the birds, the cattle, and every beast of the earth with you, as many as came out of the ark. (Gen 9:10)
>
> This is the sign of the covenant which I make between me and you and every *living creature* (*nepheš ḥayyah*) that is with you, for all future generations: (Gen 9:12)
>
> I will remember my covenant which is between me and you and every *living creature* (*nepheš ḥayyah*) of all flesh; and the waters shall never again become a flood to destroy all flesh. When the bow is in the clouds, I will look upon it and remember the everlasting covenant between God and every *living creature* (*nepheš ḥayyah*) of all flesh that is upon the earth. (Gen 9:15-16)

This, in turn, explains why *ruaḥ* (wind) is intimately linked to this vocabulary as in Genesis 6:17; 7:15 and especially 7:22

quoted above. However, by forcing an understanding of the scriptural *ruaḥ*—also or sometimes, according to their whim—as the "Spirit" of classical Christian theology, the "eternal" third person of the eternal Trinity, we Christians bound ourselves to a catch-22 situation on two levels.

On the one hand, we resorted to the preposterous gamut of translations of the one noun *ruaḥ* into wind, spirit, Spirit, breath. The most flagrant case is that of the New Jerusalem Bible where *ruaḥ* is systematically rendered as "spirit" (lower case), whereas "Spirit" (upper case) is reserved for the New Testament Greek *pnevma* (the LXX rendering of the Hebrew *ruaḥ*), perhaps with the intention of reflecting a common stand in Christian theology that the Trinity was fully revealed in the New Testament.[12] On the other hand, once *ruaḥ* has been understood as being the Christian "Spirit," one is bound to view it always as a "positive" factor or element, as the "spirit of life." A case in point is the handling by many of "the Spirit (*ruaḥ*) of God was moving over the face of the waters" (Gen 1:2) as referring to the life-giving "trinitarian" Spirit that prepares the way for God's "trinitarian" eternal "Word"—understand the pre-existing Lord Jesus Christ—to create the world, as indicated by the repeated "And God said" (Gen 1:3, 6, 9, 11, 14, 20, 24, 26). However, this exclusively positive take on the Spirit is forced since, functionally, it parallels darkness in the preceding phrase "darkness was upon the face of the deep" (1:2) where clearly "deep" corresponds to "waters" as will be confirmed in the flood story.[13] This explains why some translations, including the NRSV, skirt the issue by rendering the last phrase of Genesis 1:2 as "a mighty wind swept over the waters (NAB), " a divine wind sweeping over the waters" (NJB), "a wind from God swept over the face of the waters" (NRSV).

---

12 This reminds me of a former colleague's premise that Christ's disciples learn to "theologize" in the light of the "risen Christ" and we "theologians" have to learn from their writings, the New Testament, how to proceed in that mission of "theologizing"!

13 See earlier my comments on this matter.

As will be discussed later in my chapter "Positive Negative," the *ruaḥ* of God remains throughout *his ruaḥ* and does *his* bidding whether for the good or for the evil. Consider the following instances where God's *ruaḥ* functions negatively, from our perspective of course:

> So Moses stretched forth his rod over the land of Egypt, and the Lord brought an east wind (*ruaḥ*) upon the land all that day and all that night; and when it was morning the east wind (*ruaḥ*) had brought the locusts. And the locusts came up over all the land of Egypt, and settled on the whole country of Egypt, such a dense swarm of locusts as had never been before, nor ever shall be again. For they covered the face of the whole land, so that the land was darkened, and they ate all the plants in the land and all the fruit of the trees which the hail had left; not a green thing remained, neither tree nor plant of the field, through all the land of Egypt…And the Lord turned a very strong west wind (*ruaḥ*), which lifted the locusts and drove them into the Red Sea; not a single locust was left in all the country of Egypt. (Ex 10:13-15, 19)[14]

> Now the Spirit (*ruaḥ*) of the Lord departed from Saul, and an *evil* spirit (*ruaḥ*) from the Lord tormented him. And Saul's servants said to him, "Behold now, an *evil* spirit (*ruaḥ*) from God is tormenting you." (1 Sam 16:14-15)

> And he said, "Go forth, and stand upon the mount before the Lord." And behold, the Lord passed by, and a great and strong wind (*ruaḥ*) rent the mountains, and broke in pieces the rocks before the Lord, but *the Lord was not in the wind* (*ruaḥ*); and after the wind (*ruaḥ*) an earthquake, but the Lord was not in the earthquake; and after the earthquake a fire, but the Lord was not in the fire; and after the fire a still small voice. (1 Kg 19:11-12)

> Because, yea, because they have misled my people, saying, "Peace," when there is no peace; and because, when the people build a wall, these prophets daub it with whitewash; say to those who daub it with whitewash that it shall fall! There will be a deluge of rain, great hailstones will fall, and a *stormy wind* (*ruaḥ*

14 Notice how the same *ruaḥ* under the Lord's control has two opposite effects.

> *se'arot*)[15] break out; and when the wall falls, will it not be said to you, "Where is the daubing with which you daubed it?" Therefore thus says the Lord God: I will make a *stormy wind* (*ruaḥ se'arot*)[16] break out in my wrath; and there shall be a deluge of rain in my anger, and great hailstones in wrath to destroy it. (Ezek 13:10-13)

> But the vine was plucked up in fury, cast down to the ground; the east wind (*ruaḥ*) dried it up; its fruit was stripped off, its strong stem was withered; the fire consumed it. (Ezek 19:12)

> On the wicked he will rain coals of fire and brimstone; a scorching wind (*ruaḥ*) shall be the portion of their cup. (Ps 11:6)

This rule regarding the *ruaḥ* (Greek *pnevma*) applies to the New Testament despite all the misguided efforts of classical theology that God's Spirit is exclusively the "spirit of life" and not of death. Consider the following passage:

> It is actually reported that there is immorality among you, and of a kind that is not found even among pagans; for a man is living with his father's wife. And you are arrogant! Ought you not rather to mourn? Let him who has done this be removed from among you. For though absent in body *I am present in spirit, and as if present, I have already pronounced judgment* (Greek *kekrika* from the verb *krinein*) *in the name of the Lord Jesus* on the man who has done such a thing. When you are assembled, and *my spirit is present, with the power of our Lord Jesus, you are to deliver this man to Satan for the destruction* (Greek *olethron*) *of the flesh*, that his spirit may be saved in the day of the Lord Jesus. (1 Cor 5:1-5)

Paul's spirit is none other than the "spirit of God" (1 Cor 7:40) according to which he emits his authoritative apostolic "judgment" since he alone[17] is "the spiritual man (who) judges (*anakrinei*) all things, but is himself to be judged (*anakrinetai*) by no one." (1 Cor 2:15) The same spirit—Hebrew *ruaḥ*, Greek

---

15 The hearer cannot but recall that the "stormy wind" was introduced as *the* sign of God's presence right at the outset of the Book of Ezekiel: "As I looked, behold, a stormy wind (*ruaḥ se'arot*) came out of the north, and a great cloud, with brightness round about it, and fire flashing forth continually, and in the midst of the fire, as it were gleaming bronze." (1:4)

16 See previous note.

17 See my comments in *C-1Cor* 64-9.

pnevma—of God bestows salvation and life, on the one hand, but also, on the other hand, brings about *olethron* (destruction, ruin, death; 5:5). This noun is found in 1 Timothy in parallel with *apōleia* (destruction; perishing) from the verb *apollymai* (perish): "But those who desire to be rich fall into temptation, into a snare, into many senseless and hurtful desires that plunge men into ruin (*olethron*) and destruction (*apōleia*)." (6:9) *Apollymai* occurs in Jonah as the translation of the Hebrew *'abad* (perish) that is linked to the *ruaḥ* (wind) hurled upon the sea by none other than the Lord himself:

> But the Lord hurled a great *wind* (Hebrew *ruaḥ;* Greek *pnevma*) upon the sea, and there was a mighty tempest on the sea, so that the ship threatened to break up. Then the mariners were afraid, and each cried to his god; and they threw the wares that were in the ship into the sea, to lighten it for them. But Jonah had gone down into the inner part of the ship and had lain down, and was fast asleep. So the captain came and said to him, "What do you mean, you sleeper? Arise, call upon your god! Perhaps the god will give a thought to us, that we do not *perish* (Hebrew *no'bed;* Greek *apolōmetha*)."...Therefore they cried to the Lord, "We beseech thee, O Lord, let us not *perish* (Hebrew *no'bedah;* Greek *apolōmetha*) for this man's life, and lay not on us innocent blood; for thou, O Lord, hast done as it pleased thee." (Jon 1:4-6, 14)

Put otherwise, yet still in Pauline terms, the Spirit of God works unto life conditionally:

> There is therefore now no condemnation for those who are in Christ Jesus. For the law of the Spirit of life in Christ Jesus has set me free from the law of sin and death. For God has done what the law, weakened by the flesh, could not do: sending his own Son in the likeness of sinful flesh and for sin, he condemned sin in the flesh, *in order that the just requirement of the law might be fulfilled in us, who walk not according to the flesh but according to the Spirit.* (Rom 8:1-4)

This is an echo of Leviticus 26 and Deuteronomy 28 where God is the initiator of both blessing and curse. It is no wonder then that Satan, the "tempter," needs divine permission to test the human beings (Job 1:12a; 2:6). Just as Satan is presented as a member of the divine council (1:6; 2:1) and "goes out" on his mission "from the presence of the Lord" (1:12b; 2:7), so also the "tempter" in Genesis 3:1 is one *ḥayyat haśśadeh* (living [creature] of the field) from among *kol·ḥayyat haśśadeh* (all the living [creatures] of the field) that the Lord God fashioned out of the ground (2:19) in a similar way as he had fashioned the human being (v.7), to be the latter's companions "fit for him" (v.18). Thus, scripturally speaking, it is no wonder that, in Genesis 3, the "serpent" and the human being could "converse and understand one another." By advocating demythologization of scripture and rationalizing it according to the Platonic "reason" (Greek *logos*; Latin *ratio*), classical theological discourse created false dilemmas and tensions—such as "faith seeking reason" and "reason seeking faith"—to promote self-aggrandizing careerism in schools and universities patterned after Plato's "academy," whence our term "academia."

Theology in its totality is just a "fad" of superegos since its inception. Theologians honestly believe they are the intellectual "appropriators" of the "simplistic" scripture when, in reality, it is scripture that was already conceived to pull their leg by purposely presenting the protagonists of the New Testament writings as "fishermen" and "tentmakers." Similarly, the Old Testament authors conceived of a shepherd God residing in a tent, and not a city God residing in a temple of stone made by human hands:

> Now when the king dwelt in his house, and the Lord had given him rest from all his enemies round about, the king said to Nathan the prophet, "See now, I dwell in a house of cedar, but the ark of God dwells in a tent." And Nathan said to the king, "Go, do all that is in your heart; for the Lord is with you." But that same night the word of the Lord came to Nathan, "Go and tell my servant David, 'Thus says the Lord: Would you build me a house to dwell in? I have not dwelt in a house since the day I brought up the people of Israel from Egypt to this day, *but I have been moving about in a tent for my dwelling*.'" (2 Sam 7:1-6)

Thus says the Lord: "Heaven is my throne and the earth is my footstool; what is the house which you would build for me, and what is the place of my rest?" (Is 66:1)

To the choirmaster: according to Lilies. A Testimony of Asaph. A Psalm. *Give ear, O Shepherd of Israel, thou who leadest Joseph like a flock!* Thou who art enthroned upon the cherubim, shine forth before Ephraim and Benjamin and Manasseh! Stir up thy might, and come to save us! (Ps 80:1-2)

For the Lord is a great God, and a great King above all gods. In his hand are the depths of the earth; the heights of the mountains are his also. The sea is his, for he made it; for his hands formed the dry land. O come, let us worship and bow down, let us kneel before the Lord, our Maker! For he is our God, and *we are the people of his pasture, and the sheep of his hand.* O that today you would hearken to his voice! (Ps 95:3-7)

9

Genesis 2:1-4

> [1] Thus the heavens and the earth were finished, and all the host of them. [2] And on the seventh day God finished his work (*mela'kah*) which he had done, and he rested on the seventh day from all his work (*mela'kah*) which he had done. [3] So God blessed the seventh day and hallowed it, because on it God rested from all his work (*mela'kah*) which he had done in creation (*bara' la'aśot*; created unto/by doing). [4] These are the generations of the heavens and the earth when thy were created. In the day that the Lord God made the earth and the heavens.

In v.2, the work that God had completed/finished/fulfilled, "the work which he had done (*'asah*)," is referred to twice as *mela'kah*. In v.3 the same noun *mela'kah* is repeated as the object of both verbs *'aśah* (made) and *bara'* (created) that controlled Genesis 1. The noun *mela'kah* disappears to emerge much later in Genesis twice in 33:14 and in 39:11. The latter instance shows beyond any doubt that the term applies to any kind of work performed by God or human beings:

> But one day, when he [viz Joseph] went into the house to do his work (*mela'kah*) and none of the men of the house was there in the house. (Gen 39:11)

This understanding is confirmed by the following instances:

> Some went down to the sea in ships, doing (*'ośey* from *'aśah*) business (*mela'kah*) on the great waters; they saw the deeds (*ma'aśey*) of the Lord, his wondrous works (*niphle'ot*) in the deep. (Ps 107:23-24)

> But for me it is good to be near God; I have made the Lord God my refuge, that I may tell of all thy works (*mal'ekot* plural of *mela'kah*). (Ps 73:28)

One can only surmise—according to the rules of Semitic grammar—that the verbal root is *l'k*, although the verb *la'ak* is not found in scripture.[1] However, one does find *mal'ak*, a very common noun in scripture, which is usually translated as angel or messenger. Consonantally speaking, *mal'ak* is the grammatically masculine gender of *mela'kah*, just as *'adam* (man, human being) is the grammatically masculine gender of *'adamah* (ground). These latter nouns are undoubtedly interconnected, as is clear from the following instances:

> then the Lord God formed man (*ha'adam*) of dust (*'aphar*) from the ground (*ha'adamah*), and breathed into his nostrils the breath of life; and man became a living being. (Gen 2:7)[2]

> And to Adam (*'adam*) he said… In the sweat of your face you shall eat bread till you return to the ground (*ha'adamah*), for out of it you were taken; you are dust (*'aphar*), and to dust (*'aphar*) you shall return. (Gen 3:17, 19)

Is there a way in scripture to show a connection, meaning wise, between *mela'kah* and *mal'ak*? Providence—or rather, as usual, the authors' ingenuity—provides the answer. In Haggai we find the sole instance of a third noun *mal'akut* from the same root, which is commonly translated—in the only manner that fits the context—as "message":

> Then Haggai, the messenger (*mal'ak*) of the Lord, spoke to the people with the Lord's message (*mal'akut*), "I am with you, says the Lord." (Hag 1:13)

The original is more striking since it reflects the immediate interconnection between *mal'ak* and *mal'akut* through redundancy and sounds thus:

> Then said (spoke, addressed) Haggai the messenger of the Lord in (with, according to) the message of the Lord to the people saying, "I am with you, oracle of the Lord." (Hag 1:13)[3]

---

1 See Lisowsky, *Konkordanz zum Hebräischen Alten Testament*, and dictionaries.

2 See my comments in *ROS* 35.

3 Avoiding the redundancy of the original the LXX, alone among the translations, old and new, has: καὶ εἶπεν Αγγαιος ὁ ἄγγελος κυρίου τῷ λαῷ ἐγώ εἰμι μεθ' ὑμῶν λέγει κύριος. "And said Aggaios the messenger of the Lord to the people: I am with you says the Lord." More in tune with the original the Vulgate has: "et dixit Aggeus

The only logically plausible explanation is to perceive the root *l'k* as referring to something emitted or produced by someone, which product reflects something announcing or introducing that author by way of an introduction. It functions as a retinue or entourage would do. The retinue is assigned by its lord to both reflect and announce its lord's presence; it points to as well as surrounds or precedes the lord. As such, it serves as a delegation or an embassy would. This understanding fits Genesis 2:1-2 where the term *mela'kah* parallels functionally the term *ṣaba'* whose technical meaning is "army, armed host" and whose plural is profusely encountered in scripture in the ubiquitous phrase "*yahweh ṣeba'ot* (the Lord of hosts)":

> Thus the heavens and the earth were *finished*, and all the *host* of them. And on the seventh day God *finished* his *work* which he had done. (Gen 2:1-2)

This conclusion finds corroboration in the following seemingly difficult passage:

> But Jacob said to him, "My lord knows that the children are frail, and that the flocks and herds giving suck are a care to me; and if they are overdriven for one day, all the flocks will die. Let my lord pass on before his servant, and I will lead on slowly, according to the pace of the cattle (*mela'kah*) which are before me and according to the pace of the children, until I come to my lord in Seir." (Gen 33:13-14)

Not being able to unlock the meaning of the original, most translations, including RSV, understand *mela'kah* in the light of the previous verse that refers to "flocks and herds" after "children" and thus translate it in v.14 as "cattle", where it parallels "children."[4] However, when one takes seriously the

---

nuntius Domini de *nuntiis* Domini populo dicens ego vobiscum dicit Dominus." The Latin *nuntius* means messenger as in the papal *nuntius* (English nuncio, rendering the Italian *nunzio*). The Latin *nuntiis* is the ablative plural case of *nuntium* (announcement, message).

4 The Arabic translates it as "possessions" thus taking it as though the root is *mlk* (own, possess). However, such understanding is unwarranted since it eliminates the

entire passage building up to v.14, one would realize that the detailed enumeration of Jacob's "retinue" which, we are also told, mimics his action of bowing down to Esau, is in view of the conclusion that Jacob was "presenting" his retinue as an "offering" to his brother:

> 1 And Jacob lifted up his eyes and looked, and behold, Esau was coming, and four hundred men with him. So he divided the children among Leah and Rachel and the two maids. 2 And he put the maids with their children in front, then Leah with her children, and Rachel and Joseph last of all. 3 He himself went on before them, bowing himself to the ground seven times, until he came near to his brother. 4 But Esau ran to meet him, and embraced him, and fell on his neck and kissed him, and they wept. 5 And when Esau raised his eyes and saw the women and children, he said, "Who are these with you?" Jacob said, "The children whom God has graciously given your servant." 6 Then the maids drew near, they and their children, and bowed down; 7 Leah likewise and her children drew near and bowed down; and last Joseph and Rachel drew near, and they bowed down. 8 Esau said, "What do you mean by all this company which I met?" Jacob answered, "To find favor in the sight of my lord." 9 But Esau said, "I have enough, my brother; keep what you have for yourself." 10 Jacob said, "No, I pray you, if I have found favor in your sight, then accept my present (*berakah*) from my hand; for truly to see your face is like seeing the face of God, with such favor have you received me. 11 Accept, I pray you, my gift that is brought to you, because God has dealt graciously with me, and because I have enough." Thus he urged him, and he took it. 12 Then Esau said, "Let us journey on our way, and I will go before you." 13 But Jacob said to him, "My lord knows that the children are frail, and that the flocks and herds giving suck are a care to me; and if they are overdriven for one day, all the flocks will die. 14 Let my lord pass on before his servant, and I will lead on slowly, according to the pace of the "retinue" (my translation of the original *mela'kah*) which is *before me* and according to the pace of the children, until I come to my lord in Seir." (Gen 33:1-14)

---

consonant א (*'aleph* transliterated as ') which is inexcusable in Semitic languages. Besides, the original Hebrew refers to the *regel* (foot/feet, leg/legs)—translated as "pace"—of both the *mela'kah* and the "children."

Two features of v.14 stand out. On the one hand, the item that parallels *mela'kah* are the children and only they. This fits perfectly with Jacob's reply to Esau's inquiry about "the women and children," which reply is restricted to the mention of only the children: "And when Esau raised his eyes and saw the women and children, he said, 'Who are these with you?' Jacob said, 'The children whom God has graciously given your servant.'" (v.5) The function of such undue restriction will be revealed later in v.14. On the other hand, *mela'kah* that parallels "children" in that verse is further qualified as "before me," an addition which fits the function I assigned to that noun. The *mela'kah* precedes Jacob as an offering[5] to placate Esau's ire—assumed by Jacob—against him and thus "to find favor in the sight of my lord" (v.8b). In other words, Jacob's *mela'kah* is restrictively his children, that is, his progeny and legacy that he was willing to make Esau's. This understanding is sealed in Jacob's reference to his "present" as a "blessing" (*berakah*) in v.11. The disregard of the meaning and function of *berakah* by most modern translations that render it as "gift," making of it a redundancy with "present" (*minḥah*) in v.10, is literally shocking. The LXX, the Vulgate, and KJV adhere with the original "blessing."[6] In scripture, blessing is bestowed exclusively by a senior to a junior and never vice versa. The classic text is found in the encounter of Abimelech with Abram:

> And Melchizedek king of Salem brought out bread and wine; he was priest of God Most High. And he blessed him and said, "Blessed be Abram by God Most High, maker of heaven and earth." (Gen 14:18-19)

> For this Melchizedek, king of Salem, priest of the Most High God, met Abraham returning from the slaughter of the kings and blessed him; and to him Abraham apportioned a tenth part of

---

5 This is precisely how Jacob refers to it in v.10 *minḥah* meaning technically "offering" and translated as "present" in RSV.

6 In this regard, while the Vulgate and KJV reflect the original singular "blessing," the LXX seems to have opened up the door for the blunder of modern translations through its use of the plural "blessings" (*evlogias*).

> everything. He is first, by translation of his name, king of righteousness, and then he is also king of Salem, that is, king of peace. He is without father or mother or genealogy, and has neither beginning of days nor end of life, but resembling the Son of God he continues a priest for ever. See how great he is! Abraham the patriarch gave him a tithe of the spoils. And those descendants of Levi who receive the priestly office have a commandment in the law to take tithes from the people, that is, from their brethren, though these also are descended from Abraham. But this man who has not their genealogy received tithes from Abraham and blessed him who had the promises. *It is beyond dispute that the inferior is blessed by the superior.* (Heb 7:1-7)

This being the case, then it is inconvertible that the blessing referred to by Jacob is the blessing of heirship that Isaac, the senior, was intending to bestow on Esau, his elder son, which was stolen by Jacob through Rebecca's cunning (Gen 27). On the other hand, the blessing of heirship cannot remain effective over the ages except through the mediacy of a series of heirs, referred to as descendants or, in the original, "seed" (progeny):

> Behold, I establish my covenant with you and your descendants (*zera'*; seed) after you. (Gen 9:9)

> Then the Lord appeared to Abram, and said, "To your descendants (*zera'*; seed) I will give this land." So he built there an altar to the Lord, who had appeared to him. (Gen 12:7)

> I will make your descendants (*zera'*; seed) as the dust of the earth; so that if one can count the dust of the earth, your descendants (*zera'*; seed) also can be counted. (Gen 13:16)

> And I will establish my covenant between me and you and your descendants (*zera'*; seed) after you throughout their generations for an everlasting covenant, to be God to you and to your descendants (*zera'*; seed) after you. And I will give to you, and to your descendants (*zera'*; seed) after you, the land of your sojournings, all the land of Canaan, for an everlasting possession; and I will be their God. (Gen 17:7-8)

> God said, "No, but Sarah your wife shall bear you a son, and you shall call his name Isaac. I will establish my covenant with him as

> an everlasting covenant for his descendants (*zera'*; seed) after him." (Gen 17:19)

This explains Abram's puzzlement in Genesis 15 for he was "childless":

> After these things the word of the Lord came to Abram in a vision, "Fear not, Abram, I am your shield; your reward shall be very great." But Abram said, "O Lord God, what wilt thou give me, for I continue childless, and the heir of my house is Eliezer of Damascus?" And Abram said, "Behold, thou hast given me no offspring (*zera'*; seed); and a slave born in my house will be my heir." And behold, the word of the Lord came to him, "This man shall not be your heir; your own son shall be your heir." And he brought him outside and said, "Look toward heaven, and number the stars, if you are able to number them." Then he said to him, "So shall your descendants (*zera'*; seed) be." And he believed the Lord; and he reckoned it to him as righteousness. (Gen 15:1-6)

So, it stands to reason to understand the authors' intent as saying that Jacob was proposing to his wronged brother that Esau take Jacob's children as being his own. That was Jacob's *mela'kah* to Esau and not a herd of cattle as translations want us to believe. However, Esau declined the offer saying: "I have enough, my brother; keep what you have for yourself." (Gen 33:9) The hearers of scripture will soon understand Esau's statement when they will learn of his extensive progeny covering no less than forty-three verses (Gen 35).

I noted the importance of the authorial addition "before me" (*lephanay*; literally "to my face") in conjunction with *mela'kak* in Genesis 33:14. This feature is found again in a unique scriptural instance referring to "the angel of his (the Lord's) presence":

> I will recount the steadfast love of the Lord, the praises of the Lord, according to all that the Lord has granted us, and the great goodness to the house of Israel which he has granted them according to his mercy, according to the abundance of his steadfast love. For he said, Surely they are my people, sons who will not deal falsely; and he became their Savior. In all their

> affliction he was afflicted, and *the angel of his presence* (*mal'ak phanayw*; the angel/messenger of his face) saved them; in his love and in his pity he redeemed them; he lifted them up and carried them all the days of old. But they rebelled and grieved his holy Spirit; therefore he turned to be their enemy, and himself fought against them. (Is 63:7-10)

It is abundantly clear from the context that the *mal'ak* spoken of here is not someone who stands "to the face of" (facing) the Lord, but rather someone who goes out before or in front of him to do his bidding, just as Jacob's *mala'kah* went out before (in front of) him.

The conclusion is inescapable. The heavens and the earth and all their denizens or constituents (Gen 2:1-4) function as God's "retinue" that heralds as well as reflects him by doing his bidding, just as an army would do the bidding of its general, or in this case the bidding of "the lord of hosts" (*yahweh ṣeba'ot*). The same view is revisited at the beginning of Psalm 148 where "angels" (*mal'akim*) and "host" (*ṣaba'*) are referred to as two sides of the same reality just as *mal'akah* and *ṣaba'* are in Genesis 2:1-4:

> Praise him, all his *angels*, praise him, all his *host*! (Ps 148:2)

That the two passages are clearly phrased against the same background is revealed in the vocabulary of Psalm 148 which is reminiscent of that of Genesis 1:1-2:4

> Praise the Lord! Praise the Lord from *the heavens*, praise him in the heights! Praise him, all his angels, praise him, all his host! Praise him, *sun* and *moon*, praise him, all you shining *stars*! Praise him, you highest *heavens*, and you *waters above the heavens*! *Let them praise the name of the Lord! For he commanded and they were created* (*nibre'u*). And he established them for ever and ever; he fixed their bounds which cannot be passed. Praise the Lord from *the earth*, you *sea monsters* (*tanninim*) and all *deeps* (*tehomot*), fire and hail, snow and frost, stormy wind (*ruaḥ*; spirit) fulfilling his command! Mountains and all hills, *fruit trees* and all cedars! *Beasts* (*ḥayyah*; living beings) and all *cattle* (*behemah*; beasts), *creeping things* and flying birds! (Ps 148:1-10)

It is my conviction that the unexpected mention of *ṣaba'* in Genesis 2:1 that is not heard of again until Genesis 21:22 is intentional in that it prepares for the first reference to the deity *'elohim* in chapter 1 as *yahweh 'elohim* which is used throughout chapters 2 and 3, at the end of which we hear of his "lieutenants," the cherubim, who do his bidding, just as "the angel of his presence (face)" does in Isaiah 63:9:

> Then the Lord God said, "Behold, the man has become like one of us, knowing good and evil; and now, lest he put forth his hand and take also of the tree of life, and eat, and live for ever"—therefore the Lord God sent him forth from the garden of Eden, to till the ground from which he was taken. He drove out the man; and at the east of the garden of Eden he placed the cherubim, and a flaming sword which turned every way, to guard the way to the tree of life. (Gen 3:22-24)

Genesis 2:1-4 not only concludes the first creation narrative but also seals this narrative as indeed an introduction to the entire scripture in all its three parts: the Law, the Prophets, and the Ketubim. There is no denying that of all the crimson threads that run through scripture, the one that is literally and literarily ubiquitous and holds all its three parts together would be the Mosaic Law (Exodus-Deuteronomy). Without this law there would not have been a scriptural literature. The most impressive feature of this literature is precisely how the Prophets, the most extensive part of scripture, is woven around the Law (Pentateuch), the shortest part of scripture. Not only does the phrase "the book of the law" close Deuteronomy, the last Book of the Pentateuch (When Moses had finished writing the words of this law in a book, to the very end, Moses commanded the Levites who carried the ark of the covenant of the Lord, "Take this book of the law, and put it by the side of the ark of the covenant of the Lord your God, that it may be there for a witness against you." 31:24-26), and inaugurates Joshua, the first Book of the Prophets (This book of the law shall not depart out of your mouth, but you shall meditate on it day and night, that you may be careful to do according to all that is written in it; for then you shall make your way prosperous, and then you shall have good success. 1:8), but this "book of the law" is instated as the charter that governs all those who live in the earth of the promise *throughout the generations*, including "the next generation, the children yet unborn, *and their children*" (Ps 78:6):

> So Joshua burned Ai, and made it for ever a heap of ruins, as it is to this day. And he hanged the king of Ai on a tree until evening; and at the going down of the sun Joshua commanded, and they took his body down from the tree, and cast it at the entrance of the gate of the city, and raised over it a great heap of stones, which stands there to this day. Then Joshua built an altar in Mount Ebal to the Lord, the God of Israel, as Moses the servant of the Lord had commanded the people of Israel, as it is written in the book of the law of Moses, "an altar of unhewn stones, upon which no man has lifted an iron tool"; and they offered on it burnt offerings to the Lord, and sacrificed peace offerings. And there, in the presence of the people of Israel, he wrote upon the stones a copy of the law of Moses, which he had written. And all Israel, sojourner as well as homeborn, with their elders and officers and their judges, stood on opposite sides of the ark before the Levitical priests who carried the ark of the covenant of the Lord, half of them in front of Mount Gerizim and half of them in front of Mount Ebal, as Moses the servant of the Lord had commanded at the first, that they should bless the people of Israel. And afterward he read all the words of the law, the blessing and the curse, according to all that is written in the book of the law. There was not a word of all that Moses commanded which Joshua did not read before all the assembly of Israel, and the women, and the little ones, and the sojourners who lived among them. (Josh 8:28-35)

> But Joshua said to the people, "You cannot serve the Lord; for he is a holy God; he is a jealous God; he will not forgive your transgressions or your sins. If you forsake the Lord and serve foreign gods, then he will turn and do you harm, and consume you, after having done you good." And the people said to Joshua, "Nay; but we will serve the Lord." Then Joshua said to the people, "You are witnesses against yourselves that you have chosen the Lord, to serve him." And they said, "We are witnesses." He said, "Then put away the foreign gods which are

> among you, and incline your heart to the Lord, the God of Israel." And the people said to Joshua, "The Lord our God we will serve, and his voice we will obey." So Joshua made a covenant with the people that day, and made statutes and ordinances for them at Shechem. And Joshua wrote these words in the book of the law of God; and he took a great stone, and set it up there under the oak in the sanctuary of the Lord. And Joshua said to all the people, "Behold, this stone shall be a witness against us; for it has heard all the words of the Lord which he spoke to us; therefore it shall be a witness against you, lest you deal falsely with your God." So Joshua sent the people away, every man to his inheritance. (Josh 24:19-28)

The latter passage sets the tone for the sad story of the scriptural Judah and Israel that covers the Latter Prophets (Isaiah, Jeremiah, Ezekiel and the twelve prophets) as well as the Prior Prophets (Joshua, Judges, Samuel and Kings). As to the Ketubim, suffice it to mention the following two features. First, the lengthiest Psalm 119 in the first book of the Ketubim,[7] the Book of Psalms, is an ode to the Law artificially constructed as a "dictionary" reflecting metaphorically all the possible "words" of scriptural Hebrew. It is divided, after the twenty-two letters of the Hebrew alphabet, into twenty-two sections of eight lines each whereby each of the eight lines in each section starts with the same alphabetical consonant letter. It starts with "Blessed are those whose way is blameless, who walk in *the law* of the Lord!" (Ps 119:1) and concludes with "I have gone astray like a lost sheep; seek thy servant, for I do not forget *thy commandments*" (v. 176). Secondly, Ecclesiastes, that stands at the heart of the Ketubim[8] and ends by pointing out emphatically that, although "all is vanity," nevertheless identifies one item of central import, the divine Law:

---

7 According to the Hebrew canon.

8 In the sixth position among the eleven books, if one counts Ezra and Nehemiah as one and 1 and 2 Chronicles as one, after the manner of Samuel (1 and 2) and Kings (1 and 2).

> Vanity of vanities, says the Preacher; all is vanity. Besides being wise, the Preacher also taught the people knowledge, weighing and studying and arranging proverbs with great care. The Preacher sought to find pleasing words, and uprightly he wrote words of truth. The sayings of the wise are like goads, and like nails firmly fixed are the collected sayings which are given by one Shepherd. My son, beware of anything beyond these. Of making many books there is no end, and much study is a weariness of the flesh. *The end of the matter; all has been heard. Fear God, and keep his commandments; for this is the whole duty of man. For God will bring every deed into judgment, with every secret thing, whether good or evil.* (Eccl 12:8-14)

Such ending is hardly unexpected given that "Preacher" is the translation of the Hebrew *qohelet* which is the title of the book itself. *qohelet* is the feminine active participle of the root *qahal* that is the scriptural gathering on the sabbath day during which sections of the Law were read. The grammatically feminine *qohelet* (gatherer; caller to the gathering) has in view the *torah* which is a feminine noun in Hebrew.[9]

Considering all of the above, it is striking that the vocabulary and phraseology of Genesis 2:2-3 already presages the rest of scripture that is focused around the *torah* and the most central of its foundations, the sabbath. The sabbath day is very frequently referred as "the seventh day" in the Books of the Law. Since the institution of the sabbath is strictly a topic of the Law, the author very astutely respects that matter by referring to the sabbath obliquely in underscoring thrice the "seventh day" of creation in two verses, yet explicitly avoiding the term "sabbath": "And on the seventh day God finished his work which he had done, and he rested on the seventh day from all his work which he had done. So God blessed the seventh day and hallowed it, because on it God rested from all his work which he had done in creation." (Gen 2:2-3) Still, he indirectly hints aurally at the matter through his use twice of the verb *šabat* (rested) from the same root as the noun *šabbat* (sabbath). The original Hebrew is much more striking given that both the verb

---

9 See a detailed explanation of this in *OTI3* 134.

and the noun are, consonantally, exactly the same: *šbt*. The hearers could not possibly miss the intentionality of the linkage once they reach Exodus and hear the rationale behind the institution of the sabbath that is phrased according to the terminology of Genesis 2:2-3:

> And on the seventh day God finished his work (*mela'kah*) which he had done, and he rested on the seventh day from all his work (*mela'kah*) which he had done. So God blessed the seventh day and hallowed it, because on it God rested from all his work (*mela'kah*) which he had done in creation. (Gen 2:2-3)

> Six days you shall labor, and do all your work (*mela'kah*); but the seventh day is a sabbath (*šabbat*) to the Lord your God; in it you shall not do any work (*mela'kah*), you, or your son, or your daughter, your manservant, or your maidservant, or your cattle, or the sojourner who is within your gates; for in six days the Lord made heaven and earth, the sea, and all that is in them, and rested the seventh day; therefore the Lord blessed the sabbath (*šabbat*) day and hallowed it. (Ex 20:9-11)

Lastly, and in no way the least, surmising that God not only blessed, which is the verb used commonly in Genesis, but also hallowed (*qiddeš*; sanctified, rendered holy) the seventh day is quite unexpected, especially in view of the fact that the root *qdš* does not occur again in Genesis outside the reference to the locality Kadesh (*qadeš*)[10] and the thrice reference to Tamar as *qedešah* (female cult prostitute).[11] For the next instance of holiness one has to wait until Exodus 3:5: "Then he said, 'Do not come near; put off your shoes from your feet, for the place on which you are standing is holy ground (*'admat qodeš*).'" More importantly for our concern is the following instance: "On the first day you shall hold a holy assembly (*miqre' qodeš*), and on *the seventh day* a holy assembly (*miqre' qodeš*); no *work* (*mela'kah*) shall be done on those days; but what every one must eat, that only may be prepared by you." (Ex 12:16) Soon one will learn that

---

10 Genesis 14:7; 16:14; 20:1.
11 Genesis 31:21 (twice), 22.

this holy assembly or convocation is none other than the sabbath day: "Six days shall *work* (*mela'kah*) be done; but on *the seventh day* is a *sabbath* (*šabbat*) of *solemn rest* (*šabbaton*), a *holy convocation* (*miqre' qodeš*); you shall do no *work* (*mela'kah*); it is a *sabbath* (*šabbat*) to the Lord in all your dwellings." (Lev 23:3)

In order to seal in the hearers' ears Genesis 1:1-2:4 as an introduction to the entire Book of Genesis and, beyond it, to the entire scripture, the author uses unwarrantedly the noun *toledot* to speak of the creating, respectively making, of the heavens and the earth (2:4). In so doing the author is positing them as a backdrop for their "host" and especially his addressees, the human hearers, throughout their *toledot* that will be referred to as a refrain all through Genesis, Exodus, Numbers, and later Ruth.

10

Genesis 2:15-12:3

Having covered in minute detail what I consider the introduction to scripture, I should like to proceed with the remainder of Genesis 1-11 and linger on specific terms that were not found in Genesis 1:1-2:4 and show how the author introduces them as axial to the understanding of the rest of scripture. In other words, until the end of Genesis 11, the author proceeds with establishing the framework for the basic lexicon of the entire scripture. To quote Ecclesiastes, for those who have ears to hear the original Hebrew, after Genesis 11 "there is nothing new under the sun" (Eccl 1:9).

‘aphar *(dust)*

In Genesis 2:7 we encounter for the first time *‘aphar* (dust) in the following context: "then the Lord God formed (the) man (*ha'adam*) as[1] dust from (*min*) the ground (*ha'adamah*), and breathed into his nostrils the breath of life; and man became a living being." Since the interplay in the original language is between "(the) man" and "the ground" that are from the same root *'dm*, "dust" is clearly additional and thus intentional. A few verses later the author omits "dust" in the description of the animals formed simply "out of" (*min*) the same ground: "So *out of* (*min*) the ground the Lord God formed every beast of the field and every bird of the air, and brought them to the man to see what he would call them." (Gen 2:19) Besides the classic scriptural program of demeaning the human beings, the author clearly has in his purview the upcoming punishment of the disobedient *ha'adam*: "And to Adam he [the Lord God] said ... In the sweat of your face you shall eat bread till you return to the ground (*ha'adamah*), for *out of* (*min*) it you were taken; you are

1 RSV's "of" is incorrect and thus misleading.

dust, and to *dust* you shall return." (Gen 3:17, 19) Notice how the author splits here between the ground and the dust, whereas, they were joined in 2:7, in order to underscore the negative connotation of "dust" that, unlike the ground, can be scattered to the four winds into not so much obliteration—since dust will remain as dust, but rather oblivion away from its place of origin. Indeed, before his death, *ha'adam* will be thrown out of the garden—his original ground as well as place of origin—to "the east of Eden" where (his son) Cain's earth of Nod, the land of wandering aimlessly (*nad*), is located, away from the tree of life:

> He drove out the man; and at the *east of* the garden of *Eden* he placed the cherubim, and a flaming sword which turned every way, to guard the way to the tree of life. (Gen 3:24)

> "When you till the ground, it shall no longer yield to you its strength; you shall be a fugitive and a wanderer (*nad*) on the earth." … Then Cain went away from the presence of the Lord, and dwelt in the land of Nod (*nod*), *east of Eden*. (Gen 4:12, 16)

However, for the hearers, arrogant human beings as they are, the fate of punishment through dust will be unexpectedly redressed in Genesis 23 via *'ephron* (Ephron) the (outsider) Hittite who will prove to be the Lord God's medium for establishing *ḥebron,* the place of brotherhood, the gathering place of Abraham's descendants, which ironically will end as the inheritance, not of Joshua, but of Caleb, "the (outsider) dog" (*keleb*), in the Book of Joshua (14:13-15). The intended interconnection between the two stories is evident in their similar phraseology:

> And Sarah died at *Kiriatharba* (that is, *Hebron*) in the land of Canaan; and Abraham went in to mourn for Sarah and to weep for her. (Gen 23:2)

> Then Joshua blessed him; and he gave Hebron to Caleb the son of Jephunneh for an inheritance. So Hebron became the inheritance of Caleb the son of Jephunneh the Kenizzite to this day, because he wholly followed the Lord, the God of Israel. Now the name of *Hebron* formerly was *Kiriatharba*; this Arba was the

> greatest man among the Anakim. And the land had rest from war." (Josh 14:13-15)

The centrality of Ephron (*'ephron;* the man of dust) is evidenced in that any time a burial in Hebron is mentioned, his name is brought up along with being identified as "the Hittite":

> So the field of Ephron in Machpelah, which was to the east of Mamre, the field with the cave which was in it and all the trees that were in the field, throughout its whole area, was made over to Abraham as a possession in the presence of the Hittites, before all who went in at the gate of his city. After this, Abraham buried Sarah his wife in the cave of the field of Machpelah east of Mamre (that is, Hebron) in the land of Canaan. The field and the cave that is in it were made over to Abraham as a possession for a burying place by the Hittites. (Gen 23:17-20)

> Isaac and Ishmael his sons buried him in the cave of Machpelah, in the field of Ephron the son of Zohar the Hittite, east of Mamre, the field which Abraham purchased from the Hittites. There Abraham was buried, with Sarah his wife. (Gen 25:9-10)

> Then he charged them, and said to them, "I am to be gathered to my people; bury me with my fathers in the cave that is in the field of Ephron the Hittite, in the cave that is in the field at Machpelah, to the east of Mamre, in the land of Canaan, which Abraham bought with the field from Ephron the Hittite to possess as a burying place. There they buried Abraham and Sarah his wife; there they buried Isaac and Rebekah his wife; and there I buried Leah—the field and the cave that is in it were purchased from the Hittites." (Gen 49:29-32)

This underscoring of the Hittites presages the narrative of the Book of Joshua where the earth of the scriptural Cannan, the earth of the divine promise, is introduced straightforwardly and specifically in the first verses as "the earth of the Hittites" (Josh 1:4), rather than "the earth of the Perizzites and Canaanites" (Gen 13:7) or "the land of the Kenites, the Kenizzites, the Kadmonites, the Hittites, the Perizzites, the Rephaim, the Amorites, the Canaanites, the Girgashites and the Jebusites" (Gen 15:19-21):

> After the death of Moses the servant of the Lord, the Lord said to Joshua the son of Nun, Moses' minister, "Moses my servant is dead; now therefore arise, go over this Jordan, you and all this people, into the land which I am giving to them, to the people of Israel. Every place that the sole of your foot will tread upon I have given to you, as I promised to Moses. From the wilderness and this Lebanon as far as the great river, the river Euphrates, *all*[2] *the land of the Hittites* to the Great Sea toward the going down of the sun shall be your territory." (Josh 1:1-4)

This is even more striking when one considers that later in the book one repeatedly hears the more inclusive description of the same earth of the divine promise:

> And Joshua said, "Hereby you shall know that the living God is among you, and that he will without fail drive out from before you the Canaanites, the Hittites, the Hivites, the Perizzites, the Girgashites, the Amorites, and the Jebusites." (Josh 3:10)

> When all the kings who were beyond the Jordan in the hill country and in the lowland all along the coast of the Great Sea toward Lebanon, the Hittites, the Amorites, the Canaanites, the Perizzites, the Hivites, and the Jebusites, heard of this, they gathered together with one accord to fight Joshua and Israel. (Josh 9:1-2)

> When Jabin king of Hazor heard of this, he sent to Jobab king of Madon, and to the king of Shimron, and to the king of Achshaph, and to the kings who were in the northern hill country, and in the Arabah south of Chinneroth, and in the lowland, and in Naphothdor on the west, to the Canaanites in the east and the west, the Amorites, the Hittites, the Perizzites, and the Jebusites in the hill country, and the Hivites under Hermon in the land of Mizpah. (Josh 11:1-3)

> And these are the kings of the land whom Joshua and the people of Israel defeated on the west side of the Jordan, from Baalgad in the valley of Lebanon to Mount Halak, that rises toward Seir (and Joshua gave their land to the tribes of Israel as a possession according to their allotments, in the hill country, in the lowland, in the Arabah, in the slopes, in the wilderness, and in the Negeb,

---

2 Notice the author is underscoring the "totality."

> the land of the Hittites, the Amorites, the Canaanites, the Perizzites, the Hivites, and the Jebusites)... (Josh 12:7-8)

> And you went over the Jordan and came to Jericho, and the men of Jericho fought against you, and also the Amorites, the Perizzites, the Canaanites, the Hittites, the Girgashites, the Hivites, and the Jebusites; and I gave them into your hand. (Josh 24:11)

Even the following Book of Judges follows suit. Its first mention of the earth of the promise is that it is simply the earth of the Hittites before including the other nations:

> The house of Joseph also went up against Bethel; and the Lord was with them. And the house of Joseph sent to spy out Bethel. (Now the name of the city was formerly Luz.) And the spies saw a man coming out of the city, and they said to him, "Pray, show us the way into the city, and we will deal kindly with you." And he showed them the way into the city; and they smote the city with the edge of the sword, but they let the man and all his family go. And the man went to *the land of the Hittites* and built a city, and called its name Luz; that is its name to this day. (Judg 1:22-26)

> These are the nations: the five lords of the Philistines, and all the Canaanites, and the Sidonians, and the Hivites who dwelt on Mount Lebanon, from Mount Baalhermon as far as the entrance of Hamath. They were for the testing of Israel, to know whether Israel would obey the commandments of the Lord, which he commanded their fathers by Moses. So the people of Israel dwelt among the Canaanites, the Hittites, the Amorites, the Perizzites, the Hivites, and the Jebusites; and they took their daughters to themselves for wives, and their own daughters they gave to their sons; and they served their gods. (Judg 3:3-6)

Ephron's specter is even more overarching. His memory will emerge in the hearers' minds centuries later in the story of King David. Although the Lord's elect and beloved, David will betray and slay his top general, Uriah the Hittite,[3] who led the king's

---

3 2 Sam 11:3, 6, 17, 21, 24; 12:9, 10; 1 Kg 15:5.

army to victories in the earth of the divine promise, in order to take his wife, following the example of the "sons of God" in Genesis 6:1-2 that led to the flood as punishment. David's behavior will be revisited centuries later in the demise of his kingdom under Zedekiah, his heir (2 Kg 25). Neither David's fake repentance nor Josiah's acknowledgment of his shortcomings could save their kingdom from the divine verdict: "Nevertheless for David's sake the Lord his God gave him a lamp in Jerusalem, setting up his son after him, and establishing Jerusalem; because David did what was right in the eyes of the Lord, and did not turn aside from anything that he commanded him all the days of his life, *except in the matter of Uriah the Hittite*." (1 Kg 15:4-5)

The close interconnection between the nations and Abraham's children reflected in the story of Ephron the Hittite is further underscored in the unexpected and thus unnecessary twice reference to Zohar (*ṣoḥar*), Ephron's father (Gen 23:8 and 25:9), since that person appears only in these two instances in scripture and without any functional role in either chapter. Is it just an appendage? The function of this additional name will soon be realized when the hearers are told that Simeon, Jacob's second in line son (Gen 29:33), had a son called Zohar who is referred to on two different occasions separated by ten chapters:

> The sons of Simeon: Jemuel, Jamin, Ohad, Jachin, Zohar (*ṣoḥar*), and Shaul, the son of a Canaanitish woman. (Gen 46:10)

> The sons of Simeon: Jemuel, Jamin, Ohad, Jachin, Zohar (*ṣoḥar*), and Shaul, the son of a Canaanite woman; these are the families of Simeon. (Ex 6:15)

Throughout scripture there is only one other instance of the root *ṣḥr*, the adjective *ṣaḥor* whose meaning is tawny, yellowish-red: "Tell of it, you who ride on tawny (*ṣeḥorot*) asses, you who sit on rich carpets and you who walk by the way." (Judg 5:10) What is interesting for our discussion is that this is the color of the earth/ground and thus, just as Ephron reminds the hearer of the dust of the ground, Zohar, his father's name, reminds the same hearer of the color of the same ground. Put otherwise, in scripture's purview, the progeny of both the Gentile Ephron the Hittite and Abraham are ultimately "children of Adam" and, just as *'adam*, the progenitor of all *beney 'adam* (the children of Adam), are children (a product) of the (dust of the) *'adamah*.

One encounters a similar wordplay on the Hebrew word for "red" which is *'adom* from the same root as *'adamah*; so *'adom* is technically speaking "ground/earth-colored" and so is *'admony* (reddish). This classic wordplay is found in the story of Esau, who is linked to the territory (and people) Edom or rather his other name is Edom, just as Jacob's other name, Israel, is also the name of a territory as well as people. Here is the passage in full:

> And Isaac prayed to the Lord for his wife, because she was barren; and the Lord granted his prayer, and Rebekah his wife conceived. The children struggled together within her; and she said, "If it is thus, why do I live?" So she went to inquire of the Lord. And the Lord said to her, "*Two nations* are in your womb, and *two peoples*, born of you, shall be divided; the one shall be stronger than the other, the elder shall serve the younger." When her days to be delivered were fulfilled, behold, there were twins in her womb. The first came forth red (*'admony*), all his body like a hairy mantle; so they called his name Esau. Afterward his brother came forth, and his hand had taken hold of Esau's heel; so his name was called Jacob. Isaac was sixty years old when she bore them. When the boys grew up, Esau was a skilful hunter, a man of the field, while Jacob was a quiet man, dwelling in tents. Isaac loved Esau, because he ate of his game; but Rebekah loved Jacob. Once when Jacob was boiling pottage, Esau came in from the field, and he was famished. And Esau said to Jacob, "Let me eat some of that *red pottage* (*ha'adom ha'adom*; the red the red), for I am famished!" (Therefore his name was called *Edom* [*'edom*].) Jacob said, "First sell me your birthright." Esau said, "I am about to die; of what use is a birthright to me?" Jacob said, "Swear to me first." So he swore to him, and sold his birthright to Jacob. Then Jacob gave Esau bread and pottage of lentils,[4] and he ate

4 Lentils are red which explains why Esau referred to the pottage of lentils as "the red the red" earlier in v.30.

and drank, and rose and went his way. Thus Esau despised his birthright. (Gen 25:21-34)

śadeh *(field)*

Why would the authors bother with a third term, *śadeh*, that parallels in meaning *'ereṣ* (earth) and *'adamah* (ground)? The most plausible answer lies in the difference of connotation and thus functionality. On the one hand, *'ereṣ* would be the generic term as opposed to "heavens" as well as to "waters" since its first connotation early on is that of a dry and thus a solid surface where humans and land animals can walk and birds can alight without sinking. The case of the birds is telling in that they are primordially introduced in the following manner:[5]

> And God said, "Let the waters bring forth swarms of living creatures, and let birds fly *above* (*'al*; which means over and also [up]on) *the earth* across (*'al peney*; toward/to/on[6] the face of) the firmament of the heavens." So God created the great sea monsters and every living creature that moves, with which the waters swarm, according to their kinds, and every winged bird according to its kind. And God saw that it was good. And God blessed them, saying, "Be fruitful and multiply and fill the waters in the seas, and let birds multiply on the earth (*ba'areṣ*; in the earth)."[7] (Gen 1:20-22)

On the other hand, *'adamah* specifically underscores the link in nature between the earth and the human beings that are formed out of (*min*) it (Gen 2:7). This intimate interconnection is reflected in the tan (color) of both the earth cover and the human skin. As I indicated earlier in my discussion of *'aphar*, the adjective *'adom* ([yellowish] red) explains the reference to Esau

5 Only later the birds are referred to as *kol 'oph haššamayim* (every bird [all the birds] of the air/heavens; Gen 1:30).

6 The Hebrew *'al peney* is the exact same expression used a few verses later with both *'ereṣ* (Gen 1:29) and *'adamah* (2:6) as well as earlier with the abyss and the waters (1:2). Technically speaking, it means "facing," "looking toward," "in the direction of."

7 The preposition *b* is the most generic in Semitic languages just as our English "in" which is used not only in a strictly physical sense (in the room), but also idiomatically as "sit in the sun" and "in my eyes you look good."

as *'admony* (the reddish one): "The first came forth red, all his body like a hairy mantle; so they called his name Esau." (Gen 25:25)[8] It also explains the other name of Esau, namely Edom: "And Esau said to Jacob, 'Let me eat some of that *red* pottage, for I am famished!' (Therefore his name was called Edom.)" (25:30). Although the wordplay revolves around the root *'dm*, nowhere in the entire passage (25:21-34) is the noun *'adamah* heard nor even that of its closest correspondent *'ereṣ*. The term that is used, and twice in a row (vv.27 and 29), is the noun *śadeh* (field). To consider this matter as just whimsical on the author's part is preposterous since two chapters later and again in a passage dealing with the two brothers, the author links Esau to *śadeh*:

> When Isaac was old and his eyes were dim so that he could not see, he called Esau his older son, and said to him, "My son"; and he answered, "Here I am." He said, "Behold, I am old; I do not know the day of my death. Now then, take your weapons, your quiver and your bow, and go out to the *field* (*śadeh*), and hunt game for me, and prepare for me savory food, such as I love, and bring it to me that I may eat; that I may bless you before I die." Now Rebekah was listening when Isaac spoke to his son Esau. So when Esau went to the *field* (*śadeh*) to hunt for game and bring it … (Gen 27:1-5)

Since the wordplay on Esau's color works only with *'adamah*, the author is obviously assuming that the hearers are acquainted with the close relation between the two nouns, *'adamah* and *śadeh.* Opting for field (*śadeh*) has to do with the context of the story and is clearly functional since Esau is presented as a hunter. Early on in Genesis, shortly after the double reference to the vegetation "of the field" (2:5), the addressees hear again twice in a row that the land animals, first referred to as "beast

---

8 See also the only other instance of that adjective: "And Samuel said to Jesse, 'Are all your sons here?' And he said, 'There remains yet the youngest, but behold, he is keeping the sheep.' And Samuel said to Jesse, 'Send and fetch him; for we will not sit down till he comes here.' And he sent, and brought him in. Now he was ruddy (*'admony*), and had beautiful eyes, and was handsome. And the Lord said, 'Arise, anoint him; for this is he.'" (1 Sam 16:11-12)

(*ḥayyah*; living [being]) of the earth (*'ereṣ*)" (1:30) are introduced as "beasts of the field" in spite of the fact that they are formed out of (*min*) the ground (*'adamah*):

> So out of the *ground* (*'adamah*) the Lord God formed every *beast* (*ḥayyah*) *of the field* (*śadeh*) and every bird of the air, and brought them to the man to see what he would call them; and whatever the man called every living creature, that was its name. The man gave names to all cattle, and to the birds of the air, and to every *beast* (*ḥayyah*) *of the field* (*śadeh*); but for the man there was not found a helper fit for him. (Gen 2:19-20)

Given that Esau is a game hunter, it makes sense that the authors would opt for "field" when speaking of him, especially when they previously established the interconnectedness between "earth," "ground," and "field." The bottom line is that the use of a parallel, yet different, term is ultimately as well as primordially functional. However, before delving into the nuance and, more importantly, the function of *śadeh* in Genesis, I should like to take a long aside to show my readers not only the importance, but also in some cases, such as ours here, the necessity of studying and discussing the matter on the basis of the original Hebrew.

RSV gives the impression that it is translating the correct intent or, as many nowadays like to call it, the "spirit" of the text. In reality, it is betraying the original in that it does not reflect the interconnection between the original words. RSV—and all the translations at some point or another, including the venerable LXX and Vulgate—do that by rendering one original word into two or more different English words or, conversely, rendering two different original words into one English word. The easiest way for my readers to comprehend this is to read Genesis chapter 1:

> In the beginning God created the heavens (*šamayim*) and the earth. The earth was without form and void, and darkness was upon the face of (*'al peney*) the deep; and the Spirit of God was moving over the face of (*'al peney*) the waters. And God said, "Let there be light"; and there was light. And God saw that the light was good; and God separated the light from the darkness. God

called the light Day, and the darkness he called Night. And there was evening and there was morning, one day.

And God said, "Let there be a firmament in the midst of the waters, and let it separate the waters from the waters." And God made the firmament and separated the waters which were under the firmament from the waters which were above the firmament. And it was so. And God called the firmament *Heaven* (*šamayim*). And there was evening and there was morning, a second day.

And God said, "Let the waters under the heavens be gathered together into one place, and let the dry land appear." And it was so. God called the dry land Earth, and the waters that were gathered together he called Seas.[9] And God saw that it was good. And God said, "Let the earth *put forth* (*tadše'*; let sprout) vegetation (*deše'*),[10] plants yielding (*mazria'*; seeding) seed (*zera'*),[11] and fruit trees bearing (*'ośeh*; making)[12] fruit in which is their seed, each according to its kind, upon the earth." And it was so. The earth *brought forth* (*toṣe'*; from the root *yaṣa'* [go forth, out]) vegetation, plants yielding (*mazria'*; seeding/producing) seed (*zera'*) according to their own kinds, and trees bearing (*'ośeh*; making) fruit in which is their seed, each according to its kind. And God saw that it was good. And there was evening and there was morning, a third day.

And God said, "Let there be lights in the firmament of the heavens to separate the day from the night; and let them be for signs and for seasons and for days and years, and let them be lights in the firmament of the heavens to give light upon the earth." And it was so. And God made the two great lights, the greater light to rule the day, and the lesser light to rule the night; *he made* (added; it is not in the Hebrew) the stars also. And God set them in the firmament of the heavens to give light upon the earth, to rule over the day and over the night, and to separate the

---

9 Notice how RSV kept the original plural in Hebrew, while unwarrantedly translates the plural *šamayim* in Genesis 1:8 into the singular "Heaven" (And God called the firmament Heaven) when elsewhere throughout it uses the plural "heavens."
10 Notice the interplay between *tadše'* and *deše'* in Hebrew.
11 Notice the interplay between *mazri'a* and *zera'* in Hebrew.
12 The same verb *'asah* (made) with God as its subject found earlier in v.7 and later in 1:16, 25, 31; 2:4. See earlier my comments on this matter and its functionality—and thus intentionality—in the original.

light from the darkness. And God saw that it was good. And there was evening and there was morning, a fourth day.

And God said, "Let the waters *bring forth*[13] (*yišreṣu*; swarm [with]) swarms (*šereṣ*)[14] of living creatures, and let birds fly above the earth *across* (*'al peney*)[15] the firmament of the heavens." So God created the great *sea monsters* (*tanninim*) and every living creature that moves, with which the waters swarm (*šareṣu*),[16] according to their kinds, and every winged bird according to its kind. And God saw that it was good. And God blessed them, saying, "Be fruitful and multiply and fill the waters in the seas, and let birds multiply on the earth." And there was evening and there was morning, a fifth day.

And God said, "Let the earth bring forth (*toṣe'* as in v.12) living creatures according to their kinds: cattle (*behemah*) and creeping things and beasts (*ḥayyot*, plural of *ḥayyah*) of the earth according to their kinds." And it was so. And God made the beasts (singular generic *ḥayyah*) of the earth according to their kinds and the cattle according to their kinds, and everything that creeps upon the ground according to its kind. And God saw that it was good. Then God said, "Let us make man in our image, after our likeness; and let them have dominion over the fish of the sea, and over the birds of the air, and over the cattle, and over all the earth, and over every creeping thing that creeps upon the earth." So God created man in his own image, in the image of God he created him; male and female he created them. And God blessed them, and God said to them, "Be fruitful and multiply, and fill the earth and subdue it; and have dominion over the fish of the sea and over the birds of the air and over every living thing that moves upon the earth." And God said, "Behold, I have given you every plant yielding (*zorea'*; sowing) seed (*zera'*)[17] which is upon the face of all the earth, and every tree with seed in its fruit **yielding**

13 Earlier in v.12 RSV used "bring forth" to translate another verb *hoṣih*, the *hiphil* form of *yaṣa'*. See above my comments on the importance of this differentiation.

14 Similar wordplay as with the vegetation in v.11.

15 This same phrase was translated earlier twice as "over the face of" in v.2. See my comments earlier on the matter.

16 Translated in the previous verse as "bring forth."

17 When compared with vv.11 and 12 where we have the *hiphil* form *mazri'a*, here the author uses the *qal* form *zorea'*.

> (***zorea'*; sowing) seed (*zera'*)**;[18] you shall have them for food. And to every beast of the earth, and to every bird of the air, and to everything that creeps on the earth, everything that has the breath of life, I have given every green plant for food." And it was so. And God saw everything that he had made, and behold, it was very good. And there was evening and there was morning, a sixth day.

A specific case that would shed light on the discussion of "field" versus "earth" and "ground" is RSV's handling of the two Hebrew nouns *behemah* and *ḥayyah* which are rendered as "cattle" and "beast" respectively in vv.24 and 25. Those of my readers who know Hebrew will soon find the following when reading further into Genesis 2-11. First of all, the same *behemah* is translated as "beasts" in 6:7, as "animals" in 6:20; 7:2 (twice), 8 (twice), 23; 8:17, 20, and as "cattle" again in 7:14, 21; 9:10; secondly, *ḥayyah* is translated as "animals" in 3:14. Also, we often see in Genesis that "cattle" appears as the translation of the Hebrew *miqneh*, whose stricter meaning is acquisition, i.e., what is acquired, since it is the verbal noun of the verb *qanah* (acquire, buy).[19] However, what complicates the matter is twofold. On the one hand, at its first occurrence it is used in conjunction with tents, the abode of shepherds: "Adah bore Jabal; he was the father of those who dwell in tents and have cattle (*miqneh*)." (4:20)[20] On the other hand, at the end of the book, we encounter *miqneh* in reference to the acquiring of a landed property:

> Then he [Jacob] charged them, and said to them, "I am to be gathered to my people; bury me with my fathers in the cave that

---

18 The words in bold are omitted in RSV. The difficulty of the original is reflected in KJV that has: "And God said, Behold, I have given you every herb bearing seed, which *is* upon the face of all the earth, and every tree, in the which *is* the fruit of a tree yielding seed; to you it shall be for meat." (Gen 1:29)

19 See for instance the interplay with the name Cain: "And Adam knew Eve his wife; and she conceived, and bare Cain (*qayn*), and said, I have gotten (*qaniti*) a man from the Lord." (Gen 4:1)

20 NRSV, probably sensing the contradiction, changed "cattle" into "livestock" in this instance.

> is in the field of Ephron the Hittite, in the cave that is in the field at Machpelah, to the east of Mamre, in the land of Canaan, which Abraham bought (*qanah*) with the field from Ephron the Hittite to possess as a burying place. There they buried Abraham and Sarah his wife; there they buried Isaac and Rebekah his wife; and there I buried Leah—the field and the cave that is in it were purchased (*miqneh*) from the Hittites." (Gen 49:29-32 RSV)

> And he [Jacob] charged them, and said unto them, I am to be gathered unto my people: bury me with my fathers in the cave that *is* in the field of Ephron the Hittite, In the cave that *is* in the field of Machpelah, which *is* before Mamre, in the land of Canaan, which Abraham bought (*qanah*) with the field of Ephron the Hittite for a possession of a burying place. There they buried Abraham and Sarah his wife; there they buried Isaac and Rebekah his wife; and there I buried Leah. The purchase (*miqneh*) of the field and of the cave that *is* therein *was* from the children of Heth. (Gen 49:29-32 KJV)

Most of my readers are thinking: "What's the big deal? Animals are animals. At any rate, the most important subject in scripture, besides God himself, is the human being." As far as scripture is concerned, these are false statements that stem from theology rooted in anthropocentric Ancient Greek philosophy. Scripture underlines in an extreme way the parity between humans and the animal kingdom. Suffice it to hear the unequivocal verdict of Ecclesiastes:

> I said in my heart with regard to the sons of men that God is testing them to show them that they are but beasts (*behemah*). For the fate of the sons of men and the fate of beasts (*behemah*) is the same; as one dies, so dies the other. They all have the same breath, and man has no advantage over the beasts (*behemah*); for all is vanity. All go to one place; all are from the dust, and all turn to dust again. Who knows whether the spirit of man goes upward and the spirit of the beast (*behemah*) goes down to the earth? (3:18-21)

Notice that, unexpectedly for us today, the author speaks of the beast's "spirit".[21] Furthermore, after the flood, at the blessing of

21 See my comments on this matter earlier.

his creation, God establishes no less than his personal covenant with everything that is a *nepheš ḥayyah* (living creature) and *kol baśar* (all flesh), and even *the earth* (*'ereṣ*) in its totality, and not only with Noah, his wife, and his sons and their wives:

> Then God said to Noah and to his sons with him, "Behold, I establish my covenant with you and your descendants after you, and with every living creature that is with you, the birds, the cattle, and every beast of the earth with you, as many as came out of the ark. I establish my covenant with you, that never again shall all flesh be cut off by the waters of a flood, and never again shall there be a flood to destroy the earth." And God said, "This is the sign of the covenant which I make between me and you and every living creature that is with you, for all future generations: I set my bow in the cloud, and it shall be *a sign of the covenant between me and the earth.* When I bring clouds over the earth and the bow is seen in the clouds, I will remember my covenant which is between me and you and every living creature of all flesh; and the waters shall never again become a flood to destroy all flesh. When the bow is in the clouds, I will look upon it and remember the everlasting covenant between God and every living creature of all flesh that is upon the earth." (Gen 9:8-16)[22]

On a practical note, let us consider the English "cattle" that was introduced by KJV[23] to render the original *behemah.* The immediate meaning associated with the noun cattle in today's English language, according to Google, is the following:

1. large ruminant animals with horns and cloven hoofs, domesticated for meat or milk, or as beasts of burden; cows.

   Similar: cows, bovines, oxen, bulls, stock, livestock.

---

22 Perhaps we should desist from referring to the covenant mentioned in Genesis 6:18 and 9:8-16 as Noa(c)hic covenant since it is imprecise, and thus, misleading. At any rate, it is Noah and his sons that are addressed (9:8) and not just Noah.

23 KJV is a translation many Protestants view as divinely inspired and thus referential in itself, just as the LXX is treated by many Orthodox Christians.

2. similar animals of a group related to domestic cattle, including yak, bison, and buffalo.

The Merriam-Webster dictionary defines cattle as the following:

1. domesticated quadrupeds held as property or raised for use specifically: bovine animals on a farm or ranch
2. human beings especially en masse

This is perplexing, to say the least, since the scriptural patriarchs were shepherds and not cattlemen. After all, the scriptural setting is the Syrian wilderness and not the North American continent. Ultimately God's people are his flock—not his herd—and he their shepherd (Jer 23; Ezek 34; Ps 78; Ps 80) and, *as his flock*, they shall be his people and he their God:

> And they shall know that I, the Lord their God, am with them, and that they, the house of Israel, are my people, says the Lord God. And you are my sheep, the sheep of my pasture, and I am your God, says the Lord God. (Ezek 34:30-31)

> Then we thy people, the flock of thy pasture, will give thanks to thee for ever; from generation to generation we will recount thy praise. To the choirmaster: according to Lilies. A Testimony of Asaph. A Psalm. Give ear, O Shepherd of Israel, thou who leadest Joseph like a flock! Thou who art enthroned upon the cherubim, shine forth. (Ps 79:13-80:1)

God's bias toward shepherd life is posited early on in Genesis—at face value, for no apparent reason—with his predilection toward Abel the *shepherd of flock* (*ro'eh ṣon*; Gen 4:2) at the beginning of human life outside the garden of Eden. And when Abel is slain—again for no apparent reason in the original Hebrew—by his brother Cain the *servant of the ground* (*'obed 'adamah*; Gen 4:2) and builder of the city (v.17)—God establishes a new *seed* (*zera'*) through Seth who takes Abel's place (vv.25-26) and who becomes the first born of Adam through whom God's original plan carries on: "When Adam had lived a hundred and thirty years, he became the father of a son *in his own likeness, after his image,* and named him Seth." (5:3; see 1:26)

To go the way of excessive pedantry in trying to defend and justify KJV and its child RSV by delving into the original meaning of the English "cattle" as coming from the Old French *chattels*, referring to all the things that a person owns, does not cut it for several reasons. The usual justification in defense of translations is that the congregants hearing the readings are to perceive immediately the meaning of the text. However, after some time, let alone centuries, new translations are needed precisely in order to uphold this alleged function of a translation. One need only open the BibleWorks program and see the endless updated translations in each language, especially in the English language, and the lists are still building up, each newcomer hailing it as being the most appropriate for the times, as the comparatively recent example NRSV does. Here is the introduction on Bible Gateway under Version Information:

> The *New Revised Standard Version of the Bible* (*NRSV*) was published in 1989 and has received the widest acclaim and broadest support from academics and church leaders of any modern English translation.
>
> **The *NRSV* is truly a Bible for all Christians!**
>
> Rooted in the past, but right for today, the *NRSV* continues the tradition of William Tyndale, the *King James Version*, the *American Standard Version*, and the *Revised Standard Version*. Equally important, it sets a new standard for the 21st Century.
>
> The *NRSV* stands out among the many translations because it is "as literal as possible" in adhering to the ancient texts and only "as free as necessary" to make the meaning clear in graceful, understandable English.
>
> The *NRSV* differs from the *RSV* in four primary ways, (the third and the fourth being) making the translation more accurate, and *helping it to be more easily understood, especially when it is read out loud.*[24]

---

24 My underscoring.

How NRSV actualizes these last two objectives is questionable, unless by "making the translation more accurate," the authors mean slashing the occurrences of "cattle" in Genesis from 32 instances in RSV to 10 in NRSV, or by rendering three different Hebrew verbs into the same "produced."

> Now the man knew his wife Eve, and she conceived and bore Cain, saying, "I have produced (*qaniti* [from *qanah*]; acquired) a man with the help of the Lord." (Gen 4:1)

> the flocks bred in front of the rods, and so the flocks produced (*teladna* [from *yalad*]; gave birth to) young that were striped, speckled, and spotted. (Gen 30:39)

> During the seven plenteous years the earth produced (*ta'aś* [from *'aśah*]; did, made] abundantly. (Gen 41:47)

And why not, in keeping with the spirit of the original and its wordplay, translate Cain into "produce"? After all, a name is a name; at least this translation would be in line with the intent of the original wordplay. This is not a facetious comment. For how can NRSV succeed in making "the text more easily understood, especially when it is read out loud" in the case of the names of Jacob's children in Genesis 29-30? How could English speaking hearers understand that these two chapters are basically constructed on wordplay unless someone explains to them the meaning of the original Hebrew names? In this particular case, not even Greek Orthodox hearers can fathom the intent of their LXX when it is read out loud to them. And neither North Americans nor Greeks together with the French and the Italians and the Spaniards will ever be able to connect the name "Abel" (*hebel*) in Genesis 4 with the same exact noun *hebel* translated as "vanity" which pervades the Book of Ecclesiastes. Only a Greek speaking person can readily hear and see the interplay between *Khristos* (Anointed, Messiah, Christ) and *khrēstos* (meek, gentle) in the original Greek New Testament. Only someone conversant with scriptural Hebrew—and not any Hebrew—will be able to dot the i's and cross the t's of the Hebrew Old Testament.

If this is the reality of the matter on the ground, so to speak, those interested in promoting the "words" of God and not their own "theologies,"[25] dubbed as "tradition of men" by both Jesus and the Apostle, should desist from all the long years of efforts in updating all translations or coining new ones—as though theirs are more valid than the old ones—and use any available old ones to teach their constituents or followers the original Hebrew text. In the original Old Testament text, even God speaks scriptural Hebrew and only scriptural Hebrew. One may not make, let alone force, him to be heard in any other language. In my estimation it is sheer blasphemy.[26] Notice what self-promoting scholars try to do with Paul's speech to the people around him in Jerusalem where he purportedly addressed them in "the Hebrew language" (Acts 21:40; 22:2) by re-translating the Greek that all of us hear and read into an original Hebrew to capture the historically actual address of Paul![27] The same applies to the following Old Testament episode:

> Then Eliakim the son of Hilkiah, and Shebnah, and Joah, said to the Rabshakeh, "Pray, speak to your servants in the Aramaic

---

25 See my comments on all the negatively assessed "-logies" (*mōrologia; pithanologia; aiskhrologia; genealogia; mataiologia; antilogia*) in my commentaries on Paul's epistles.

26 The scriptural God may well know perfect English and Arabic and thus may well understand our prayer. But all his responses to all our prayers are already inscribed in scriptural Hebrew in the Old Testament and in scriptural Greek in the New Testament. He is not going to change his mind—and give new answers in each of our todays: "For truly, I say to you, till heaven and earth pass away, not an iota, not a dot, will pass from the law until all is accomplished." (Mt 5:18) And the "Jesus Christ" who "is the same yesterday and today and for ever" (Heb 13:8) is encountered exclusively in the "iotas" and "dots" of the New Testament where his original voice is heard fully and completely: "I glorified thee on earth, having accomplished (*teleiōsas*) the work which thou gavest me to do." (Jn 17:4) Even, according to that same Jesus Christ, "And in praying do not heap up empty phrases as the Gentiles do; for they think that they will be heard for their many words. Do not be like them, for your Father knows what you need before you ask him." (Mt 6:7-8) Then he commands us to pray at all times the shortest possible prayer "Our Father who art in heaven... Thy will be done" (vv.9-10) in order for us to have enough remaining energy to implement God's will.

27 Is that at all possible? Any attempt would be conjecture since scholars will never be able to reach a consensus. Besides, does this mean that, upon reaching the start of Acts 22, we should lay aside scripture and not venture into listening to the remainder of Acts, the Pauline epistles, and the rest of the New Testament until the theologians have reached a consensus concerning Acts 22?

> language, for we understand it; do not speak to us in the language of Judah within the hearing of the people who are on the wall." But the Rabshakeh said to them, "Has my master sent me to speak these words to your master and to you, and not to the men sitting on the wall, who are doomed with you to eat their own dung and to drink their own urine?" Then the Rabshakeh stood and called out in a loud voice in the language of Judah: "Hear the word of the great king, the king of Assyria!" (2 Kg 18:26-28)

The listeners to the following message hear solely and exclusively scriptural Hebrew, and not Aramaic or the language of Judah, let alone English.

An extreme example of overcooked, if not outright misguided, scholarship is the strange case of "the Jerusalem Bible." The huge success of the original French "Jerusalem Bible" (La Bible de Jérusalem) published in 1956 gave the impetus for emulation in the English-speaking Roman Catholic world where the English "Jerusalem Bible" was published in 1966. With the obvious intent to defend the originality of the latter, we are told in the Editor's Foreword that, for a small number of Old Testament books, the first draft of the English translation was made directly from the French, and then the General Editor (Alexander Jones) produced a revised draft by comparing this word-for-word to the Hebrew or Aramaic texts. This gave rise to the consensus thereafter that the Jerusalem Bible was not a translation from the French; rather, it was an original translation heavily influenced by the French. However, this is clearly contradicted by the editor of the revised "New Jerusalem Bible," Henry Wansbrough, in his Foreword.

With all this in mind let us now turn to the real task at hand and follow the itinerary of *śadeh* (field) in the original text in order for us to learn from that text the meaning of the noun *śadeh* and its specific function especially when compared with the related *'ereṣ* and *'adamah*. Earlier I have pointed out that all three nouns in Genesis 1 and 2 are used practically interchangeably, since all three terms refer to the same reality of the domain of daily life for human beings, albeit from three different perspectives. In the passage concerning Esau and his skin color (Gen 27:1-5) I indicated that, since the wordplay on Esau's color works only with *'adamah* rather than with *śadeh*, the author's choice of the latter assumes that the hearers are acquainted with the close relation between the two nouns. This predilection for *śadeh* is further evident in the following passage where Esau, in contrast to his brother Jacob who led an itinerant shepherd life, is presented as a man of the earth/ground referred to as field:

> When the boys grew up, Esau was a skilful hunter, a man of the *field*, while Jacob was a quiet man, dwelling in tents. Isaac loved Esau, because he ate of his game; but Rebekah loved Jacob. Once when Jacob was boiling pottage, Esau came in from the *field*, and he was famished. And Esau said to Jacob, "Let me eat some of that red pottage, for I am famished!" (Therefore his name was called Edom.) Jacob said, "First sell me your birthright." Esau said, "I am about to die; of what use is a birthright to me?" Jacob said, "Swear to me first." So he swore to him, and sold his birthright to Jacob. Then Jacob gave Esau bread and pottage of lentils, and he ate and drank, and rose and went his way. Thus Esau despised his birthright. (Gen 25:27-34)

What is important for our discussion is that a few verses earlier we have a double express reference to "the field of Ephron" (Gen 25:9-10) which is the subject matter of an entire chapter, Genesis 23. In turn, what is striking for an attentive hearer is that after the frequent occurrence of *śadeh* in the *toledot* of the heavens and the earth (Gen 1-4)—no less than eight times—the term disappears completely, except for a curious passing mention in 14:7 (in the original Hebrew),[28] not to reappear until chapter 23 where it is heard no less than seven times, virtually as often as in Genesis 1-4. The importance of this topic—the field of Ephron—is sealed in that the entire Book of Genesis signs off with a sextuple reference to it (49:29, 30 twice, 32; 50:13 twice). Such cannot possibly be happenstance. So, what

---

28 Then they turned back and came to Enmishpat (that is, Kadesh), and subdued all the country (*śadeh*) of the Amalekites, and also the Amorites who dwelt in Hazazontamar. (Gen 14:7 RSV)

is the story of *śadeh* that literally brackets the first book of scripture as no other word does?[29]

The leap from Genesis 1-4 to chapter 23 in the high incidence mention of *śadeh* is obviously intentional. The first four instances (2:5 twice, 19 and 20) make it clear that *śadeh* is the earth or ground inasmuch as they are connected to life, whether vegetative (v.5) or animalic (19, 20). In this sense the English field reflects the same connotation: it is a piece of land (earth) or ground that supports vegetation which, in turn, supports the animals that consume that vegetation. In other words, *śadeh* is the earth or ground as being the source of and support for life. Notice in this regard that the animals in Genesis 2 are said to be *kol ḥayyat haśśadeh* (every "living" [adjective feminine] of the field) which would be more technically rendered as "every animated (being, creature) of the field."[30] In this sense *śadeh* in Genesis 2 presages the *śadeh* of chapters 25 and 27 where it functions as the source for food as well as a hunting locale:

> Afterward his brother came forth, and his hand had taken hold of Esau's heel; so his name was called Jacob. Isaac was sixty years old when she bore them. When the boys grew up, Esau was *a skilful hunter, a man of the field*, while Jacob was a quiet man, dwelling in tents. Isaac loved Esau, because *he ate of his game*; but Rebekah loved Jacob. Once when Jacob was *boiling pottage*, Esau came in *from the field*, and he was famished. And Esau said to Jacob, "*Let me eat some of that red pottage*, for I am famished!" (Therefore his name was called Edom) … Then Jacob gave Esau *bread and pottage of lentils*, and he ate and drank, and rose and went his way. (Gen 25:26-30, 34)

> When Isaac was old and his eyes were dim so that he could not see, he called Esau his older son, and said to him, "My son"; and he answered, "Here I am." He said, "Behold, I am old; I do not know the day of my death. Now then, take your weapons, your

29 The last instances of both *'ereṣ* and *'adamah* in Genesis occur in chapter 47.
30 Anyone knowledgeable of Latin will have guessed that the Latin *animal* reflects the same meaning. The Latin *anima* refers to a current of air, wind, air, breath, and thus *animal* refers to a breathing (independently moving) being. Hence our English "animal life."

> quiver and your bow, *and go out to the field, and hunt game for me, and prepare for me savory food*, such as I love, and *bring it to me that I may eat*; that I may bless you before I die." (Gen 27:1-4)

However, a sudden twist away from the positiveness of the *śadeh* starts when the serpent is introduced as "more subtle than *kol ḥayyat haśśadeh* (any other wild creature, RSV; any beast of the field, KJV; any other wild animal, NRSV) that the Lord had made (Gen 3:1). This introduction brings about an avalanche of bad news:

> The Lord God said to the serpent, "Because you have done this, *cursed* are you among all animals and among *all wild creatures* (*kol ḥayyat haśśadeh*; all animal [breathing] *of the field*); upon your belly you shall go, and *dust* (*'aphar*) you shall eat all the days of your life. (Gen 3:14)

> And to the man he said, "Because you have listened to the voice of your wife, and have eaten of the tree about which I commanded you, 'You shall not eat of it,' *cursed* is the ground because of you; in toil you shall eat of it all the days of your life; thorns and thistles it shall bring forth for you; and you shall eat the *plants of the field* (*haśśadeh*). (Gen 3:17-18)

It culminates with the consummate fratricide, for no apparent reason, which ends with a curse as in the case of the serpent, and the ground in conjunction with Adam:

> The Lord said to Cain, "Why are you angry, and why has your countenance fallen? If you do well, will you not be accepted? And if you do not do well, *sin* is couching at the door; its desire is for you, but you must master it."

> Cain said to Abel *his brother*, ~~"Let us go out to the field."~~ (not in the original Hebrew and supplied by the LXX) And when they were *in the field* (*baśśadeh*), Cain rose up against *his brother* Abel, and killed him. Then the Lord said to Cain, "Where is Abel your brother?" He said, "I do not know; am I my brother's keeper?" And the Lord said, "What have you done? The voice of your brother's blood is crying to me *from the ground*. And now you are *cursed from the ground*, which has opened its mouth to receive your brother's blood from your hand. (Gen 4:6-11)

Notice how the curse against the sinner Cain originates in the ground that was earlier cursed due to the disobedient Adam (Gen 3:17).

This situation of curse will be reversed in Genesis 23 through the medium of the ultimate assumed enemy, Ephron (the man of *'aphar*) the Hittite, when the *śadeh*—still the earth[31] of dust to which every human returns (3:19)—will become Hebron, the place of full brotherhood,[32] where Sarah (23:19), Abraham (25:9-10), Isaac (35:27-29), Rebekah and Leah (49:31) and Jacob (49:29-33; 50:12-14) are buried. Notice in this regard the full brotherhood between not so friendly people. Rebekah who betrayed her husband Isaac (Gen 27) was buried with him. Notice also how Rachel, Jacob's beloved wife, is buried in Bethlehem (35:19) while it is Leah, the "less loved" and even hated one (29:30-33), who ends up with her husband. Notice moreover how the field of Ephron brought together the two inimical brothers Isaac and Ishmael. Ishmael, who was cast out with his mother Hagar by Sarah (Gen 21), resurfaces and together with Isaac bury their father Abraham *in the field of Ephron the son of Zohar the Hittite*:

> Abraham breathed his last and died in a good old age, an old man and full of years, and was gathered to his people. Isaac and Ishmael his sons buried him in the cave of Machpelah, in the field of Ephron the son of Zohar the Hittite, east of Mamre, the field which Abraham purchased from the Hittites. There Abraham was buried, with Sarah his wife. (Gen 25:8-10)

This role of the field as building a bridge between inimical brothers and even between a Hittite and Abraham is prepared for in the very curious instance found in an even more curious chapter that seems hanging on its own:[33]

---

31 Notice the use of *'ereṣ* in Genesis 23 (vv.2, 7, 12, 13, 15, 19).

32 This is the meaning of the Hebrew *ḥebron.*

33 Try to read Genesis either by yourself or to others by moving from the end of chapter 13 to the start of chapter 15, thus omitting completely chapter 14, and you will soon realize that neither you nor they will miss it since it does not seem to add anything to the movement of the Genesis story.

> In the fourteenth year Chedorlaomer and the kings who were with him came and subdued the Rephaim in Ashterothkarnaim, the Zuzim in Ham, the Emim in Shavehkiriathaim, and the Horites in their Mount Seir as far as Elparan on the border of the wilderness; then they turned back and came to Enmishpat (that is, Kadesh), and subdued all the *śadeh* (country, RSV, KJV and NRSV) of the Amalekites, and also the Amorites who dwelt in Hazazontamar. (Gen 14:5-7)

One cannot be but perplexed by the unwarranted use of *śadeh* to speak of the "country" or "region" of a group or people, a unique instance in scripture. Add to this that *śadeh* is specifically the area of the Amalekites who are not only descendants of Esau (Gen 36:12, 16), Jacob/Israel's nemesis, but also and more importantly they are the perennial enemies of the scriptural Judah and Israel.[34]

Early in Genesis we hear the author using the appellation of *śadeh*, that is, the earth as life supporting (2:5, 19, 20), and then applying it to the living area of the Amalekites, well before the story of Ephron the Hittite (Gen 23) and the story of the two brothers Esau and Jacob (Gen 25, 27). In other words, early on in chapter 14, the author magisterially preempts the hearers from concluding that the special story about their ancestor, Abram, and his superman feats, makes them different from other peoples, especially their sworn adversaries. So from the beginning of the story, the author impresses upon the addressees that the *'ereṣ* which God created (1:1) and which is also *'adamah* (1:25) does not become the *'adamah* out of which *ha'adam* (any and every human being) is formed (2:7) until it has been introduced as *śadeh*, a place of vegetation, the food for the human being (1:29):

> … when no plant of the field (*śadeh*) was yet in the earth and no herb of the field (*śadeh*) had yet sprung up -- for the Lord God had

34 Ex 17:8-16; Num 14:45; Deut 25:17-19; Judg 3:13; 6:3, 33; 7:12; 10:12; 1 Sam 15; 1 Sam 30.

> not caused it to rain upon the earth (*'ereṣ*), and there was no man to till (*'abad*; serve) the ground (*'adamah*) (Gen 2:5)

Put simply, the area where the Amalekites are living is of the same fabric as the area out of whose dust (*'aphar*) *ha'adam*, the progenitor of both Abram and the Amalekites, was formed (2:7) and, consequently, into which both Abram and the Amalekites will turn (3:19). The hearers will soon be hit again with this reality when they will be barraged with the lengthy chapter 23 where Abraham will purchase the *śadeh* of Ephron (the man of dust) in order to bury *as dust* no less than Sarah who was impregnated with God's word of promise. If this is not a technical knockout against human propensity towards arrogance, what is?

gabar *(might/power)*

Human hubris is a pervading topic in scripture and is dealt with right from the beginning. In Genesis 1-2, the author demeans the humans by presenting and considering them on par not only with animal life, but also with vegetation. In the following chapter, the author takes the bull by the horns and attacks the matter head on by presenting the same human beings as prone to consider themselves equal to the deities or, at the very least, are tempted to entertain such a proposition, and do so at the instigation of a *ḥayyat haśśadeh*, an inferior being in their eyes.

For anyone knowledgeable of scripture, rather than the serpent, it is the author who is cunningly setting the trap for the readers and preparing for their later verdict in Job:

> Now the serpent was more subtle (*'arum*) than any other wild creature (*ḥayyat haśśadeh*) that the Lord God had made (Gen 3:1)

> As for me, I would seek God, and to God would I commit my cause; who does great things and unsearchable, marvelous things without number: he gives rain upon the earth and sends waters upon the fields; he sets on high those who are lowly, and those

who mourn are lifted to safety. He frustrates the devices of the *crafty* (*'arumim*), so that their hands achieve no success. He takes the wise in *their own craftiness* (*'ormam*); and the schemes of the wily are brought to a quick end. (Job 5:8-13)[35]

But you are doing away with the fear of God, and hindering meditation before God. For your iniquity teaches your mouth, and you choose the tongue of the *crafty* (*'arumim*) (Job 15:4-5)[36]

Still one does not need to wait until Job since the topic of human hubris is immediately revisited in Genesis 6-11 through the wordplay on the root *gabar* whose connotation is might (power) as is reflected in the term *gibbor* which is usually translated as "mighty."[37] The hearers of scripture will soon discover that the only one who is ultimately in control of *gabar* is the scriptural God.

In one of the most compelling passages against the humans whose behavior prompted God's frustration[38] and his decision to blot out all life from the face of the ground (Gen 6:1-7), we encounter the first instance of the root *gabar* in conjunction with the unbridled wickedness of man:

The Nephilim were on the earth in those days, and also afterward, when the sons of God came in to the daughters of men,

---

35 The interconnectedness between the temptation of Eve into falling for human wisdom and the teaching of the Book of Job was magisterially captured by Paul in his letters to the inhabitants of Corinth, the capital of Roman Greece (Province Achaia), which letters are aimed at belittling Greek wisdom. At the beginning of the Corinthian correspondence, his critique of Greek wisdom culminates in his quoting Job 5:13a (He takes the wise in their own craftiness) in 1 Corinthians 3:19b (For it is written, "He catches the wise in their craftiness [*panourgia*]"); see on this matter *C-1Cor* 81-2. And toward the end of this same correspondence he refers to Eve's being beguiled by the serpent in the following terms: "But I am afraid that as the serpent deceived Eve by his cunning (*panourgia*)." (2 Cor 11:3)

36 The wordplay in the original in Genesis 2-3 is compellingly unmissable. Both Adam and Eve realized they were "naked" (*'arummim*) upon their eating from the fruit of the tree of the knowledge of the good and the evil, and made themselves aprons from fig leaves (3:7) to cover the nakedness they were not ashamed of earlier (2:25). Shame in scripture is an expression of divine punishment (passim in the Prophets).

37 Gen 6:4; 10:8, 9; Josh 10:2; 1 Sam 2:4; 2 Sam 1:25; 10:7; 23:8-9, 16-17, 22.

38 See my comments on the Hebrew *wayyit'aṣṣeb* (and it grieved him to his heart; Gen 6:6) in *C-Gen* 88.

> and they bore children to them. These were the mighty men (*gibborim*) that were of old, the men of renown. The Lord saw that the wickedness of man was great in the earth, and that every imagination of the thoughts of his heart was only evil continually. And the Lord was sorry that he had made man on the earth, and it grieved him to his heart. (Gen 6:4-6)

The story of the flood is literarily conceived as punishment against humans using their might to subjugate others (the nephilim—as *gibborim*—were the product of the men—as sons of God—imposing themselves on women—as daughters of man). This is evident in the frequent use of the root *gabar* in the flood narrative in chapter 7 to describe God's handyman, the waters (vv.18, 19, 20 and 24):

> The flood continued forty days upon the earth; and the waters increased, and bore up the ark, and it rose high above the earth. The waters prevailed (*wayyigberu*) and increased greatly upon the earth; and the ark floated on the face of the waters. And the waters prevailed (*gaberu*) so mightily upon the earth that all the high mountains under the whole heaven were covered; the waters prevailed (*gaberu*) above the mountains, covering them fifteen cubits deep. And all flesh died that moved upon the earth, birds, cattle, beasts, all swarming creatures that swarm upon the earth, and every man; everything on the dry land in whose nostrils was the breath of life died. *He blotted out every living thing that was upon the face of the ground, man and animals and creeping things and birds of the air; they were blotted out from the earth.*[39] Only Noah was left, and those that were with him in the ark. And the waters prevailed (*wayyigberu*) upon the earth a hundred and fifty days. (Gen 7:17-24)[40]

The scriptural bias against human might is picked up in the last two chapters of Genesis 1-11. Suddenly in the enumeration of the nations and their peopling the earth we encounter a

---

39 The enactment of his promise in Genesis 6:7: "So the Lord said, 'I will blot out man whom I have created from the face of the ground, man and beast and creeping things and birds of the air, for I am sorry that I have made them.'"

40 Again a most compelling example where the aural link between the original "mighty" and "prevail" is lost in translation. Ergo, while scripture is the word/s of God, translations thereof are hardly so even by any stretch of the imagination.

lengthy aside concerning a certain Nimrod set in the following terms:

> Cush became the father of Nimrod; he was the first on earth to be a mighty man (*gibbor*). He was a mighty hunter before the Lord; therefore it is said, "Like Nimrod a mighty (*gibbor*) hunter before the Lord." The beginning of his kingdom was Babel, Erech, and Accad, all of them in the land of Shinar. (Gen 10:8-10)

This text is astutely phrased so that it looks backward and forward at the same time. Looking backward, Nimrod is the first named *gibbor* among the *gibborim* introduced in chapter 6. Even his name *nimrod* fits the context since it is from the root *marad* (stand tall, rebel) and literally means "we rebel." Even the plural reflected in the "we" seems appropriate since his kingdom covered three major cities, Babel, Erech, and Accad. Looking forward, the mention of Babel first and, more to the point, the additional and unnecessary "all of them in the land of Shinar" at the end of verse clearly points to the episode of the tower of Babel at the beginning of chapter 11 where again Shinar is clearly additional and functions to prepare the hearers for the location of the tower as being in the city of Babel:

> And as men migrated from the east, they found a plain[41] in the land of Shinar and settled there ... Then they said, "Come, let us build ourselves a city, and a tower with its top in the heavens, and let us make a name for ourselves, lest we be scattered abroad upon the face of the whole earth." ... Therefore its name was called Babel. (Gen 11:2, 4, 9)

41 The noun *biq'ah* (plain) is not found again until Deuteronomy 8:7. The patient hearers will be gratified when they will hear in Ezekiel that the same God will appear in the *biq'ah* (plain) by the River Chebar (*kebar*) which means also "great, mighty": "In the thirtieth year, in the fourth month, on the fifth day of the month, as I was among the exiles by the river Chebar, the heavens were opened, and I saw visions of God ... And the hand of the Lord was there upon me; and he said to me, 'Arise, go forth into the *plain*, and there I will speak with you.' So I arose and went forth into the *plain*; and, lo, the glory of the Lord stood there, like the glory which I had seen by the river Chebar; and I fell on my face." (Ezek 1:1; 3:22-23)

In turn this episode harks back, terminology wise, to the passage where one hears the root *gabar* for the first time:

> When men began to multiply *on the face of the ground*, and daughters were born to them, the sons of God saw that the daughters of men were fair; and they took to wife such of them as they chose. Then the Lord said, "My spirit shall not abide in man for ever, for he is flesh, but his days shall be a hundred and twenty years." The Nephilim were on the earth in those days, and also afterward, when the *sons of God* came in to the daughters of men, and they bore children to them. These were the *mighty men (gibborim)* that were of old, *the men of renown (name)*. The Lord saw that the wickedness of man was great in the earth, and that every imagination of the thoughts of his heart was only evil continually. And the Lord was sorry that he had made man on the earth, and it grieved him to his heart. So the Lord said, "I will blot out man whom I have created *from the face of the ground*, man and beast and creeping things and birds of the air, for I am sorry that I have made them." (Gen 6:1-7)

> And as men migrated from the east, they found a plain in the land of Shinar and settled there. And they said to one another, "Come, let us make bricks, and burn them thoroughly." And they had brick for stone, and bitumen for mortar. Then they said, "Come, let us build ourselves a city, and a tower with its top in the heavens, and *let us make a name for ourselves*, lest we be scattered abroad *upon the face of the whole earth*." And the Lord came down to see the city and the tower, which *the sons of men* had built. And the Lord said, "Behold, they are one people, and they have all one language; and this is only the beginning of what they will do; and nothing that they propose to do will now be impossible for them. Come, let us go down, and there confuse their language, that they may not understand one another's speech." So the Lord scattered them abroad from there *over the face of all the earth*, and they left off building the city. (Gen 11:2-8)

11
Families

The uniqueness of Noah's scriptural character lies in that his *toledot* or scriptural chapter is not defined by the parameters of his birth, the birth of his first son, and his death, as was the case of his predecessors throughout the *toledot* of Adam. The *toledot* of Noah are defined by the flood.

> These are the generations (*toledot*) of Noah. Noah was a righteous man, blameless in his generation; Noah walked with God. And Noah had three sons, Shem, Ham, and Japheth. Now the earth was corrupt in God's sight, and the earth was filled with violence. And God saw the earth, and behold, it was corrupt; for all flesh had corrupted their way upon the earth. ... For behold, I will bring a flood of waters upon the earth, to destroy all flesh in which is the breath of life from under heaven; everything that is on the earth shall die. (Gen 6:9-12, 17)

> The sons of Noah who went forth from the ark were Shem, Ham, and Japheth. ... After the flood Noah lived three hundred and fifty years. All the days of Noah were nine hundred and fifty years; and he died. (Gen 9:18; 9:28-29)

In other words, the *toledot* of Noah do not extend over his progeny as in the case of Adam and later of Shem and Terah, but is co-extensive with the story of the flood. The scriptural Noah exists only in conjunction with the flood in the sense that all the authors allow us to know concerning this literary character is in relation to another literary construct of theirs, the scriptural flood. This is similar to Jules Verne's Captain Nemo, who is who he is within the parameters of "Twenty Thousand Leagues under the Sea." Although both stories revolve around the waters of the seas, in Jules Verne's epic the sea monster is an essential character in the story, whereas, in the flood story, the *tanninim* (great sea monsters) that have a place of eminence in Genesis 1 are conspicuous by their total absence. Nevertheless, the sea animals control the entire plot in that, at the end, the human beings are blessed by being granted to "swarm" (9:17) as the fish have all along been doing since they were created by God (1:21).

Just as the character of Noah straddles over the end of Adam's *toledot* and the start of his own, so also the characters of his three sons straddle over the end of Noah's *toledot* and the start of their own:

> But Noah found favor in the eyes of the Lord. These are the generations (*toledot*) of Noah. Noah was a righteous man, blameless in his generation (*dorot*); Noah walked with God. And Noah had three sons, Shem, Ham, and Japheth. (Gen 6:8-10)

> The sons of Noah who went forth from the ark were Shem, Ham, and Japheth. Ham was the father of Canaan. These three were the sons of Noah; and from these the whole earth was peopled. … After the flood Noah lived three hundred and fifty years. All the days of Noah were nine hundred and fifty years; and he died. These are the generations (*toledot*) of the sons of Noah, Shem, Ham, and Japheth; sons were born to them after the flood. (Gen 9:18-19; 9:28-10:1)

However, in the latter case, one hears of a comparatively lengthy aside of eight verses (Gen 9:20-27) that relates an anecdote that does not seem to have anything to do with either what precedes it or what follows it. If this passage were absent, the flow of the narration does not suffer at all:

> The sons of Noah who went forth from the ark were Shem, Ham, and Japheth. Ham was the father of Canaan. These three were the sons of Noah; and from these the whole earth was peopled … These are the generations (*toledot*) of the sons of Noah, Shem, Ham, and Japheth; sons were born to them after the flood. (Gen 9:18-19; 10:1)

The intentionality of these additional verses (Gen 9:20-27) is sealed through the comment "Ham was the father of Canaan" at the end of 9:18. This out of the blue mention of Canaan by the authors is obviously a teaser to pique the hearers' curiosity about Canaan who, a few verses later, will have, next to Cush (10:7-14; six verses), a lion's share among the "sons of Ham"

(10:15-19; five verses). The curiosity of the hearers will be immediately satisfied since Canaan is mentioned no less than five times (9:18, 22, 25, 26, 27). Canaan is introduced twice as "son of Ham" (Ham was the father of Canaan; 9:18 and 9:22) in view of Canaan's curse: "Cursed be Canaan; a slave of slaves shall he be to his brothers ... and let Canaan be his (Japheth's) slave ... and let Canaan be his (Shem's) slave." (9:25, 26, 27)

Let us listen to the entire addition:

> The sons of Noah who went forth from the ark were Shem, Ham, and Japheth. Ham was the father of Canaan (*weḥam hu' 'abi kena'an*); And Ham, he, the father of Canaan). These three were the sons of Noah; and from these the whole earth was peopled. Noah was the first tiller of the soil. He planted a vineyard; and he drank of the wine, and became drunk, and lay uncovered in his tent. And Ham, the father of Canaan, saw the nakedness of his father, and told his two brothers outside. Then Shem and Japheth took a garment, laid it upon both their shoulders, and walked backward and covered the nakedness of their father; their faces were turned away, and they did not see their father's nakedness. When Noah awoke from his wine and knew what his youngest son had done to him, he said, "Cursed be Canaan; a slave of slaves shall he be to his brothers." He also said, "Blessed by the Lord my God be Shem; and let Canaan be his slave. God enlarge Japheth, and let him dwell in the tents of Shem; and let Canaan be his slave." After the flood Noah lived three hundred and fifty years. All the days of Noah were nine hundred and fifty years; and he died. (Gen 9:18-29)

The tone is set in v.18 through the codicil "And Ham—mind you, I mean—the father of Canaan" which clearly looks ahead to v.22 where we are told that the one who committed the sacrilegious action of looking at his father's nakedness was not simply Ham, but specifically Ham the father of Canaan.[1]

---

1 See Leviticus 18:6-7: "None of you shall approach any one near of kin to him to uncover nakedness. I am the Lord. You shall not uncover the nakedness of your father, which is the nakedness of your mother; she is your mother, you shall not uncover her nakedness."

Beyond that, it looks ahead to vv.25-27 where the one who is cursed is not Ham, but Canaan. In order to fathom what is going on, one is to open one's "Hebrew" ears. In the list of nations (chapter 10) one notices that the territories of Ham and Shem overlap and thus, as I explained in *The Rise of Scripture*, those two brothers are two sides of the same coin: curse on the one hand, and blessing, on the other hand. The one and the same Lord is the bestower of both the blessing and the curse upon the same people. In Hebrew, *šem* (Shem) means "name" and ultimately the name of God:

> Now an Israelite woman's son, whose father was an Egyptian, went out among the people of Israel; and the Israelite woman's son and a man of Israel quarreled in the camp, and the Israelite woman's son blasphemed the Name (*haššem*), and cursed. And they brought him to Moses. His mother's name was Shelomith, the daughter of Dibri, of the tribe of Dan. And they put him in custody, till the will of the Lord should be declared to them. And the Lord said to Moses, "Bring out of the camp him who cursed; and let all who heard him lay their hands upon his head, and let all the congregation stone him. And say to the people of Israel, Whoever curses his God shall bear his sin. He who blasphemes the name of the Lord shall be put to death; all the congregation shall stone him; the sojourner as well as the native, when he blasphemes the Name (*haššem*), shall be put to death." (Lev 24:10-16)

Notice the full equivalence between "the Name" and God himself. "Cursed" is appended to "blasphemed the Name" (Lev 24:11) in view of "curses his God" (Lev 24:15), which parallels "blasphemes the name of the Lord" (Lev 24:16). Thus Shem reflects the divine blessing as is clear from Genesis 9:26-27 where he is blessed "by the Lord, my God" (v.26) while Japheth shares in this one blessing—which is not repeated—by "entering the tents of Shem" (v.27). On the other hand, *ḥam* (Ham) means "hot"[2] and thus reflects "divine ire"

---

2 Josh 9:12 (Here is our bread; it was still warm (*ḥam*; hot) when we took it from our houses as our food for the journey, on the day we set forth to come to you, but now,

and, by extension, "curse." The classic texts concerning this matter are found in Leviticus 26 and Deuteronomy 28 where God is the source of both blessing and curse.

When one considers that the one territory of both Shem and Ham covers the area that is presented as the "earth of (the scriptural) Canaan," then it becomes clear that Japheth is the outsider who had to dwell in the tents of Shem in order for him and his descendants to enjoy the divine blessing. Moreover, the scriptural primary interest is not so much Ham or even Shem, but Japheth. Notice how he is introduced systematically as third in line after Shem and Ham (Gen 5:32; 6:10; 7:13; 9:18; 10:1). Yet, after the introduction to the table of nations that follows the traditional order, Shem, Ham, and Japheth (These are the generations [*toledot*] of the sons of Noah, Shem, Ham, and Japheth; sons were born to them after the flood; 10:1) the author suddenly starts with Japheth who is linked to the "coastland peoples" or, more accurately "the islands/coastlands of the nations" (*'iyyey haggoyim*), which are said to "have spread" (*niphredu*) (10:2). Moreover, it is Japheth's "spreading" (*pharad*) that sets the tone for the movement of "all the families of the sons of Noah: "These are the families of the sons of Noah, according to their genealogies, in their nations (*goyim*); and from these the nations (*goyim*) spread abroad (*pharad*) on the earth after the flood." (Gen 10:32) In this regard RSV is misleading because it gives the impression that "spreading" applies also to the Canaanites: "Afterward the families of the Canaanites spread (*phuṣ*) abroad." (Gen 10:18) However, the Hebrew verb *phuṣ* used here later describes—and no less than three times—a movement with the negative connotation of "scatter," and in the last two instances referring to an act of punishment by God:

> Then they said, "Come, let us build ourselves a city, and a tower with its top in the heavens, and let us make a name for ourselves,

---

behold, it is dry and moldy.) and Job 37:16-17 (Do you know the balancings of the clouds, the wondrous works of him who is perfect in knowledge, you whose garments are hot (*ḥammim*) when the earth is still because of the south wind?).

> lest we be scattered abroad (*phuṣ*) upon the face of the whole earth." (Gen 11:4)

> So the Lord scattered (*phuṣ*) them abroad from there over the face of all the earth, and they left off building the city. Therefore its name was called Babel, because there the Lord confused the language of all the earth; and from there the Lord scattered (*phuṣ*) them abroad over the face of all the earth. (Gen 11:8-9)

So, the author very astutely was already referring to the Canaanites in chapter 10 as being under the curse emitted against them by Noah (Gen 9:25). When the hearers take into consideration that Canaan is presented as a son of Ham, then they cannot miss the fact that in the following chapter, Ham's other son Cush is the father of Nimrod, King of Babel, who will prove to be the reason behind the Lord's scattering of the sons of Adam as a punishment for their arrogance that clearly emulates that of Nimrod:

> Cush became the father of Nimrod; he was the first on earth to be a mighty man. He was a mighty hunter before the Lord; therefore it is said, "Like Nimrod a mighty hunter before the Lord." The beginning of his kingdom was Babel, Erech, and Accad, all of them in the land of Shinar. (Gen 10:8-10)

> Now the whole earth had one language and few words. And as men migrated from the east, they found a plain in the land of Shinar and settled there. And they said to one another, "Come, let us make bricks, and burn them thoroughly." And they had brick for stone, and bitumen for mortar. Then they said, "Come, let us build ourselves a city, and a tower with its top in the heavens, and let us make a name for ourselves, lest we be scattered abroad upon the face of the whole earth." And the Lord came down to see the city and the tower, which the sons of men had built. And the Lord said, "Behold, they are one people, and they have all one language; and this is only the beginning of what they will do; and nothing that they propose to do will now be impossible for them. Come, let us go down, and there confuse their language, that they may not understand one another's speech." So the Lord scattered them abroad from there over the face of all the earth, and they left off building the city. Therefore its name was called Babel, because there the Lord confused the

> language of all the earth; and from there the Lord scattered them abroad over the face of all the earth. (Gen 11:1-9)

The intended connection between these two passages is sealed by the fact that "the Lord" (*yahweh*) occurs only in them throughout chapters 9 and 10. The conclusion imposes itself. Through his two children, Cush and Canaan, Ham's name is chosen intentionally: *ḥam* carries God's ire. Thus, one can conclude that through the legacy of his two children, Cush and Canaan, the name Ham was intentionally chosen to reflect God's ire.

However, those who live in the Syro-Arabian wilderness, the shared territory by Shem and Ham, according to the will of *haššem* (The Name) will come under the blessing granted to their forefather *šem* (Shem; 9:26). The scriptural Shemites are not the historical Semites since, in scripture, the same Semites can end up Hamites rather than Shemites. In *The Rise of Scripture*, I detailed this view that is supported by Ham being the father of both Canaan, associated with the Syrian wilderness, and Cush, associated with the Arabian wilderness. The Syro-Arabian wilderness is a continuous area that encompasses the scriptural world described in the second creation narrative as circumscribed by Havilah—Southern Arabia (Gen 2:11-12), Cush—Egypt (v.13), on the one hand, and the Tigris and the Euphrates (v.14), on the other hand.

Still, literarily speaking, Japheth rather than Shem seems to be the main character in chapter 10. Note that Japheth is suddenly moved into the first position (v.2) after the classic order "Shem, Ham, and Japheth" (v.1). Further, the description of the movement of the Japhethites as "spreading" (v.5) is taken up at the closure of the chapter to describe the "spreading" of all other families and nations (v.32). The primacy of Japheth even over Shem is sealed in that, at the start of his genealogy, Shem is introduced as being the brother of Japheth despite the fact that he was the elder: "To Shem also, the father of all the children of Eber, the elder brother of Japheth, children were born." (v.21). The oddity of the additional phrase "the elder brother of Japheth" is twofold: the hearers already know that the two are brothers (5:32; 6:10; 7:13; 9:18; 10:1), and usually it is the older brother that defines the younger and not vice versa. This primary interest of the author in Japheth is not unexpected when one realizes that it has been deftly prepared for a few verses earlier at the close of chapter 9:

> He also said, "Blessed by the Lord (*yahweh*) my God be Shem; and let Canaan be his slave. God (*'elohim*) enlarge Japheth, and let him dwell in the tents of Shem; and let Canaan be his slave." After the flood Noah lived three hundred and fifty years. (vv.26-28)

Not only are Noah's last words made in conjunction with Japheth (v.27) rather than with Shem (v.26), but also, whereas the appeal concerning Shem is made to *yahweh* who is connected with the Mosaic Law and the scriptural Israel,[3] the prayer concerning Japheth is made to *'elohim* the "universal" scriptural deity. So, the entire scenario seems to suggest that the blessing of Shem by *the Lord* is made so that *God* will lead Japheth into dwelling in the tents of Shem and thus share in this blessing. This is precisely, in a nutshell, the entire scriptural story culminating at the end of Isaiah where the servant of the Lord would serve as his messenger to the scriptural nations as well as to the remnant of the scriptural Israel (Is 42; 49; 50). The scriptural Israel ended up dispersed in exile among the nations away from its scriptural home, "the earth of Canaan."

So once again, the author is looking ahead to Isaiah, just as was the case with *bara'* and *tohu wabohu* at the opening of scripture in Genesis 1:1-2. This is expressed here in the reference to the descendants of Japheth as originating in the *'iyye haggoyim* (the isles/coastlands of the nations; 10:5).[4] The intentional link between Genesis 10 and Isaiah is more readily

---

3 And God said to Moses, "I am the Lord. I appeared to Abraham, to Isaac, and to Jacob, as God Almighty, but by my name the Lord I did not make myself known to them." (Ex 6:2-3)

4 Whereas KJV keeps closer to the original with its "the isles of the Gentiles," RSV has the insipid "the coastland peoples."

noticeable and thus more striking than the case between Genesis 1 and Isaiah. Consider the following:

1. After Genesis 1 the verb *bara'* is heard again in 2:4 and 5:2 and occurs only in Exodus 34:10;[5] Numbers 16:30; and Deuteronomy 4:32 before its subsequent use twenty-one times in Isaiah.
2. The same applies to *tohu* and *bohu*. After Genesis 1:2 the noun *tohu* is used in Deuteronomy 32:10 and twice in 1 Sam 1:21 before its following frequent occurrence (eleven times) in Isaiah. As for *bohu* it occurs three times in the entire scripture (Gen 1:2; Is 34:11; Jer 4:23)
3. On the hand, *'iyyim*, which occurs only in the plural form of *'iy*, it disappears completely from the scriptural horizon after Genesis 10:5 until it overwhelms the hearers no less than seventeen times in Isaiah. Such a literary feature can in no way be happenstance.

It is no wonder then that, in the last chapter of Isaiah just before the entire creation is subsumed into the new scriptural reality of "the new heavens and the new earth which I will make (*'aśah*)"[6] (66:22), we suddenly hear not only *goyim* as a refrain, but also, in tandem, the names of Japhethite nations from Genesis 10 that will be incorporated into the new Zion, God's city, together and on the same footing with the children of Israel:

> For I know their works and their thoughts, and I am coming to gather all nations (*goyim*)[7] and tongues (*lešonot*);[8] and they shall come and shall see my glory, and I will set a sign among them.

---

5 "Behold, I make a covenant. Before all your people I will do marvels, such as have not been wrought (*nibre'u*; passive form) in all the earth or in any nation."
6 The same verb heard several times in Genesis 1:1-2:4.
7 Genesis 10:5 (twice in Hebrew), 20, 31. In Hebrew, Genesis 10:5 reads: "From these the coastland peoples (*goyim*) spread. These are the sons of Japheth in their lands, each with his own language, by their families, in their nations (*goyim*)." (Gen 10:5)
8 Gen 10:5, 20, 31. RSV has in all three cases "languages."

> And from them I will send survivors to the nations (*goyim*), to Tarshish, Put, and Lud, who draw the bow, to Tubal and Javan, to the coastlands (*'iyyim*)[9] afar off, that have not heard my fame or seen my glory; and they shall declare my glory among the nations (*goyim*). And they shall bring all your brethren from all the nations (*goyim*) as an offering to the Lord, upon horses, and in chariots, and in litters, and upon mules, and upon dromedaries, to my holy mountain Jerusalem, says the Lord, just as the Israelites (children of Israel) bring their cereal offering in a clean vessel to the house of the Lord. And some of them also I will take for priests and for Levites, says the Lord. (Is 66:18-21)

The stress on Japheth is evident in that, in Isaiah 66:19, after the names of one son of Japheth, Tarshish (Gen 10:4), one son of Ham, Put (v.6), and one son of Shem, Lud (v.22)—that is to say, after the order that is followed in Genesis 10—Isaiah adds specifically two names, Tubal and Javan, that are mentioned in the list of the sons of Japheth in Genesis 10:2. Moreover, the first name in Isaiah's list, Tarshish, is the son of Javan (Gen 10:4) that refers specifically to Greece (*Hellas*, *Hellada*),[10] the nation of isles (v.5). See also Joel 3:6 where "Greeks" is the translation of the Hebrew *yewanim* (Javanites; plural of *yawan* [Javan]). In turn, this explains why the New Testament writings use *Hellēnes* (Hellenes, Greeks) and *ethne* (*goyim*; nations) interchangeably:

> I want you to know, brethren, that I have often intended to come to you (but thus far have been prevented), in order that I may reap some harvest among you as well as among the rest of the Gentiles (*ethnesin*; nations). I am under obligation both to Greeks (*Hellēsin*) and to barbarians, both to the wise and to the foolish: so I am eager to preach the gospel to you also who are in Rome. (Rom 1:13-15)

---

9 Gen 10:5.

10 This is precisely how the LXX renders it in both Isaiah 66:19 and Ezekiel 27:13. See also Zechariah 9:13; Daniel 8:21; 11:20; 1:2.

Revisiting the Parity between Animals and Human Beings

The matter of parity between the animal kingdom and humans is so much on the authors' mind that it remains a focus of theirs in the subsequent chapters of Genesis 5-11, where it is stressed in two opposite directions. On the one hand, when speaking of the pairs of animals that entered the ark the author very unexpectedly refers to them twice in a row as *'iš we'išto* (man and his wife; 7:2). This is striking since (1) these two nouns—*'iš* and *'iššah*—are strictly reserved to the male and, respectively, female human beings in the rest of scripture; (2) the author could have easily repeated the classic "male and female" (*zakar uneqebah*) which he uses profusely of the animals in the flood story (6:19; 7:3, 9, 16) and he used twice earlier to speak of the human beings (1:27; 5:2). The intentionality is unmissable: the animal pair is as much "man and his wife" as the human pair:

> So the Lord God caused a deep sleep to fall upon the man, and while he slept took one of his ribs and closed up its place with flesh; and the rib which the Lord God had taken from the man he made into a woman (*'iššah*) and brought her to the man. Then the man said, "This at last is bone of my bones and flesh of my flesh; she shall be called Woman (*'iššah*), because she was taken out of Man." Therefore a man leaves his father and his mother and cleaves to his wife (*'išto*), and they become one flesh. And the man and his wife (*we'išto*) were both naked, and were not ashamed. (Gen 2:21-25)

On the other hand, later on, when introducing for the first time the noun *mišpaḥot* (families) that will be the classic word for human collectives (10:5, 18, 20, 31, 32), the author uses it in conjunction with animals: "And every beast, every creeping thing, and every bird, everything that moves upon the earth, went forth by families out of the ark." (8:19) In this case, the human being is defined according to the animal and not vice versa. This will become pertinent at hearing Genesis 12:3 where the all-encompassing divine promise to Abram and, through him, to all nations is cast in the same way:

> And I will bless them that bless thee, and curse him that curseth thee: and in thee shall all families of the earth be blessed. (Gen 12:3 KJV)

> I will bless those who bless you, and him who curses you I will curse; and by you all the families of the earth shall bless themselves. (Gen 12:3 RSV)

> I will bless those who bless you, and the one who curses you I will curse; and in you all the families of the earth shall be blessed. (Gen 12:3 NRS)[11]

The intentionality behind the use of "families" here is immediately corroborated two verses later in the description of Abram's company:

> And Abram took Sarai his wife, and Lot his brother's son, and all their possessions (*rekuš*) which they had gathered (*rakašu*), and the persons (*nepheš ḥayyah*) that they had gotten (*'aśu*; made) in Haran; and they set forth to go to the land of Canaan. (Gen 12:5)

rekuš refers to the inanimate property as opposed to *miqneh* that is usually the animate property. Notice how here the author differentiates between *rekuš* and *nepheš ḥayyah* that obviously refers to the animate belongings since this expression has been established as referring to humans as well as animals in Genesis 1. So, rendering it as "persons" is misleading because, then, the animals are to be counted as *rekuš*, which would be counterintuitive. The inclusiveness of *nepheš ḥayyah* is further confirmed in the following instances of listing the "belongings" of a patriarch where the animals are mentioned *before* the human beings:

> And for her sake he dealt well with Abram; and he had sheep, oxen, he-asses, menservants, maidservants, she-asses, and camels. (Gen 12:16)

---

11 Notice in this regard the bias of both the LXX and the Vulgate. Although they both render *mišpaḥot* as *phylai* (Greek) and, respectively, *familiai* (Latin) throughout Genesis 10 and as *phylai* (Greek) and, respectively, *cognationes* (kindreds; Latin) in Gen 12:3, they have the generic *genos* (class, kind; Greek) and *genus* (class, kind; Latin) in 7:2.

> Then Abimelech took sheep and oxen, and male and female slaves, and gave them to Abraham, and restored Sarah his wife to him. (Gen 20:14)

> The Lord has greatly blessed my master, and he has become great; he has given him flocks and herds, silver and gold, menservants and maidservants, camels and asses. (Gen 24:35)

> For he had possession (*miqneh*) of flocks, and possession (*miqneh*) of herds, and great store of servants: and the Philistines envied him. (Gen 26:14 KJV)[12]

Since the patriarchs are expressly spoken of as "shepherds of flock" (*ro'eh ṣon*; Gen 30:36; 37:2; 46:32, 34; 47:3) as Abel was (Gen 2:4)—and as ultimately God Almighty himself, "the Mighty One of Jacob," is addressed as "Shepherd" (Gen 49:24)—the hearers are already on their way to readily receive and comprehend Nathan's message to David:

> There were two men in a certain city, the one rich and the other poor. The rich man had very many flocks (*ṣon*) and herds; but the poor man had nothing but one *little ewe lamb* (*kibsah*), which he had bought. *And he brought it up, and it grew up with him and with his children; it used to eat of his morsel, and drink from his cup, and lie in his bosom, and it was like a daughter to him.* (2 Sam 12:1-3)

12 RSV omits the repetition of *miqneh* in the original Hebrew: "He had possessions of flocks and herds, and a great household, so that the Philistines envied him."

12
Positive Negative

The dilemma of good (*tob*) versus evil (*ra'*) is a perennial issue brought about by the lingering human fascination with ethics or morals. However one looks at it, an ultimate solution to the dilemma is unattainable since it will always be bogged down with definitions, differentiations, limits, and the like, and these will always remain fluid in that they are dependent on one's premises concerning good and evil. The scriptural authors were obviously aware of the conundrum as is clear from their introduction to the debate in Genesis 2 under the heading of "the tree of the *knowledge* of good and evil" (v.17). In other words, they were aware that the real issue was the discernment between the two. However—and that is the striking feature of scripture—instead of dealing with this matter that is at the heart of all religions and philosophies throughout the ages, they took a stand against the grain. At the outset—at the first mention of the matter—they made it unequivocally clear that the human beings were prohibited from engaging in debate on this subject and added the unexpected threat of capital punishment, to boot:

> And the Lord God commanded the man, saying, "You may freely eat of every tree of the garden; but of the tree of the knowledge of good and evil you shall not eat, for in the day that you eat of it you shall die." (Gen 2:16-17)

As though that extreme proposition was not enough, the authors developed their first story of human mental activity and conversation with words around that prohibited subject in no less than a full chapter (Genesis 3) that sets the tone as well as main subject for the remainder of scripture: the contravention of the scriptural God's commandment. It is as though they were stressing that that subject was the subject of subjects—the "mother of all subjects"—for human beings who—the authors a few verses earlier stressed—were the only beings who "were made in God's image and after his likeness" (Gen 1:26) and "created after his own image" (v.27) with the express purpose of their "having dominion over the fish of the sea and over the birds of the air and over every living thing that moves upon the earth" (v.28), that is to say, in the scriptural God's stead. My readers should notice that the scriptural authors are more cunning than they give the impression in that they preempted the critique of human philosophy and its parody, theology,[1] by making it precisely the argument of the serpent of their story: "Dear Woman (*'iššah*), God is pulling your leg since his true intention is not to have you and the Man (*ha'adam*) be like him; he is actually jealous of you now that he had made you look like him and is trying to renege on his original intention":

> Now the serpent was more subtle than any other wild creature that the Lord God had made. He said to the woman, "Did God say, 'You shall not eat of any tree of the garden'?" And the woman said to the serpent, "We may eat of the fruit of the trees of the garden; but God said, 'You shall not eat of the fruit of the tree which is in the midst of the garden, neither shall you touch it, lest you die.'" But the serpent said to the woman, "You will not die. For God knows that when you eat of it your eyes will be opened, and you will be *like God, knowing good and evil.*" (Gen 3:1-5)

The first unavoidable conclusion is that, *in scripture*, the human being is not God, albeit the human being is "like" God. This is at its clearest, literarily speaking, in the, literarily speaking, central Psalm 82:[2]

---

1 Theology, as usual, tries to soften the scriptural God's harshness by making him "look good" and conceived the ill-conceived (pun intended) ridiculous proposition of *liberum arbitrium* ([human] free will) not realizing that the scriptural authors' serpent preceded theologians on that path and, in a way, led them on that path! And how could not theologians fall prey to this trap since they are merely the progeny of their forebears, "the man" and his "woman": "And he said to me, 'Son of man, I send you to the people of Israel, to a nation of rebels, who have rebelled against me; they and their fathers have transgressed against me to this very day.'" (Ezek 2:3)

2 If one takes into consideration the lengthy Psalm 119, made out of 176 verses, then Psalm 82 falls roughly speaking at the center of the Psalter.

> 1 A Psalm of Asaph. God has taken his place in the divine council; in the midst of the gods he holds judgment (*yišpoṭ*): 2 "How long will you judge (*tišpeṭu*) unjustly and show partiality to the wicked? *Selah* 3 Give justice to the weak (*dal*) and the fatherless; maintain the right of the afflicted and the destitute. 4 Rescue the weak (*dal*) and the needy; deliver them from the hand of the wicked." 5 They have neither knowledge (*lo' yade'u*; from the same root as *da'at*) nor understanding, they walk about in darkness; all the foundations of the earth are shaken. 6 I say, "*You are gods*, sons of the Most High, all of you; 7 nevertheless, you shall die (*temutun*) like men (*'adam*; man), and fall (*tippolu* from *naphal*) like any prince." 8 Arise, O God, judge (*šopṭah*) the earth; for to thee belong all the nations!

The scriptural God is threatening all other deities with death just as he did man in Genesis 2:17 (Ps 82:7a), and with falling (*naphal*; v.7b) just like the Nephilim (*nephilim*), the progeny of the "sons of God" (Gen 6:4), although the deities are "gods, sons of the Most High" (Ps 82:6). Moreover, the reason for their harsh judgment by God (vv.1 and 8) is that their judging is unjust and partial (v.2) in that they side with the wicked against the weak (*dal*), fatherless, afflicted, destitute, and needy (vv.3-4). What is impressive is that the word that is repeated at the start of v.3 and v.4 is *dal* whose technical meaning is "base, lowly, insignificant, unworthy of mention, worth nothing."[3] The hearers cannot avoid reminiscing the story of Cain (*qayn*; acquirer and thus rich, powerful), forefather of the king Lemech, and Abel (*hebel*; vanity, nothingness, vapor) (Gen 4).

This turning of the situation on its head, so to speak, is encountered in Psalm 8 that was used in Patristic theology to speak of the human being's high value in God's plan. In a classic example of text proofing, theologians like to quote verse 5 out of context to uphold the special value of the human being—in their eyes of course: "Yet thou hast made him (the human being; *'enoš*; *'adam*) little less than God, and dost crown him with glory and honor." However, the careful hearer of scripture will immediately detect a touch of irony like the one that is heard in

---

3 *dhalil* in Arabic.

Psalm 82. There the “gods, sons of the Most High” (v.5) are “nevertheless (*’aken;* truly, indeed)” ultimately treated—and, more specifically, brought under divine judgment—as “mortal men” (v.6). However, in order to follow the subtler line of thought in Psalm 8, one is to hear it in the original Hebrew. So I am asking my readers’ indulgence in this matter. Here is the RSV text:

> 1 To the choirmaster: according to The Gittith. A Psalm of David.
> O Lord, our Lord, how majestic is thy name in all the earth! Thou
> whose glory above the heavens is chanted 2 by the mouth of babes
> and infants, thou hast founded a bulwark because of thy foes, to
> still the enemy and the avenger. 3 When I look at thy *heavens*, the
> work (*ma‘asey* from the verb *‘aśah* [make]) of thy fingers, *the moon*
> *and the stars* which thou hast established; 4 what is man (*’enoš*) that
> thou art mindful of him, and the son of man (*ben ‘adam*) that thou
> dost care for him? 5 Yet thou hast made him little less (*ḥisser*;
> diminished him) than God (*’elohim*), and dost crown him with
> glory and honor. 6 Thou hast given him dominion over the works
> (*ma‘aśey;* from the verb *‘aśah* [make]) of thy hands; thou hast put
> *all things* (*kol*; all, everything) under his feet, 7 all sheep and oxen,
> and also *the beasts of the field* (*bahamot śadeh*), 8 *the birds (ṣippor) of the*
> *air* (*šamayim;* heavens), *and the fish of the sea (degey hayyam)*, whatever
> passes along the paths of the sea. 9 O Lord, our Lord, how
> majestic is thy name in all the earth! (Ps 8:1-9)

Hearing the English of Psalm 8:4-5 one easily tends to perceive verse 5 in a totally positive light, especially due to the additional “yet” at its beginning. The final result sounds thus: “Although the human being is not worth your attention (v.4), *yet* you made sure to bestow upon him a glory (v.5) reserved to God alone” (v.1). Add to this the use of the verb “make” that describes the divine actions in Genesis 1, and one cannot but draw the connection since the terminology of the rest of the psalm is clearly reminiscent of that chapter. However, the original Hebrew uses the verb *ḥisser* (the *piel* form of *ḥasar*) whose meaning is “make someone lack something;” “deprive someone of something."[4] A second connotation is "lessen," "diminish (someone)." This can be gathered from that the *qal* form *ḥasar* means "diminish" (intransitive), "abate," "fail," "lack":

> … and the waters receded from the earth continually. At the end of a hundred and fifty days the waters had abated (*wayyaḥseru*) … And the waters continued to abate (*weḥasor*) until the tenth month; in the tenth month, on the first day of the month, the tops of the mountains were seen. (Gen 8:3 and 5)

> Suppose five of the fifty righteous are lacking (*yaḥserun*)? Wilt thou destroy the whole city for lack of five? (Gen 18:28)

The negative connotation of *ḥisser* in Psalm 8:5 is preserved in both the LXX and Vulgate. The LXX has *ēlattōsas* from *elattoō* (diminish, make inferior): *ēlattōsas avton brachy ti par' angelous*. The Vulgate uses *minuisti* (diminish). The Vulgate is interesting in that it reinforces the connotation of the verb by adding *minus* to *minuisti*: "*minuisti eum paulo minus ab angelis*." Furthermore, the use of the plural "angels" by both venerable translations to render the original *'elohim* betrays their correct understanding of that noun as referring not to the one scriptural God, but rather to the plurality of the other deities:

> ἠλάττωσας αὐτὸν βραχύ τι παρ' ἀγγέλους (**'elohim**) δόξῃ καὶ τιμῇ ἐστεφάνωσας αὐτόν (LXX)

> minuisti eum paulo minus ab angelis (*'elohim*) gloria et honore coronasti eum (VUL)

My readers are reminded that the original Hebrew 'elohim can be either singular or plural as is evident in the following passage: "And Joshua said to all the people, 'Thus says the Lord, the God

---

4 See for instance the only other occurrence of *ḥisser* in scripture: "Again, I saw vanity under the sun: a person who has no one, either son or brother, yet there is no end to all his toil, and his eyes are never satisfied with riches, so that he never asks, 'For whom am I toiling and depriving (*meḥasser*) myself of pleasure?' This also is vanity and an unhappy business." (Eccl 4:7-8)

(*'elohey*)[5] of Israel, Your fathers lived of old beyond the Euphrates, Terah, the father of Abraham and of Nahor; and they served other gods (*'elohim*).'" (Josh 24:2) In other words, both the LXX and the Vulgate understood that the scriptural author was not comparing the human beings to God, but rather to "divine" beings as in the phrase "sons of God" (understand "divine beings") when referring to men: "When men (*ha'adam*; [generic singular] the human being/s) began to multiply on the face of the ground, and daughters were born to them, the sons of God (*beney ha'elohim*; the sons of the God/gods) saw that the daughters of men were fair; and they took to wife such of them as they chose." (Gen 6:1-2)

The conclusion is that Psalms 8 and 82 are singing the same tune in that they are both conceived to remind the humans and the deities that, notwithstanding all appearances, they both are ultimately accountable for their behavior to the sole scriptural God. The message of Psalm 82 is straightforward, whereas that of Psalm 8 is more subtle. I underscored appearances because the human beings seem to be highly positioned to the extent that they rule over everything (*kol*; all, all things, v.6). However, such is perceived only by theologians who, under the spell of Ancient Greek philosophy, tend to view the human being as the culmination of existence on earth, if not of the universe. However, a closer and more attentive *hearing* of the Psalm will readily show the fallacy of this thesis. I stressed "hearing" because, ultimately, scripture is a literary text and not a philosophical treatise à la Plato's dialogues. I should like then to invite my readers to become hearers while I lead them through Psalm 8.

- The most striking as well as readily detectable feature of this psalm is that it is a recollection of Genesis 1-9 and more specifically chapter 1: the

5 This is the so-called "construct form of a noun," that is, the form that a noun takes when it is followed by a noun complement. For instance, the plural *melakim* becomes *malkey* in the phrase "the kings of Israel."

earth,[6] the heavens,[7] work/works of God,[8] the moon and the stars, *'enoš* (man),[9] *ben 'adam* (son of man),[10] dominion,[11] "all" (*kol*),[12] beasts of the field,[13] birds of the air,[14] fish of the sea.[15]

- If the author is intentionally inviting the hearers to recollect/reminisce Genesis 1-9 while listening to Psalm 8, then the obvious aim is to remind them that the human being failed miserably in his assignment to rule over creation in God's stead. More specifically, his failure was due to his having been lured by the serpent to assume that he could become "like God/gods": "But the serpent said to the woman, 'You will not die. For God knows that when you eat of it your eyes will be opened, and you will be *like God* (*ke'lohim*), knowing good and evil.'" (Gen 3:4-5) The parallelism is even more compelling once one notices that in Genesis 3, the hearers are also faced with the same predicament as in Psalm 8: the Hebrew *'elohim* can refer to either God or gods.

---

6 Throughout Genesis 1:1-2:4.
7 Throughout Genesis 1:1-2:4.
8 The singular work (Ps 8:3) and works (v.6) render the same original plural *ma'aśey* which is from the verb *'aśah* (make) found numerous times in Genesis 1:1-2:4.
9 See the name Enosh (*'enoš*) in Genesis 4:25.
10 See "sons of man" in Genesis 11:5 as well as all the instances of *'adam* and *ha'adam* in Genesis 1-9.
11 From the root *mašal* whose meaning is to rule. Although the verb is not used in conjunction with the human beings in Genesis 1:28, still it describes the rule of the sun and moon over the day and the night in Gen 1:16 and 18.
12 Throughout Genesis 1 and 2.
13 Gen 2:19, 20.
14 The Hebrew *ṣippor šamayim* (birds of the air [heavens]) is a mix of *'oph haššamayim* (birds of the air [heavens]; Gen 1:26, 28, 30); and "every winged bird (*kol 'oph kanaph*) according to its kind" (Gen 1:21); and "every bird (*kol ha'oph*) according to its kind, every bird of every sort (*kol ṣippor kol kanaph*)" (Gen 7:14).
15 Compare *degey hayyam* (the fish/es of the sea; Ps 8:8) with *degat hayyam* (the fish of the sea; Gen 1:26 and 28). *degey* is plural (fishes) and *degat* is generic singular (fish).

- When discussing the terminology of Genesis 1:28 in my commentary on Genesis I have shown that the two verbs used to speak of the human being's rule over the rest of creation reflected kingly rule.[16] In Psalm 45 the king is addressed unequivocally as *'elohim* in v.6: "Your throne, O God (*'elohim*), endures forever and ever. Your royal scepter is a scepter of equity, you love righteousness and hate wickedness." (NRSV)[17] Notice that, a few verses later, he is qualified as *'adon* (lord, master), the same title used of other gods as well as of God throughout scripture.[18] What is interesting in this regard is that the king "as divine being" is no less accountable for upholding equity and righteousness, and fighting wickedness, than the "gods" in Psalm 82. This accountability is fleshed out in another Psalm dealing with kingship:

  > A Psalm of Solomon. Give the king thy justice, O God, and thy righteousness to the royal son! May he judge thy people with righteousness, and thy poor with justice! Let the mountains bear prosperity for the people, and the hills, in righteousness! May he defend the cause of the poor of the people, give deliverance to the needy, and crush the oppressor! … May he have dominion

---

16 *C-Gen* 44-46.

17 RSV has the deferential "Your divine throne endures for ever and ever. Your royal scepter is a scepter of equity."

18 See, e.g., Josh 3:11-13: "Behold, the ark of the covenant of the Lord (*'adon*) of all the earth is to pass over before you into the Jordan. Now therefore take twelve men from the tribes of Israel, from each tribe a man. And when the soles of the feet of the priests who bear the ark of the Lord (*yahweh*), the Lord (*'adon*) of all the earth, shall rest in the waters of the Jordan, the waters of the Jordan shall be stopped from flowing, and the waters coming down from above shall stand in one heap."

(*weyerd*)[19] from sea to sea, and from the River to the ends of the earth! … For he delivers the needy when he calls, the poor and him who has no helper. He has pity on the weak and the needy, and saves the lives of the needy. From oppression and violence he redeems their life; and precious is their blood in his sight." (Psa 72:1-4, 8, 12-14).

- One will readily notice in Psalm 8 that the heavens, the domain of the divine, are beyond the human reach and dominion here as well as in Genesis where the author's interest revolves around the earth, the human domain (Gen 1:2).[20] The entire psalm is conceived as an *inclusio*: "O Lord, our Lord, how majestic is thy name in all the earth! … O Lord, our Lord, how majestic is thy name in all the earth!" (Ps 8:1a, 9) However, the two domains, the divine and the human, are split between the heavens (vv.1b-3), whose denizens, the moon and stars, are beyond the human being's reach—just as is the case in Genesis 1—and the earth, whose denizens are in the latter's care (vv.5-8). The author even uses a literary twist to draw the hearers' attention to the intended differentiation: the heavens are the work (*ma'aśey*) of God's *fingers* (v.3) whereas the human being's dominion is over the works (*ma'aśey*) of God's *hands* (v.6)!

The parallelism in thought between Genesis 1 and Psalm 8 is corroborated if one follows the Book of Psalms as a literary "book" where the individual chapters (psalms) are interrelated

---

19 The original Hebrew uses the same verb *radah* (rule, have dominion over) as the one found in Genesis 1:28: "And God blessed them, and God said to them, 'Be fruitful and multiply, and fill the earth and subdue it; and have dominion (*redu*) over the fish of the sea and over the birds of the air and over every living thing that moves upon the earth.'"

20 See my comments earlier on the earth being the domain of human life, pp. 45-46.

into one story, which I would dub "the story of God and his city Jerusalem," in the same way as I view the Book of Isaiah,[21] and not as a collection of independent proof texts as is the case in patristic thought and in theology throughout the centuries. Psalm 8 is sandwiched between two psalms that set it up to be heard as a "divine judgment" over the king *together with the nations*, just as Psalm 82 is a "divine judgment" over the gods *of the nations*: "Arise, O God, judge the earth; for to thee belong all the nations!" (v.8) Let us hear the three psalms 7, 8, and 9 in tandem. To make matters simpler for my readers I am setting in bold lettering the words and phrases that secure the intimate link between them:

> **Psalm 7:1** A Shiggaion of David, which he sang to the Lord concerning Cush a Benjaminite. O Lord my God, in thee do I take refuge; save me from all my pursuers, and deliver me,
> 2 lest like a lion they rend me, dragging me away, with none to rescue.
> **3 O Lord my God, if I have done this, if there is wrong in my hands,**
> 4 if I have requited my friend with evil or plundered my enemy without cause,
> **5 let the enemy pursue me and overtake me, and let him trample my life to the ground, and <u>lay my soul</u>** (*kabod*, glory as in Ps 8:5) **<u>in the dust</u>.** *Selah*
>
> 6 **Arise** (*qumah*, [emphatic imperative] as in Ps 82:8)**, O Lord, in thy anger,** lift thyself up against the fury of my enemies; awake, O my God; **thou hast appointed a judgment.**
> **7 Let the assembly of the peoples** (*'ummim*)[22] **be gathered about thee; and over it take thy seat on high.**
> **8 The Lord judges the peoples** (*'ammim*)**; judge me, O Lord, according to my righteousness and according to the integrity that is in me.**[23]

21 *OTI3* 98-104.
22 *'ummim, 'ammim* and *goyim* are equivalent and refer to peoples, nations, related human groupings.
23 Notice how it is the same divine judgment that both David and the peoples must submit to. See also Psalm 9:19-20.

9 O let the evil of the wicked come to an end, but establish thou
the righteous, thou who triest the minds and hearts, thou
righteous God.
10 My shield is with God, who saves the upright in heart.
11 **God is a righteous judge, and a God who has
indignation every day.**
**12 If a man does not repent, God will whet his sword;
he has bent and strung his bow;**
**13 he has prepared his deadly weapons, making his
arrows fiery shafts.**
14 Behold, the wicked man conceives evil, and is pregnant with
mischief, and brings forth lies.
15 He makes a pit, digging it out, and falls into the hole which he
has made.
16 His mischief returns upon his own head, and on his own pate
his violence descends.
17 I will give to the Lord the thanks due to his righteousness, and
I will sing praise to **the name of the Lord**,[24] the Most High.

Psalm 8:1 To the choirmaster: according to The Gittith. A Psalm of David. O Lord, our Lord, how majestic is **thy name** in all the earth! Thou whose glory above the heavens is chanted

2 by the mouth of babes and infants, thou hast founded a bulwark
because of thy foes, to still the enemy and the avenger.
3 When I look at thy heavens, **the work of thy fingers**, the
moon and the stars which thou hast established;
4 what is man (*'enoš*) that thou art mindful of him, and the son of
man that thou dost care for him?
5 Yet thou hast made him little less than God, and dost crown
him with **glory** (as in Ps 7:5) and honor.
6 Thou hast given him dominion over **the works of thy
hands**; thou hast put all things under his feet,
7 all sheep and oxen, and also the beasts of the field,
8 the birds of the air, and the fish of the sea, whatever passes
along the paths of the sea.
9 O Lord, our Lord, how majestic is **thy name** in all the earth!

---

24 That brackets the following psalm as an *inclusio.*

Psalm 9:1 To the choirmaster: according to Muthlabben. A Psalm of David. I will give thanks to the Lord with my whole heart; I will tell of all thy wonderful deeds.
2 I will be glad and exult in thee, I will **sing praise to thy name**, O Most High.
3 When my enemies turned back, they stumbled and perished before thee.
4 For thou hast maintained my just cause; **thou hast sat on the throne giving righteous judgment.**
5 Thou hast rebuked the **nations** (*goyim*), thou hast destroyed the wicked; thou hast blotted out their name for ever and ever.
6 The enemy have vanished in everlasting ruins; their cities thou hast rooted out; the very memory of them has perished.
7 But the Lord sits enthroned for ever, he has established his throne for judgment;
8 and he judges the world with righteousness, he judges the **peoples** (*'ummim*) with equity.
9 The Lord is a stronghold for the oppressed, a stronghold in times of trouble.
10 And those who know thy name put their trust in thee, for thou, O Lord, hast not forsaken those who seek thee.

11 Sing praises to the Lord, who dwells in Zion! Tell among the **peoples** (*'ammim*) his deeds!
12 For he who avenges blood is mindful of them; he does not forget the cry of the afflicted.
13 Be gracious to me, O Lord! Behold what I suffer from those who hate me, O thou who liftest me up from the gates of death,
14 that I may recount all thy praises, that in the gates of the daughter of Zion I may rejoice in thy deliverance.
15 The **nations** (*goyim*) have sunk in the pit which they made; in the net which they hid has their own foot been caught.
16 The Lord has made himself known, **he has executed judgment**; the wicked are snared in the work of their own hands. *Higgaion. Selah*
17 The wicked shall depart to Sheol, all the **nations** (*goyim*) that forget God.
18 **For the needy shall not always be forgotten, and the hope of the poor shall not perish for ever.**
19 **Arise** (*qumah*)**, O Lord! Let not man** (*'enoš*) **prevail; let the nations be judged before thee!**

[20] **Put them in fear, O Lord! Let the nations know that they are but men** (*'enoš*)**!** *Selah*

The use of *'enoš* (man) in Psalm 8:4 clearly prepares for the judgment of the same *'enoš* at the end of Psalm 9 where it is used in parallel with "nations": "Arise (*qumah*), O Lord! Let not man (*'enoš*) prevail; let the nations (*goyim*) be judged before thee! Put them in fear, O Lord! Let the nations (*goyim*) know that they are but men (*'enoš*)!" (vv.19-20) These two verses, which function as the closing statement of all three psalms, are important for the following reasons.

1. They are constructed as chiasm A (*'enoš*), B (*goyim*), B' (*goyim*), A' (*'enoš*) and thus are undeniably intended to lump "nations" with every "human being."
2. Since the term *'enoš* is restricted to these verses and (earlier) Psalm 8:4—where it parallels *ben 'adam* (son of man)—it is obvious that the intended is not only every human being, but also and more specifically the human being *as "ruler"* (8:6) *and thus king.*
3. Arise (*qumah*) not only brackets the trilogy of these three psalms (7:6 and 9:20), but is also found in the ending of Psalm 82.

The conclusion is that Psalms 7, 8, and 9 function as a trilogy that parallels in intention and scope Psalm 82: the clearly harsh judgment of all nations together with their rulers, human or divine, because these have failed the muster set up by God for them, the care for the needy, which is his defining trait: "The Lord is a stronghold for the oppressed, a stronghold in times of trouble … The Lord has made himself known, he has executed judgment; the wicked are snared in the work of their own hands. The wicked shall depart to Sheol, all the nations (*goyim*) that forget God. For the needy shall not always be forgotten, and the hope of the poor shall not perish for ever." (Ps 9:9, 16-18)

That Psalm 8 is to be heard in the light of Genesis 1-11 is particularly confirmed in that the judgment of the nations and that of "man" (*'enoš*; [*ben*] *'adam*) are factually one and the same. The evidence is manifold:

- All humankind is subsumed in the repetitive *ha'adam* (*the* human being) that pervades Genesis 1-11 (no less than thirty-six times). This explains why we do not hear of an explanation—sought by many a reader of scripture—as to where Cain's wife came from: "Cain knew his wife, and she conceived and bore Enoch." (Gen 4:17). Add to this that humanity (all human beings) is referred to as *beney ha'adam* (the sons [children] of the human being; Gen 11:5), that is "those pertaining to *ha'adam*, those who are of the kind of *ha'adam*."

- All the *beney ha'adam* are already posited as being in the environment in which we human beings all live, that is to say, already outside the "garden" since "*ha'adam* knew Eve his wife/woman" in Genesis 4:1 after they were both "sent forth from the garden" (3:23) and "driven out of" it (v.24).

- Even after hearing a long list of names of specific individuals (Gen 4-5), the story of the first "universal" punishment has throughout *ha'adam* as the main character, besides God:

  "When men (*ha'adam*) began to multiply on the face of the ground, and daughters were born to them, the sons of God saw that the daughters of men (*ha'adam*) were fair; and they took to wife such of them as they chose. Then the Lord said, "My spirit shall not abide in man (*ha'adam*) for ever, for he is flesh, but his days shall be a hundred and twenty years." The Nephilim were on the earth in those days, and also afterward, when the sons of

> God came in to the daughters of men (*ha'adam*), and they bore children to them. These were the mighty men that were of old, the men of renown. The Lord saw that the wickedness of man (*ha'adam*) was great in the earth, and that every imagination of the thoughts of his heart was only evil continually. And the Lord was sorry that he had made man (*ha'adam*) on the earth, and it grieved him to his heart. So the Lord said, "I will blot out man (*ha'adam*) whom I have created from the face of the ground, man (*'adam*)[25] and beast and creeping things and birds of the air, for I am sorry that I have made them." (Gen 6:1-7)

- The nations mentioned in Genesis 10 are introduced as the *toledot* (birthings) of *beney noaḥ* (the sons of Noah; v.1). Noah is the last descendent in the *toledot* (birthings) of Adam (5:1, 29). Moreover, given the detailed enumeration of the different human groupings, one is to conclude that they are to be taken as all of the "nations" (10:5 twice,[26] 20, 31, 32 twice) or the "families" (10:5, 18, 20, 31, 32) known to the authors and living around their world, the Syro-Arabian wilderness described in Genesis 2:8-14.

The centrality of the divine judgment in scripture is underscored very early on and several times in Genesis at the start of human history: chapters 3 (the man and his wife), 4 (Cain), 6-9 (the entire creation), 11 (the entire humanity gathered around Babel). Such is hardly coincidental despite the absence of the actual classic root *šapaṭ* associated with judgment, which is found twice in Psalm 7, five times in Psalm 9, and four times in Psalm 82. If God is able to judge righteously, it is

25 In this case without the definite article *ha(l)-* (the) because it starts a series of nouns that are used in the generic singular without article, which fits a description of the different "kinds" of "living beings."

26 The first instance is translated as "peoples" in RSV.

because he alone knows how to discern between good and evil, for such knowledge—even the serpent conceded—is reserved to God: "For God knows (*yodea'*; active participle singular; (is) knowing) that when you eat of it your eyes will be opened, and you will be *like God, knowing* (*yode'ey*; active participle plural) *good and evil.*" (Gen 3:5) Notice that, in the original, what is heard is a full correspondence between God, on the one hand, and *ha'adam* and his *woman* (*iššah*), on the other hand. And this is precisely where—for the hearers, the actual addressees of scripture—*ha'adam* and his *woman* proved their foolishness in endorsing the serpent's proposition. The hearers *know* very well from Genesis 1:1-2:5—to which Adam and Eve are not privy, since Adam is formed only two verses later in 2:7 and his woman still much later in v.22—that the only *'elohim* until now is the scriptural *'elohim* who not only created *ha'adam* as male and female in 1:27, but also—as *yahweh 'elohim*—planted the tree of the knowledge of good and evil (2:9).

What is striking is that it is only in this verse that one hears the first time a reference to "evil," whereas "good" has been hammered into the ears of the hearers no less than seven times (1:4, 10, 12, 18, 21, 25, 31) besides the one time immediately preceding "good and evil" in 2:9: "And out of the ground the Lord God made to grow every tree that is pleasant to the sight and *good* for food, the tree of life also in the midst of the garden, and the tree of the knowledge of *good and evil.*" In scripture this knowledge is restricted to the scriptural God exclusively since the other deities (*'elohim*), let alone humans, do not possess it. Consequently, they are judged by the scriptural God in Psalm 82. Moreover, we hear in the same Book of Psalms statements explaining why these deities are incapable of discerning between good and evil. The reason is that—per the scriptural authors and not in accordance with a philosophical or theological mental premise—they do not make use of their "senses":

> Not to us, O Lord, not to us, but to thy name give glory, for the sake of thy steadfast love and thy faithfulness! Why should the nations say, "Where is their God?" Our God is in the heavens; *he*

> *does whatever he pleases.* Their idols are silver and gold, the work of men's hands. They have mouths, but do not speak; eyes, but do not see. They have ears, but do not hear; noses, but do not smell. They have hands, but do not feel; feet, but do not walk; and they do not make a sound in their throat. Those who make them are like them; so are all who trust in them. (Ps 115:1-8)

> The idols of the nations are silver and gold, the work of men's hands. They have mouths, but they speak not, they have eyes, but they see not, they have ears, but they hear not, nor is there any breath in their mouths. Like them be those who make them!—yea, every one who trusts in them! (Ps 135:15-18)

Philosophy and theology do not speak in this manner about idols or false deities. These two branches of human endeavor do not even speak in this manner of the scriptural God himself since, according to both, God is a "pure spirit" if not *the* ultimate and quintessential spirit. Not so the scriptural God since he does whatever he pleases (Ps 115:3) *including smelling*:

> And when the Lord smelled the pleasing odor, the Lord said in his heart, "I will never again curse the ground because of man, for the imagination of man's heart is evil from his youth; neither will I ever again destroy every living creature as I have done. While the earth remains, seedtime and harvest, cold and heat, summer and winter, day and night, shall not cease." (Gen 8:21-22)

Were it not for his sense of smell (humorous pun intended) there would have been no hope for humanity or for the entire world. And for those who still do not take seriously that the scriptural God enjoys humor, let me quote how the Book of Psalms describes God while he is emitting his judgment against his enemies, nations as well as individuals:

> [1] Why do the nations conspire, and the peoples plot in vain? [2] The kings of the earth set themselves, and the rulers take counsel together, against the Lord and his anointed, saying, [3] "Let us burst their bonds asunder, and cast their cords from us." [4] *He who*

> *sits in the heavens*[27] *laughs; the Lord has them in derision.* 5 Then he will
> speak to them in his wrath, and terrify them in his fury, saying, 6
> "I have set my king on Zion, my holy hill." 7 I will tell of the decree
> of the Lord: He said to me, "You are my son, today I have
> begotten you. 8 Ask of me, and I will make the nations your
> heritage, and the ends of the earth your possession. 9 You shall
> break them with a rod of iron, and dash them in pieces like a
> potter's vessel." 10 Now therefore, O kings, be wise; be warned, O
> rulers of the earth. 11 Serve the Lord with fear, with trembling 12
> kiss his feet, lest he be angry, and you perish in the way; for his
> wrath is quickly kindled. Blessed are all who take refuge in him.
> (Ps 2:1-12)

To top it all off, whereas the other deities have "feet, but do not walk (*hillek;* walk intently, with assurance; [the *piel* form of *halak*, walk]; Ps 115:7) he—without having feet—"walks back and forth, ambles to and fro" (*hithallek;* the *hiphil* form of *halak*) and no less "in the cool of the day" (Gen 3:8). Not only that, but he requires from his "elect" to follow his example:

> Enoch walked (*hithallek*) with God after the birth of Methuselah three hundred years, and had other sons and daughters. Thus all the days of Enoch were three hundred and sixty-five years. Enoch walked (*hithallek*) with God; and he was not, for God took him. (Gen 5:22-24)

> But Noah found favor in the eyes of the Lord. These are the generations of Noah. Noah was a righteous man, blameless in his generation; Noah walked (*hithallek*) with God. (Gen 6:8-9)

> The Lord said to Abram … Arise, walk (*hithallek*) through the length and the breadth of the land, for I will give it to you (Gen 13:17)

> When Abram was ninety-nine years old the Lord appeared to Abram, and said to him, "I am God Almighty; walk (*hithallek*) before me, and be blameless. And I will make my covenant between me and you, and will multiply you exceedingly." (Gen 17:1-2)

---

27 Compare with "God has taken his place in the divine council; in the midst of the gods he holds judgment" (Ps 82:1).

13

The Book of Jonah and God's Total Control

To hear that the scriptural God has total control over the waters and its sea monster, Leviathan, the *tannin*, is definitely the ultimate relief even though the seas are not the natural habitat of the human beings who live on the dry land. However, this aspect of the scriptural God should not come as a surprise for anyone who listened carefully to Genesis 1:21-22 and chapters 6-8 because they presage the final victory of God's rule over all nations as well as the creation where the nations subsist.

For the humans, the *tannin* of the seas may seem threatening, however, it was "created" (*bara'*) *in the sea* and blessed by God to multiply (Gen 1:21-22), and even formed (*yaṣar*) *in the sea* in order to "sport" in it (Ps 104:25-26) as a fish would do in a pond. After all, the "great sea monsters" (Gen 1:21) are nothing else than "fish of the sea" (vv.26, 28) in God's eyes. This, in turn, explains how the same terrifying "great sea monsters" can be used by the same God to further a mission of good will toward the nations. A study of the Book of Jonah will confirm this. By the same token, it will confirm that the authors of Genesis 1 and 6-8 were already preparing vocabulary-wise for Jonah, which will substantiate that, from the outset, scripture was conceived as a unitary product.

In the case of Jonah, the argument is overwhelming; even the vocabulary of the LXX which follows a different path than the original Hebrew arrives at the same result. Such cannot be explained unless one endorses that the authors of the LXX understood what the original Hebrew was endeavoring to do or, more along the lines of my conviction, that the two texts were produced by the same authors.[1] Only the original author can take such liberty and yet succeed in linking two scriptural books so far apart in the canon.

The Hebrew Book of Jonah presents the following striking features. Earlier I pointed out how *gedolim* (great) as adjective qualifying *tanninim* (sea monsters) is as unwarranted as it is awkward. Nowhere else in scripture is *tannin* (sea monster) qualified with any adjective. It is as though there is no need to aggrandize it. But, as I repeatedly maintain, any unwarranted addition cannot but be intended and thus functional. Nowadays where writing is electronic and any additional words are not costly, the spell check of the Microsoft Office program still keeps suggesting the elimination of unnecessary additional wording by highlighting it and commenting, "Consider using concise language," with a few suggestions.[2] Now imagine how much more important it is to be concise when writing is done on expensive parchment with equally expensive ink, not to mention the painstaking calligraphy. The clue to any unwarranted addition, especially in the opening chapter of such a huge literature as scripture, is often not found until much later in the manuscript. This is precisely what I have been trying to show and defend in this study of the beginning chapters of Genesis. So, the strange addition of *gedolim* in Genesis 1:21 functions as a teaser whose resolution will not be found until the Book of Jonah, where we encounter a parallel strangeness.

The Book of Jonah sounds as though it is sprinkled all over with the adjective *gadol* (great). It is used, in the Hebrew original, fourteen times over forty-eight verses, that is, once every three and a half verses—the highest percentage in the entire scripture. Moreover, one cannot possibly miss the close similarity in vocabulary between Jonah, on the one hand, and Genesis 1-2 and 6-8, on the other hand.

---

1 See my argument in *ROS* 39-40.

2 E.g., consider using the straightforward "in this case" instead of the wordy "in this particular case."

- In the beginning God created the heavens (*haššamayim*) and the earth ... And God said, "Let the waters under the heavens be gathered together into one place, and let the dry land (*hayyabbašah*) appear." And it was so. God called the dry land (*hayyabbašah*) Earth, and the waters that were gathered together he called Seas (*yammim*). And God saw that it was good. (Gen 1:1, 9-10)

  I am a Hebrew; and I fear the Lord, the God of heaven (*haššamayim*), who made the sea (*yam*) and the dry land (*hayyabbašah*)." (Jon 1:9)

- The earth was without form and void, and darkness was upon the face of the deep (*tehom*); and the Spirit (*ruaḥ*) of God was moving over the face of the waters (*mayim*). (Gen 1:2)

  But the Lord hurled a great wind (*ruaḥ*) upon the sea, and there was a mighty tempest on the sea. (Jon 1:4) The waters (*mayim*) closed in over me, the deep (*tehom*) was round about me. (Jon 2:5).

- So the Lord God caused a deep sleep (*tardemah*) to fall upon the man. (Gen 2:21)

  But Jonah had gone down into the inner part of the ship and had lain down, and was fast asleep (*wayyeradam*). So the captain came and said to him, "What do you mean, you sleeper (*yirdam*)?" (Jon 1:5-6)

- Then God said, "Let us make man in our image, after our likeness; and let them have dominion over the fish of the sea (*degat hayyam*), and over the birds of the air, and over the cattle, and over all the earth, and over every creeping thing that

> creeps upon the earth." So God created man in his own image, in the image of God he created him; male and female he created them. And God blessed them, and God said to them, "Be fruitful and multiply, and fill the earth and subdue it; and have dominion over the fish of the sea (*degat hayyam*) and over the birds of the air and over every living thing that moves upon the earth." (Gen 1:26-28)

> And the Lord appointed a great fish (*dag gadol*) to swallow up Jonah; and Jonah was in the belly of the fish (*haddag*) three days and three nights. Then Jonah prayed to the Lord his God (*yahweh 'elohayw*)[3] from the belly of the fish (*haddag*) … And the Lord spoke to the fish (*laddag*), and it vomited out Jonah upon the dry land (*hayyabbašah*)." (Jon 1:17-2:1, 10)

It is specifically this last comparison that brings with it the resolution to the enigma of the addition of "great" before "sea monsters" in Genesis 1:21. The use of the adjective *gadol* in conjunction with a singular fish in Jonah 1:17 is a necessary ingredient for the plausibility of the story. For those familiar with scriptural Hebrew, the intentionality is unmissable in that the noun *dag* and its counterpart *dagah* are generic singulars, just as the English fish or deer indicates a plurality of fish or deer as well as a singular animal. In scripture *dag* referring to a single fish, and no less than four times in a row, occurs only in Jonah. An attentive and even not so attentive hearer can hardly miss the reference to one of the "great sea monsters" (*tanninim*) of Genesis 1:21 especially that, in that context, these *tanninim* parallel the generic singular *dagah* of verses 26 and 28.[4] Notice that in Jonah the hearer's attention is drawn to that individual fish per se in that it appears all four times on its own and not in

---

3 See the repeated "the Lord God" (*yahweh 'elohim*) in Genesis 2 and 3.

4 *degat* heard in those verses is the construct form of *dagah*, which is the form a noun takes when followed by another noun as its complement, as in "the fish of the sea."

grammatical relation to the "sea" that occurs in 1:15—two verses before verse 17—or "seas" that occur in 2:3—two verses after 2:1 and seven verses before 2:10.

That the writers of Genesis 1 had in mind the Book of Jonah is further evident in the use of the adjective *gadol* (great) to expressly qualify Nineveh in Genesis 10:

> Cush became the father of Nimrod; he was the first on earth to be a mighty man. He was a mighty hunter before the Lord; therefore it is said, "Like Nimrod a mighty hunter before the Lord." The beginning of his kingdom was Babel, Erech, and Accad, all of them in the land of Shinar. From that land he went into Assyria, and built Nineveh, Rehobothir, Calah, and Resen between Nineveh and Calah; that is the great city (*hw' [hi'] ha'ir haggedolah*) (vv.8-12)

The intentional reference to Nineveh and as a great city, to boot, is undeniable. Until the Book of Jonah, where it occurs nine times in four chapters, three of which as specifically "that great city," Nineveh is heard of only twice in a copycat passage in 2 Kings 19:36 and Isaiah 37:37: "Then Sennacherib king of Assyria departed, and went home, and dwelt at Nineveh."[5] Moreover, the mention of Nineveh in Genesis 10:11-12 is clearly an unnecessary aside after the reference to Nimrod's city Babel in the land of Shinar which is shortly going to be the topic of an entire episode (Gen 11:1-9):

> And as men migrated from the east, they found a plain *in the land of Shinar* and settled there. And they said to one another, "Come, let us make bricks, and burn them thoroughly." And they had brick for stone, and bitumen for mortar. Then they said, "Come, let us build ourselves a city, and a tower with its top in the heavens, and let us make a name for ourselves, lest we be scattered abroad upon the face of the whole earth." … So the Lord scattered them abroad from there over the face of all the earth, and they left off building the city. Therefore its name was called *Babel*, because there the Lord confused the language of all

---

5 Isaiah 36-37 is a verbatim copy of 2 Kings 18:13-19:47.

> the earth; and from there the Lord scattered them abroad over the face of all the earth. (vv.2-4, 8-9)

In other words, Genesis 10 was phrased with Jonah already in mind.

Earlier I pointed out that the qualification of the *tanninim* (sea monsters) as *gedolim* (great) in Genesis 1:21 sounded redundant, if not oxymoronic. The LXX will show how it used this as an opportunity to prepare for the message of the Book of Jonah in a manner that reflects the consistency of scripture. Let us compare the two texts:

> So God created the great sea monsters (Hebrew *hattanninim haggedolim*; Greek, *ta kētē ta megala*) and every living creature that moves, with which the waters swarm, according to their kinds, and every winged bird according to its kind. (Gen 1:21)

> Then God said, "Let us make man in our image, after our likeness; and let them have dominion over the fish of the sea (Hebrew *degat hayyam*; Greek, *tōn ikhthyōn tēs thalassēs*) and over the birds of the air, and over the cattle, and over all the earth, and over every creeping thing that creeps upon the earth." So God created man in his own image, in the image of God he created him; male and female he created them. And God blessed them, and God said to them, "Be fruitful and multiply, and fill the earth and subdue it; and have dominion over the fish of the sea (Hebrew *degat hayyam*; Greek, *tōn ikhthyōn tēs thalassēs*) and over the birds of the air and over every living thing that moves upon the earth." (Gen 1:27-28)

So, to render the Hebrew *tanninim* in Genesis 1:21 the LXX opted for *kētē* (the plural of *kētos*) rather than *drakontes* (dragons), the plural of *drakōn* (dragon), a term that is found profusely in the LXX to speak of Leviathan (Is 27:1 [twice]; Job 40:25; 41:1; Ps 73:14; 103:26;), serpents (Ex 7:9, 10, 12; Is 27:1; Am 9:6; Job 26:13), and even sea monsters (Deut 32:33; Jer 28:34; Lam 4:3; Ezek 29:3; 32:2; Job 7:12; Ps 73:13; 90:13; 148:7). In Job the LXX used the singular *kētos* to translate Leviathan (3:8) and Rahab (26:12) and the plural *kētē* to render the "helpers of Rahab" (9:13).

In the case of Jonah, what is unique is that the LXX used, no less than three times, *kētos* to speak of the fish whose original Hebrew is the singular *dag* which is precisely from the same root as *dagah* that occurs in Genesis 1:26 and 28 parallel to the *tanninim* of verse 21. In other words, in its own way and independently of the Hebrew, the LXX draws the hearers' attention to Genesis 1. The LXX translators understood the intention of the Hebrew, namely, that it was looking ahead to the Book of Jonah, and in this case took their liberties, which militates support for my thesis that they are themselves the authors of the original Hebrew. They took seriously that the "fish" in Jonah was "great," and not just any fish, in order for it to function in the story as having "swallowed" the prophet. It is then, in both the Hebrew and the Greek, that the link lies in the additional adjective "great" that is heard in both languages in Genesis 1:21 as qualifying an already "large animal" in view of the Jonah story.

yabbašah *(dry land)*

An additional feature of Jonah—and unimpressive at first hearing—will confirm that the authors of Genesis 1 had in mind that later book in the canon. No hearer of Genesis can possibly miss the unique phraseology associated with the formation of the earth. Whereas all other components of the world are created (*bara'*), made (*'aśah*), or commanded to be (*yehi*), the only exception is the earth whose formation is coined as being as an "appearance" in that it was wrenched out of the all-encompassing hegemony of the waters of the seas that had to be "gathered together in one place" to allow the earth to "appear, be seen":

> The earth (*'eres*) was without form and void, and darkness was upon the face of *the deep*; and the Spirit of God was moving over the face of *the waters*. (Gen 1:2)

> And God said, "Let the waters under the heavens be gathered together (*yiqqawu*) into one place, and let the dry land (*yabbašah*)

> appear (*wetera'eh*; be seen)." And it was so. God called the dry land (*yabbašah*) Earth (*'ereṣ*), and the waters that were gathered together he called Seas. And God saw that it was good. (Gen 1:9-10)

Moreover, since the noun *'ereṣ* was used earlier (v.1), the author introduced the noun *yabbašah* (dry land) to qualify specifically the "non-watery" aspect of the ground upon which land animals and birds as well as humans will live. Still, the name "earth," by which that dry land was to be known, was given to it by God himself, which explains the rarity of the term *yabbašah* in scripture (a total of sixteen instances), whereas, the term *'eres* is ubiquitous. Understandably, *yabbašah* is used six times in the episode of the exodus from Egypt (Ex 14:16, 22, 29; 15:19; Ps 66:6; Neh 9:11) and once in its counterpart, the crossing of the Jordan River (Josh 4:22). Its use in Psalm 95:5 is reminiscent of Genesis 1: "The sea is his, for he made it; for his hands formed the dry land." What is truly remarkable are the three instances it is found in Jonah (four chapters with a mere forty verses), compared to the six times it is used in Exodus (forty chapters with a total of 1213 verses).

> And he said to them, "I am a Hebrew; and I fear the Lord, the God of heaven, who made the sea and the dry land." (Jon 1:9)

> Nevertheless the men rowed hard to bring the ship back to land (*yabbašah*), but they could not, for the sea grew more and more tempestuous against them. (Jon 1:13)

> And the Lord spoke to the fish, and it vomited out Jonah upon the dry land. (Jon 2:10)

The latter two instances are understandable in that they refer to the rescue of Jonah from the raging waters, which is the theme of chapters 1 and 2. It is then the first instance (1:9) that is unexpected and, consequently, intentionally pointing to Genesis 1 through the reference not only to sea and dry land, which are functional in the story, but also and more importantly to heaven (*šamayim*)[6] and in a striking way. The Lord is referred

---

6 The Hebrew does not differentiate between "heavens" and "heaven" and uses the one *šamayim* throughout scripture.

to as essentially "the God of heaven" who (also) "made the sea and the dry land." This statement corresponds perfectly to Genesis 1 where "heaven/s" is heard in the opening verse (In the beginning God created the heavens and the earth) and again in verse 8, whereas the nouns "dry land" and "sea" are first mentioned in verses 9 and 10, respectively. Still what is ingenious about Jonah 1:9 is the seemingly totally irrelevant "I am a Hebrew," that points to the Book of Exodus where we hear no less than six times the phrase "the Lord, the God of the Hebrews" in conjunction with the planning of the exodus from Egypt (Ex 3:18; 5:3; 7:16; 9:1, 13; 10:3). The conclusion, or at least the distinct impression, is that, out of the blue, the Book of Jonah reaches out beyond the Prophets, Prior as well as Latter, and the last three books of the Law (Leviticus, Numbers, and Deuteronomy), all the way back to Exodus and Genesis in a way that is not encountered in any other Old Testament book. What is astounding, however, is that this reach is not only topical but also, and more so, terminological. It is as though Genesis 1 was written the way it was *in view of* Jonah.

Why is the Book of Jonah so special?

That Jonah holds a place of honor among the canonical prophets is evident in that he is the only one who is referred to in the Prior Prophets and, to boot, under his full appellation "Jonah the son of Amittai" just as in the title of the Book of Jonah:[7]

> In the fifteenth year of Amaziah the son of Joash, king of Judah, Jeroboam the son of Joash, king of Israel, began to reign in Samaria, and he reigned forty-one years. And he did what was evil in the sight of the Lord; he did not depart from all the sins of Jeroboam the son of Nebat, which he made Israel to sin. *He restored the border of Israel from the entrance of Hamath as far as the Sea of the Arabah, according to the word of the Lord, the God of Israel, which he*

7 The case of Isaiah does not negate this assertion since he is mentioned repeatedly in a lengthy episode 2 Kings 18:13-20:19 which is a verbatim copy of Is 36-39.

> *spoke by his servant Jonah the son of Amittai, the prophet*, who was from Gathhepher. For the Lord saw that the affliction of Israel was very bitter, for there was none left, bond or free, and there was none to help Israel. But the Lord had not said that he would blot out the name of Israel from under heaven, so he saved them by the hand of Jeroboam the son of Joash. Now the rest of the acts of Jeroboam, and all that he did, and his might, how he fought, and how he recovered for Israel Damascus and Hamath, which had belonged to Judah, are they not written in the Book of the Chronicles of the Kings of Israel? And Jeroboam slept with his fathers, the kings of Israel, and Zechariah his son reigned in his stead. (2 Kg 14:23-29)

This story is evidently functional since it sheds light on the frustration of the same prophet with his assigned mission to Nineveh by "the word" of the same "Lord God" (Jon 1:9; 2:1, 6; 4:6). Nineveh, the capital city of the Assyrians that—according to scriptural chronology—two decades later would sack Samaria, the capital city of the Kingdom of Israel that was restored to the glory it enjoyed under David and Solomon by Jeroboam "according to the word of the Lord, the God of Israel, which he spoke by his servant Jonah the son of Amittai, the prophet" (2 Kg 14:25). So, the hearers are prepared to understand, but not excuse, the prophet's recalcitrance in the Book of Jonah.

The unique feature of the Book of Jonah is that it is the only one among the Prophetic Books that relates a story "against the grain." In all the other books the addressees refuse, to the chagrin of the prophet, his message of repentance. In Jonah we witness the exact opposite: the addressees accept the call for repentance and enact such, to the chagrin of the prophet! Add to this that the addressees in this case are the Lord God's as well as the prophet's "enemies," as witnessed in the two following Books of Nahum (1:1; 2:8; 3:7) and Zephaniah (2:13). Also of interest is the totally unexpected phraseology of the kingly decree:

> 4 Jonah began to go into the city, going a day's journey. And he
> cried, "Yet forty days, and Nineveh shall be overthrown!" 5 And

> the people of Nineveh believed God; they proclaimed a fast, and
> put on sackcloth, from the greatest of them to the least of them. 6
> Then tidings reached the king of Nineveh, and he arose from his
> throne, removed his robe, and covered himself with sackcloth,
> and sat in ashes. 7 And he made proclamation and published
> through Nineveh, "By the decree of the king and his nobles: Let
> neither man (*ha'adam*) nor beast (*habbehemah*), herd (*habbaqar*) nor
> flock (*haṣṣon*), taste (*yiṭ'amu*) anything; let them not feed (*yir'u*), or
> *drink* water, 8 but let man (*ha'adam*) and beast (*habbehemah*) be
> covered with sackcloth, and let them cry (*yiqre'u*) mightily
> (*beḥozqah*) to God; yea, let every one (*'iš*) turn from his evil (*hara'ah*)
> way (*darko*) and from the violence (*ḥamas*) which is in his hands. 9
> Who knows, God (*ha'elohim*) may yet repent (*niḥam*) and turn from
> his fierce anger, so that we perish (*no'bed*) not?" (Jon 3:4-9)

A close and detailed analysis of this passage will readily show that it is a compressed version of both Genesis 1-9 and the crucial chapter 34 of Ezekiel. This is no menial feat given that Genesis is the constitutional book of the entire scripture, and Ezekiel is the "father of scripture" whose presence is unmistakably detectable in the episode of the tower of Babel (Gen 11:1-9) where we hear unwarrantedly that the building of the city (Babel) and its tower took place in the *biq'ah* (plain; Gen 11:2) that is a staple of the Book of Ezekiel. Following are the main striking features of Jonah 3:4-9.

1. The most impressive feature is the inclusion of the animals in the act of repentance, which is unique in scripture. However, their eventual punishment is in accordance with a divine rule that is found early in Genesis: "Only you shall not eat flesh with its life, that is, its blood. *For your lifeblood I will surely require a reckoning; of every beast I will require it and of man*; of every man's brother I will require the life of man." (9:4-5) That is why, and despite its strangeness, they are to join the human beings in their crying out (*qara'*) to God (Jon 3:8). The verb *qara'* (spell out; call; read

aloud) is reserved to God and humans in scripture. Notice also, when speaking of every "one," human or animal, the author uses *iš* which is usually used of the male human being. This corroborates the link to the flood episode where we hear *'iš we'išto* (human male and his woman) to describe the animal pairs (Gen 7:2).

2. The importance given this matter is evident on two levels. On the one hand, twice in Jonah 3:7 and 8 both "man" and "beast" are introduced with the definite article *ha(l)*. On the other hand, although *behemah* (beast; cattle) is encompassing of land mammals as in Genesis 1:24, 25, 26; 2:20; 3:14; 7:14, 21; 8:1; 9:10, the author seems intent to stress the totality of all land mammals by adding "herd" and "flock"—also preceded by the definite article—perhaps with the intention of saying that the Ninevites are no different than the Hebrew forebears of Jonah "the Hebrew" (Jon 1:9) who are repeatedly introduced as having "flock" and "herd" (Gen 12:6; 13:5; 20:14; 21:27; 24:35; 26:14; etc.).

3. The inclusion of the flock (Jon 3:7) is probably triggered by what the hearers faced earlier in Ezekiel concerning the misbehavior of sheep toward fellow sheep (34:17-22), especially in view of the similar phraseology. While the use of the verb *ra'ah* (graze; feed on the grass) is natural in the context of a flock, in Jonah it is doubled up with the verb *ṭa'am* (taste; eat). This doubling is clearly intentional since "drink" occurs only once and with no counterpart. It is as though drinking applies to both humans and animals, whereas tasting has in view humans, and grazing is specifically aimed at the herd and the flock. Whenever the verb *ra'ah* is used of humans, it

means "shepherd, feed the sheep." This is precisely what is heard in Ezekiel 34 where the verb *ra'ah* occurs in both senses, in conjunction with the shepherds and, respectively, the sheep. Still, what is important for our discussion is that the passage in which the sheep are judged on their behavior uses twice the verbs "feed" and "drink" in parallel, just as is the case in Jonah 3:7 where they also appear in parallel:

> As for you, my *flock*, thus says the Lord God: Behold, I judge between sheep and sheep, rams and he-goats. Is it not enough for you to *feed* (*ra'ah*) on the good pasture (*mir'eh*; same root as *ra'ah*), that you must tread down with your feet the rest of your pasture (*mir'eh*; same root as *ra'ah*); and to *drink* of clear water, that you must foul the rest with your feet? And must my sheep *eat* (*ra'ah*) what you have trodden with your feet, and *drink* what you have fouled with your feet? Therefore, thus says the Lord God to them: Behold, I, I myself will judge between the fat sheep and the lean sheep. Because you push with side and shoulder, and thrust at all the weak with your horns, till you have scattered them abroad, I will save my *flock*, they shall no longer be a prey; and I will judge between sheep and sheep. (Ezek 34:17-22)

This can hardly be considered happenstance. The unnecessary use of the extremely rare adverb *beḥozqah* (mightily)—from the root *ḥazaq*—to qualify the cry of prayer in Jonah 3:8 may well be a deft allusion to the name of the Prophet *yeḥezqe'l* (Ezekiel) from the same root *ḥazaq*. The only other three instances of *beḥozqah* are

Judges 4:3;[8] 8:1[9] and 1 Samuel 2:16,[10] and in all three cases with the connotation of "violently, oppressively." In turn, this goes hand in hand with Jonah's reference to the evil actions of humans and animals as acts of "violence" (*ḥamas*) in the same verse 8 of chapter 3.

4. The terminology and phraseology used to introduce the first major universal calamity in scripture (Gen 6) provides the pieces for the terminology and phraseology heard in Jonah 3:8-9:

> The Lord saw that the wickedness (*ra'at*; evil) of man was great in the earth, and that every imagination of the thoughts of his heart was only evil (*ra'*) continually. And the Lord was sorry (*wayinnaḥem*; from the root *niḥam*) that he had made man on the earth, and it grieved him to his heart. So the Lord said, "I will blot out man whom I have created from the face of the ground, man (*'adam*) and beast (*behemah*) and creeping things and birds of the air, for I am sorry (*niḥamti*) that I have made them." But Noah found favor in the eyes of the Lord. These are the generations of Noah. Noah was a righteous man, blameless in his generation; Noah walked with God (*ha'elohim*). And Noah had three sons, Shem, Ham, and Japheth. Now the earth was corrupt in God's (*ha'elohim*) sight, and the earth was filled with violence (*ḥamas*). And God saw the earth, and behold, it was corrupt; for all flesh (*baśar*; singular masculine) had corrupted their[11] way (*darko*) upon the earth. And God said to Noah, 'I have determined to make an end of all flesh; for the earth

---

8 Then the people of Israel cried to the Lord for help; for he had nine hundred chariots of iron, and oppressed the people of Israel *cruelly* for twenty years.
9 And the men of Ephraim said to him, "What is this that you have done to us, not to call us when you went to fight with Midian?" And they upbraided him *violently*.
10 And if the man said to him, "Let them burn the fat first, and then take as much as you wish," he would say, "No, you must give it now; and if not, I will take it *by force*."
11 "his" masculine singular in Hebrew; hence *darko* (his way) as in Jonah 4:8 where the referent is *'iś* (each one) that is masculine singular.

> is filled with violence (*ḥamas*) through them; behold, I will destroy them with the earth. (Gen 6:5-13)
>
> But let man and beast be covered with sackcloth, and let them cry mightily to God; yea, let every one turn from his evil (*ra'ah*) way (*darko*) and from the violence (*ḥamas*) which is in his hands. Who knows, God may yet repent (*niḥam*) and turn from his fierce anger, so that we perish not? (Jon 3:8-9)

The Jonah Story and the Flood Story

The connection of the Book of Jonah to Genesis 1-11 is overarching. We have seen that, besides Genesis 1, the book of Jonah recalls Genesis 10 through the repeated mention of the Hamite Nineveh and the Japhethite Tarshish. Yet the most direct connection between the two books lies in the prophet's name *yonah*—whose meaning is "dove"[12]—that plays a pivotal role at the conclusion of the flood story:

> At the end of forty days Noah opened the window of the ark which he had made, and sent forth a raven; and it went to and fro until the waters were dried up (*yebošet*) from the earth. Then he sent forth a *dove* from him, to see if the waters had subsided from the face of the ground; but the *dove* found no place to set her foot, and she returned to him to the ark, for the waters were still on the face of the whole earth. So he put forth his hand and took her and brought her into the ark with him. He waited another seven days, and again he sent forth the *dove* out of the ark; and the *dove* came back to him in the evening, and lo, in her mouth a freshly plucked olive leaf; so Noah knew that the waters had subsided from the earth. Then he waited another seven days, and sent forth the *dove*; and she did not return to him any more. In the six hundred and first year, in the first month, the first day of the month, the waters were dried from off the earth; and Noah

12 *yonah* is a feminine noun given to a man. Although strange, we have a similar case in Arabic. The feminine noun *bisharat* meaning "good news, gospel, annunciation" is bestowed only on men.

> removed the covering of the ark, and looked, and behold, the face of the ground was dry. In the second month, on the twenty-seventh day of the month, the earth was dry (*yabešah*). (Gen 8:6-14)

The intended parallelism between the two "doves" is unmissable:

- In both cases, Jonah and the dove reach the end of their "stories" when they have accomplished the "mission" for which they were sent.
- In both cases, the end of the mission is linked to the *yabbašah* (dry land): "Nevertheless the men rowed hard to bring the ship back to land (*yabbašah*; dry land), but they could not, for the sea grew more and more tempestuous against them. (Jon 1:13);" "And the Lord spoke to the fish, and it vomited out Jonah upon the dry land (*yabbašah*)." (2:10)
- In Genesis, the dove's message was delivered when it found vegetative *life* on the "dry land." In the case of Jonah it is the drying up of a plant—and thus a sign of *death*—that gave the clue to the prophet as to what his message was all about: "But when dawn came up the next day, God appointed a worm which attacked the plant, so that it withered (*yibaš*)." (Jon 4:7)
- Lastly, and most importantly, in both cases, we have a full inclusion of all humanity. The three sons of Noah were together in the ark. In the Book of Jonah, we have Shem, the father of all the children of *'eber* (Eber; Gen 10:21), that is the *'abarim* (Hebrews) among whom is Jonah the *'ibri* (Hebrew; Jon 1:9); Ham is represented by Nineveh; and Japheth is represented by Tarshish.

It would be worth our while at this point to investigate in more detail the scriptural interplay between the two stories (the flood story and the story of Jonah) to show how the authors had the Book of Jonah in mind while penning Genesis 6-8.

Let me start with the least conspicuous aspect of universality since, for obvious reasons, it is handled only in an oblique way, yet skillfully enough for a sensitive ear. In a short book of merely forty-eight verses one hears the verb *'abad* ([utterly] perish) four times, twice very early on the lips of the sailors, once as a statement, and the other time as request not to perish:

> So the captain came and said to him, "What do you mean, you sleeper? Arise, call upon your god! Perhaps the god will give a thought to us, that we do not perish (*lo' no'bad*)." (Jon 1:6)

> Therefore they cried to the Lord, "We beseech thee, O Lord, let us not perish (*'al-na' no'bedah*) for this man's life, and lay not on us innocent blood; for thou, O Lord, hast done as it pleased thee." (Jon 1:14)

> And he [the King of Nineveh] made proclamation and published through Nineveh ... Who knows, God may yet repent and turn from his fierce anger, so that we perish not (*lo' no'bad*)?" (Jon 3:7, 9)

> And the Lord God appointed a *plant*, and made it come up over Jonah, that it might be a shade over his head, to save him from his discomfort. So Jonah was exceedingly glad because of the *plant*. But when dawn came up the next day, God appointed a worm which attacked the *plant*, so that it withered. When the sun rose, God appointed a sultry east wind, and the sun beat upon the head of Jonah so that he was faint; and he asked that he might die, and said, "It is better for me to die than to live." But God said to Jonah, "Do you do well to be angry for the *plant*?" And he said, "I do well to be angry, angry enough to die." And the Lord said, "You pity the *plant*, for which you did not labor, nor did you make it grow, which came into being in a night, and perished (*'abad*) in a night. And should not I pity Nineveh, that great city, in which there are more than a hundred and twenty thousand

> persons who do not know their right hand from their left, and also much cattle (*behemah*)?" (Jon 4:6-11)

The sailors' perishing under the raging waters of the sea, as well as the perishing of the Ninevites and their animals on dry land, combined with the mention of a plant—all of which is said to have been done at God's command—cannot but recall God's decision to "blot out" everything that lives from the face of the ground (Gen 6:6-7). Still it is striking that the "plant," whose Hebrew original *qiqayon* (gourd; pumpkin) is found only here in scripture, is referred to no less than five times in five verses right at the end of the story where life on the earth of the Ninevites is spared, just as that of the sailors at the beginning of the story. The intentionality of this feature cannot be fathomed except by hearers cognizant of scriptural Hebrew. Not even the Greek and the Latin translations can reflect what is heard in Hebrew. The name of the prophet *yonah* is exactly the same word that is used to refer to the dove that plays the most important role in the announcement of the end of the flood and in conjunction with the vegetation, that is, plant life, to boot:

> At the end of forty days Noah opened the window of the ark which he had made, and sent forth a raven; and it went to and fro until the waters were dried up from the earth. Then he sent forth a dove (*yonah*) from him, to see if the waters had subsided from the face of the ground; but the dove (*yonah*) found no place to set her foot, and she returned to him to the ark, for the waters were still on the face of the whole earth. So he put forth his hand and took her and brought her into the ark with him. He waited another seven days, and again he sent forth the dove (*yonah*) out of the ark; and the dove (*yonah*) came back to him in the evening, and lo, in her mouth a freshly plucked olive leaf; so Noah knew that the waters had subsided from the earth. Then he waited another seven days, and sent forth the dove (*yonah*); and she did not return to him any more. (Gen 8:6-12)

To consider this matter as mere happenstance is belied by the fact that "dove" is mentioned *five times in five verses* just as the "plant" is in the Book of Jonah. I have no doubt that many Christian and Jewish scholars, as well as "believers" schooled in the Platonic ways of theology, would dismiss my argument regarding the connection between the flood and Jonah as fanciful and having nothing to do with the essentially anthropocentric message of scripture. However, my hope lies with the scriptural God and those who still have "ears to hear" instead of "minds to think." For whatever the "thoughts" of great thinkers, or even not so great thinkers, they are not the Lord's "thoughts" which are already written—that is, *scripturalized* for the ages:

> For my thoughts are not your thoughts, neither are your ways my ways, says the Lord. For as the heavens are higher than the earth, so are my ways higher than your ways and my thoughts than your thoughts. *For as the rain and the snow come down from heaven, and return not thither but water the earth, making it bring forth and sprout, giving seed to the sower and bread to the eater, so shall my word be that goes forth from my mouth; it shall not return to me empty, but it shall accomplish that which I purpose, and prosper in the thing for which I sent it.* (Is 55:8-11)

The underscored words above describe precisely what happens at the end of the two stories, of the flood and of Jonah. Both "doves" disappear at the end of their short stories not to be heard of again in the Old Testament to allow God's plan to unfold on his earth, including the repentant and pardoned Nineveh, the destroyer of Samaria, the capital of Israel, despite the pouting Jonah: "While the earth remains, seedtime and harvest, cold and heat, summer and winter, day and night, shall not cease." (Gen 8:22)

My readers are to never forget the reason for Jonah's pouting and fleeing to Tarshish, which is in the opposite direction of Nineveh, that triggered the entire story:

> But it displeased Jonah exceedingly, and he was angry. And he prayed to the Lord and said, "I pray thee, Lord, is not this what I said when I was yet in my country? That is why I made haste to flee to Tarshish; for I knew that thou art a gracious God and merciful, slow to anger, and abounding in steadfast love, and repentest of evil." (Jon 4:1-2)

Jonah and the Tablets of the Law

The reason Jonah gave for his decision to flee to Tarshish and not follow God's prompting to go to Nineveh with a call to repentance is taken from words out of the Lord's mouth describing himself in Exodus:

> And he prayed to the Lord and said, "I pray thee, Lord, is not this what I said when I was yet in my country? That is why I made haste to flee to Tarshish; for I knew that thou art a gracious God and merciful, slow to anger, and abounding in steadfast love, and repentest of evil." (Jon 4:2)

> The Lord passed before him, and proclaimed, "The Lord, the Lord, a God merciful and gracious, slow to anger, and abounding in steadfast love and faithfulness, keeping steadfast love for thousands, forgiving iniquity and transgression and sin, but who will by no means clear the guilty, visiting the iniquity of the fathers upon the children and the children's children, to the third and the fourth generation." And Moses made haste to bow his head toward the earth, and worshiped. (Ex 34:6-8)

This declaration is made toward the end of the episode of the golden calf (Ex 32-34) when Aaron and his followers betrayed the first covenant by worshipping a calf of gold they made and considered as their god in contravention of the first commandment (32:1-6). Moses had to break the tablets of the Law indicating the rescinding of God's covenant, which covenant had to be reestablished through a new set of tablets (34:1-5). This renewal of the same covenant was made possible due to divine "mercy and graciousness, slowness to anger and steadfast love" and not to any worthiness on the part of the people. However, the guilty will have to repent and redress their "way"; otherwise the Lord, still the equitable judge, will visit the perpetrators' "iniquity" to "the third and the fourth generation." So, Jonah was familiar with God's generosity, yet he decided not to relay it to the Ninevites although that was the mission assigned to him by "the word of the Lord" (Jon 1:1). In so doing, Jonah became the prototype for Christians as well as Jews who traditionally practice entitlement in that they appropriate for themselves the "favorable" scriptural promises while hurling the "condemnatory" ones upon the heads of the outsiders. It as though they view themselves "worthy" of divine mercy *because* (they say) they repented when, in scripture, God's mercy *precedes* repentance for a very simple reason: were God not merciful and gracious and slow to anger, no one would even have had the chance to repent and change one's evil way (Jon 3:8). That is why the new covenant in Ezekiel is cast after the mold of Exodus 32-34:

> And I will give them one heart, and put a new spirit within them; I will take the stony heart out of their flesh and give them a heart of flesh, *that they may walk in my statutes and keep my ordinances and obey them*; and they shall be my people, and I will be their God. (Ezek 11:19-20)

> A new heart I will give you, and a new spirit I will put within you; and I will take out of your flesh the heart of stone and give you a heart of flesh. And I will put my spirit within you, *and cause you to walk in my statutes and be careful to observe my ordinances.* (Ezek 36:26-27)

Nineveh, Tarshish, and the Hebrew Jonah

Besides Nineveh, a great city, whose mention nine times is understandable, it is the reference to Tarshish three times in a row at the outset of the book (Jon 1:3) that is striking:

> Now the word of the Lord came to Jonah the son of Amittai, saying, "Arise, go to Nineveh, that great city, and cry against it; for their wickedness has come up *before me* (*lephanay*)." But Jonah rose to flee to Tarshish *from the presence of the Lord* (*milliphney yahweh*). He went down to Joppa and found a ship going to Tarshish; so he paid the fare, and went on board, to go with them to Tarshish, *away from the presence of the Lord* (*milliphney yahweh*). But the Lord hurled a great wind (*ruaḥ*) upon the *sea*, and there was a mighty tempest (*sa'ar*) on the *sea*, so that the ship threatened to break up. (Jon 1:1-4)

This repetition is paralleled by the thrice reference to the Lord's *phanim* (face; presence). Technically speaking, all three instances have to do with the "judging" face (presence) of the Lord that Jonah was trying to dodge. The author's verdict regarding the possibility of evading such an endeavor is revealed in the divine action that is taken immediately without a breather:[13] "But the Lord hurled a great wind upon the sea, and there was a mighty tempest on the sea, so that the ship threatened to break up." In their hurry to board the ship for Tarshish with Jonah the hearers may have forgotten to take along their copies of the Book of Genesis where they could have read that Cain, the first human born outside the garden, tried unsuccessfully, to "hide from the Lord's face":

> Cain said to the Lord, "My punishment is greater than I can bear. Behold, thou hast driven me this day away from the ground; and *from thy face* (*miphphaneka*) *I shall be hidden*; and I shall be a fugitive and a wanderer on the earth, and whoever finds me will slay me." Then the Lord said to him, "*Not so*! If any one slays Cain, vengeance shall be taken on him sevenfold." And the Lord put a mark on Cain, lest any who came upon him should kill him. (Gen 4:13-15)

However, as is the case in the never ending repetitiveness of scripture itself, the hearers are reminded here in Jonah, preemptively, that, *in scripture*, God controls completely and at will the destiny of all, everyone, and everything—humans, land animals, birds, sea animals and even wind and waters—until his purpose is realized: "… so shall my word be that goes forth from my mouth; it shall not return to me empty, but it shall accomplish that which I purpose, and prosper in the thing for

---

13 Pun intended since the *ruaḥ* (wind) connotes also "breath" and "breathing" as in Ecclesiastes: "For the fate of the sons of men and the fate of beasts is the same; as one dies, so dies the other. They all have the same breath (*ruaḥ*), and man has no advantage over the beasts; for all is vanity (*hebel*; vanishing breath). All go to one place; all are from the dust, and all turn to dust again. Who knows whether the spirit (*ruaḥ*) of man goes upward and the spirit (*ruaḥ*) of the beast goes down to the earth?" (3:19-21)

which I sent it." (Is 55:11) The phraseology of this reminder (Jon 1:4) cannot but recall the second verse of scripture:

> The earth was without form and void, and darkness was *upon the face ('al phenay)* of the *deep (tehom)*; and the *Spirit (ruaḥ)* of God was moving *over the face ('al phenay)* of the *waters (mayim)*." (Gen 1:2)

> But Jonah rose to flee to Tarshish *from the presence of the Lord (milliphney yahweh*; from the face of the Lord). He went down to Joppa and found a ship going to Tarshish; so he paid the fare, and went on board, to go with them to Tarshish, *away from the presence of the Lord (milliphney yahweh*; from the face of the Lord). But the Lord hurled a great wind *(ruaḥ)* upon the *sea*, and there was a mighty tempest *(sa'ar)* on the *sea*, so that the ship threatened to break up. (Jon 1:3-4)

Although *ruaḥ* does not appear again until later in the book as a "sultry east wind" (Jon 4:8), the following verses of chapter 1 are replete with words of the root *sa'ar* as well as and "sea":

> Then the mariners were afraid, and each cried to his god; and they threw the wares that were in the ship into the sea, to lighten it for them. ... Then they said to him, "What shall we do to you, that the *sea* may quiet down for us?" For the *sea* grew more and more tempestuous *(so'er)*. He said to them, "Take me up and throw me into the *sea*; then the *sea* will quiet down for you; for I know it is because of me that this great tempest *(sa'ar)* has come upon you." Nevertheless the men rowed hard to bring the ship back to land, but they could not, for the *sea* grew more and more tempestuous *(so'er)* against them. ... So they took up Jonah and threw him into the *sea*; and the *sea* ceased from its raging. (Jon 1:5, 11-13, 15)

As for the pair "deep" *(tehom)* and "waters" *(mayim)* of Genesis 1:2 they are heard *as a pair* in Jonah's prayer: "The waters *(mayim)* closed in over me, the deep *(tehom)* was round about me; weeds were wrapped about my head." (Jon 2:5)

Still, I am convinced that the Book of Jonah subtly harks back to Genesis 10 in a way that establishes the importance, if not centrality, of the sea animals in furthering and accomplishing

God's purpose. Jonah's unexpected introduction of himself as "a Hebrew" (*'ibri* from the verb *'abar*) in conjunction with his statement reminiscent of Genesis 1 (I fear the Lord, the God of heaven, who made the sea and the dry land; Jon 1:9) seems out of line unless one remembers my caveat that any seemingly "out of order" addition must be highly functional. The link to Genesis is repeated in the following instance of the verb *'abar* which again is heard on Jonah's lips: "For thou didst cast me into the deep (*meṣulah*),[14] into the heart of the *seas* (*yammim*; plural of *yam*), and the flood was round about me; all thy waves and thy billows passed (*'abaru*) over me." (Jon 2:3)[15] The first instance ever of "Hebrew" in scripture occurs with the definite article "the" (*ha'ibri*) in apposition to Abram (Gen 14:13) who is the son of Terah (Gen 11:26), the last in the *toledot* of Shem (Gen 11:10-25). So, scripturally speaking, a Hebrew is, by definition, a Shemite. On the other hand, Tarshish is a Japhethite via Javan (Gen 10:2-4) whereas Nineveh is a city built by King Nimrod, a Hamite via Cush (Gen 10:6-12).

In Genesis 10 the entire scriptural world is presented as the *one* world of the three sons of Noah that are lumped into *one toledot*, a unique instance in Genesis where *toledot* is usually followed by the name of an individual:[16] "These are the generations (*toledot*) of *the sons of Noah*, Shem, Ham, and Japheth; sons were born to *them* after the flood." (v.1) The priority given

14 Compare with the following instances where *meṣulah* occurs in conjunction with *yam* (sea): "Thou wilt cast all our sins into the depths (*meṣulot*) of the sea (*yam*)" (Mic 7:19); "The Lord said, 'I will bring them back from Bashan, I will bring them back from the depths (*meṣulot*) of the sea (*yam*)'" (Ps 68:22); "Some went down to the sea (*yam*) in ships, doing business on the great *waters*; they saw the deeds of the Lord, his wondrous works in the deep (*meṣulah*)." (Ps 107:23-24).

15 The only other occurrence of *'abar* in the book concerns the king's disrobing himself of his royal garment: "Then tidings reached the king of Nineveh, and he arose from his throne, removed (*ya'aber*) his robe, and covered himself with sackcloth, and sat in ashes." (Jon 3:6)

16 Adam (Gen 5:1), Noah (6:9), Shem (11:10), Terah (11:27), Ishmael (25:12), Isaac (25:19), Esau (36:1 and 9), Jacob (37:2).

Japheth[17] is not to be equated with being given precedence time wise; after all Japheth is third in line and will have to wait his turn to dwell in the tents of Shem (Gen 9:27). At the same time, the door was left open for Ham to repent of his abominable deed (v.22) in that Noah circumvented him by cursing his son, Canaan, instead (v.25).

As I have pointed out repeatedly, Shem and Ham function as the two sides of the same coin in that their names describe not two different entities, but rather two different behaviors. So, Ham describes the same Shemites whenever they misbehave and earn God's ire (*ḥam*; heat, hotness) instead of the blessing inherent to the "name" (*šem*). In the meantime, the Japhethites will have to wait until the Shemites *as* Hamites are punished into exile among the nations, representative of the Japhethites, who will join the "remnant" of the Shemites and *together with them* will be given a "second chance" in the new Zion, which is nothing else than the "tent" of Sarah and her children:

> Hearken to me, you who pursue deliverance, you who seek the Lord; look to the rock from which you were hewn, and to the quarry from which you were digged. Look to Abraham your father and to Sarah who bore you; for when he was but one I called him, and I blessed him and made him many. For the Lord will comfort Zion; he will comfort all her waste places, and will make her wilderness like Eden, her desert like the garden of the Lord; joy and gladness will be found in her, thanksgiving and the voice of song. (Is 51:1-3)

> Sing, O barren one, who did not bear; break forth into singing and cry aloud, you who have not been in travail! For the children of the desolate one will be more than the children of her that is married, says the Lord. Enlarge the place of your tent, and let the curtains of your habitations be stretched out; hold not back, lengthen your cords and strengthen your stakes. For you will spread abroad to the right and to the left, and your descendants

17 In Genesis 10, although Japheth is the third in line (v.1), the author starts by enumerating his progeny (vv.2-5) followed by that of Ham (vv.6-20) and then that of Shem (vv.21-31).

> will possess the nations and will people the desolate cities. Fear not, for you will not be ashamed; be not confounded, for you will not be put to shame; for you will forget the shame of your youth, and the reproach of your widowhood you will remember no more. For your Maker is your husband, the Lord of hosts is his name; and the Holy One of Israel is your Redeemer, the God of the whole earth he is called. (Is 54:1-5)

> And now the Lord says, who formed me from the womb to be his servant, to bring Jacob back to him, and that Israel might be gathered to him, for I am honored in the eyes of the Lord, and my God has become my strength—he says: "It is too light a thing that you should be my servant to raise up the tribes of Jacob and to restore the preserved of Israel; I will give you as a light to the nations, that my salvation may reach to the end of the earth." Thus says the Lord, the Redeemer of Israel and his Holy One, to one deeply despised, abhorred by the nations, the servant of rulers: "Kings shall see and arise; princes, and they shall prostrate themselves; because of the Lord, who is faithful, the Holy One of Israel, who has chosen you." (Is 49:5-7)

> For I know their works and their thoughts, and I am coming to gather all nations and tongues; and they shall come and shall see my glory, and I will set a sign among them. And from them I will send survivors to the nations, to Tarshish, Put, and Lud, who draw the bow, to Tubal and Javan, to the coastlands afar off, that have not heard my fame or seen my glory; and they shall declare my glory among the nations. And they shall bring all your brethren from all the nations as an offering to the Lord, upon horses, and in chariots, and in litters, and upon mules, and upon dromedaries, to my holy mountain Jerusalem, says the Lord, just as the Israelites bring their cereal offering in a clean vessel to the house of the Lord. And some of them also I will take for priests and for Levites, says the Lord. (Is 66:18-21)

However, if the new Zion will be patterned after Eden (51:3) this means precisely that it will be lawful and not lawless. It was in the scriptural Eden that the first and arguably the harshest commandment (Gen 2:17) was issued which did not allow the human beings to cogitate and assess and then choose to obey—as the nations trained in Plato's school do—but rather simply to submit and obey. This aspect was quintessentially captured by

Paul, the Apostle to the nations, who dubbed his gospel to them as a gospel of *hypakoē* (submission in obedience; Rom 1:5; 15:18; 16:19, 26). In other words, once Japheth dwells in the tents of Shem, he becomes bound by the house rules. That is why the nations as well as the redeemed of Israel (Shem) will be bound *unconditionally* to the divine commandment and law:

> And I will give them one heart, and put a new spirit within them; I will take the stony heart out of their flesh and give them a heart of flesh, that they may walk in my statutes and keep my ordinances and obey them; and they shall be my people, and I will be their God. (Ezek 11:19-20)

> A new heart I will give you, and a new spirit I will put within you; and I will take out of your flesh the heart of stone and give you a heart of flesh. And I will put my spirit within you, and cause you to walk in my statutes and be careful to observe my ordinances. (Ezek 36:26-27)

Again, the Apostle to the nations captured the Ezekelian teaching and unflinchingly bound his nations to it:

> But I say, walk (*peripateite*; amble) by the Spirit, and do not gratify the desires of the flesh ... And those who belong to Christ Jesus have crucified the flesh with its passions and desires. If we live by the Spirit, let us also walk (*stoikhōmen*; *walk in line army style*) by the Spirit. (Gal 5:16, 24-25)

> So the law is holy, and the commandment is holy and just and good ... For *the law of the Spirit of life* in Christ Jesus has set me free from the law of sin and death. (Rom 7:12; 8:2)

The strictness of the "new" covenant is reflected in Jeremiah's description of it:

> Behold, the days are coming, says the Lord, when I will make a new covenant with the house of Israel and the house of Judah, not like the covenant which I made with their fathers when I took them by the hand to bring them out of the land of Egypt, my covenant which they broke, though I was their husband, says the Lord. But this is the covenant which I will make with the house of Israel after those days, says the Lord: I will put my law within

> them, and I will write it upon their hearts; and I will be their God, and they shall be my people. And no longer shall each man teach his neighbor and each his brother, saying, "Know the Lord," for they shall all know me, from the least of them to the greatest, says the Lord; for I will forgive their iniquity, and I will remember their sin no more. (Jer 31:31-34)

Unlike the Mosaic covenant that was written on tablets of stone that could be broken and replaced (Ex 32-34), should the new covenant be "broken" by the people it is their hearts *as tablets* that will have to be "broken," and this is precisely the sight that is offered from the new Zion that includes the nations:

> For as the new heavens and the new earth which I will make shall remain before me, says the Lord; so shall your descendants and your name remain. From new moon to new moon, and from sabbath to sabbath, all flesh shall come to worship before me, says the Lord. *And they shall go forth and look on the dead bodies of the men that have rebelled against me; for their worm shall not die, their fire shall not be quenched, and they shall be an abhorrence to all flesh.* (Is 66:22-24)

In the meantime

If the primary interest of scripture is bringing the nations of the Mediterranean Sea under the tent of Shem, the consummate shepherd of the Syrian wilderness, why did the scriptural authors resort to a tediously long and repetitious story detailing the failings of Shem's descendants throughout the centuries? Simply put, to address the nations in any other direct way, à la Plato's dialogues, would have been to follow the "thoughts and ways" of the human beings which are presented as not being the "thoughts and ways" of the scriptural God (Is 55:8-9), that is to say, to submit to Plato's "unfruitful" *logos* instead of submitting to God's "fruitful" *dabar*:

> For as the rain and the snow come down from heaven, and return not thither but water the earth, making it bring forth and sprout, giving seed to the sower and bread to the eater, so shall my word (*dabar*) be that goes forth from my mouth; it shall not return to me empty, but it shall accomplish that which I purpose, and prosper in the thing for which I sent it. (Is 55:10-11)

It is not simple to convince arrogant human beings, shaped by anthropocentric and ego-serving Ancient Greek philosophy that blossomed around the apparently fertile "isles" of the Aegean Sea, to accept receiving the "water" and "bread" of life in a *dabar* originating in the arid Syrian *midbar* (wilderness) that the Macedonian Greek Alexander subjugated. As I explained in detail in *The Rise of Scripture*, the scriptural authors devised an epic surpassing the word count of the Iliad and Odyssey put together, as well as the works of Plato. In this epic, their main aim was to free the nations from their bondage to their self-aggrandizing literature and subjugate them to the bondage of the scriptural God. However, in order to do that without giving the Shemites free rein to gloat, those Shemites had to undergo the same experience:

> I am the Lord your God, who brought you out of the land of Egypt, out of the house of bondage (*'abadim*; slaves). You shall have no other gods before me. (Ex 20:2-3)

> For to me the people of Israel are servants (*'abadim*; slaves), they are my servants (*'abaday*; slaves) whom I brought forth out of the land of Egypt: I am the Lord your God. (Lev 25:55)

Such a proposition is almost impossible for human beings to accept as is shown in the writings of the Christian Greco-Roman theologians of Alexandria, the city founded by Alexander of Macedon. Upon accepting the gospel and having become, so they say, the "Israel of God" (Gal 6:16), they reverted to their old "Greek" ways and exchanged the scriptural *dabar* for Plato's *logos*, thus "perverting the gospel of Christ" they received from Paul (Gal 1:7). This is the fate of all theologies, including the so-called *sola scriptura* theologies and "confessions (of faith)" of the so-called Reformation. While the Apostle to the nations berated Greek philosophy (1 Cor 1-2), Alexandrian theologians—and all theologies after them—became enslaved to their own perverted interpretation of the "spoils" of Egypt as inclusive of "ideas," besides jewelry and clothing. They indulged in Greek philosophy to better comprehend—so they say—the "intent" of the message in the following scriptural statements:

> And I will give this people favor in the sight of the Egyptians; and when you go, you shall not go empty, but each woman shall ask of her neighbor, and of her who sojourns in her house, jewelry of silver and of gold, and clothing, and you shall put them on your sons and on your daughters; thus you shall despoil the Egyptians. (Ex 3:21-22)

> The people of Israel had also done as Moses told them, for they had asked of the Egyptians jewelry of silver and of gold, and clothing; and the Lord had given the people favor in the sight of the Egyptians, so that they let them have what they asked. Thus they despoiled the Egyptians. (Ex 12:35-36)

In so doing, they fell and are still falling under Paul's judgment of their undertaking as foolishness in the garb of wisdom (1 Cor 1-2). Luckily, scripture is still there and, for the "ecumenical" among the Protestants as well as for the Orthodox and Roman Catholics, it includes the Prologue to Sirach with its caveat *against* assuming that knowledge of Greek secures the intent of the original Hebrew. And if Paul as apostle was able to communicate the prophetic message of the Old Testament in the way he did, by demeaning his addressees, the nations, right from the start, it is because he understood correctly that openly conveying the scriptural message to the Japhethites is, as Isaiah taught in his last chapter, a sign of the end times. Thus, the nations do not have a second chance as the scriptural Israel did. The reason is straightforward: by accepting the scriptural teaching, the nations have already been in and out of Egypt, that is, they are already *posited* as having had their first chance:

> I want you to know, brethren, that our fathers were all under the cloud, and all passed through the sea, and all were baptized into Moses in the cloud and in the sea, and all ate the same supernatural food and all drank the same supernatural drink. For they drank from the supernatural Rock which followed them, and the Rock was Christ. Nevertheless with most of them God was not pleased; for they were overthrown in the wilderness. Now these things are warnings for us, not to desire evil as they did. Do

> not be idolaters as some of them were; as it is written, "The people sat down to eat and drink and rose up to dance." We must not indulge in immorality as some of them did, and twenty-three thousand fell in a single day. We must not put the Lord to the test, as some of them did and were destroyed by serpents; nor grumble, as some of them did and were destroyed by the Destroyer. *Now these things happened to them as a warning, but they were written down for our instruction, upon whom the end of the ages has come.* (1 Cor 10:1-11)

Still, Paul did not appear out of the blue. After all, as I have shown in *The Rise of Scripture*, he is as much a textual character as are the Old Testament Prophets and their God. It is in the *Book* of Acts, written as a "word"[18] to be read aloud, that the story of Paul is found,[19] just as the story of Jonah is found in the Book of Jonah. After the opening of the entire scripture in Genesis 1-11 where Japheth *and his families* (10:5, 32) are set up to dwell *at one point* "in the tents of Shem" (9:27), scripture announces at the beginning of chapter 12 that this prediction will be realized *at one point* through the story of Abram the Hebrew (shepherd) Shemite in words reminiscent of chapter 9 where we have heard of "blessing" and "curse" and chapter 10 where we have heard of "families":

> When Noah awoke from his wine and knew what his youngest son had done to him, he said, "Cursed be Canaan; a slave of slaves shall he be to his brothers." He also said, "Blessed by the Lord my God be Shem; and let Canaan be his slave. God enlarge Japheth, and let him dwell in the tents of Shem; and let Canaan be his slave." (Gen 9:24-27)

> From these the coastland peoples spread. These are the sons of Japheth in their lands, each with his own language, by their families, in their nations … These are the families of the sons of Noah, according to their genealogies, in their nations; and from

---

18 In the first book [*logon*], O Theophilus, I have dealt with all that Jesus began to do and teach. (Acts 1:1)

19 The Pauline letters contain bits and pieces of Paul's story, but not a continuous narrative as in Acts.

> these the nations spread abroad on the earth after the flood. (Gen 10:5, 32)
>
> Now the Lord said to Abram, "Go from your country and your kindred and your father's house to the land that I will show you. And I will make of you a great nation, and I will bless you, and make your name great, so that you will be a blessing. I will bless those who bless you, and him who curses you I will curse; and by you all the families of the earth shall bless themselves." (Gen 12:1-3)

In order to prepare the nations for their final encounter with the scriptural God in a way that they would accept his judgment as impartial, the authors devised an epic where the Shemites, time and again throughout their generations, must choose between blessing and curse (Lev 26; Deut 28) or, in the terminology of Genesis 10, choose to be followers of Shem or followers of Ham *on the same ground* of the Syrian wilderness. Should they follow Ham's way, then they will be forced into another exile in Mesopotamia like the one they experienced in Egypt (Ezek 20). My readers are reminded that, according to Genesis 10, Egypt is a son of Ham (v.6) while Babel and Nineveh are cities founded by Nimrod grandson of Ham via Cush (vv.6-12). It is *in exile in Babel* that Alexander and his Macedonians will find the Shemites punished by none other than their *Savior* himself! Should the Macedonians inquire about that strangely acting savior, they will learn that he is none other than the God who saved their common progenitor Noah together with his sons Shem, Ham, and Japheth only because "Noah (*noaḥ*) found favor in the eyes of the Lord" (Gen 6:8). And, lest anyone forgets, the respite (*nuaḥ*) accorded all the nations of the earth hinged solely on the behavior of Noah (*noaḥ*) and not his sons, the forebears of all those nations. Notice that the statement, "Noah was a righteous man, blameless in his generation; Noah walked with God" (v.9b), unduly interrupts the expected flow between "These are the generations of Noah" (v.9a) and "Noah had three sons, Shem, Ham, and Japheth (v.10), as is the case elsewhere when one hears of the *toledot* of so and so. The hearer cannot but be aurally struck by the quintuple mention of Noah in three verses compared to the one mention of his three sons:

> But Noah found favor in the eyes of the Lord. These are the generations of Noah. Noah was a righteous man, blameless in his generation; Noah walked with God. And Noah had three sons, Shem, Ham, and Japheth. (Gen 6:8-10)

As for Japheth, it only through the blessing of Noah, the father of all three brothers, that he will abide in the tents of Shem and not Ham. In other words, the blessing of Japheth is conditioned on his readiness to hear and obey the *dabar* of the scriptural God that originates in the *midbar* (wilderness) of Syria which encompasses Sinai, and not from his cities on the isles surrounding the Great (Western) Sea, the Mediterranean.

Jonah again

What is the role of the Book of Jonah in this scenario? Against the background I just delineated, the sin of the anti-prophet Jonah is threefold. First and foremost, he betrayed his calling that is encrypted in his name *yonah*, dove, the harbinger of good tidings of life in peace, which was established in Noah's times. However, it is Jonah's pouting that is significant. On the one hand, he, the Hebrew and thus Shemite by the will of the God of heavens, maker of the sea and the dry land (Jon 1:9), refused to convey this same God's offer of repentance to the Hamite Nineveh (Gen 9:6-12). Perhaps he was irked by the fact that, according to his canonical predecessors—Isaiah through Obadiah—, none of the Hebrew recipients accepted that same offer. The opening of Isaiah says it all, in that it functions as an overarching description of the prophetic literature:

> The vision of Isaiah the son of Amoz, which he saw concerning Judah and Jerusalem in the days of Uzziah, Jotham, Ahaz, and Hezekiah, kings of Judah. Hear, O heavens, and give ear, O earth; for the Lord has spoken (*dibber* from the root *dabar*): "Sons have I reared and brought up, but they have rebelled against me. The ox knows its owner, and the ass its master's crib; but Israel

> does not know, my people does not understand." (Is 1:1-3)

On the other hand, and more importantly, Jonah decided to flee to Tarshish, the farthest ends of the domain of Japheth, that is frequently mentioned in conjunction with ships and with Tyre, the queen city of the Mediterranean in those times (Is 23; Ezek 26-28):

> For the king (Solomon) had a fleet of ships of Tarshish at sea with the fleet of Hiram (King of Tyre). Once every three years the fleet of ships of Tarshish used to come bringing gold, silver, ivory, apes, and peacocks. (1 Kg 10:22)

> Jehoshaphat made ships of Tarshish to go to Ophir for gold; but they did not go, for the ships were wrecked at Eziongeber. (1 Kg 22:48)

So, going there to forego the "presence of the Lord" (Jon 1:3) is an outright insult to the Lord himself. It is not as though the isle nation could protect anyone from the Lord who "has a day against all that is proud and lofty, against all that is lifted up and high … against all the ships of Tarshish, and against all the beautiful craft" (Is 2:12, 16), and who "by the east wind shattered the ships of Tarshish" (Ps 48:7). The same Lord declared to his city Zion through his prophet Isaiah: "For the coastlands (*'iyyim*) shall wait for me, the ships of *Tarshish first*, to bring your sons from far, their silver and gold with them, for the name of the Lord your God, and for the Holy One of Israel, because he has glorified you." (60:9)

The link to the Book of Isaiah is more direct that one imagines, which is a credit to the astuteness of the scriptural authors. A mere four chapters after the end of Jonah one hears a passage in Micah 4 which is a carbon copy of a passage in Isaiah describing the end of the scriptural odyssey when the nations will join Israel to listen to the law of the Lord on his holy mountain in the same way as they will join them at the end of Isaiah in his holy city Zion (Is 66):

> It shall come to pass in the latter days that the mountain of the house of the Lord shall be established as the highest of the mountains, and shall be raised above the hills; and all the nations shall flow to it, and many peoples shall come, and say: "Come, let us go up to the mountain of the Lord, to the house of the God of Jacob; that he may teach us his ways and that we may walk in his paths." For out of Zion shall go forth the law, and the word of the Lord from Jerusalem. He shall judge between the nations, and shall decide for many peoples; and they shall beat their swords into plowshares, and their spears into pruning hooks; nation shall not lift up sword against nation, neither shall they learn war any more. O house of Jacob, come, let us walk in the light of the Lord. (Is 2:2-5)

> It shall come to pass in the latter days that the mountain of the house of the Lord shall be established as the highest of the mountains, and shall be raised up above the hills; and peoples shall flow to it, and many nations shall come, and say: "Come, let us go up to the mountain of the Lord, to the house of the God of Jacob; that he may teach us his ways and we may walk in his paths." For out of Zion shall go forth the law, and the word of the Lord from Jerusalem. He shall judge between many peoples, and shall decide for strong nations afar off; and they shall beat their swords into plowshares, and their spears into pruning hooks; nation shall not lift up sword against nation, neither shall they learn war any more; but they shall sit every man under his vine and under his fig tree, and none shall make them afraid; for the mouth of the Lord of hosts has spoken. For all the peoples walk each in the name of its god, but we will walk in the name of the Lord our God for ever and ever. (Mic 4:1-5)

The authors' choice of the name Micah fits the scenario since the Hebrew *mikah* is a shortened form of the original *mikayehu* (who is like Yahweh?)—after the pattern of *yešaʿyahu* (the Lord will save; Isaiah)—forcing the hearer to wonder in amazement: "Who is like Yahweh capable of pulling a stunt like this, bringing the Japhethites from the far away isles of the Great Sea to dwell in the tents of Shem under the blessing granted in the divine law?" This is precisely what the hearer will be forced to intone with Zion, "Who is a God like thee?"[20], at the closing of the book:

> But as for me, I will look to the Lord, I will wait for the God of my salvation; my God will hear me. Rejoice not over me, O my enemy; when I fall, I shall rise; when I sit in darkness, the Lord will be a light to me. I will bear the indignation of the Lord because I have sinned against him, until he pleads my cause and executes judgment for me. He will bring me forth to the light; I shall behold his deliverance. Then my enemy will see, and shame will cover her who said to me, "Where is the Lord your God?" My eyes will gloat over her; now she will be trodden down like the mire of the streets. A day for the building of your walls! In that day the boundary shall be far extended. In that day they will come to you, from Assyria to Egypt, and from Egypt to the River, from sea to sea and from mountain to mountain … The nations shall see and be ashamed of all their might; they shall lay their hands on their mouths; their ears shall be deaf; they shall lick the dust like a serpent, like the crawling things of the earth; they shall come trembling out of their strongholds, they shall turn in dread to the Lord our God, and they shall fear because of thee. Who is a God like thee (*mi 'el kamoka*), pardoning iniquity and passing over transgression for the remnant of his inheritance? He does not retain his anger for ever because he delights in steadfast love. (Mic 7:7-12; 16-18)

Notice how the ending corresponds to that of Jonah: "And he prayed to the Lord and said, 'I pray thee, Lord, is not this what I said when I was yet in my country? That is why I made haste to flee to Tarshish; for I knew that thou art a gracious God and merciful, slow to anger, and abounding in steadfast love, and repentest of evil.'" (Jon 4:2)

In order to make his point to the hearer as well as to Jonah, the "God of heaven, sea, and dry land" (Jon 1:9), that is the God of Genesis 1, uses a "great fish," one of the *tanninim* (sea monsters) he created and blessed (Gen 1:21-22)[21] to swallow his

---

20 *mikah* could be also construed as a shortened form of *mika'el* (Who is like God?; Michael [Num 13:13; Dan 10:13]).

21 See above my discussion of the interplay on nouns between the Hebrew and the LXX Greek.

prophet and bring him back to the dry land that will lead him to Nineveh. The first question that comes to the hearer's mind is: "Why did God choose this medium instead of just calming the winds and the waves so that the mariners could return to the dry land and drop Jonah off there?" But God did not allow them to do this: "but they could not, for the sea grew more and more tempestuous against them." (Jon 1:13) He kept unleashing the waves of the sea, over which he had total control (Ps 93:3-4), so that the mariners would throw Jonah off board into the raging sea (Jon 1:15a). That this was indeed God's intention is confirmed since immediately thereafter "the sea ceased from its raging" (v.15b). However, it was not the mariners' safety that God was interested in, although they may have concluded as much since, from their perspective, Jonah "perished" in exchange for their lives: "We beseech thee, O Lord, let us not perish for this man's life, and lay not on us innocent blood; for thou, O Lord, hast done as it pleased thee ... Then the men feared the Lord exceedingly, and they offered a sacrifice to the Lord and made vows." (vv.14, 16) God's interest was not even in Jonah, per se, let alone his spiritual life or his growth in thanksgiving. Rather he was interested in the prophet's mission, which is coined in the same noun *mel'akah* as that twice used to define God's work and in a context where we are told, again twice, that he accomplished it:

> Thus the heavens and the earth were finished, and all the host of them. And on the seventh day God finished his work (*mel'akah*) which he had done, and he rested on the seventh day from all his work which he had done. So God blessed the seventh day and hallowed it, because on it God rested from all his work (*mel'akah*) which he had done in creation. These are the generations of the heavens and the earth when they were created. In the day that the Lord God made the earth and the heavens, (Gen 2:1-4)

> Then they said to him, "Tell us, on whose account this evil has come upon us? What is your occupation (*mel'akah*)? And whence do you come? What is your country? And of what people are you?" (Jon 1:8)

The rarity of the word *mel'akah* in the scroll of the Twelve (Minor) Prophets militates for its intentional use in Jonah. It is encountered only once more in Haggai 1:14 where again the work done by human beings was "stirred up" by the Lord himself and where intentionality on the authors' part is unmissable in both the quintuple use of "the Lord" and the thrice use of the root *mal'ak* over two verses:

> Then Haggai, the messenger (*mal'ak*) of the Lord, spoke to the people with the Lord's message (*mal'akut*), "I am with you, says the Lord." And the Lord stirred up the spirit of Zerubbabel the son of Shealtiel, governor of Judah, and the spirit of Joshua the son of Jehozadak, the high priest, and the spirit of all the remnant of the people; and they came and worked (*wayya'śu mel'akah*; and they did work) on the house of the Lord of hosts, their God. (Hag 1:13-14)

At any rate, in order to leave nothing to the hearer's imagination, the authors made sure that Jonah's reply referred back to Genesis 1-2:

> And he said to them, "I am a Hebrew; and I fear the Lord, the God of heaven, who made the sea and the dry land." (Jon 1:9)

Jonah's mission was to the Hamite Nineveh and not to the Japhethites, and this mission was of utmost importance. Since Shem and Ham are two sides of the same coin, a forgiven and repentant Hamite would forego the divine curse and become a Shemite under God's blessing. This amounts to killing two birds with one stone. On the one hand, the Japhethites are invited to accept more readily the message of the scriptural God because they now know that he is, in one breath, the merciful and compassionate par excellence as well as the avenger par excellence or, more succinctly put, he is the just judge, and the hope of all lies precisely in this, his defining feature or rather *function*. On the other hand, the Japhethites will not be allowed to look down at the forgiven "Shemites" since it is in their shepherd tents that the Japhethites are invited to dwell and, by the same token, will have to forego their Macedonian "conquering" tents. Both they and the Shemites will be dwelling around and in the vicinity of the "tent of meeting" wherever it may lead them since it will be the tent of their "new" leader:

> Then the cloud covered the tent of meeting, and the glory of the Lord filled the tabernacle. And Moses was not able to enter the tent of meeting, because the cloud abode upon it, and the glory of the Lord filled the tabernacle. Throughout all their journeys, whenever the cloud was taken up from over the tabernacle, the people of Israel would go onward; but if the cloud was not taken up, then they did not go onward till the day that it was taken up. For throughout all their journeys the cloud of the Lord was upon the tabernacle by day, and fire was in it by night, in the sight of all the house of Israel. (Ex 40:34-38)

> The Lord said to Moses and Aaron, "The people of Israel shall encamp each by his own standard, with the ensigns of their fathers' houses; they shall encamp facing the tent of meeting on every side." (Num 2:1-2)

These two aspects of the scriptural message will be picked up in the magisterial letter to the "Japhethite" Romans who overran the legacy of Alexander of Macedon:

> Then what advantage has the Jew? Or what is the value of circumcision? Much in every way. To begin with, the Jews are entrusted with the oracles of God. What if some were unfaithful? Does their faithlessness nullify the faithfulness of God? By no means! Let God be true though every man be false, as it is written, "That thou mayest be justified in thy words, and prevail when thou art judged." But if our wickedness serves to show the justice of God, what shall we say? That God is unjust to inflict wrath on us? (I speak in a human way.) By no means! For then how could God judge the world? (Rom 3:1-6)

> But if some of the branches were broken off, and you, a wild olive shoot, were grafted in their place to share the richness of the olive tree, do not boast over the branches. If you do boast, remember it is not you that support the root, but the root that supports you. You will say, "Branches were broken off so that I might be grafted in." That is true. They were broken off because of their unbelief, but you stand fast only through faith. So do not become proud, but stand in awe. For if God did not spare the natural branches,

> neither will he spare you … For the gifts and the call of God are irrevocable. Just as you were once disobedient to God but now have received mercy because of their disobedience, so they have now been disobedient in order that by the mercy shown to you they also may receive mercy. For God has consigned all men to disobedience, that he may have mercy upon all. (Rom 11: 17-21, 29-32)

The Role of the Great Fish

I have established that scripture leads the attentive hearers of both the Hebrew original and the LXX Greek to realize that the great fish of the Book of Jonah reflects Leviathan or Rahab, a "monster" or "dragon" more specifically associated with the sea rather than with the dry land. Although "dragon" can refer, as we have seen, to a "serpent," however, as Leviathan or Rahab, God's ultimate archenemy,[22] it is associated with the sea. To understand this scriptural creature, it is imperative to realize that Leviathan or Rahab impersonates the sea waters in their state of raging and threatening waves which pose a threat to sailing ships and their passengers, as well as to life on the isles of the dry land. In other words, they represent a threat to the world as God's creation according to Genesis 1. Suffice it here to listen to Psalm 93, especially verses 3 and 4:

> [1] The Lord reigns; he is robed in majesty (*ge'ut*); the Lord is robed, he is girded with strength (*'oz*). Yea, the world (*tebel*; habitation) is established (*kun*); it shall never be moved; [2] thy throne is established (*kun*) from of old (*me'olam*); thou art from everlasting. [3] The floods have lifted up (*naśa'*), O Lord, the floods have lifted up (*naśa'*) their voice, the floods lift up (*naśa'*) their roaring. [4] Mightier than the thunders of many waters, mightier than the waves (*mišbarim* [breakers] form the root *šabar*) of the sea, the Lord on high (*marom*; from the root *rum*) is mighty! [5] Thy decrees are very sure; holiness befits thy house, O Lord, for evermore. (Ps 93:3-4)

---

22 God made him and yet in his arrogance, like that of the human being, he may stand against God. See, e.g., the king of Tyre who was granted to be in Eden and yet stood against God (Ezek 28:13-19). See also Gen 11:1-9 where it is *beney ha'adam* (v.5; sons of man) that decide to build the city and its tower.

Notice how the Lord establishes the habitation *against* the raging waters. This goes hand in hand with the terminology that portrays the showdown between God and Leviathan or Rahab in psalms whose subject is also the establishment of the world:

> Yet God is my king from of old, working salvation in the earth. You divided the sea by your might (*'oz*); you broke (*šabar*) the heads of the dragons (*tanninim*) in the waters. You crushed the heads of Leviathan, thou didst give him as food for the creatures of the wilderness . . . you established (*kun*) the luminaries and the sun. (Ps 74:12-14,16b)

> You rule the raging (*ge'ut*; majesty; height, arrogance) of the sea; when its waves rise (*naśa'*), you still them. You crushed Rahab like a carcass; you scattered your enemies with your mighty arm (the arm of your might [*'oz*]) ... the world (*tebel*; habitation) and all that is in it—you have founded them . . . You have a mighty arm; strong is (*'oz*) your hand, high is (*rum*) your right hand. (Ps 89:9-10, llb, 13)

If the waves of Leviathan or Rahab cannot be overcome except by God himself, then, without him, they represent sure death, which is precisely what Jonah experienced while "in the belly of the fish" (Jon 1:17; 2:1) away "from the Lord's presence" (1:3):

> And the Lord appointed a great fish to swallow up Jonah; and Jonah was in the *belly of the fish* three days and three nights. Then Jonah prayed to the Lord his God from the *belly of the fish*, saying, "I called to the Lord, out of my distress, and he answered me; out of the *belly of Sheol* I cried, and thou didst hear my voice. For thou didst cast me into the deep, into the heart of the seas, and the flood was round about me; all thy waves and thy billows passed over me. Then I said, 'I am cast out *from thy presence*; how shall I again look upon thy holy temple?' The waters closed in over me, the deep was round about me; weeds were wrapped about my head." (Jon 1:17-2:5)[23]

---

23 The preciseness of the Hebrew is remarkable. In reference to the fish we have *me'ey* (bowels, entrails, intestines) whereas in conjunction with the Sheol we have the more general *beṭen* (belly, abdomen, interior). In Arabic "padding" is from the same root *bṭn*.

That Sheol corresponds to death is evident in the following passage that parallels Jonah terminologically: "For the waves of death encompassed me, the torrents of perdition assailed me; the cords of Sheol entangled me, the snares of death confronted me." (2 Sam 22:5-6//Ps 18:4-5) In the Baal cycle of Ugaritic literature whence this imagery is taken, Baal's opponent is the Sea whose name is *mot* which is death in Semitic languages. In *The Rise of Scripture* I have argued that the scriptural Yahweh has Baalic traits as is evident in the classic passage of Hosea:

> Therefore I will hedge up her way with thorns; and I will build a wall against her, so that she cannot find her paths. She shall pursue her lovers, but not overtake them; and she shall seek them, but shall not find them. Then she shall say, "I will go and return to my first husband, for it was better with me then than now." And she did not know that it was I who gave her the grain, the wine, and the oil, and who lavished upon her silver and gold which they used for Baal. Therefore I will take back my grain in its time, and my wine in its season; and I will take away my wool and my flax, which were to cover her nakedness. Now I will uncover her lewdness in the sight of her lovers, and no one shall rescue her out of my hand. And I will put an end to all her mirth, her feasts, her new moons, her sabbaths, and all her appointed feasts. And I will lay waste her vines and her fig trees, of which she said, "These are my hire, which my lovers have given me." I will make them a forest, and the beasts of the field shall devour them. And I will punish her for the feast days of the Baals when she burned incense to them and decked herself with her ring and jewelry, and went after her lovers, and forgot me, says the Lord. (Hos 2:6-13)

If God can control the sea monster Leviathan whom he has "formed" to "sport" in the sea waters (Ps 104:26), then he can, at will, say "a word of command for him to obey": "And the Lord spoke (*yawwo'mer*; said) to the fish, and it vomited out Jonah upon the dry land." (Jon 2:10) The simple "said" without an object in the original Hebrew brings to mind the series of the divine commands "And God said: 'Let…'" in Genesis 1 (vv.3, 6, 9, 11, 14, 20, 24). This is precisely what the LXX captures when it systematically refers to the fish in Jonah as *kētos* (1:17

[twice]; 2:1, 10), which is the same noun it uses in Genesis 1:21 to render the Hebrew *tannin* immediately after the statement: "And *God said*, '*Let the waters bring forth swarms of living creatures*, and let birds fly above the earth across the firmament of the heavens.'" (Gen 1:20)

14

Fish as a Sign of Life in the New Jerusalem

Not only is the fish, as in the story of Jonah, instrumental in allowing the message of repentance to the Hamite Nineveh to be carried out as planned, and not only is the tamed "sea monster" a sign of submission of the Japhethites to the authority of the scriptural God, but, in Ezekiel, they are also depicted as playing an integral part in the new Jerusalem and the renewed "earth" of the scriptural Israel (*'ereṣ yisra'el*) into becoming the "ground of Israel" (*'admat yisra'el*) for every *'adam* (human being) including the nations.[1]

In chapter 28, when describing the greatness and the beauty of Tyre, Ezekiel uses the "garden of God" in Eden as muster for comparison:

> You (king of Tyre) were in Eden, the garden of God; every precious stone was your covering, carnelian, topaz, and jasper, chrysolite, beryl, and onyx, sapphire, carbuncle, and emerald; and wrought in gold were your settings and your engravings. On the day that you were created they were prepared. (Ezek 28:13)

He does the same when speaking of Egypt in chapter 31:

> I made it beautiful in the mass of its branches, and all *the trees of Eden* envied it, that were in the garden of God. … I will make the nations quake at the sound of its fall, when I cast it down to Sheol with those who go down to the Pit; and all *the trees of Eden*, the choice and best of Lebanon, all that drink water, will be comforted in the nether world. They also shall go down to Sheol with it, to those who are slain by the sword; yea, those who dwelt under its shadow among the nations shall perish. Whom are you thus like in glory and in greatness among *the trees of Eden*? You

1 See my discussion of this matter in *C-Ezek* 114-7.

> shall be brought down with the trees of Eden to the nether world; you shall lie among the uncircumcised, with those who are slain by the sword. "This is Pharaoh and all his multitude, says the Lord God." (Ezek 31:9, 16-18)

Notice, however, in this case the thrice mention of "the trees of Eden" which are an essential feature of that *life-giving* as well as *living* garden in Genesis 2:

> And the Lord God planted a garden in Eden, in the east; and there he put the man whom he had formed. And out of the ground the Lord God made to grow every tree that is pleasant to the sight and *good for food*." (vv.8-9)

The ultimate referential value of Eden is sealed in the passages that describe the New Jerusalem in the terms of "the garden of God" in the two Prophetic Books that speak of that city as encompassing the nations as well as the scriptural Israel, as I pointed out earlier.[2] In Isaiah the reference is straightforward: "For the Lord will comfort Zion; he will comfort all her waste places, and will make her wilderness like Eden, her desert like the garden of the Lord; joy and gladness will be found in her, thanksgiving and the voice of song." (51:3) Ezekiel who already dealt with Eden in these terms twice in chapters 28 and 31 goes on a different tangent whereby he picks up on the centrality of the river flowing out of the garden and spreading into four major rivers that cover the entire scriptural world:

> A river flowed out of Eden to water the garden, and there it divided and became four rivers (*ra'šim*; heads). The name of the first is Pishon; it is the one which flows around the whole land of Havilah, where there is gold; and the gold of that land is good; bdellium and onyx stone are there. The name of the second river is Gihon; it is the one which flows around the whole land of Cush. And the name of the third river is Tigris, which flows east of Assyria. And the fourth river is the Euphrates. (Gen 2:10-14)

Let us listen in turn to Ezekiel's words just before the closing lengthy passage of the book where he details the boundaries of

---

2 Pp. 217; 267-270.

the new "earth—*as in dry land*—of inheritance" (Ezek 47:13-48:35):

> 1 Afterward he brought me again unto the door of the house; and, behold, waters issued out from under the threshold of the house eastward: for the forefront of the house *stood toward* the east, and the waters came down from under from the right side of the house, at the south *side* of the altar. 2 Then brought he me out of the way of the gate northward, and led me about the way without unto the utter gate by the way that looketh eastward; and, behold, there ran out waters on the right side. 3 And when the man that had the line in his hand went forth eastward, he measured a thousand cubits, and he brought me through the waters; the waters *were* to the ankles. 4 Again he measured a thousand, and brought me through the waters; the waters *were* to the knees. Again he measured a thousand, and brought me through; the waters *were* to the loins. 5 Afterward he measured a thousand; *and it was* a river that I could not pass over: for the waters were risen, waters to swim in, a river that could not be passed over. 6 And he said unto me, 'Son of man, hast thou seen *this*?' Then he brought me, and caused me to return to the brink of the river. 7 Now when I had returned, behold, at the bank of the river *were* very many trees on the one side and on the other. 8 Then said he unto me, 'These waters issue out toward the east country, and go down into the desert, and go into the sea: *which being* brought forth into the sea, the waters shall be healed. (*nirphe'u*). 9 And it shall come to pass, *that* every thing that liveth, which moveth, whithersoever the rivers shall come, shall live: and there shall be a very great multitude of fish, because these waters shall come thither: for they shall be healed; and every thing shall live whither the river cometh. 10 And it shall come to pass, *that* the *fishers* shall stand upon it from Engedi even unto Eneglaim; they shall be a *place* to spread forth nets; their fish shall be according to their kinds, as the fish of the great sea, exceeding many. 11 But the miry places thereof and the marshes thereof shall not be healed (*yeraphe'u*); they shall be given to salt. 12 And by the river upon the bank thereof, on this side and on that side, shall grow all trees for meat, whose leaf shall not fade, neither shall the fruit thereof be consumed: it shall bring forth new fruit according to his months, because their waters they issued out of the sanctuary: and the fruit

thereof shall be for meat, and the leaf thereof for medicine' (*teruphah*; healing). (Ezek 47:1-12 KJV)[3]

This passage is very impressive for the following reasons. Despite its stress on the waters (vv.1-5), the trees are still an integral part of the scenario where we hear over two verses that there are many trees growing on both banks of the river (vv.6-7). Their importance can be seen in that their extended following mention in the closing verse 12 underscores their role in providing "food" just as in Genesis 2:9. However, they are able to function as such "because the water for them flows from the sanctuary," which will enhance their role as being not only "for food" in their fruit but also "for healing" in their leaves. All this is understandable in a context where the stress is on the "living" earth that will have to support the twelve tribes of the renewed scriptural Israel (Ezek 47:13-48:35).

Those cognizant of Hebrew will have detected the inclusion of the land animals in the two names Engedi and Eneglaim. Given that the Hebrew *ʿen gedi* means "the fountain of the kid" and *ʿen ʿeglaym* "the fountain of the two calves," these two nouns ostensibly stand for a region where there is enough water to support plenty of flock and cattle. Still, what is totally unexpected in this scenario is the inclusion of the fish over two verses and in these terms:

> And it shall come to pass, *that* every thing that liveth, which moveth, (*nepheš ḥayyah ʾašer yišroṣ*; every living creature which swarms [RSV]) whithersoever the rivers shall come, shall live: and there shall be a very great multitude of *fish* (*dagah*), because these waters shall come thither: for they shall be healed (*yeraphe'u*); and every thing shall live whither the river cometh. And it shall come to pass, *that* the fishers (*dawwagim*) shall stand upon it from Engedi even unto Eneglaim; they shall be a *place* to spread forth nets; their *fish* shall be according to their kinds (*minah*), as *the fish of the great sea*, exceeding many. (Ezek 47:9-10 KJV)

---

3 I opted for KJV because in this case RSV takes so many liberties that the original is literally *unrecognizable*. This should be taken as a case in point for my stand against translations for the "study" of scripture.

Their inclusion is unexpected for the following reasons:

1. The importance given Eden in Ezekiel and the fact that the inheritance is an "earth" (Ezek 47:13-48:35) are obviously connected to the information in Genesis 2 regarding the river, the trees, and the land animals (kids and calves).

2. Although the main element that controls the narrative throughout Ezekiel 47:1-12 is the one river (vv.5 [twice], 6, 7, 9, 12), we suddenly hear also of the "rivers" in verse 9. This cannot be except a reflection of what is said of the river of the garden that divides into four rivers.

3. However, in Genesis 2 there is no mention of "fish" that are referenced only in Genesis 1:21, 26, and 28 and then disappear until 9:2, that is after the flood, since they play no role whatsoever in the flood story.

4. So, in order to include the fish the authors resorted to Genesis 1 as is clear from the terminology of Ezekiel 47:9-10: "every thing that liveth, which moveth"[4] (Gen 1:21), "fish (vv.26 and 28)," "kinds (v.21)," and "sea (vv.22, 26, 28)." Notice that the authors were aware of the artificiality of the matter since they felt it necessary to speak of the river fish as being "like the fish of the great sea." The noun "sea" occurs only here at the end of the two verses.[5]

5. Still the authors resort to another subterfuge to underscore their intent of making "the fish of the great sea" an integral part of the eschatological "garden of the Lord" through the mention of

4 "every living creature which swarms" (RSV).

5 RSV unwarrantedly adds it twice before, once after "waters" in v.9 and once instead of "it" in v.10.

> "fishers" standing on the river bank and thus on dry land (Ezek 47:10). The function of this unnecessary "addition" is to include indirectly the fish of the river and sea as an integral part of the "garden of the Lord," which could not have possibly been the case in Genesis 2. That the additional "fishers" (*dawwagim*; from the same root as *dag* [fish]) is intentional is evident from the fact that this noun is exceedingly rare in the Old Testament. It is found elsewhere only in Isaiah 19:8 and Jeremiah 16:16 where it appears as the alternate form *dayyagim.* So, formally, the Ezekelian *dawwagim* is unique in scripture.

In my study of Genesis 1-2 in *The Rise of Scripture,* I showed how the scriptural authors projected their actual world, which is the Syro-Arabian wilderness of Genesis 2:8-14, as the "universal" world of Genesis 1, which explains the overlapping of information between the two accounts of creation. And this is precisely what they did here in Ezekiel, which militates for the oneness of authorship of the entire scripture.

In scripture, then, it is the authors' Shemite world of Genesis 2, which is lacking fish and, by extension, the sea and its isles, that "informs" the world at large of Genesis 1 which includes the fish, the sea and its isles. Put otherwise, the authors are inviting the world at large to pattern itself after the authors' world and not vice versa. This thesis will be revisited with more clarity in the story of Noah's sons where it is the Japhethites, the authors' primary interest, that will find blessing only whenever they ultimately "dwell in the tents of Shem" (Gen 9:27) and thus enter into the "garden of God" of Genesis 2:8-14. This is precisely what Ezekiel is depicting as the last act in the scriptural story. Notice how it is the waters of the river that (1) water the trees—of the Shemite "garden"—*for healing* as well as food (Ezek 47:12), and at the same time (2) bring *healing* to its fish (v.9) that are "like the fish of the great sea" (v.10).

With this ending of the Book of Ezekiel one can see how the dilemma of unexpected "esteem" in which Genesis 1 held the "sea monsters" in that they are the only "living creature" (*nepheš ḥayyah*) that were "created" (v.21) *before* the human being (*ha'adam*)—also a *nepheš ḥayyah* (2:7)— was "created" (1:28), is resolved. As the Leviathan of the sea waters and, by extension, of their isles where the Japhethites reside, the "sea monster" is to be ultimately overcome. But overcoming can take the aspect of "taming" as in the case of Psalm 104:

> Yonder is the sea, great and wide, which teems with things innumerable, living things both small and great. There go the ships, and Leviathan which thou didst form to sport in it. (vv.25-26)

The sea monster, after all, is a sea denizen just as "every living creature that moves, with which the waters swarm, according to their kinds" (Gen 1:21; Ezek 47:9-10 KJV) and, as such, is included in the "fish of the sea" (Gen 1:26, 28; Ezek 47:9-10). As we have seen, this view of the matter is at its clearest in the story of Jonah where the "great fish" is rendered in the LXX as *kētos* (2:1 [twice], 2, 11)[6] which is the same noun it used to render *tannin* (sea monster) in Genesis 1:21. Jonah's mission was to the Hamite Nineveh, so he was not allowed to jump the gun by going to Tarshish. By using the "great fish" to re-route Jonah, God was reminding him that the matter was under control but had to wait for the end of times when God will send his messenger, the "Servant of the Lord," to the Japhethite nations (Is 42:1-7; 49:1-6).

The implementation of God's ultimate plan is the subject of the last book of the New Testament canon and, by the same token, the concluding book of the entire scripture. Following the lead of Ezekiel 47, the author writes:

> Then he showed me the river of the water of life, bright as crystal, flowing from the throne of God and of the Lamb through the

6 Corresponding to RSV 1:17 [twice]; 2:1, 10.

> middle of the street of the city; also, on either side of the river, the tree of life with its twelve kinds of fruit, yielding its fruit each month; and the leaves of the tree were *for the healing of the nations.* (Rev 22:1-2)

And just as the *biblion* (book, scroll) that "had writing on the front and on the back" (Ezek 2:10), to which nothing could be added and from which nothing could be subtracted, contained the "word of the Lord" that was handed to Ezekiel (1:3) the "prophet" (2:5), the "words of the prophecy" (Rev 1:3) handed to John (v.1) the "prophet"[7] were handed to him as a *biblion* (book, scroll) to which nothing could be added and from which nothing could be subtracted:

> And he said to me, "These *words* are trustworthy and true. And the Lord, the God of the spirits of the prophets, has sent his angel to show his servants what must soon take place. And behold, I am coming soon." Blessed is he who keeps *the words of the prophecy of this book* (*bibliou*). ... And he said to me, "Do not seal up *the words of the prophecy of this book* (*bibliou*), for the time is near." ... I warn (*martyrō*; testifies to) every one who hears *the words of the prophecy of this book* (*bibliou*): if any one adds to them, God will add to him the plagues described in this book (*bibliō*), and if any one takes away from *the words of the book* (*bibliou*) *of this prophecy*, God will take away his share in the tree of life and in the holy city, which are described in this book (*bibliō*). He who testifies to (*martyrōn*) these things says, "Surely I am coming soon." Amen. Come, Lord Jesus! (Rev 22:6-7, 10, 18-20)

In turn, due to Revelation's interest in the end times, it stands to reason that this book allocates a lion's share to the "dragon" (*drakōn*)—both "sea monster" and "serpent"—of the LXX. Here again the author uses the interplay between God's opponent being active on earth as "serpent" (*naḥaš*) and in the sea as "sea monster" (*tannin*) as one hears in Isaiah:

---

7 Blessed is he who keeps the words of the prophecy of this book. I John am he who heard and saw these things. And when I heard and saw them, I fell down to worship at the feet of the angel who showed them to me; but he said to me, "You must not do that! *I am a fellow servant with you and your brethren the prophets*, and with those who keep the words of this book. Worship God." (Rev 22:7-9)

> In that day the Lord with his hard and great and strong sword will punish Leviathan the fleeing serpent (Hebrew *naḥaš*; Greek *ophis*), Leviathan the twisting serpent (Hebrew *naḥaš*; Greek *ophis*), and he will slay the dragon (Hebrew *tannin*; Greek *drakonta*) that is in the sea. (Is 27:1)

This explains the following phraseology in Revelation 12 where "dragon" and "serpent" (vv.9, 14, 15) are interchangeable and even presented as the same reality as in Isaiah: "And the great dragon was thrown down, that ancient serpent." (Rev 12:9) Still the entire passage offers more than meets the ear at first hearing:

> And a great portent appeared in heaven, a woman clothed with the sun, with the moon under her feet, and on her head a crown of twelve stars; she was with child and she cried out in her pangs of birth, in anguish for delivery. And another portent appeared in heaven; behold, a great red *dragon, with seven heads and ten horns, and seven diadems upon his heads*. His tail swept down a third of the stars of heaven, and cast them to the earth. And the dragon stood before the woman who was about to bear a child, that he might devour her child when she brought it forth; *she brought forth a male child, one who is to rule all the nations with a rod of iron*, but her child was caught up to God and to his throne, and *the woman fled into the wilderness, where she has a place prepared by God, in which to be nourished* for one thousand two hundred and sixty days. Now war arose in heaven, Michael and his angels fighting against the dragon; and the dragon and his angels fought, but they were defeated and there was no longer any place for them in heaven. And the great dragon was thrown down, *that ancient serpent*, who is called the Devil and Satan, the deceiver of the whole world -- he was thrown down to the earth, and his angels were thrown down with him. ... But the woman was given the two wings of the great eagle that she might fly from the *serpent into the wilderness, to the place where she is to be nourished* for a time, and times, and half a time. The *serpent* poured water like a river out of his mouth after the woman, to sweep her away with the flood. But the earth came to the help of the woman, and the earth opened its mouth and swallowed the river which the dragon had poured from his mouth. Then the dragon was angry with the woman, and *went off to make war on the rest of her offspring*, on those who keep the commandments of God

> and bear testimony to Jesus. *And he stood on the sand of the sea.* (Rev 12:1-9, 14-17)
>
> And I saw a *beast* (*thyrion*) rising out of the sea, *with ten horns and seven heads, with ten diadems upon its horns* and a blasphemous name upon its heads. And the beast that I saw was like a leopard, its feet were like a bear's, and its mouth was like a lion's mouth. *And to it the dragon gave his power and his throne and great authority.* (Rev 13:1-2)

The "heavenly" dragon that battled the woman and her offspring on the *earth*, and more specifically, the wilderness, is introduced as "serpent" (vv.9, 14, 15). However, when it embarks on waging war against the woman's remaining offspring, it does so while standing *on the sand of the sea* and calling upon its surrogate, or alter ego, the beast (*thyrion*) that *comes out of the sea*.[8] The hearers are surprised because, at the outset, in Genesis, they had encountered the dragon (*drakōn*) as sea denizen (1:21) while land animals as repeatedly *thyria* (beasts).[9] Yet the author of Revelation has no qualms switching the roles so to speak. In other words, the ultimate enemy remains the same. It is its area of activity that differs. The earth as dry land and, more specifically, the wilderness is the "domain" of the Shemite scriptural Israel whereas the sea and its isles (the sand of the sea) are the "domain" of the Japhethite "nations." Notice the sequence in the dragon's activity, first the wilderness, and then the sea. The "healing" of the nations (Rev 22:2), in God's and not Jonah's time, is the ultimate goal of scripture as was made clear in Genesis 10 where Japheth, the youngest among Noah's sons, was given the place of honor in the *toledot* of the three brothers. Put scripturally, it is the scriptural "nations,"

---

8 In Acts we find another instance of the exchangeability between "serpent" and "beast/creature": "Paul had gathered a bundle of sticks and put them on the fire, when a *viper* came out because of the heat and fastened on his hand. When the natives saw the creature (*thyrion*) hanging from his hand, they said to one another, 'No doubt this man is a murderer. Though he has escaped from the sea, justice has not allowed him to live.' He, however, shook off the creature (*thyrion*) into the fire and suffered no harm." (Act 28:3-5)

9 Gen 1:24, 25, 30; 2:19, 20; 3:1, 14 and throughout Genesis 6-9.

and not the scriptural Israel, that bracket the scriptural odyssey between Genesis and Revelation.

15

Jonah in the Gospel of Matthew

In the New Testament writings, Jonah is mentioned by name only in Matthew and Luke and, in both cases, in conjunction with the "sign of Jonah" (Mt 12; 16; Lk 11). It would be worth our while to go in depth as to how the matter is handled in Matthew for the following reasons:

1. There is nothing heard in Luke 11:29-32 that is not found in Matthew 12:38-42.
2. In addition to the "sign" of the repentance of the Ninevites that is found in Luke, Matthew refers to the sign of Jonah's spending "three days and three nights in the belly of the whale" (12:40; see Jon 1:17).
3. In Matthew 16 we have another instance of the "sign of Jonah" (v.4) followed shortly thereafter by Jesus calling Peter "Simon Barjona" (Aramaic, meaning son of Jonah; v.17).

Throughout my entire work on the New Testament literature I have repeatedly indicated that the Gospel of Matthew is for the New Testament what the Book of Genesis is for the Old Testament. In this present volume I have refined my thesis in *The Rise of Scripture* that the entire message of scripture is contained not only in the Book of Genesis as a whole, but in its first few chapters. In the same way, the Gospel of Matthew subsumes the entire message of the New Testament. That it was intentionally construed as such can be readily seen in the title itself: "The book of Genesis (*biblos geneseōs*) of Jesus Christ, son of David, son of Abraham." (Mt 1:1). That this choice of vocabulary was intended is evident in that the writer repeats it verbatim at the start of the "story of the birth of Jesus Christ": "Now the birth (*genesis*; genesis) of Jesus Christ took place in this way." (1:18) Had the authors intended to say "birth" they could have readily used the Greek noun *gennēsis*, especially since just two verses earlier they used the verb *egennēthē*, which is from the same root *genn*— to speak of Jesus' birth: "and Jacob the father of Joseph the husband of Mary, of whom Jesus was born (*egennēthē*), who is called Christ." (v.16).

For all intents and purposes, virtually all translations present us with a classic case of misrepresentation, if not outright distortion, of the original text. The two exceptions, to my knowledge, are the French translations, *La Bible de Jérusalem* and *Traduction Oecuménique de la Bible*, that stick to the original: *genèse* (vv.1 and 18) in the first case and *origines* (v.1) and *origine* (v.18) in the second case. One can, with a grain of salt, understand and possibly even excuse the rendering of *genesis* in verse 18 into "birth" due to its proximity with *egennēthē* (was born) in verse 16. However, the hearer will still miss the authors' intentional connection between verses 1 and 18. How would the hearer of a translation at least consider that the authors of Matthew intended to link *materially* this Gospel with the LXX Book of Genesis where the phrase *hē biblos geneseōs* occurs twice, in Genesis 2:4 and 5:1. Its use in Genesis 2:4 is definitely intentional in that (1) the LXX 5:1 (*hē biblos geneseōs*) is a literal translation of the original Hebrew *sepher toledot* (the book of the *toledot*), whereas (2) although the Hebrew 2:4 is simply *toledot*, which the LXX usually renders as *hai geneseis* (the origins, the makings; 6:8; 10:1; 11:10, 27), in this case it added *biblos* before *geneseis* so that the result was a carbon copy of 5:1. In so doing the LXX wanted to draw the hearer's attention to the fact that scripture is treating the heavens and the earth in the same vein as the human beings *in spite* of the oddity of such a comparison.

Thus, the LXX translators, being themselves the authors of the Hebrew, rendered explicitly in Greek what was implicit in Hebrew, namely, that Genesis 1-4 was a "book"—a closed chapter—and the *toledot* of Adam (5:1-6:8) formed the *second* "chapter" in the story consigned in the Book of Genesis. I am convinced that, along the same lines and through its choice of words, the Gospel of Matthew was establishing itself as the *first*—and thus institutional—book of the New Testament canon, just as the Book of Genesis functions that way in the Old Testament canon. If so, then, in the light of my study of the two books of Genesis and Jonah, it becomes understandable that Matthew allocates a great importance to the latter.

Let us start with Matthew's first reference to the "sign of Jonah," which corresponds to the one instance in Luke:

> When the crowds were increasing, he began to say, "This generation is an evil generation; it seeks a sign, but no sign shall be given to it except the sign of Jonah. For as Jonah became a sign to the men of Nineveh, so will the Son of man be to this generation. The queen of the South will arise (*egerthēsetai*) at the judgment with the men of this generation and condemn them; for she came from the ends of the earth to hear the wisdom of Solomon, and behold, something greater than Solomon is here. The men of Nineveh will arise (*anastēsontai*) at the judgment with this generation and condemn it; for they repented at the preaching of Jonah, and behold, something greater than Jonah is here." (Lk 11:29-32)

> Then some of the scribes and Pharisees said to him, "Teacher, we wish to see a sign from you." But he answered them, "An evil and adulterous generation seeks for a sign; but no sign shall be given to it except the sign of the prophet Jonah. For as Jonah was three days and three nights in the belly of the whale, so will the Son of man be three days and three nights in the heart of the earth. The men of Nineveh will arise (*anastēsontai*) at the judgment with this generation and condemn it; for they repented at the preaching of Jonah, and behold, something greater than Jonah is here. The queen of the South will arise (*egerthēsetai*) at the judgment with this generation and condemn it; for she came from the ends of the earth to hear the wisdom of Solomon, and behold, something greater than Solomon is here." (Mt 12:38-42)

Matthew clearly expands on Luke's "For as Jonah became a sign to the men of Nineveh, so will the Son of man be to this generation" (11:30). However, Luke understood the basic message of the Book of Jonah along the same lines of my interpretation. The Ninevites, as Hamites, live together with their Shemite counterparts in the scriptural world that extends over the entire Syrian-Arabian wilderness in both its parts, the Northern or Syrian wilderness and the Southern or Arabian wilderness, as evidenced in both Genesis 2 and Genesis 10:

> A river flowed out of Eden to water the garden, and there it divided and became four rivers. The name of the first is Pishon; it is the one which flows around the whole land of Havilah, where there is gold; and the gold of that land is good; bdellium and onyx stone are there. The name of the second river is Gihon; it is the one which flows around the whole land of Cush. And the name of the third river is Tigris, which flows east of Assyria. And the fourth river is the Euphrates. (Gen 2:10-14)

> The sons of Cush: Seba, Havilah, Sabtah, Raamah, and Sabteca. The sons of Raamah: Sheba and Dedan. … To Shem also, the father of all the children of Eber, the elder brother of Japheth, children were born. The sons of Shem: Elam, Asshur, Arpachshad, Lud, and Aram. The sons of Aram: Uz, Hul, Gether, and Mash. Arpachshad became the father of Shelah; and Shelah became the father of Eber. To Eber were born two sons: the name of the one was Peleg, for in his days the earth was divided, and his brother's name was Joktan. Joktan became the father of Almodad, Sheleph, Hazarmaveth, Jerah, Hadoram, Uzal, Diklah, Obal, Abimael, Sheba, Ophir, Havilah, and Jobab; all these were the sons of Joktan. (Gen 10:7, 21-29)

The division of the scriptural "earth"—the Syro-Arabian wilderness—into North and South is already evident in Genesis 2. The hearers were familiar with the geography of the Rivers Euphrates and Tigris that are lumped together in one verse where Assyria is named by name. As for Cush, it is also familiar to the hearers in that it refers to Egypt and Ethiopia. Notice how the authors do not name the southern rivers but give them generic names Pishon (*pišon*) and Gihon (*giḥon*) connoting gushing and bursting as waters do, most probably because they wanted to avoid naming the Nile which flows in Africa, East of the Red Sea, and not within the range of the Syro-Arabian wilderness.

Genesis 10 takes the matter one step further to spell out the division of the scriptural earth in two between the two sons of Shem's descendant Eber (*'eber*)—whence *'ibri* (Hebrew) and the quintessential representative of the Shemites—Peleg and Yoktan: "To Eber were born two sons: the name of the one was Peleg (*peleg*), for in his days *the earth was divided* (*niplegah*), and his brother's name was Joktan (*yoqtan* from *qatan* [young, younger, lesser])." (Gen 10:25) So Peleg, the carrier of Shem's progeny (11:16-19) and, through Terah and Abram, a resident of the Syrian wilderness, the region of the Two Rivers, sets the tone. Joktan, the progenitor of the peoples of the Arabian wilderness through Sheba (10:28) and Havilah (v.29), follows suit. His area is still a matter of concern in scripture, which is evident in the story of the queen of Sheba coming to learn of Solomon's wisdom (1 Kg 10:1-13). In the Book of Jonah, Nineveh was representative of the Syrian and, by extension, the Arabian wilderness, in contradistinction to the sea that is reflective of the domain of the Japhethites. Thus, Luke correctly understood the message of that book and included in the "sign of Jonah" the invitation for repentance to Sheba as well as to Nineveh.

Matthew endorsed Luke's view and elaborated on it in a way that would fit his overall purview. The two verbs "arise" (Lk 11:31, 32) referring to the rising of the dead unto judgment (Dan 12:2; see also Jn 5:29; 1 Cor 11:31-32) are *egerthēsetai* (will be raised) and *anastēsontai* (will stand up), which are the two verbs found in the Pauline corpus to speak of the resurrection of Christ. This allowed Matthew to refine the "sign of Jonah" by adding another component to which he gave precedence, namely, the resurrection of the Son of man mentioned in Luke. This fits the function of the New Testament Son of Man who was launched by Mark and patterned after Ezekiel, the "son of man," who taught in parables and who was dubbed "the 'parabler' of parables" (*memaššel mešalim*; maker of allegories, Ezek 20:49). That is why the people, we are told, "were astonished at Jesus' teaching (*didakhē*)" (Mk 1:22) rather than at him, which was picked up by Matthew:

> And they went into Capernaum; and immediately on the sabbath he entered the synagogue and taught. And *they were astonished at his teaching* (*didakhē*), for he taught them as one who had authority, and not as the scribes. (Mk 1:21-22)

> And they were all amazed, so that they questioned among themselves, saying, "What is this? A new teaching (*didakhē*)! With authority he commands even the unclean spirits, and they obey him." (Mk 1:27)

> And he taught them many things in *parables*, and in his teaching (*didakhē*) he said to them. (Mk 4:2)

> And the chief priests and the scribes heard it and sought a way to destroy him; for they feared him, because *all the multitude* (*okhlos*) *was astonished at his teaching* (*didakhē*). (Mk 11:18)

> And when Jesus finished these sayings, *the crowds* (*okhloi*) *were astonished at his teaching* (*didakhē*), for he taught them as one who had authority, and not as their scribes. (Mt 7:28-29)

> Then the disciples came and said to him, "Why do you speak to them in *parables*?" (Mt 13:10)

> And when the crowd (*okhloi*; crowds) heard it, they were astonished at his teaching (*didakhē*). (Mt 22:33)

This, in turn, explains why, in the Gospels, the title most used by an interlocutor when addressing Jesus is "teacher." And this is precisely what is heard at the start of the first Matthean episode regarding the "sign of Jonah": "Then some of the scribes and Pharisees said to him, 'Teacher, we wish to see a sign from you.'" (Mt 12:38) This pinning down of Jesus *as teacher* against the scribes and the Pharisees will be picked up again in the lengthy harangue against them that is special to Matthew 23: the scribes and the Pharisees "love being called rabbi by men. But you are not to be called rabbi, for you have *one teacher*, and you are all brethren." (vv.7-8) Still, what is more important is the expansion of the sign so as to include the "risen Son of man:" "For as Jonah was three days and three nights in the belly of the whale, so will the Son of man be three days and three nights in the heart of the earth." (Mt 12:40) This, in turn, will find its ultimate resolution in yet another account, again special to Matthew, which describes the judgment of *all nations* by the "glorious" Son of man:

> When the Son of man comes in his glory, and all the angels with him, then he will sit on his glorious throne. Before him will be gathered all the nations, and he will separate them one from another as a shepherd separates the sheep from the goats, and he will place the sheep at his right hand, but the goats at the left. (Mt 25:31-33)

This judgment is guaranteed to be equitable and just since, according to that same Gospel, by that time, those nations will have been forewarned by Jesus' disciples: "Go therefore and make disciples of all nations, baptizing them in the name of the Father and of the Son and of the Holy Spirit, *teaching them to observe all that I have commanded you*; and lo, I am with you always, to the close of the age." (Mt 28:19-20) That is why the excuse presented by the sheep as well as the goats that they did not know (Mt 25:37-39, 44) is at best ludicrous! They should have heeded Jesus' disciples' teaching just as the king and the citizens of Nineveh heeded Jonah's call (Jon 3:5-9).

So, the "sign of Jonah," that is, the message of the Book of Jonah is played out again in the Gospel of Matthew. This is corroborated in a second passage, special to Matthew, where we again encounter the "sign of Jonah":

> And the Pharisees and Sadducees came, and to test him they asked him to show them a sign from heaven. He answered them, "When it is evening, you say, 'It will be fair weather; for the sky is red.' And in the morning 'It will be stormy today, for the sky is red and threatening.' You know how to interpret the appearance of the sky, but you cannot interpret the signs of the times. An evil and adulterous generation seeks for a sign, but no sign shall be given to it except the sign of Jonah (*Iōna*)." So he left them and departed. (Mt 16:1-4)

This passage sounds as a bland repeat of the previous one at first hearing. However, it is interesting on two counts. On the one hand, in Matthew the pair "Pharisees and Sadducees" is the crimson thread (Mt 16:1, 6, 11, 12) that holds together the entire episode (Mt 16:1-12) which culminates in a summation that is an open criticism of their "teaching": "Then they understood that he did not tell them to beware of the leaven of bread, but of the teaching (*didakhēs*) of the Pharisees and Sadducees." (v.12) On the other hand, the only other instance in the Gospel where we encounter the pair "Pharisees and Sadducees," just as we have in Matthew 12:38-42, is in conjunction with both repentance and final judgment as well as resurrection:

> But when he saw many of the Pharisees and Sadducees coming for baptism, he said to them, "You brood of vipers! Who warned you to flee from *the wrath to come*? Bear fruit that befits *repentance*, and do not presume to say to yourselves, 'We have Abraham as our father'; for I tell you, God is able from these stones to *raise up* (*egeirai*) children to Abraham." (Mt 3:7-9)

A striking feature of Matthew 16:1-12 is that it precedes the episode of Peter's confession of Christ (vv.13-20), which is much lengthier (eight verses) than its parallel counterparts in Mark 8:27-30 (four verses) and Luke 9:18-21 (four verses) due to its expansion concerning Simon Peter and his role in the church. The additional lengthy insertion in Matthew between Peter's confession (Mt 16:16; Mk 8:29; Lk 9:20) and Jesus' charge to his disciples not to tell anyone about him (Mt 16:20; Mk 8:30; Lk 9:21) reads thus:

> And Jesus answered him, "Blessed are you, Simon Barjona (*bariōna*)! For flesh and blood has not revealed this to you, but my Father who is in heaven. And I tell you, you are Peter, and on this rock I will build my church, and the powers of death shall not prevail against it. I will give you the keys of the kingdom of heaven, and whatever you bind on earth shall be bound in heaven, and whatever you loose on earth shall be loosed in heaven." (Mt 16:17-19)

Besides the reference to the "church," the Matthean addition begins with Jesus' addressing Peter as Simon Barjona. Not only is the noun *ekklēsia* (church) reserved in the Gospels only to Matthew, once in 16:18 and twice in 18:17, but, more importantly for our discussion, it contains the appellation

Simon Barjona unique throughout scripture, both Old and New Testaments. The intentionality is unmissable. In the former case, one would have to wait until chapter 18 to figure out the meaning and function of "church" in Matthew 16:18. But, in the latter case, *Bariōna* cannot but recall the sound *Iōna* just heard a few verses earlier (16:4). The hearer's ear is drawn to the obvious connection due to the use of the Semitic *Simon Barjona* (v.17). Notice how the author piqued the hearer's attention by referring to Peter in the previous verse as "Simon Peter"—also a unique instance in Matthew[1]—as compared to simply "Peter" in Mark and Luke:

> Simon Peter replied, "You are the Christ, the Son of the living God." (Mt 16:16)
>
> Peter answered him, "You are the Christ." (Mk 8:29)
>
> And Peter answered, "The Christ of God." (Lk 9:20)

Given that *bar yonah* is Aramaic for "son of Jonah," which means "someone taking after Jonah, someone similar to Jonah, someone the like of Jonah," there can be no doubt that Peter here is likened to Jonah. The author's intention to cast Peter as "another" Jonah in conjunction with his assignment as carrier of a message of repentance has been already deftly prepared for in another uniquely encompassing Matthean chapter during which the "first" "Simon, who is called Peter" and his colleagues were "called" to be "sent out" as "doves," which is the only occurrence of that noun outside the baptism of Jesus episode in all four Gospels (Mt 3:16; Mk 1:10; Lk 3:22; Jn 1:22):[2]

> And he called to him his twelve disciples and gave them authority over unclean spirits, to cast them out, and to heal every disease and every infirmity. The names of the twelve apostles are these: first, Simon, who is called Peter, and Andrew his brother; James the son of Zebedee, and John his brother; Philip and Bartholomew; Thomas and Matthew the tax collector; James the

1 In Matthew 4:18 and 10:2 we have "Simon, who is called Peter."
2 See my comments further below.

son of Alphaeus, and Thaddaeus; Simon the Cananaean, and Judas Iscariot, who betrayed him. These twelve Jesus sent out, charging them … "Behold, I send you out as sheep in the midst of wolves; so be wise (*phronimoi*) as serpents and innocent (*akeraioi*) as *doves*."[3] (Mt 10: 1-5, 16)

Still, in which sense would Peter be "like Jonah"? Since the author intentionally used the Semitic noun Simon, the answer lies in the meaning of the root of that name which could be either *šamaʿ* (hear, listen, obey), as in the name *šimʿon* (Simeon; Gen 29:33), or *šaman/šamen* (be fat, be thick) with a negative connotation as in all the instances of that verb in the Old Testament:

But Jeshurun waxed fat (*yišman*), and kicked; you waxed fat (*šamanta*), you grew thick, you became sleek; then he forsook God who made him, and scoffed at the Rock of his salvation. (Deut 32:15)

Make the heart of this people *fat* (*hašmen*), and their ears heavy, and shut their eyes; lest they see with their eyes, and hear with their ears, and understand with their hearts, and turn and be healed. (Is 6:10)

Like a basket full of birds, their houses are full of treachery; therefore they have become great and rich, they have grown fat (*šamenu*) and sleek. They know no bounds in deeds of wickedness; they judge not with justice the cause of the fatherless, to make it prosper, and they do not defend the rights of the needy. (Jer 5:27-28)

And they captured fortified cities and a rich land, and took possession of houses full of all good things, cisterns hewn out, vineyards, olive orchards and fruit trees in abundance; so they ate, and were filled and became fat (*yašminu*), and delighted themselves in thy great goodness. Nevertheless they were disobedient and rebelled against thee and cast thy law behind their back and killed thy prophets, who had warned them in order

---

3 One can readily detect the Pauline source of that statement: "For while your obedience is known to all, so that I rejoice over you, I would have you wise (*sophous*) as to what is good and guileless (*akeraious*) as to what is evil." (Rom 16:19)

> to turn them back to thee, and they committed great blasphemies. (Neh 9:25-26)

Either way one takes it, the message is sarcastic and fits the story of Jonah who was chosen by God to be his prophet and yet ended up trying to renege on his mission. The same applies here to "Simon, who is called Peter," who was introduced as "first" in the list of Jesus' twelve apostles: "The names of the twelve apostles are these: *first* (*prōtos*), Simon, who is called Peter, and Andrew his brother; James the son of Zebedee, and John his brother." (Mt 10:2) Yet, his zeal to steer his master away from an ignominious death (God forbid, Lord! This shall never happen to you; 16:22) will prove not only misplaced, but also reveal that he himself was not ready to face the challenge of having been called to become "the rock" of the church, which explains why Simon was given the name "Peter" as a calling: "And I tell you, you are Peter (*Petros*), and on this rock (*petra*)[4] I will build my church, and the powers of death shall not prevail against it." (16:18) As the newly named Peter, the rock, he will nevertheless renege on his mission, as Jonah tried to do before him, by turning his back on his master three times just after his solemn pledge not to be like the others:

> Peter declared to him, "Though they all fall away because of you, I will never fall away." Jesus said to him, "Truly, I say to you, this very night, before the cock crows, you will deny me three times." Peter said to him, "Even if I must die with you, I will not deny you." And so said all the disciples. (Mt 26:33-35)

> Now Peter was sitting outside in the courtyard. And a maid came up to him, and said, "You also were with Jesus the Galilean." But he denied it before them all, saying, "I do not know what you mean." And when he went out to the porch, another maid saw him, and she said to the bystanders, "This man was with Jesus of

---

4 The intended pun in Greek is evident. See the previous double occurrence of "rock" in Matthew: "Every one then who hears these words of mine and does them will be like a wise man who built his house upon the rock (*petran*); and the rain fell, and the floods came, and the winds blew and beat upon that house, but it did not fall, because it had been founded on the rock (*petran*)." (Mt 7:24-25)

> Nazareth." And again he denied it with an oath, "I do not know the man." After a little while the bystanders came up and said to Peter, "Certainly you are also one of them, for your accent betrays you." Then he began to invoke a curse on himself and to swear, "I do not know the man." And immediately the cock crowed. And Peter remembered the saying of Jesus, "Before the cock crows, you will deny me three times." And he went out and wept bitterly. (Mt 26: 69-75)

Just as in the case of Jonah, the mission assigned shall be realized despite Peter's recalcitrance. Moreover, his mission will top that of Jonah who was sent to relay *God's words* to the Hamite Nineveh *despite his unwillingness* and being forbidden from reaching the Japhethite Tarshish. Peter's mission will go beyond that of Jonah in that he, along with his colleagues, will be sent to relay *Jesus' words* to "all" the Japhethite nations, *despite their indecisiveness*:

> Now the eleven disciples went to Galilee, to the mountain to which Jesus had directed them. And when they saw him they worshiped him; *but some doubted.*[5] And Jesus came and said to them, "All authority in heaven and on earth has been given to me. Go therefore and make disciples of *all nations*, baptizing them in the name of the Father and of the Son and of the Holy Spirit, teaching them to observe *all that I have commanded you*; and lo, I am with you always, to the close of the age." (Mt 28:16-20)

It is understandable then, due to its all-encompassing nature, that the mission of Peter and his colleagues will extend until "the close of the age" at which time the Son of man will enact the divine judgment on all:

> He answered, "He who sows the good seed is the Son of man; the field is the world, and the good seed means the sons of the kingdom; the weeds are the sons of the evil one, and the enemy who sowed them is the devil; the harvest is the close of the age,

---

5 The original Greek *hoi de edistasan* is better translated as "yet these (they) doubted." All the translations, beginning with the Vulgate, avoid the "scandal" by hearing it as "(only) some doubted." Adducing the argument, "If all doubted, how could the Lord send them forth as his apostles?" does not hold water since God did the same with Jonah despite his outright recalcitrance.

> and the reapers are angels. Just as the weeds are gathered and burned with fire, so will it be at the close of the age. The Son of man will send his angels, and they will gather out of his kingdom all causes of sin and all evildoers, and throw them into the furnace of fire; there men will weep and gnash their teeth. ... So it will be at the close of the age. The angels will come out and separate the evil from the righteous." (Mt 13:37-42, 49)

What is striking in this regard is that the only other instance of "the close of the age" in this Gospel is found in conjunction with "sign" and "coming"—to fulfill a mission—in between chapters 13 and 28: "As he sat on the Mount of Olives, the disciples came to him privately, saying, 'Tell us, when will this be, and what will be the sign of your coming and of the close of the age?'" (Mt 24:3)

Jonah the Dove

There can be no doubt, for those who have "ears to hear," that the mission of "the prophet" Jonah (2 Kg 14:25) presented in the Book of Jonah offered the author of Matthew a blue print for the continuation of the mission to the nations. In the New Testament, Jonah is dubbed as "the prophet" only in Matthew and at his first mention (12:39), that is, he was *introduced* as "the prophet." At this occasion, in conjunction with describing Jonah's mission among the Ninevites, Jesus ends by saying "and behold, something greater than Jonah is here." (v.41) Later, at his entry into Jerusalem, and only in Matthew, we hear of Jesus as follows:

> And the crowds that went before him and that followed him shouted, "Hosanna to the Son of David! Blessed is he who comes in the name of the Lord! Hosanna in the highest!" And when he entered Jerusalem, all the city was stirred, saying, "Who is this?" And the crowds said, "This is *the prophet* Jesus from Nazareth of Galilee." (Mt 21:9-11)

The importance of the additional "from Nazareth of Galilee" after "the prophet Jesus" will become clear to the Gospel's addressees when they will soon hear the comments of the two maids in the courtyard:

> Now Peter was sitting outside in the courtyard. And a maid came up to him, and said, "You also were with Jesus *the Galilean.*" But he denied it before them all, saying, "I do not know what you mean." And when he went out to the porch, another maid saw him, and she said to the bystanders, "This man was with Jesus *of Nazareth.*" And again he denied it with an oath, "I do not know the man." (Mt 26:69-72)

This is a clear invitation for us to remember the beginning of Matthew's Gospel where one is repeatedly reminded no less than seven times in three chapters that Galilee is the "homeland" of Jesus (2:22; 3:13; 4:12, 15, 18, 23, 25) and, more specifically, that Nazareth is his "hometown":

> But when he heard that Archelaus reigned over Judea in place of his father Herod, he was afraid to go there, and being warned in a dream he withdrew to the district of *Galilee*. And he went and dwelt in a city called Nazareth, that what was spoken by the prophets might be fulfilled, "He shall be called a *Nazarene.*" (Mt 2:22-23)[6]

At one point, Jesus' "homeland" is referred to as "Galilee of the Gentiles (*ethnōn*; nations)" in a quotation taken from the *prophet* Isaiah:

> Now when he heard that John had been arrested, he withdrew into Galilee; and leaving Nazareth he went and dwelt in Capernaum by the sea, in the territory of Zebulun and Naphtali, that what was spoken by *the prophet* Isaiah might be fulfilled: "The land of Zebulun and the land of Naphtali, toward the sea, across the Jordan, *Galilee of the Gentiles* (*ethnōn*; nations)—the people who sat in darkness have seen a great light, and for those who sat in the region and shadow of death light has dawned." (Mt 4:12-16)

So, according to Matthew, it is Jesus "the prophet" who fulfills the mission started by Jonah "the prophet" in that he was assigned to reach out to the Japhethite nations. Notice the stress

---

6 See also 3:13; 4:12, 15, 18, 23, 25.

on the "sea" twice: "by the sea" (v.15) and "toward the sea" (v.16).

When one listens to the above quoted text (Mt 4:12-16) in its larger context one will realize that the "sign of Jonah" was alluded to at the start of the Gospel of Matthew and thus informs that Gospel, which, in turn, explains the later double reference to that sign, unique to Matthew, in chapters 12 and 16. Add to this that chapter 12 looks ahead to the end of the Gospel through the reference to the resurrection, and chapter 16 harks back to the beginning of the Gospel through the phrase "the Pharisees and Sadducees" (3:7) and one cannot but at least suspect that the "sign of Jonah" and, by extension, the Book of Jonah was on the mind of the author of the Book of Matthew.

In other "scripturally coined" words, the Book of Jonah stretches like a fisher's net over the Book of Matthew. Let us consider the broader context of Matthew 4:12-16:

> But when he saw many of the *Pharisees and Sadducees* coming for baptism, he said to them, "You brood of vipers! Who warned you to flee from the wrath to come? Bear fruit that befits *repentance*, and do not presume to say to yourselves, 'We have Abraham as our father'; for I tell you, God is able from these stones to raise up children to Abraham. Even now the axe is laid to the root of the trees; every tree therefore that does not bear good fruit is cut down and thrown into the *fire*. I baptize you with water for *repentance*, but he who is coming after me is mightier than I, whose sandals I am not worthy to carry; he will baptize you with the *Holy Spirit* and with *fire*. His winnowing fork is in his hand, and he will clear his threshing floor and *gather his wheat* into the granary (*apothēkēn*), but the chaff he will burn with unquenchable *fire*." Then Jesus came from Galilee to the Jordan to John, to be baptized by him. John would have prevented him, saying, "I need to be baptized by you, and do you come to me?" But Jesus answered him, "Let it be so now; for thus it is fitting for us to fulfil all righteousness." Then he consented. And when Jesus was baptized, he went up immediately from the water, and behold, the heavens were opened and he saw *the Spirit of God descending like a dove*, and alighting on him; and lo, a voice from heaven, saying,

> "This is my beloved Son, with whom I am well pleased." Then Jesus was led up by the Spirit into the wilderness to be tempted by the devil. And he *fasted forty days and forty nights*, and afterward he was hungry. (Mt 3:7-4:2)

> Now when he heard that John had been arrested, he withdrew into Galilee; and leaving Nazareth he went and dwelt in Capernaum by the sea, in the territory of Zebulun and Naphtali, that what was spoken by the prophet Isaiah might be fulfilled: "The land of Zebulun and the land of Naphtali, toward the sea, across the Jordan, Galilee of the Gentiles—the people who sat in darkness have seen a great light, and for those who sat in the region and shadow of death light has dawned." From that time Jesus began to preach, saying, "*Repent*, for the kingdom of heaven is at hand." As he walked by the Sea of Galilee, he saw two brothers, *Simon who is called Peter* and Andrew his brother, casting a net into the sea; for they were *fishermen*. And he said to them, "Follow me, and I will make you *fishers of men*." Immediately they left their nets and followed him. And going on from there he saw two other brothers, James the son of Zebedee and John his brother, in the boat with Zebedee their father, mending their nets, and he called them. Immediately they left the boat and their father, and followed him. And he went about all Galilee, teaching in their synagogues and preaching the gospel of the kingdom and *healing* every disease and every infirmity among the people. So his fame spread throughout all *Syria*, and they brought him all the sick, those afflicted with various diseases and pains, demoniacs, epileptics, and paralytics, and he *healed* them. And great crowds followed him *from Galilee and the Decapolis and Jerusalem and Judea and from beyond the Jordan*. (Mt 4:12-25)

Notice the following features of these two passages that introduce the "mission" of "the prophet Jesus from Nazareth of Galilee" (Mt 21:11):

- The phrase "Pharisees and Sadducees" occurs four more times in Matthew, all of which in the episode (16:1-12) immediately preceding that of Simon Peter's confession at Caesarea Philippi (vv.13-23) where we hear of John the Baptist (v.14) as well as of Barjona (v.17).

- "Repentance," the key word in Jonah, is heard three times (3:8, 11; 4:17).

- The phrase "will gather (*synaxei* from *synagō*) *his* wheat (*siton*) into the granary (*apothēkēn*)" (3:12) occurs in the New Testament twice more, once in the Lukan parallel 3:17 and the other time in Matthew 13:30: "but gather (*synagagete*) the wheat (*siton*) into *my* barn (*apothēkēn*)." The link between the two is further enhanced by "fire" that is repeated in both passages (3:10, 11, 12; 13:40, 42, 50), and more specifically the phrase "burn with fire" (3:12; 13:40). My readers are reminded that, through the phrase "the close of the age" (Mt 13:39, 40, 49), Matthew 13 looks ahead to the Gospel's ending (and lo, I am with you always, to the close of the age; Mt 28:20) as well as to Jesus' statement concerning the "sign" of his "coming" as "Son of man" to judge all nations (25:31-46): "Tell us, when will this be, and what will be the sign of your coming and of the close of the age? … As were the days of Noah, so will be the coming of the Son of man. (24:3, 37)

- The Holy Spirit, which is the "sign" that differentiates Jesus' baptism from John's (3:11), takes the form of a "dove" (Hebrew *yonah*), that is, of Jonah.

- Another striking double feature of Matthew is the evangelist's statement in 4:2: "And he fasted forty days and forty nights." Two indicators point to Jonah. While Luke has "ate nothing" during "forty days," which explains Jesus' hunger (4:1), Matthew uses specifically the verb "fasted" (*nēstevsas*), which cannot but bring to mind the Book of Jonah: "Jonah began to go into the city, going a day's journey. And he cried, 'Yet *forty days*, and Nineveh shall be overthrown!' And the people of Nineveh believed God; they proclaimed a *fast* (*nēsteian*), and put on sackcloth, from the greatest of them to the least of them." (Jon 3:4-5) Furthermore, while both Mark (1:12) and Luke (4:1) refer to the wilderness period as "forty days" Matthew has "forty days and forty nights" (4:2), noticeably patterned after the "three days and three nights" of Jonah's stay "in the belly of the fish" (Jon 1:17). That this is on Matthew's mind here will be confirmed in chapter 12 where we shall hear of the only such verbatim reference to the Book of Jonah in the New Testament: "For as Jonah was three days and three nights in the belly of the whale, so will the Son of man be three days and three nights in the heart of the earth." (v.40)

- The "beginning" of Jesus' public preaching to the Gentiles (nations; 4:15), after his stay of forty days and forty nights in the wilderness and his temptation (vv.1-11), is subsumed in the summons "Repent" (*metanoeite*; v.17), which is similar to Jonah's call to the Hamite Nineveh, after his stay of three days and three nights in the belly of the fish, to change their ways of "wickedness" (Jon 1:2) so that God may "repent" of his decision to destroy that city:

  > "Who knows, God may yet *repent* (*metanoēsei*) and turn from his fierce anger, so that we perish not?" When God saw what they did, how they turned from their evil way, God *repented* (*metenoēsen*) of the evil which he had said he would do to them; and he did not do it. But it displeased Jonah exceedingly, and he was angry. And he prayed to the Lord and said, "I pray thee, Lord, is not this

> what I said when I was yet in my country? That is why I made haste to flee to Tarshish; for I knew that thou art a gracious God and merciful, slow to anger, and abounding in steadfast love, and *repentest* (*metanoōn*) of evil. (Jon 3:9-4:2)

In order to present Jesus going beyond Jonah in that his mission is ultimately to the Japhethites, Matthew very astutely resorts to Ezekiel 47:

- Jesus' first action was to recruit "fishermen" whose area was the inland Sea of Galilee, an expansion of the River Jordan (Mt 4:18-20), which corresponds to Ezekiel 47:10: "Fishermen will stand beside the sea; from Engedi to Eneglaim it will be a place for the spreading of nets; its fish will be of very many kinds, like the fish of the Great Sea."

- Jesus' choice is disciples who ultimately would carry on his mission beyond Matthew 28:19-20, however, according to the terms of that Gospel: "Go therefore and make disciples of all nations … *teaching them to observe all that I have commanded you.*" Since the reason behind Jesus' call to repentance is the proximity of the kingdom of heaven (4:17) Matthew titles itself "the gospel of the kingdom" that is to be preached before the end comes: "And *this* gospel of the kingdom will be preached throughout the whole world, as a testimony to all nations; and then the end will come." (Mt 24:14)

- As in Ezekiel 47:8, 9, 11, 12 Jesus' mission among the nations is one of "healing": "And he went about all Galilee, teaching in their synagogues and preaching the gospel of the kingdom and *healing* every disease and every infirmity among the people. So his fame spread throughout all Syria, and they brought him all the sick, those afflicted with various diseases and pains, demoniacs, epileptics, and paralytics, and he *healed* them." (Mt 4:23-24)

- Following the lead of Ezekiel, who expands the domain of the landlocked waters into that of the open sea through the medium of the fish—the fish of the river were "like the fish of the Great Sea" (47:10), Matthew does the same through the medium of Jesus' fishermen. Upon calling them to become "fishers of men" (4:19) he leads them into "Syria" (v.24), the Roman province bordering the Mediterranean (Great) Sea. Luke has his own way to suggest the same by mentioning the "seacoast" of Tyre and Sidon, Mediterranean port cities, located in the Roman province Syria that was known to Luke: "In those days a decree went out from Caesar Augustus that all the world should be enrolled. This was the first enrollment, when Quirinius was governor of Syria." (2:1-2). Compare the two renditions where "Jerusalem and Judea" join areas of the nations in following Jesus and his disciples:

  > So his fame spread throughout all Syria, and they brought him all the sick, those afflicted with various diseases and pains, demoniacs, epileptics, and paralytics, and he healed them. And great crowds followed him from *Galilee and the Decapolis* and Jerusalem and Judea and from beyond the Jordan. (Mt 4:24-25)

  > And he came down with them and stood on a level place, with a great crowd of his disciples and a great multitude of people from all Judea and Jerusalem and *the seacoast of Tyre and Sidon*, who came to hear him and to be healed of their diseases. (Lk 6:17)

Matthew's special interest in the Mediterranean (Great) Sea is betrayed in his phraseology in the passage depicting Jesus' crossing to the other side of the "sea" of Galilee into the Gentile country of the Gadarenes. The Gadarenes were obviously Gentile since they herded swine, which is forbidden in the Mosaic law. Although Matthew (8:23-27) and Luke (8:22-25) follow the lead of Mark in this pericope, Matthew overbids Mark (4:35-41) in that he mentions "sea" three times over five verses, whereas Mark uses it only twice over seven verses. Luke, on the other hand, prefers the term "lake" since carrying the gospel message to the nations across the "sea" is reserved to his second volume where he speaks of Paul's maritime journey to Rome.[7]

Payment of the Temple Tax

> When they came to Capernaum, the collectors of the half-shekel tax went up to Peter and said, "Does not your teacher pay the tax?" He said, "Yes." And when he came home, Jesus spoke to him first, saying, "What do you think Simon? From whom do kings of the earth take toll or tribute? From their sons or from others?" And when he said, "From others," Jesus said to him, "Then the sons are free. However, not to give offence to them, go to the sea and cast a hook, and take the first fish that comes up, and when you open its mouth you will find a shekel; take that and give it to them for me and for yourself." (Mt 17:24-27)

This episode, solely in Matthew, sums up in a unique way that Gospel's message concerning the "one" gospel to both Jews and Gentiles. This matter was already hinted at in chapter 10 where we have the overarching missionary commission of Jesus Christ to his "twelve apostles" (vv.2-4) with the following introductory remarks:

> Go nowhere among the Gentiles, and enter no town of the Samaritans, but go rather to the lost sheep of the house of Israel.

---

7 See my comments on this matter in the following chapter "The Ezekielian School and the Pauline School."

> And preach as you go, saying, "The kingdom of heaven is at hand." (Mt 10:5-7)

Yet, in the actual discourse we hear:

> Behold, I send you out as sheep in the midst of wolves; so be wise as serpents and innocent as *doves*. Beware of men; for they will deliver you up to councils, and flog you in their synagogues, and you will be dragged *before governors and kings* for my sake, *to bear testimony before them and the Gentiles*. (Mt 10:16-18)

Matthew's intention is betrayed by the fact that he combines in his "one" mission to Jews and Gentiles the elements that are found in Mark and Luke. They pertain to the mission to those whom Matthew refers to as "the lost sheep of the house of Israel"[8] (Mk 6:7-13; Lk 9:1-6; in Mt 10:5-15) along with elements of the mission linked to the gospel to the nations in conjunction with the destruction of the temple of Jerusalem (Mk 13:9-13; Lk 21:12-17; in Mt 10:16-24).

Matthew's special episode regarding the temple tax follows the second foretelling of the Son of man's resurrection (16:22-23). The first such foretelling (16:23) followed the episode of Peter's confession where he was likened to Jonah as Barjona.[9]

In the episode under discussion, the hearer cannot miss the central role played by a fish "whose mouth was opened" by Peter the "fisherman" upon Jesus' summons (17:27), which action brought about the resolution of the story's dilemma, just as the great fish was ordered by the Lord God (Jon 1:9) to "vomit out Jonah" (2:10), an action that brought about the solution to the story's dilemma. Given the uniqueness of the episode it would be worthwhile to examine the original phraesology to "hear out" its message.

The intention of the passage is to invite Peter, and with him the entire church leadership, to endorse the mission to the Gentiles. In Capernaum, which is in the "Galilee of the nations," Peter is challenged by the collectors of the didrachma,

---

8 Matthew 10:5; see also 15:24.

9 See my comments earlier.

the temple tax imposed by the Law (Ex 30:13-16)[10] and secured by the Roman authorities in support of the maintenance of the Jerusalem temple. Just as Peter earlier confessed that Jesus was the messiah, yet misunderstood its true meaning, here also he was right in saying that Jesus did fulfill his duty toward the temple, yet erred in understanding how. The story revolves around a wordplay connected with the Greek root *tel*—. The verb *teleō*, whose meaning is "finish, complete," is used in the sense of both "fulfill, bring to an end" as well as "fulfill one's duty" as in paying taxes (hence *telei ta didrakhma* [half-shekel] in Mt 17:24 means "pays the temple tax"). Consequently, the noun *telos* can mean "end, aim, fulfillment" as in "the end of the Law" (*telos nomou*, Rom 10:4) or "tax, toll" as in "taxes to whom taxes are due" (*tō to telos to telos*, Rom 13:7).

First Jesus leads Simon to state the obvious: the earthly kings collected taxes from the strangers, outsiders (*allotriōn*), i.e., the vanquished who were subdued and who, in order to forego slavery and secure their continued welfare under their conquerors, were forced to pay tribute to the latter in money or in kind (Mt 17:25). As for those of the household or of the conquering nation, they were free from those taxes and benefited from the tribute of the vanquished (v.26). The freedom of the children is a central theme in Paul's gospel.[11] Yet, as he himself taught, it is not to be used egotistically, thus ending up being a reason of offense to the weaker brethren: "Therefore, if food is a cause of my brother's falling, I will never eat meat, lest I cause my brother to fall (*skandalizei*)." (1 Cor 8:13)[12] Speaking later of what true apostleship entails Paul writes:

---

10 Each who is numbered in the census shall give this: half a shekel according to the shekel of the sanctuary (the shekel is twenty gerahs), half a shekel as an offering to the Lord. (Ex 30:13)

11 Rom 8:1-2; Gal 4:21-5:1.

12 See also: "Who is weak, and I am not weak? Who is made to fall (*skandalizetai*), and I am not indignant?" (2 Cor 11:29)

> Am I not free? Am I not an apostle? ... If we have sown spiritual good among you, is it too much if we reap your material benefits? If others share this rightful claim upon you, do not we still more? Nevertheless, we have not made use of this right, but we endure anything rather than *put an obstacle in the* way of the gospel of Christ ... For though I am free from all men, I have made myself a slave to all, that I might win the more. *To the Jews I became as a Jew, in order to win Jews; to those under the law I became as one under the law—though not being myself under the law—that I might win those under the law.* To those outside the law I became as one outside the law—not being without law toward God but under the law of Christ—that I might win those outside the law. To the weak I became weak, that I might win the weak. I have become all things to all men, that I might by all means save some. *I do it all for the sake of the gospel*, that I may share in its blessings." (1 Cor 9:1, 11-12, 19-23)

Here, in Matthew, Jesus follows the same path: "Then the sons are free. However, not to give offense to (*skandalisōmen*) them, go to the sea and cast a hook, and take the first fish that comes up, and when you open its mouth you will find a shekel; take that and give it to them for me and for yourself." (Mt 17:26-27) Although Jesus and his followers are sons and thus free from paying any taxes, he orders Peter to do so in order "not to give offense to" the Jews. Yet, he implicitly teaches Peter that their offering is none other than the offering of the Gentiles, and thus bound to the gospel and its requirements.[13] This is clear from the wording of Matthew 17:27: Peter is sent (*porevtheis*) to the (Roman) sea just as the apostles will be sent (*porevthentes*) to make disciples of all nations (Mt 28:19). Earlier he was prohibited from fishing in the sea, but now that he has been taught true discipleship, Peter is asked to go fishing again. Compare the terminology of his calling with the one here:

> As he walked by the Sea of Galilee, he saw two brothers, Simon who is called Peter and Andrew his brother, *casting* (*ballontas*) *a net* into the sea; for they were fishermen. And he said to them,

---

13 See *NTI₁* and *NTI₂* on the relation between the preaching of the gospel and the offering of the Gentiles.

> "Follow me, and I will make you fishers of men." Immediately they left their nets and followed him. (Mt 4:18-20)

> ... go to the sea and *cast* (*bale*) *a hook*, and take the first fish that comes up... (Mt 17:27)

If the fish of the sea represent the Gentiles, the shekel that is taken from *its mouth* represents their offering. This offering is acceptable since it is based on the Gentiles' confession of faith as can be seen from the correspondence between our text in Matthew and Romans 10:8-10:

> The word is near you, on your lips and in your heart (that is, the word of faith which we preach); because, if you confess with your lips that Jesus is Lord and believe in your heart that God raised him from the dead, you will be saved. For man believes with his heart and so is justified, and he confesses with his lips and so is saved.

It is possible to extract a further conclusion from this text. The fish in the sea are the Gentiles. Taking the first fish is tantamount to taking *any* fish, meaning that the Gentiles are to be accepted as they are without any kind of discrimination. The offering of both Peter and Jesus is one and the same—one shekel instead of two didrachmas (half-shekels)—underscoring the oneness of the gospel, which is the gospel to the Gentiles preached by Paul as evidenced in Galatians: "but on the contrary, when they saw that I had been entrusted with the gospel to the uncircumcised, just as Peter to the circumcised, for he who worked through Peter for the apostleship to the circumcised worked through me also for the Gentiles."[14] Since

---

14 I am following closely the Greek that does not repeat the terms "entrusted," "gospel," and "apostleship," stressing thus the oneness of the gospel to both Paul and Peter, namely the one whose content is Paul's preaching to the Gentiles (see my comments on these verses in *Gal* 69-70). RSV waters down the matter: "but on the contrary, when they saw that I had been entrusted with the gospel to the uncircumcised, just as Peter had been entrusted with *the gospel* to the circumcised (for he who worked through Peter for the mission to the circumcised worked through me also for the Gentiles)."

the numeral four is symbolic of the temple (building),[15] one may also add that the one offering amounting to four drachmas[16] may be intended to say that Jesus' and Peter's one offering was made to the temple of the new Jerusalem where the gospel offering was laid:

> But on some points I have written to you very boldly by way of reminder, because of the grace given me by God to be a minister of Christ Jesus to the Gentiles in the priestly service of the gospel of God, so that the offering of the Gentiles may be acceptable, sanctified by the Holy Spirit. (Rom 15:15-16)

My last suggestion fits perfectly with the notion of fulfillment, central in Matthew. Here Jesus fulfills[17] the temple of Jerusalem with the new eschatological one, just as he fulfills the Mosaic Law (Mt 5:17) with the eschatological law of the messiah.[18] The following text of Matthew 18 is itself a compendium of the Messiah's law.

---

15 See my comments in *NTI₁* 141-3, 147. See also my comments on Matthew 4:18-22 in *NTI₄* 126-7.

16 The drachma was the basic Hellenistic monetary unit (see Lk 15:8-9).

17 See earlier my comments on Matthew's use of the verb *telei* (fulfills) to speak of the payment of the temple tax.

18 See my comments on Matthew 5:1-20 in *NTI₄* 129-34.

16

The Ezekelian School and the Pauline School

Time and again I have referred to Ezekiel as the "father of scripture" in that his Book is the major influence over at least the Books of Genesis and Leviticus. By extension, I have dubbed the authors that produced the Old Testament the "Ezekelian" school." I have discussed this matter in detail in my commentaries on Ezekiel and Genesis and in *The Rise of Scripture*. Similarly, I view Paul as the "father of the New Testament" in that the thoughts expressed in the letters bearing his name are imprinted in the rest of that literature. By the same token, I dubbed the school of its authors as the "Pauline" school.

The parallelism between the two—or rather the Pauline school's mimicking the Ezekelian school—is evident in the similarity of their socio-geographical settings. Ezekiel was active as the prophet of the universal deity *'elohim* in the vicinity of Babylon where the Old Testament was produced. This literature was conceived and written at the time when the Shemite/Hamite Babylon was under the aegis of Alexander's successors, the Japhethite Seleucids. The Japhethites imagined that they were in control of the area surrounding the Syrian wilderness, just as they were the masters of their own area of origin, the "isles" of the East Mediterranean Sea. The Ezekelian school conceived an epic literature meant to subvert their claim by professing that their deities were just puppets:

> The ironsmith fashions it and works it over the coals; he shapes it with hammers, and forges it with his strong arm; he becomes hungry and his strength fails, he drinks no water and is faint. The carpenter stretches a line, he marks it out with a pencil; he fashions it with planes, and marks it with a compass; he shapes it into the figure of a man, with the beauty of a man, to dwell in a

house. He cuts down cedars; or he chooses a holm tree or an oak and lets it grow strong among the trees of the forest; he plants a cedar and the rain nourishes it. Then it becomes fuel for a man; he takes a part of it and warms himself, he kindles a fire and bakes bread; also he makes a god and worships it, he makes it a graven image and falls down before it. Half of it he burns in the fire; over the half he eats flesh, he roasts meat and is satisfied; also he warms himself and says, "Aha, I am warm, I have seen the fire!" And the rest of it he makes into a god, his idol; and falls down to it and worships it; he prays to it and says, "Deliver me, for thou art my god!" (Is 44:12-17)

Bel bows down, Nebo stoops, their idols are on beasts and cattle; these things you carry are loaded as burdens on weary beasts. They stoop, they bow down together, they cannot save the burden, but themselves go into captivity. (Is 46:1-2)

Hear the word which the Lord speaks to you, O house of Israel. Thus says the Lord: "Learn not the way of the nations, nor be dismayed at the signs of the heavens because the nations are dismayed at them, for the customs of the peoples are false. A tree from the forest is cut down, and worked with an axe by the hands of a craftsman. Men deck it with silver and gold; they fasten it with hammer and nails so that it cannot move. Their idols are like scarecrows in a cucumber field, and they cannot speak; they have to be carried, for they cannot walk. Be not afraid of them, for they cannot do evil, neither is it in them to do good." ... Every man is stupid and without knowledge; every goldsmith is put to shame by his idols; for his images are false, and there is no breath in them. They are worthless, a work of delusion; at the time of their punishment they shall perish. (Jer 10: 1-5, 14-15)

The idols of the nations are silver and gold, the work of men's hands. They have mouths, but they speak not, they have eyes, but they see not, they have ears, but they hear not, nor is there any breath in their mouths. Like them be those who make them!—yea, every one who trusts in them! (Ps 135:15-18; see also the parallel passage 115:2-8)

The other major and more important facet of the Ezekelian thesis which is usually brushed aside, or at least sidelined, in Christian as well as Jewish circles, is the intentional demeaning of the main protagonists of the story, the scriptural Israel, by the authors, who were themselves part and parcel of the scriptural Israel, and its leaders, to boot.[1] Even those who still endorse the documentary thesis to explain the perceived "differences" or "repetitions" in the scriptural narrative end up by submitting to the evident: the "Priests," as "redactors" or "editors," are the ultimate "authors" of scripture as it stands in our hands today. But this is precisely what scripture itself has repeatedly asserted in so many ways. The text of the divine law, which was delivered by God "at the hand of Moses" (*beyad mošeh*; Ex 9:35; 35:29; Lev 8:36; 10:11; 26:49; Num 4:37, 45, 49; 9:23; 10:13; 15:23; 16:40; 27:23;36:13) translated usually blandly as "through Moses" or "by Moses," was to be kept in the custody of the "Levitical priests," the "sons" of Aaron, "the high priest" (Ex 28-29), or conversely his "brethren":

> But the Levites were not numbered by their ancestral tribe along with them. For the Lord said to Moses, "Only the tribe of Levi you shall not number, and you shall not take a census of them among the people of Israel; but appoint the Levites over the tabernacle of the testimony, and over all its furnishings, and over all that belongs to it; they are to carry the tabernacle and all its furnishings, and they shall tend it, and shall encamp around the tabernacle. When the tabernacle is to set out, the Levites shall take it down; and when the tabernacle is to be pitched, the Levites shall set it up. And if any one else comes near, he shall be put to death. The people of Israel shall pitch their tents by their companies, every man by his own camp and every man by his own standard; but the Levites shall encamp around the tabernacle of the testimony, that there may be no wrath upon the congregation of the people of Israel; and the Levites shall keep charge of the tabernacle of the testimony." (Num 1:47-53)

> And Moses said to Korah, "Hear now, you sons of Levi: is it too small a thing for you that the God of Israel has separated you from the congregation of Israel, to bring you near to himself, to do service in the tabernacle of the Lord, and to stand before the

1 I discussed this matter extensively in *ROS*.

> congregation to minister to them; and that he has brought you near him, and all your brethren the sons of Levi with you? And would you seek the priesthood also? Therefore it is against the Lord that you and all your company have gathered together; what is Aaron that you murmur against him?" (Num 16:8-11)

> And when he (the king) sits on the throne of his kingdom, he shall write for himself in a book a copy of this law, from that which is in the charge of the Levitical priests. (Deut 17:18)

> Then Joshua built an altar in Mount Ebal to the Lord, the God of Israel, as Moses the servant of the Lord had commanded the people of Israel, as it is written in the book of the law of Moses, "an altar of unhewn stones, upon which no man has lifted an iron tool"; and they offered on it burnt offerings to the Lord, and sacrificed peace offerings. And there, in the presence of the people of Israel, he wrote upon the stones a copy of the law of Moses, which he had written. And all Israel, sojourner as well as homeborn, with their elders and officers and their judges, stood on opposite sides of the ark before the Levitical priests who carried the ark of the covenant of the Lord, half of them in front of Mount Gerizim and half of them in front of Mount Ebal, as Moses the servant of the Lord had commanded at the first, that they should bless the people of Israel. And afterward he read all the words of the law, the blessing and the curse, according to all that is written in the book of the law. There was not a word of all that Moses commanded which Joshua did not read before all the assembly of Israel, and the women, and the little ones, and the sojourners who lived among them. (Josh 8:30-35)

How could leaders write literature that castigates their own people and, worse, themselves? This is the question asked by many of my students over the years, both in the Middle East and in North America, and by many of my hearers at conferences and talks throughout Europe, East and West, and in South America as well. The answer is simple: they wrote against the grain because, literarily, they were forced to do so. They cast themselves not as authors, but as preservers of the *debarim* (words) of the Law with no leeway for them to edit or rephrase it—as theologians and preachers assume is their sworn duty. The authors themselves are part of the addressees and characters within the literature.[2] They assert the Law was delivered to them for safekeeping "at the hand of Moses" the "prophet" and his "brethren" the "prophets":

> Then Amaziah the priest of Bethel sent to Jeroboam king of Israel, saying, "Amos has conspired against you in the midst of the house of Israel; the land is not able to bear all his words. For thus Amos has said, 'Jeroboam shall die by the sword, and Israel must go into exile away from his land.'" And Amaziah said to Amos, "O seer, go, flee away to the land of Judah, and eat bread there, and prophesy there; but never again prophesy at Bethel, for it is the king's sanctuary, and it is a temple of the kingdom." Then Amos answered Amaziah, "I am no prophet, nor a prophet's son; but I am a herdsman, and a dresser of sycamore trees, and the Lord took me from following the flock, and the Lord said to me, 'Go, prophesy to my people Israel.' Now therefore hear the word of the Lord. You say, 'Do not prophesy against Israel, and do not preach against the house of Isaac.' Therefore thus says the Lord: 'Your wife shall be a harlot in the city, and your sons and your daughters shall fall by the sword, and your land shall be parceled out by line; you yourself shall die in an unclean land, and Israel shall surely go into exile away from its land.'" (Am 7:10-17)

The prophetic literature is replete ad nauseam with criticism of the priests who did not convey to the people the content of the Law (*torah*) that contained the "words" of the Lord and that was in their "charge" (Deut 17:18). Suffice it here to quote a few instances:

> The priests did not say, "Where is the Lord?" Those who handle the law did not know me (Jer 2:8)[3]

---

2 See *ROS* 33-126: *Part One: What triggered the writing of scripture.*

3 A renowned Israeli biblical scholar at a biblical conference in London, UK in September 1972 which I was attending, insisted more than once that he considered the Prophet Jeremiah a traitor to his people for his having prompted them not to take arms against Nebuchadnezzar of Babylon (Jer 27). Scripturally speaking, at that point, that scholar was simply siding with Hananiah, the other "prophet" in the Book of Jeremiah.

Her priests have done violence to my law and have profaned my holy things; they have made no distinction between the holy and the common, neither have they taught the difference between the unclean and the clean, and they have disregarded my sabbaths, so that I am profaned among them. (Ezek 22:26)

My people are destroyed for lack of knowledge; because you have rejected knowledge, I reject you from being a priest to me. And since you have forgotten the law of your God, I also will forget your children. The more they increased, the more they sinned against me; I will change their glory into shame. They feed on the sin of my people; they are greedy for their iniquity. And it shall be like people, like priest; I will punish them for their ways, and requite them for their deeds. They shall eat, but not be satisfied; they shall play the harlot, but not multiply; because they have forsaken the Lord to cherish harlotry (Hos 4:6-10)

Hear this, O priests! Give heed, O house of Israel! Hearken, O house of the king! For the judgment pertains to you; for you have been a snare at Mizpah, and a net spread upon Tabor. And they have made deep the pit of Shittim; but I will chastise all of them. (Hos 5:1-2)

A son honors his father, and a servant his master. If then I am a father, where is my honor? And if I am a master, where is my fear? says the Lord of hosts to you, O priests, who despise my name. (Mal 1:6)

And now, O priests, this command is for you. If you will not listen, if you will not lay it to heart to give glory to my name, says the Lord of hosts, then I will send the curse upon you and I will curse your blessings; indeed I have already cursed them, because you do not lay it to heart. Behold, I will rebuke your offspring, and spread dung upon your faces, the dung of your offerings, and I will put you out of my presence. So shall you know that I have sent this command to you, that my covenant with Levi may hold, says the Lord of hosts. My covenant with him was a covenant of life and peace, and I gave them to him, that he might fear; and he feared me, he stood in awe of my name. True instruction was in his mouth, and no wrong was found on his lips. He walked with me in peace and uprightness, and he turned many from iniquity. For the lips of a priest should guard knowledge, and men should seek instruction from his mouth, for he is the messenger of the

> Lord of hosts. But you have turned aside from the way; you have caused many to stumble by your instruction; you have corrupted the covenant of Levi, says the Lord of hosts, and so I make you despised and abased before all the people, inasmuch as you have not kept my ways but have shown partiality in your instruction. (Mal 2:1-9)

The Ezekelian blueprint was copied by the Pauline school. Ezekiel was portrayed as the prophet of God active in Babylon, where he and his people were exiled,[4] away from Jerusalem, in an area that would be overtaken by Alexander of Macedon. Paul is portrayed as being from Tarsus of Cilicia in Asia Minor (Acts 22:3) and as having established his headquarters in Ephesus, also in Asia Minor, that is, away from both Jerusalem, the city of the "men of repute," his equals (Gal 2:1-10), and Antioch—founded by the Seleucid leader Seleucus I Nicator—where "the disciples were for the first time called Christians" (Acts 11:26). The Pauline school realized that to faithfully continue the legacy of the Ezekelian school, it had to forget about the internal conflicts of the Judaism of the time, in Judea and Syria, and "leave the dead bury their dead" (Mt 8:22; Lk 9:60). The Jewish leadership that controlled both Jerusalem and Antioch (Gal 2:1-10, 11-14) was under the boot of the Romans. They submitted to Herod, a client of Rome, in order to erect the temple of Jerusalem, a building of stone that Ezekiel's God had castigated.

For the Ezekelian school, Jerusalem was "rubble" of the past, and the divine word was to be proclaimed to the descendants of Alexander, Gog of the land of Magog, with the aim of bringing his descendants into submission. The Pauline school viewed the "Macedonian" Antioch as "rubble" of the past in that it was subdued by Rome. It set its eyes on Rome, the capital of the new Japhethites, in order to bring that city and its emperor into submission (*hypakoē*, obedience; Rom 1:5) to the scriptural God

4 Son of man, your brethren, even your brethren, your fellow exiles, the whole house of Israel, all of them… (Ezek 11:15).

by relaying to them the "gospel of (that) God" (v.1) and reminding them that this gospel, and not Caesar, is the source of true power that ensures their salvation: "so I am eager to preach the gospel to you also who are in Rome. For I am not ashamed of the gospel: it is the power of God for salvation to every one who has faith, to the Jew first and also to the Greek." (vv.15-16). Halfway between Jerusalem and Antioch, on the one hand, and Rome, on the other hand, was Ephesus, the capital of the very important Roman province Asia, as well as the city of the temple of Artemis, Apollo's twin sister. It was fitting that it would be coined in the New Testament as the Pauline headquarters. Geographically, as a port city on the Aegean Sea, it understandably became the central commercial hub of the Mediterranean during the Roman period. That the Pauline mission was eyeing not only Rome, the capital, but the *entire* Mediterranean, the sea of the Japhethite "isles" (Gen 10:5), is evidenced in what the Apostle wrote to the Romans:

> I hope to see you in passing as I go to Spain, and to be sped on my journey there by you, once I have enjoyed your company for a little. At present, however, I am going to Jerusalem with aid for the saints. For Macedonia and Achaia have been pleased to make some contribution for the poor among the saints at Jerusalem; they were pleased to do it, and indeed they are in debt to them, for if the Gentiles have come to share in their spiritual blessings, they ought also to be of service to them in material blessings. When therefore I have completed this, and have delivered to them what has been raised, I shall go on by way of you to Spain; and I know that when I come to you I shall come in the fulness of the blessing of Christ. (Rom 15:24-29)

Spain was the westernmost part of the empire. The importance of Spain is reflected in the following passage of 1 Maccabees:

> Now Judas heard of the fame of the Romans, that they were very strong and were well-disposed toward all who made an alliance with them, that they pledged friendship to those who came to them, and that they were very strong. Men told him of their wars and of the brave deeds which they were doing among the Gauls, how they had defeated them and forced them to pay tribute, and

> what they had done in the land of Spain to get control of the silver and gold mines there, and how they had gained control of the whole region by their planning and patience, even though the place was far distant from them. They also subdued the kings who came against them from the ends of the earth, until they crushed them and inflicted great disaster upon them; the rest paid them tribute every year. (1 Macc 8:1-4)

I am convinced that Spain in the New Testament functions similarly to Tarshish in the Old Testament. Both point to the western Mediterranean, at the other end of the world of the Syrian wilderness and the landmass to the east of it. Put in contemporary terms, Tarshish and Spain for the scriptural authors would have functioned as the Americas for Europeans. Linking functionally the New Testament Spain and the Old Testament Tarshish is not as farfetched as it may seem considering that the New Testament casts Rome in terms of the Old Testament Babylon in the Book of Revelation:

> Then one of the seven angels who had the seven bowls came and said to me, "Come, I will show you the judgment of the great harlot who is seated upon many waters, with whom the kings of the earth have committed fornication, and with the wine of whose fornication the dwellers on earth have become drunk." And he carried me away in the Spirit into a wilderness, and I saw a woman sitting on a scarlet beast which was full of blasphemous names, and it had seven heads and ten horns. The woman was arrayed in purple and scarlet, and bedecked with gold and jewels and pearls, holding in her hand a golden cup full of abominations and the impurities of her fornication; and on her forehead was written a name of mystery: "*Babylon the great*, mother of harlots and of earth's abominations." And I saw the woman, *drunk with the blood of the saints and the blood of the martyrs of Jesus*. When I saw her I marveled greatly. (Rev 17:1-6)

Paul and Jonah

Both Paul's journey to Rome and Jonah's intended journey to Tarshish revolve around a ship as a main component of the story. Comparing the two accounts, we end with the following results:

- In Jonah 1:3-5 we hear four times a reference to a sea vessel, all rendered as "ship" in RSV.[5] The Greek has the same word *ploion* in all four instances, however, the original Hebrew has *'oniyyah* in vv.3, 4, 5a and *sephinah* in v.5b.[6] It is interesting, in this regard, that the phrase *'oniyyot taršiš* (the ships of Tarshish) is encountered repeatedly in the Old Testament (Is 2:16; 23:1, 14; 60:9; Ezek 27:25; Ps 48:8; 2 Chr 9:21) which is, in my eyes, an indirect indication that Tarshish is the last main port in the West Mediterranean and thus the farthest "isles of the nations" (Gen 10:5) from the Syrian wilderness. This explains why that phrase fits perfectly in the description of the extent and expanse of Solomon's area of commerce:

  > All King Solomon's drinking vessels were of gold, and all the vessels of the House of the Forest of Lebanon were of pure gold; silver was not considered as anything in the days of Solomon. For the king's ships went to Tarshish with the servants of Huram; once every three years the ships of Tarshish used to come bringing gold, silver, ivory, apes, and peacocks. Thus King Solomon excelled all the kings of the earth in riches and in wisdom. And all the kings of the earth sought the presence of Solomon to hear his wisdom, which God had put into his mind. Every one of them brought his present, articles of silver and of gold, garments, myrrh, spices, horses, and mules, so much year by year. And Solomon had four thousand stalls for

---

5 The fifth occurrence of that noun in v.13 is an addition. KJV supplies an italicized *it.*

6 This is the only instance of that noun in the entire Old Testament. My readers who know Arabic will have guessed that it corresponds to the Arabic *saphinat* whose meaning is "ship."

> horses and chariots, and twelve thousand horsemen, whom he stationed in the chariot cities and with the king in Jerusalem. (2 Chr 9:20-25)

- In its description of Paul's maritime journey from the East Mediterranean coast to Rome, Acts uses the noun "ship" (Greek *ploion*), as a refrain, twelve times over forty-four verses (Acts 27). If one adds "vessel" (*naun/navn*) in v.41 and the three occurrences of "boat" (*skaphē*) in vv.16, 30, and 32 in conjunction with a shipwreck, then the hearer cannot escape the feeling of being overwhelmed, if not hammered, with the continual reference to a sea vessel. Aurally, the hearer of the original Greek cannot miss also the nouns from the same root *nau/nav*—whence our English nautical: *navklērō* (owner of the ship; v.11) and *navtai*, respectively *navtōn*, (sailors) in v.27 and 30. Instead of Tarshish, the old Japhethtite queen city of the Western Mediterranean, Paul is heading toward Rome, the new, equally Japhethite, queen city of the Western Mediterranean. Jonah did not reach Tarshish because his mission was to Nineveh. Paul's mission is to inform the leaders of Rome, the capital of the "Gentiles" (nations) that "the times of the Gentiles (nations)" are about to be "fulfilled" (Lk 20:21):[7] "But the Lord

7 My readers are reminded that both the Gospel of Luke and Acts were penned by the same author: "Inasmuch as many have undertaken to compile a narrative of the things which have been accomplished among us, just as they were delivered to us by those who from the beginning were eyewitnesses and ministers of the word (*logou*), it seemed good to me also, having followed all things closely for some time past, to write an orderly account for you, most excellent Theophilus, that you may know the truth concerning the things of which you have been informed" (Lk 1:1-4); "In the first book (*logon*; word, account), O Theophilus, I have dealt with all that Jesus began to do and teach, until the day when he was taken up, after he had given commandment through the Holy Spirit to the apostles whom he had chosen." (Acts 1:1-2)

said to him (Ananias), 'Go, for he (Paul) is a chosen instrument (*skevos*) of mine to carry my name before the Gentiles and kings and the sons of Israel.'" (Acts 9:15)

- An extra interesting feature of the Book of Acts in conjunction with our discussion is the back to back use of two different renditions of the same word, once in the masculine (*skevos*) and the other time in the feminine (*skevē*), in chapter 27 (vv.17 and 19): "after hoisting it up, they took measures to undergird the ship (*ploion*); then, fearing that they should run on the Syrtis, they lowered the gear (*skevos*), and so were driven. As we were violently storm-tossed, they began next day to throw the cargo overboard; and the third day they cast out with their own hands the tackle (*skevēn*) of the ship (*ploiou*)." It is the only instance of the feminine *skevē* in the New Testament. On the other hand, the masculine *skevos* has been heard earlier in Acts four times. The first time it is in conjunction with the Lord's assignment of Paul as his "instrument" in the mission to the Gentiles in the passage quoted above (9:15). The other three times it occurs in reference to the "sheet" filled with "all kinds of animals and reptiles and birds of the air" (10:12) in the lengthy passage in which Peter is forced into submitting to the inclusion of the Gentiles in the gospel preaching: "And he (Peter) became hungry and desired something to eat; but while they were preparing it, he fell into a trance and saw the heaven opened, and something (*skevos ti*) descending, like a great sheet, let down by four corners upon the earth. In it were all kinds of animals and reptiles and birds of the air. … This happened three times, and the thing (*to skevos*) was taken up at once to heaven. … I was in the city of Joppa praying; and in a trance I saw a vision, something (*skevos ti*) descending, like a great sheet, let down from heaven by four corners; and it came down to me." (10:10-12, 16; 11:5) A hearer of the original cannot possibly miss the intentional choice of *skevos* in 9:15 in view of Paul's maritime journey in Acts 27.

- The central difference between Jonah's journey and that of Paul is that the tempestuous waves God raises work against Jonah's plans to turn his back on the mission assigned to him, whereas the same raging waters fail to derail Paul from fulfilling his mission. The same "Lord, the God of heaven, who made the sea and the dry land" (Jon 1:9) is in full control of the "deep" and the "waters" (Gen 1:2) that he uses at will to his advantage. The same scenario is depicted in the case of Jesus's crossing the "sea" of Galilee on his way to Gentile land where swine, forbidden by the Law, are raised:

> One day he got into a *boat* with his disciples, and he said to them, 'Let us go *across to the other side of the lake*.' So they set out, and as they *sailed* he fell asleep. And a *storm of wind* came down on the lake, and they were filling with water, and were in danger. And they went and woke him, saying, 'Master, Master, we are perishing!' And he awoke and rebuked *the wind and the raging waves*; and they ceased, and there was a calm. He said to them, 'Where is your faith?' And they were afraid, and they marveled, saying to one another, 'Who then is this, that he commands even *wind and water*, and they obey him?' Then they arrived at the country

> of the Gerasenes, which is opposite Galilee. (Lk 8:22-26)[8]

Luke intentionally avoids referring to the body water in Galilee as "sea" as do Mark and Matthew, reserving it to later describe Paul's journey to Rome through the Mediterranean in Acts 27. Still Luke has this matter in mind, namely, that Jesus is crossing into Roman land. This is evident in that he kept the Markan reference to the name of the unclean spirit as "legion" (Mk 5:9, 15; Lk 8:30). An original hearer could not have possibly missed the insinuation to the Roman army legion, especially (1) when this term, in the singular, is found only in these three instances in the New Testament; (2) most importantly, the second instance in Mark shows beyond any shred of a doubt that the "name" of the unclean spirit (5:8-9) is intended in a metaphorical sense: "And they came to Jesus, and saw the demoniac sitting there, clothed and in his right mind, *the man who had had the legion*; and they were afraid" (v.15); and (3) the plural "legions" occurs only once where the connotation in context is clearly to "armed forces" (Hebrew *ṣeba'ot*; Greek *dynameis*):

> While he was still speaking, Judas came, one of the twelve, and with him a great crowd with swords and clubs, from the chief priests and the elders of the people. Now the betrayer had given them a sign, saying, "The one I shall kiss is the man; seize him." And he came up to Jesus at once and said, "Hail, Master!" And he kissed him. Jesus said to him, "Friend, why are you here?" Then they came up and laid hands on Jesus and seized him. And behold, one of those who were with Jesus stretched out his hand and drew his sword, and struck the

---

8 I chose the Lukan narrative because Luke and Acts have the same author.

> slave of the high priest, and cut off his ear. Then Jesus said to him, "Put your sword back into its place; for all who take the sword will perish by the sword. Do you think that I cannot appeal to my Father, and he will at once send me more than *twelve legions* of angels (*angelōn*)?" (Mt 26:47-53)[9]

Matthew was "Romanizing" the original Hebrew of Psalm 102 (LXX 103): "Bless the Lord, O you his angels (Greek *angeloi*; Hebrew *mal'akim*), you mighty ones who do his word, hearkening to the voice of his word! Bless the Lord, all his hosts (Greek *dynameis*; Hebrew *ṣeba'ot*), his ministers that do his will!"

It is worth noting that Jonah and Paul are the only two scriptural protagonists who declare that they are Hebrews:

> And he said to them, I am a Hebrew; and I fear the Lord, the God of heaven, who made the sea and the dry land. (Jon 1:9)

> (I, Paul) circumcised on the eighth day, of the people of Israel, of the tribe of Benjamin, a Hebrew born of Hebrews; as to the law a Pharisee… (Phil 3:5)

In the Book of Jonah, the intention was to cast the prophet as a Shemite, a child of Abram the "Hebrew" (Gen 14:13), who was called upon by the Lord to convey the call of repentance to the Hamite Nineveh. In contravening God's will in this matter, Jonah sought protection from God's wrath in Japhethite Tarshish. With Paul the "Hebrew," the message of repentance is extended to the Japhethite Rome, the New Testament Tarshish.[10] This time around Paul acted in accordance with "God's will" (1 Cor 1:1; 2 Cor 1:1; Eph 1:1; Col 1:1; 2 Tim 1:1) and not against it. Still, one might ask, "What is the function of the additional 'I am a Hebrew' in each case since it does not seem to add anything to the flow of the story line?"

---

9 Jesus was not about to fall in the trap laid to him earlier by the devil: "If you are the Son of God, throw yourself down; for it is written, 'He will give *his angels* charge of you,' and 'On their hands they will bear you up, lest you strike your foot against a stone (Ps 91:11-12).'" (Mt 4:6)

10 See my comments above.

In Jonah's case, he is replying to the sailors' question: "What is your occupation (*mela'kah*)? And whence do you come? What is your country (*'ereṣ;* earth)? And of what people (*'am*) are you?" (Jon 1:8) Their question is conceived along the lines of urban societies that "define" and "confine" their constituency within a perimeter of walls, i.e., predetermined concepts. As such, the tenure of the question parallels that of Amaziah's statement to Amos, Jonah's colleague among the Twelve Prophets:[11] "O seer, go, flee away to the land of Judah, and eat bread there, and prophesy there; but never again prophesy at Bethel, for it is the king's sanctuary, and it is a temple of the kingdom." (Am 7:12-13) Since Amos was "prophesying" Amaziah, "the priest of Bethel" (v.10), assumed that he was a "seer" (*ḥozeh;* visionary) of a sanctuary by profession (v.12). However, Amos replied that his occupation was herding, and it is the Lord "who took him from following the flock and assigned him to prophesy to Israel" (v.15).

In scriptural Hebrew terminology, the *mela'kah* (work, profession, occupation) of a "prophet," as Jonah was (2 Kg 14:25), is to be a *mal'ak* (messenger; Greek *angelos* [angel]), a carrier of a *mal'akut* (message). This is clearly stated in the Book of Haggai, another colleague of Jonah's: "Then Haggai, the messenger (*mal'ak*) of the Lord, spoke to the people with the Lord's message (*mal'akut*), 'I am with you, says the Lord.'" (Hag 1:13) So Jonah, at least verbally, got it right. He was supposed to be a *'ibri* (Hebrew), from the verb *'abar* (cross through, pass through), and thus be a wilderness wanderer, as a shepherd would be, as his forefather Abram the *'ibri* (Gen 14:13) actually was. So the author is leading a hearer with a keen ear to ask: "If so, then why are you, Jonah, sailing the sea instead of crossing (*'abar*) the Syrian wilderness in the direction of Nineveh—as assigned by the Lord God whom, you say, you fear—just as Abram the Hebrew crossed the same wilderness in

---

11 My readers are reminded that the Twelve Minor Prophets were lumped as one scroll in the Hebrew canon, which is reflected in the LXX under the name *dōdekaprophēton* (the twelve prophet [scroll]).

obedience to that same Lord God (Gen 12:1-4)?"[12] To teach him a lesson, the Lord had to use the sea against Jonah to remind him of his original mission: "For thou didst cast me into the deep, into the heart of the seas, and the flood was round about me; all thy waves and thy billows *passed* (*'abaru*) over me." (Jon 2:3)

Contrariwise, Paul the Apostle, who was carrying the "gospel of obedience (submission)" to the Romans (Rom 1:5; 15:18), submitted faithfully to God's command, which is reflected in that his journey over the Mediterranean (Acts 27-28) was done while he was "in chains" (26:29) as a "slave (*doulos*) of Christ" (Gal 1:10; Phil 1:1) and a "slave (*doulos*) of God" (Tit 1:1).[13] And yet, although a Roman, and thus supposedly an urban citizen (Acts 22:25-29; 23:27), he was, by profession, a "tentmaker": "And he found a Jew named Aquila, a native of Pontus, lately come from Italy with his wife Priscilla, because Claudius had commanded all the Jews to leave Rome. And he went to see them; and because he was of the same trade he stayed with them, and they worked, for by trade they were tentmakers." (18:2-3) And if tentmaker, then "Hebrew" as he presents himself in Philippians 3:5. What is striking, however, is that Paul stresses this point. Instead of simply saying "a Hebrew" Paul writes "a Hebrew born of Hebrews"; the original Greek *'Ebraios ex 'Ebraiōn* means "Hebrew from (out of) Hebrews." This is clearly meant as a stress underscoring his origins and not only his actual status. Comparing the two parallel passages of Philippians and Romans one realizes that "Hebrew from Hebrews" corresponds to "out of the seed of Abraham," that is, Abraham "the Hebrew" (Gen 14:13):

---

12 Notice that Abram's first action in his new "earth" of residence was to "pass through" it: "Abram passed through (*wayya'abor* from *'abar*) the land to the place at Shechem, to the oak of Moreh." (Gen 12:6)

13 RSV renders *doulos* as "servant" in all these instances.

> (I, Paul) circumcised on the eighth day, of the people of Israel, of the tribe of Benjamin, a Hebrew born of (*out of*) Hebrews (*ex 'Ebraiōn*). (Phil 3:5)

> I myself am an Israelite, a descendant of Abraham (*ek spermatos Abraam*;[14] out of the seed of Abraham), a member of the tribe of Benjamin. (Rom 11:1)

This understanding is confirmed in what Paul writes in 2 Corinthians: "Are they Hebrews? So am I. Are they Israelites? So am I. Are they descendants of Abraham (*sperma Abraam;* seed of Abraham)? So am I." (11:22) In *The Rise of Scripture,* I have shown that Paul repeatedly used this terminology to dissociate himself from the narrow Judaism of his time associated with Jerusalem and Judea whose leaders wanted to control the followers of the Torah throughout the Roman empire with the aim of forcing them to support the maintenance of the Jerusalem temple through the didrachma taxation. Even more, those leaders wanted to subjugate the "diaspora" followers of the Law by imposing on them circumcision in the flesh as the ultimate sign of being a "Jew" rather than obedience to the dictates of the Law. Paul reacted against this misconception so many times and in so many ways in his correspondence, most impressive among which is his statement in Romans:

> Circumcision indeed is of value if you obey the law; but if you break the law, your circumcision becomes uncircumcision. So, if a man who is uncircumcised keeps the precepts of the law, will not his uncircumcision be regarded as circumcision? Then those who are physically uncircumcised but keep the law will condemn you who have the written code and circumcision but break the law. For he is not a ~~real~~ (added by RSV) Jew who is one outwardly, nor is ~~true~~ (added by RSV) circumcision something external and physical. He is a Jew who is one inwardly, and ~~real~~ (added by RSV) circumcision is a matter of the heart, spiritual and not literal. His praise is not from men but from God. (Rom 2:25-29)

---

14 The Greek preposition *ek* becomes *ex* before a vowel as in the case of *'Ebraiōn* in Philippians.

This is nothing else than "the law of the Spirit of life in Christ Jesus" (Rom 8:2). Ezekiel, Paul's predecessor, described this new spirit in the following way:

> And I will give them one heart, and put a new spirit within them; I will take the stony heart out of their flesh and give them a heart of flesh, *that they may walk in my statutes and keep my ordinances and obey them*; and *they shall be my people, and I will be their God.* (Ezek 11:19-20)

> A new heart I will give you, and a new spirit I will put within you; and I will take out of your flesh the heart of stone and give you a heart of flesh. And I will put my spirit within you, and *cause you to walk in my statutes and be careful to observe my ordinances.* (Ezek 36:26-27)

The corollary is obviously the following:

> Only, let every one lead the life which the Lord has assigned to him, and in which God has called him. This is my rule in all the churches. Was any one at the time of his call already circumcised? Let him not seek to remove the marks of circumcision. Was any one at the time of his call uncircumcised? Let him not seek circumcision. For neither circumcision counts for anything nor uncircumcision, *but keeping the commandments of God.* Every one should remain in the state in which he was called. (1 Cor 7:17-20)

> For as many of you as were baptized into Christ have put on Christ. There is neither Jew nor Greek, there is neither slave nor free, there is neither male nor female; for you are all one in Christ Jesus. And if you are Christ's, then you are Abraham's offspring, heirs according to promise. (Gal 3:27-29)

> Here there cannot be Greek and Jew, circumcised and uncircumcised, barbarian, Scythian, slave, free man, but Christ is all, and in all. (Col 3:11)

With this, the door is wide open for the Japhethite Romans to dwell in the tents of Shem and receive the blessing of the scriptural God who liberates them from their slavery to Caesar, just as he liberated the scriptural Hebrews from slavery to Pharaoh by inviting them to become God's "slaves" (Lev 25:55):

> Do you not know that if you yield yourselves to any one as obedient slaves, you are slaves of the one whom you obey, either of sin, which leads to death, or of obedience, which leads to righteousness? But thanks be to God, that you who were once slaves of sin have become obedient from the heart to the standard of teaching to which you were committed, and, having been set free from sin, have become slaves of righteousness. I am speaking in human terms, because of your natural limitations. For just as you once yielded your members to impurity and to greater and greater iniquity, so now yield your members to righteousness for sanctification. When you were slaves of sin, you were free in regard to righteousness. But then what return did you get from the things of which you are now ashamed? The end of those things is death. But now that you have been set free from sin and *have become slaves of God*, the return you get is sanctification and its end, eternal life. For the wages of sin is death, but the free gift of God is eternal life in Christ Jesus our Lord. (Rom 6:16-23)

17

Where Should We Go From There?

As I noted in *The Rise of Scripture*, since the original addressees and subsequent hearers of scripture are posited as sheep, then their only possible reaction, if at all, to the scriptural message is an unconditional "baa." Sheep we are and sheep—or goats—we shall remain until judgment day (Ezek 37:17-22; Mt 25:31-46) and even, beyond the judgment, in the Kingdom of God:

> Before him will be gathered all the nations, and he will separate them one from another as a shepherd separates the sheep from the goats, and *he will place the sheep at his right hand*, but the goats at the left. Then the King will say to *those at his right hand*, "Come, O blessed of my Father, inherit the kingdom prepared for you from the foundation of the world." (Mt 25:32-34)

Man-made theology could not accept such an insult to the assumed superior intellect of its promoters and ended up, as in the classical passage of the Orthodox Church baptismal service, speaking of "reason-endowed (logic-al) sheep (*probaton logikon*) of the holy flock of your Christ." A sheep having its own mind would start questioning the voice of its master, the shepherd, and ultimately end up wandering to its death. The story of the good shepherd who goes after the lost sheep does not include a map with annotated directions that the presumably "reason-endowed" sheep would refer to any time it is lost! Being a cradle Orthodox, I can assure my readers that the adjective *logikon*—as per the translation—refers to the Platonic *logos* and not to the scriptural *dabar*. If it did, no human would be happier than I since, then, the adjective *logikon* would be understood "according to the gospel 'word'" preached by the Apostle Paul. Note the following passage that is, unfortunately, usually translated Platonically in KJV and NJB:

> I beseech you therefore, brethren, by the mercies of God, that ye present your bodies a living sacrifice, holy, acceptable unto God, *which is* your *reasonable*[1] service (*logikēn latreian*). (Rom 12:1 KJV)

> I urge you, then, brothers, remembering the mercies of God, to offer your bodies as a living sacrifice, dedicated and acceptable to God; that is the kind of worship for you, *as sensible people*. (Rom 12:1 NJB)

RSV, notoriously unbound by the original text, skirts the issue by using "spiritual," which usually renders from the original *pnevmatikēn*:

> I appeal to you therefore, brethren, by the mercies of God, to present your bodies as a living sacrifice, holy and acceptable to God, which is your *spiritual* worship. (Rom 12:1 RSV)

Yet in another striking example, RSV translates the same *pnevmatikon* into "supernatural":

> I want you to know, brethren, that our fathers were all under the cloud, and all passed through the sea, and all were baptized into Moses in the cloud and in the sea, and all ate the same supernatural food and all drank the same supernatural (*pnevmatikon*) drink. For they drank from the supernatural (*pnevmatikēs*) Rock which followed them, and the Rock was Christ. (1 Cor 10:1-4)

So, the best possible rendering of *logikēn latreian* (Rom 12:1) is "a worship patterned after the gospel 'word' or (Pauline) 'preaching.'" Examples of such are found in Paul's letters:

> And do not get drunk with wine, for that is debauchery; but be filled with the Spirit, addressing one another in psalms and hymns and spiritual songs, singing and making melody to the Lord with all your heart, always and for everything giving thanks in the name of our Lord Jesus Christ to God the Father. (Eph 5:18-20)

> Let the word of Christ dwell in you richly, teach and admonish one another in all wisdom, and sing psalms and hymns and

---

1 So also the German *vernünftiger* from *Vernunft* (reason).

> spiritual songs with thankfulness in your hearts to God. (Col 3:16)[2]

A Platonic hearing of the original would prove totally faulty in the case of the only other instance of the adjective *logik*— in the New Testament:

> Like newborn babes, long for the pure spiritual (*logikon*) milk, that by it you may grow up to salvation. (1 Pet 2:2 RSV)

One can "hear" the original reflected in KJV that tries, as best it can,[3] to be literal:

> As newborn babes, desire the sincere milk *of the word*, that ye may grow thereby. (1 Pet 2:2 KJV)

However, Plato rules Christianism across the board. Killing ourselves with updated translations will never solve the dilemma.[4] We should resign ourselves to reading any translation—doomed to be imperfect by definition—but then explain to our hearers the content of the *original* Hebrew or Greek, respectively. Let me illustrate with an example. Frustrated with the English "terrible" to speak of God in our liturgical texts, recent translators opted for "awesome" in order to avoid the equally unpalatable "dreadful"—although the latter was kept in conjunction with "Christ's seat of judgment." All was well until one day, upon hearing that God was "awesome" during liturgy, one of my altar boys said to me: "So, Father Paul, God is awesome. That's awesome!" Obviously, eminent colleagues would suggest I explain to him the

---

2 In order not to assume that Paul is referring to the religious services of the Reformation churches, please refer to my comments in *C-Col* 84-7.

3 Since all translations are, by definition, marred by the theological preconceptions of the translators.

4 A striking example of how ludicrous even "revered" translations, like KJV, can be is that, among English-speaking "Christians" until today, the Spirit of God is a "ghost." Holy, to be sure, but still a "ghost"! Even German-speaking folks do not fare better with their *Geist.* Just imagine a title of a book or pamphlet that would read "The theology of the Holy Ghost," especially if it is sold at the entrance of Disneyland at a stand run by zealous believers.

"meaning" of the original. Well, I could have done the same with "terrible" and "dreadful."

Hearing the original entails first and foremost listening and submitting to it as a closed document that has been written and sealed by the authors within their historical, socio-political, and *geographical* context of the time of writing. If the writing has any "universal" value—a jargon we all are enamored with—that value has to be perceived within the original context. Take the quite simple example of the common statement "love your neighbor." In order to understand what the authors are "saying" one is to be able to fathom what the noun "neighbor" not so much *connotes* to us the hearers, but rather *connoted* at the time—in the "times"—of writing. This being the case, one can imagine the disaster that can ensue from the liberty taken by the Europeans to enslave the Africans by perceiving themselves as Japhethites (descendants of Japheth, Noah's son) and the Africans as Hamites (descendants of Ham, Noah's son), and then applying Noah's curse against Canaan, mind you, and not against Ham (Gen 9:25-27), on the Africans in order to justify modern slavery and, no less, in the name of the scriptural God! Just consider this map conceived in Europe in 1818:

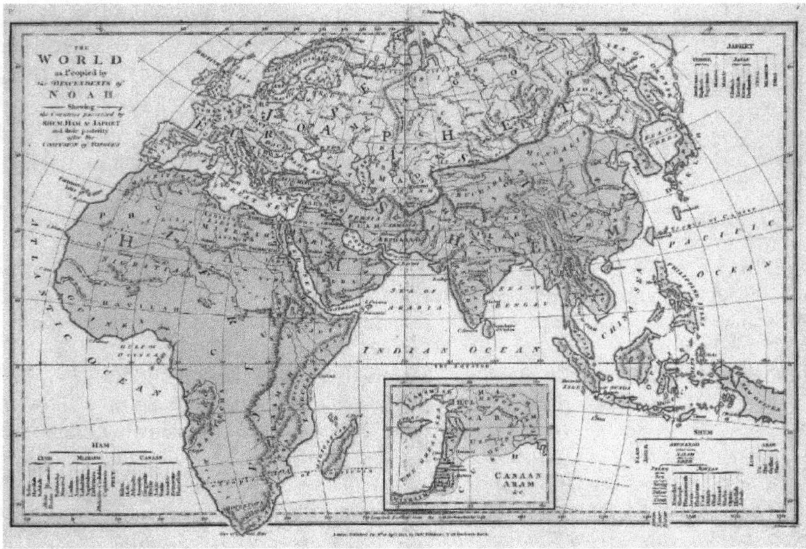

Just as the theologians, their predecessors, stretched the historical boundaries of scripture into their own times to cajole their egos by considering themselves as the "progeny" of the Apostles, if not "equal" to them—an endeavor I criticized and shown its falsehood in *The Rise of Scripture*—these "Christian" European pseudo-scientists misused the Bible for their own greedy avaricious socio-political purposes. Only the Christian East Asians (according to this map) will be happy to learn that they are Shemites. I am not sure if their non-Christian brethren *kata sarka* (according to the flesh) would be happy to learn that, especially when the twentieth century Europeans came up with their theory of the "Yellow Peril." The fact of the matter is that the East Asians and the North and South Americans as well as Central, Western, and South Africans, are not within the purview of the scriptural authors, even if one assumes that these authors were aware of those peoples and their regions, which is highly improbable or at least yet to be proven. At least the Latter-Day Saints were consistent in respecting the scriptural "reality" in that it is not inclusive of the North American continent. So they came up with the "Book of Mormon"—a written text, mind you—that contains old prophecies delivered on the North American continent at the same time as the scriptural prophets were delivering their messages between the Mediterranean Sea and the Tigris River. So, Joseph Smith got it right: scripture does not apply to North America. I hope my readers will not deduce that I agree with what he did. Instead of toying with a "new revelation" in a "strange language" that he had to translate, he should have settled on learning consonantal scriptural Hebrew. However, he was the product of theology. Theologians before him produced their theology by appealing to scores and scores of books written in Greek and Latin and, later English, German, French, and Spanish, and then quoting those books to tell us what the consonantal scriptural Hebrew text was saying.

Before rushing to denigrate the Latter-Day Saints, the rest of us, Christians, should realize that we did and still do the same, including those of us who give lip service to the slogan sola scriptura and then come up with an additional source(s) of our choosing:

- The Christian Orthodox uphold scripture *and* Holy Tradition that is also consigned in writings.
- The Roman Catholics uphold God's ten commandments *and* the church's five commandments and/or other precepts.
- The Anglicans' references are scripture *and* the Thirty-Nine Articles of Religion.
- The Lutherans are most flagrant in that they hold *only* to scripture *and* Luther's teachings and his 95 Theses. I should like to share an actual anecdote with my readers. At a special "smaller" consultation sponsored by the Faith and Order Commission on "Towards a Confession of the Common Faith" in Venice, Italy, in 1978 a renowned German Lutheran theologian, author of many books, allowed himself to rudely interrupt a Canadian Roman Catholic priest with the statement, "And who nowadays can still believe that a human being is infallible," obviously referring to the pope. Without skipping a beat, the Canadian priest retorted: "Lutherans do; they believe Martin Luther is infallible." One could hear a pin drop for a quite simple reason: the participants, including the Lutheran theologian, knew that the latter statement was factual.
- The churches of the Reformed tradition hold onto scripture *and* Calvin's "Institutes of the Christian Religion." The title of his original Latin work has the singular *Institutio* (the Institution) which could be taken as meaning "the instituting/founding (of the Christian

Religion)" and thus betraying that the work's content functions as a "foundation" of the Christian faith just as the Pauline gospel is (1 Cor 3:12). Yet it is Calvin's misunderstanding of Paul, especially the series of the Greek "aorists" in Romans 8:29-30, that gave rise to the unscriptural doctrine of "predestination."

- The same practices apply to the Methodist church, the Baptist church, the Pentecostal church. Ultimately, in all denominations of the Reformation, the "Spirit" is supposed to illumine the individual's mind and heart to accept the scriptural message as, mind you, penned in the translations. Thus, one can wonder why they bother with services and sermons, let alone theological treatises. An extreme case is found in Pentecostalism where the common service, including the sermon, seems to function as an opportunity to trigger the "Spirit" in the individual. In this regard, the Quakers (Friends) are the most logical since in their meetings the "sound" of the Spirit is not even heard, and yet one of them founded the city of Philadelphia (Brotherhood, Friendship).

The only way out of the impasse

The calamity of Christianity is that its "theology" went the way of Greek philosophy that was devised by people who divided humanity between the superior Hellene and the lesser in value outsider Barbarian who, in our European and North American style lingo, is the equivalent of "Savage," that is, "not tamed" into European civilization. The twin phenomena of the Renaissance and the Reformation reinforced this. While the Renaissance was spearheaded in the Roman Catholic Italy looking for the Greco-Roman heritage of Greek philosophy, city-state polity, and impressive architecture, the Reformation took roots in the non-Mediterranean and thus non-Roman Europe, that is the Europe that had been viewed as "barbarian" by ancient Rome. Central and Northern European countries or entities yearned for emancipation from the papacy that held sway over them just as Ancient Rome did. So, the Reformation "used" the scripture, especially the Letter to the Galatians—where Paul champions freedom from Jerusalem—as a rallying point for freedom from Rome. However, they missed Paul's stress on his being a "slave of Christ" early in Galatians (1:10)[5] as the basis for the rest of their argumentation. Hence the Reformation, across the board, held the flag of freedom and independence over and above the banner of the gospel of "submission" (*hypakoē;* obedience), which was stressed at the outset in Paul's letter to the Romans in 1:5, well before v.17, the classic text the Reformation used as their central focus: "For in it (the gospel) the righteousness of God is revealed through faith for faith; as it is written, 'He who through faith is righteous shall live.'"

Factually speaking and counter-intuitively, the Reformation thrived in the areas of Charlemagne's Frankish "Holy Roman empire." However, in scriptural terms, instead of following Paul's lead in rejecting his Juda*ism* (*ioudaismos*; Gal 1:14) and even accusing Peter of clinging to it (how can you compel the Gentiles to *live like Jews* [*ioudaizein*]?; Gal 2:14), the Reformation created and clung unto their own Christian*ism* (*khristianismos*). Once one stresses one's value around the "city" (civilization) as one's realization, as Cain did in Genesis 4:17 and the human beings did in Genesis 11:1-9, one is bound to justify it. This is precisely what the post-Renaissance and post-Reformation European and North American world did since then and is still doing. Just have a mental tour of the gigantic buildings—mainly cathedrals—that would put to shame the

5 As usual RSV has "servant" instead of "slave" that is the correct rendering of the Greek *doulos*.

tower of Babel of Genesis 11.[6] The Orthodox should refrain from gloating since they insist, whether true or not, that without the philosophical and architectural advances of Byzantium, there would not have been a European Renaissance. So, the result is the same. All civilizations follow in "the way of Cain" (Jude 1:11) whose progeny line culminated in an all-encompassing civilization that was discarded unto total oblivion[7] by the scriptural authors, who opted for a "new" *toledot* of Adam via Seth whom Eve conceived to take the place of Abel, the shepherd of flock:

> Now Adam knew Eve his wife, and she conceived and bore Cain … Cain knew his wife, and she conceived and bore Enoch; and he built a city, and called the name of the city after the name of his son, Enoch. … And Lamech took two wives; the name of the one was Adah, and the name of the other Zillah. Adah bore Jabal; he was the father of those who dwell in tents and have cattle. *His brother's name was Jubal; he was the father of all those who play the lyre and pipe. Zillah bore Tubalcain; he was the forger of all instruments of bronze and iron.* … And Adam knew his wife again, and she bore a son and called his name Seth, for she said, "*God has appointed for me another child instead of Abel*, for Cain slew him." To Seth also a son was born, and he called his name Enosh. At that time men began to call upon the name of the Lord. This is the book of the generations of Adam. When God created man, he made him in the likeness of God. Male and female he created them, and he blessed them and named them Man when they were created. When Adam had lived a hundred and thirty years, he became the father of a son in his own likeness, after his image, and named him Seth. The days of Adam after he became the father of Seth

---

6 It may well be that when the Lord said, "nothing that they propose to do will be impossible for them" (Gen 11:6), he was intending, "tongue in cheek," the Roman Catholic Cathedral of Seville since, according to the legend, the builders of the Cathedral declared: "Let us create such a building that future generations will take us for lunatic." Add to this that the gold of the impressive gilded altarpiece was stolen from the Americas in "the (golden) Age of Discovery."

7 Cain is mentioned again, besides Jude 1:11, only in 4 Maccabees 18:11, Hebrews 11:4, and 1 John 3:12 in reference to Genesis 4.

> were eight hundred years; and he had other sons and daughters. (Gen 4:1, 17, 19-22, 25-26; 5:1-4)

The authors' predilection for shepherdism over civilization will be confirmed without any doubt in the *toledot* of Shem (11:10-26) that follows immediately the debacle of civilization in the episode of the tower of Babel (vv.1-9). And yet, we, Christians as well as Jews, refer to and quote incessantly that same scripture to uphold the "work of our hands and minds." All one has to do is to hear through my ears, the cradle Orthodox, the non-ending litany of praise by my co-religionaries for the *sacred* (holy) architecture, the *sacred* (holy) space, the *sacred* (holy) iconology, the *sacred* (holy) music,[8] the *sacred* (holy) liturgical services, even the *sacred* (holy) priestly "movements" according to an article just published on a church website.[9] And all that unto the "great glory" of a God who is a shepherd. It is no wonder that he is sitting on his throne laughing at all the tumult of the nations:

> Give ear, O Shepherd of Israel, thou who leadest Joseph like a flock! Thou who art enthroned upon the cherubim, shine forth before Ephraim and Benjamin and Manasseh! Stir up thy might, and come to save us! (Ps 80:1-2)

> Arise, O God, judge the earth; for to thee belong all the nations! (Ps 82:8-1)

> Why do the nations conspire, and the peoples plot in vain? The kings of the earth set themselves, and the rulers take counsel together, against the Lord and his anointed, saying, "Let us burst their bonds asunder, and cast their cords from us." He who sits in the heavens laughs; the Lord has them in derision. (Ps 2:1-4)

---

8 Recently, I learned, an international workshop strangely—or not so strangely for the Orthodox—entitled "Music as Liturgy" was held at a prestigious institution of Orthodox Theology. My readers have already guessed that the organizers, the speakers, and the attendees were "musicians" extolling one another for the "work of their hands" as a "liturgy" offered to the Most High who expressly said through Isaiah that he didn't need such in the most stringent phraseology (Is 1:10-17; 66:1-3).

9 Which sounds exactly like mystery religions.

And for those of us who think that this is just Old Testament "stuff," let us listen to that same God's plenipotentiary messenger:

> And when you pray, you must not be like the hypocrites; for they love to stand and pray in the synagogues and at the street corners, that they may be seen by men. Truly, I say to you, they have received their reward. But when you pray, go into your room and shut the door and pray to your Father who is in secret; and your Father who sees in secret will reward you. And in praying do not heap up empty phrases as the Gentiles (*hoi ethnikoi;* those who follow the way of the nations) do; for they think that they will be heard for their many words. Do not be like them, for your Father knows what you need before you ask him. (Mat 6:5-8)

Both Jews and Christians should learn from the Muslim tradition. Although they built mosques, some of which are very impressive—the Blue Mosque of Istanbul beats its neighbor the Aghia Sophia in splendor—yet their ornamentation is restricted to "words" since their scripture, the *Qur'an*, just as ours, is a writ. My wish is that my co-religionaries, the Orthodox Christians, would take seriously their *own* liturgical tradition where, at the entrance, we bow down to a Christ who is not an eternal Platonic *logos*, but rather a book, that is, a collection of "words" (*logoi*) or "oracles, sayings" (*logia*) just as Paul viewed the Old Testament scripture: "To begin with, the Jews are entrusted with the oracles (*logia*) of God." (Rom 3:2) And we express trust (*pistis;* faith) by being faithful to those *logia* and not to a theological fabrication of our own minds as idols would be. Notice the play on the same root *pist*— in the original:

> Then what advantage has the Jew? Or what is the value of circumcision? Much in every way. To begin with, the Jews are entrusted (*epistevsēsan*) with the oracles of God. What if some were unfaithful (*ēpistēsan*)? Does their faithlessness (*apistia*) nullify the faithfulness (*pistin*, the same word for trust or faith on our part) of God? By no means! Let God be true though every man be false, as it is written, "That thou mayest be justified *in thy words* (*logois*), and prevail when thou art judged." But if our wickedness serves

> to show the justice of God, what shall we say? That God is unjust to inflict wrath on us? (I speak in a human way.) By no means! For then how could God judge the world? (Rom 3:1-6)

Any hearing of an older text in the light of a newer terminology is, to all purposes, an imposition of our own "twists" on the original text. Any terminology or phraseology that is not found in the original text in the original language should be totally discarded from our "theological" jargon. This applies primordially to a jargon that has become the "meat" of theological discourse and theological symposia, such as "divinity," "trinity," "eternal logos,"[10] "the spirit as a person," "incarnation (*ensarkōsis*)," "becoming man (*enanthrōpēsis*)," "bearer of God (*theotokos*)" in conjunction with Mary, "becoming god or godlike (*theosis*)," "orthodoxy" (let alone Lutheranism, Presbyterianism, and Methodism), and the like.

One of the most common fads among Christians is using "Jesus Christ"—whatever that means in the mind of each speaker—as a sort of master key that one holds in one's back pocket to unlock the "obscure" passages of the Old Testament. This brought about the even more ridiculous common fad, "Reading the Old Testament—and the New Testament, for that matter—in the 'light of Christ,'" a Christ that has already been preconceived in each speaker's mind. Scriptural "realities" are to be *extracted* out of the original scriptural terminology and phraseology. The logical corollary is that anyone who does not know ***scriptural*** Hebrew that was concocted by the scriptural authors to pour into it their intent and thought, should develop "ears to hear" but should never be allowed to pontificate about scripture. Here again, in this matter, we Christians should learn from the Muslims. A Muslim *'imam* (standing at the head of and thus leading) ***must*** be cognizant of the *Qur'anic Arabic* and its grammatical rules, and not, according to the Christian jargon, someone who has been moved by the Spirit to accept the "call" that has been etched in one's name since eternity, especially if

10 Just think of the common view, at least among Orthodox Christians, that Jesus Christ as "eternal logos" was "the Lord" that spoke to Moses on Mount Horeb.

one subscribes to "predestination." Notice how that kind of "calling" is subjected to the individual that has been called since ultimately, "Who are you to tell me if I have been called by God or not?"

We Orthodox are usually prone to fooling ourselves by saying that we consulted with our "spiritual father (or mother)" to make sure. Well, obviously those spiritual leaders are understandably interested in recruiting seminarians to ensure the following generation of clergy, "spiritual leaders" who, in their turn, will decide on the "call" of others. And, in this matter, what applies to the Orthodox applies to all Christians. The reason is quite simple: we all have "schools" made by the "hands of man," that cannot survive without continual ever fresh enrollment. Hence the gimmicks of "alma mater" and "class reunions" in our Western civilization that are used by the schools to perpetuate themselves on the back of their students and then project themselves as being "in the service" of those same students. All one must do to convince oneself is to re-read once a month the story of Solomon who was "filled with divine wisdom." He enslaved his own people (1 Kg chapter 5) in order to build—for God's great glory, so he says—a temple (*hekal*) worthy of that God and which that God did not need. Solomon's aim was to build a next-door palace (*hekal*) for himself on the back of those same people (1 Kg 7:1-12). Notice how the ingenious authors slipped that short notice in between the description of the building of God's temple (1 Kg 6:1-17 and 1 Kg 7:13-51). Again, all one needs to do is to look at the campuses of theological schools. The church building is one, usually the smallest, building among many more majestic structures of library, administration, dormitories, refectories, gyms, auditorium, and the like. And those schools pay lip service to God by printing in their pamphlets that the "small" church building is the center and the "beating heart" of the life of the school.

Unless a proposed solution to address this dilemma is based on the inner tradition of the scriptural text itself, then it is bound to go the way of "theologies" that are to be discarded once and for all. In scripture, God's messenger has a unique status that the hearers do not have. I am aware that most of my readers know already what I am about to say regarding the Old Testament Prophets and the Apostle in the New Testament, and yet most of us end up more often than not by assuming that we could, or at least—in all humility of course—might, be, or act as another Moses, or another Isaiah, or another Jeremiah, or another Ezekiel, or another Jonah, or another Paul, forgetting that those scriptural characters are one of a kind and, thus, unrepeatable and unmatchable. And they are so, not "essentially," but rather "functionally," within the setting of the scriptural story that is, and should forever remain, our only valid reference.

In the Book of Isaiah the protagonist Isaiah is a unique instance since he is presented as the only human, though sinful as all the others are (6:6), who becomes a member of the divine council: "And I heard the voice of the Lord saying, 'Whom shall I send, and who will go *for us*?' Then I said, 'Here am I! Send me.'" (v.8) Only Satan *in the Book of Job* is functionally equal to Isaiah presented *in the Book of Isaiah* (Job 1:6; 2:1).

In the Book of Ezekiel the protagonist Ezekiel, though a mere "son of man" as his hearers, is not functionally accountable in the same way as his hearers. Whereas the hearers will be judged based on whether or not they will have *acted* according to Ezekiel's message, Ezekiel himself will be judged based on whether or not he will have *delivered* the message verbatim. In other words, Ezekiel's "action" is to do the will of God *for him*, while the hearers' "action" is to do the will of God *for them*. In other words, Ezekiel is bound by the words of God, while the hearers are bound by the "words of Ezekiel":

> And at the end of seven days, the word of the Lord came to me: "Son of man, I have made you a watchman for the house of Israel; whenever you hear a word from my mouth, you shall give

> them warning from me. If I say to the wicked, 'You shall surely die,' and you give him no warning, nor speak to warn the wicked from his wicked way, in order to save his life, that wicked man shall die in his iniquity; but his blood I will require at your hand. But if you warn the wicked, and he does not turn from his wickedness, or from his wicked way, he shall die in his iniquity; but you will have saved your life. Again, if a righteous man turns from his righteousness and commits iniquity, and I lay a stumbling block before him, he shall die; because you have not warned him, he shall die for his sin, and his righteous deeds which he has done shall not be remembered; but his blood I will require at your hand. Nevertheless if you warn the righteous man not to sin, and he does not sin, he shall surely live, because he took warning; and you will have saved your life." (Ezek 3:16-21)

The same rule or mechanism is found in chapter 37 where Ezekiel is bound by God's word to him, while the bones are bound to Ezekiel's words to them:

> And he said to me, "Son of man, can these bones live?" And I answered, "O Lord God, thou knowest." Again he said to me, "Prophesy to these bones, and say to them, O dry bones, hear the word of the Lord. Thus says the Lord God to these bones: Behold, I will cause breath to enter you, and you shall live. And I will lay sinews upon you, and will cause flesh to come upon you, and cover you with skin, and put breath in you, and you shall live; and you shall know that I am the Lord." So I prophesied as I was commanded; and as I prophesied, there was a noise, and behold, a rattling; and the bones came together, bone to its bone. And as I looked, there were sinews on them, and flesh had come upon them, and skin had covered them; but there was no breath in them. Then he said to me, "Prophesy to the breath, prophesy, son of man, and say to the breath, Thus says the Lord God: Come from the four winds, O breath, and breathe upon these slain, that they may live." So I prophesied as he commanded me, and the breath came into them, and they lived, and stood upon their feet, an exceedingly great host. (Ezek 37:3-10)

In the Book of Jeremiah the protagonist Jeremiah is incomparable to any other character in the book. On the one hand, both he and Hananiah were equally prophets: "Then the prophet

Jeremiah spoke to Hananiah the prophet in the presence of the priests and all the people who were standing in the house of the Lord." (Jer 28:5). Still, the words of the Lord were put in the mouth of Jeremiah and not Hananiah (1:9). On the other hand, and more importantly for my argument, Jeremiah was a priest of Anathoth, a small village in Benjamin, and not a priest of Jerusalem (1:1), yet he was assigned by the Lord to speak at the entrance of the temple of Jerusalem (7:2; 26:1-2). This is definitely strange considering what Amaziah, the priest of Bethel in Samaria said to Amos of Judah: "And Amaziah said to Amos, "O seer, go, flee away to the land of Judah, and eat bread there, and prophesy there; but never again prophesy at Bethel, for it is the king's sanctuary, and it is a temple of the kingdom." (Am 7:12-13) This explains the lengthy passages in the Book of Jeremiah where the prophet had to stand trial for what he was doing (chapter 26 and 28).

This scenario is taken up in the New Testament in the description of its two main protagonists, Jesus and Paul. Both of them were identified as originating far from Jerusalem. Jesus was from far off Nazareth of Galilee (Mt 21:11); Paul was from an even farther locality, Tarsus of Cilicia (Acts 9:11). Still, this did not deter the scriptural God from assigning both to deliver God's message to Jerusalem and its leaders. However, a major difference between Jesus and Paul, on the one hand, and the Old Testament Prophets, on the other hand, is the medium though which God communicates with his assignees. The Prophet is given the words that he is supposed to regurgitate. Hence the classic "Thus says the Lord" that is repeated throughout the Prophetic literature and which is followed by statements in which the "I" is the divine "I," reflecting the fact that the Prophet is repeating verbatim what the Lord has told him to say:

> Thus says the Lord: "For three transgressions of Moab, and for four, *I* will not revoke the punishment; because he burned to lime the bones of the king of Edom. So *I* will send a fire upon Moab, and it shall devour the strongholds of Kerioth, and Moab shall die amid uproar, amid shouting and the sound of the trumpet; *I*

> will cut off the ruler from its midst, and will slay all its princes with him," says the Lord. (Am 2:1-3 RSV)

Notice how the phrase "Says the Lord" brackets the divine statement and thus functions as our quotation marks before and after the quotation.

As for Jesus and Paul their reference to God's words was scripture, an already written text:

> And Jesus answered him, "It is written, 'Man shall not live by bread alone.'" (Lk 4:4)

> And he came to Nazareth, where he had been brought up; and he went to the synagogue, as his custom was, on the sabbath day. And he stood up to read; and there was given to him the book of the prophet Isaiah. He opened the book and found the place where it was written, "The Spirit of the Lord is upon me ..." (Lk 4:16-18)

> He said to him, "What is written in the law? How do you read?" (Lk 10:26)

> For truly, I say to you, till heaven and earth pass away, not an iota, not a dot, will pass from the law until all is accomplished. (Mt 5:18)

> Paul, a servant of Jesus Christ, called to be an apostle, set apart for the gospel of God which he promised beforehand through his prophets in the holy scriptures. (Rom 1:1-2)

> For what does the scripture say? "Abraham believed God, and it was reckoned to him as righteousness." (Rom 4:3)

> Tell me, you who desire to be under law, do you not hear the law? (Gal 4:21)

> But what does the scripture say? "Cast out the slave and her son; for the son of the slave shall not inherit with the son of the free woman." (Gal 4:30)

Add to this all the instances of "As it is written" in the Pauline letters.

Accordingly, John Chrysostom is the only "Christian" who got it right and taught by "expounding" the scriptural writ. He stressed in the preface of his homilies the utmost importance of abiding by the scriptural narrative *as it stands*:

> It were indeed meet for us not at all to require the aid of the written Word, but to exhibit a life so pure, that the grace of the Spirit should be instead of books to our souls, and that as these are inscribed with ink, even so should our hearts be with the Spirit. But, since we have utterly put away from us this grace, come, *let us at any rate embrace the second best course*.
>
> For that the former was better,God has made manifest, both by His words, and by His doings. Since unto Noah, and unto Abraham, and unto his offspring, and unto Job, and unto Moses too, He discoursed not by writings, but Himself by Himself, finding their mind pure. But after the whole people of the Hebrews had fallen into the very pit of wickedness, then and thereafter was *a written word, and tables*, and the admonition which is given by these.
>
> And this one may perceive was the case, not of the saints in the Old Testament only, but also of those in the New. For neither to the apostles did God give anything in writing, but instead of written words He promised that He would give them the grace of the Spirit: for He, says our Lord, shall bring all things to your remembrance. And that you may learn that this was far better, hear what He says by the Prophet: I will make a new covenant with you, putting my laws into their mind, and in their heart I will write them, and, they shall be all taught of God. And Paul too, pointing out the same superiority, said, that they had received a law not in tables of stone, but in fleshy tables of the heart.
>
> But since in process of time they made shipwreck, some with regard to doctrines, others as to life and manners, there was again need that they should be put in remembrance by *the written word*.
>
> Reflect then how great an evil it is for us, who ought to live so purely as not even to need written words, but to yield up our hearts, as books, to the Spirit; now that we have lost that honor, *and have come to have need of these, to fail again in duly employing even this second remedy*. For if it be a blame to stand in need of written words,

> and not to have brought down on ourselves the grace of the Spirit; *consider how heavy the charge of not choosing to profit even after this assistance, but rather treating what is written with neglect, as if it were cast forth without purpose, and at random, and so bringing down upon ourselves our punishment with increase.*
>
> But that no such effect may ensue, *let us give strict heed unto the things that are written*; and let us learn how the Old Law was given on the one hand, how on the other the New Covenant.[11]

It is fitting that this preface stands at the start of Chrysostom's homilies on the Gospel of Matthew where we hear the following unexpected statement:

> Then said Jesus to the crowds and to his disciples, "The scribes and the Pharisees sit on Moses' seat; so practice and observe whatever they tell you, but not what they do; for they preach, but do not practice." (Mt 23:1-3)

This Gospel's addressees are members of the communities established by Paul as is obvious from the fact that the noun "church" occurs thrice and only in this book among the Gospels:

> And I tell you, you are Peter, and on this rock I will build my *church*, and the powers of death shall not prevail against it. (Mt 16:18)
>
> If your brother sins against you, go and tell him his fault, between you and him alone. If he listens to you, you have gained your brother. But if he does not listen, take one or two others along with you, that every word may be confirmed by the evidence of two or three witnesses. If he refuses to listen to them, tell it to the *church*; and if he refuses to listen even to the *church*, let him be to you as a Gentile and a tax collector. (Mt 18:15-17)

By the same token, "the scribes and the Pharisees" of Matthew 23 are *functionally speaking* none other than the "scribes and

---

11 E.B. Pusey, John Keble & Charles Marriott, eds., *Homilies of S John Chrysostom, Archbishop of Constantinople, on the Gospel According to St. Matthew, Homily I*, volume of *A Library of Fathers of the Holy Catholic Church, Anterior to the Division of the East & West*, trans. Frederic Field (Oxford: J.H. Parker, 1839-1874) 1-2. Italics are mine.

Pharisees" of the church where the voice of the Apostle is heard even in his absence:

> It is actually reported that there is immorality among you, and of a kind that is not found even among pagans; for a man is living with his father's wife. And you are arrogant! Ought you not rather to mourn? Let him who has done this be removed from among you. *For though absent in body I am present in spirit,* and as if present, I have already pronounced judgment in the name of the Lord Jesus on the man who has done such a thing. When you are assembled, *and my spirit is present,* with the power of our Lord Jesus, you are to deliver this man to Satan for the destruction of the flesh, that his spirit may be saved in the day of the Lord Jesus. (1 Cor 5:1-5)

> I wrote to you in my letter not to associate with immoral men; not at all meaning the immoral of this world, or the greedy and robbers, or idolaters, since then you would need to go out of the world. But rather I wrote to you not to associate with any one who bears the name of brother if he is guilty of immorality or greed, or is an idolater, reviler, drunkard, or robber -- not even to eat with such a one. For what have I to do with judging outsiders? *Is it not those inside the church whom you are to judge?* God judges those outside. "Drive out the wicked person from among you." (I Cor 5:9-13)

> Therefore, my beloved, as you have always obeyed, so now, not only as in my presence but *much more in my absence,* work out your own salvation with fear and trembling. (Phil 2:12)

> Give my greetings to the brethren at Laodicea, and to Nympha and the church in her house. And when this letter has been read among you, have it read also in the church of the Laodiceans; and see that you read also the letter from Laodicea. (Col 4:15-16)

Thus, what is heard by the congregants is the voice of the Apostle who, himself, quoted scripture. And the church leaders are—just as Chrysostom did—to convey the content of the scriptures, regardless of whether they themselves hearken to its teaching or not, as was etched for the ages *by God himself* way before Jesus and Paul:

> A Maskil of Asaph. Give ear, O my people, to my teaching; incline your ears to the words of my mouth! I will open my mouth

> in a parable; I will utter dark sayings from of old, things that we have heard and known, that our fathers have told us. We will not hide them from their children, but tell to the coming generation the glorious deeds of the Lord, and his might, and the wonders which he has wrought. He established a testimony in Jacob, and appointed a law in Israel, which he commanded our fathers to teach to their children; that the next generation might know them, the children yet unborn, and arise and tell them to their children, so that they should set their hope in God, and not forget the works of God, but keep his commandments; and *that they should not be like their fathers, a stubborn and rebellious generation, a generation whose heart was not steadfast, whose spirit was not faithful to God.* (Ps 78:1-8)

My proposition

The task of dismantling the pseudo-validity of theologies conceived outside of the scriptural text would be quite difficult, to say the least, if not practically unattainable. I believe the way to give this matter the best possible chance of succeeding is to have as "scribes and Pharisees" individuals who have been least affected by "theological" bias. They would have to be non-Christians who have been untainted when it comes to scripture, that is, people who in no way, shape, or form have been tainted by Christianism.

The classic Christian retort to this is that one needs to have faith to comprehend the "real" meaning of scripture. This does not hold water for the following blatant reasons:

1. This is a statement found on the lips of us arrogant Christians, especially in the West, who accept the strange fact that a good number of us are university professors of Judaism, Islam, Buddhism, Hinduism, and other "religions" including so-called "agnosticism," and even allow ourselves to teach followers of those religions their own religion and grant them a degree when they pass our tests. Why? Simply

because we are convinced of our superiority to assess matters "objectively."

2. As of late, we even allow Jews to be professors of New Testament at some of our universities because we suddenly decided, after the experience of the European holocaust we initiated, that they and we are "brethren" and even that, de facto, they are God's "chosen people" while we are only the "newcomer" Gentiles.
3. Many of us even decided recently that a Jew is "elect" even when that person is avowedly agnostic or atheist. My readers are to remember that such assessments are ours. We, especially in the West, decide for the others. Just look at the world map of 1818 above.

We, Christians of the West, created the universities. The name itself is reflective of total hegemony—to control the human "conversation" just as the Ancient Greeks attempted to do. For an "outsider," "barbarian," "savage" to take part, that person must be "Hellenized" or "civilized" under our aegis. My readers are invited to check the renowned series *Great Books of the Western World* where there is a leap from Augustine of Hippo to Thomas Aquinas, bypassing the "unworthy of mention" Byzantine, Arab, and Jewish scholars between the fifth and thirteenth centuries, including the two contemporaries, the Muslim Averroes, dubbed "The Master" by Aquinas, and the Jew Maimonides!

If one considers that scripture is viewed in and by the West as the best "best seller" and Augustine of Hippo's "Confessions," "the City of God," "on Christian Doctrine," and Aquinas' "Summa Theologica" were included in *The Great Books* series, then why not invite a non-Christian Vietnamese or Korean willing to study scriptural Hebrew to tell us what that text is actually saying. At least, as is done in the selection of jury members in the United States to make sure that all the jurors are "unbiased," that person would fit best the condition. Add to this that, according to the "educated" map produced in Europe in 1818, a Vietnamese or Korean would top even a European since Europeans are just Japhethites, whereas Vietnamese and Koreans are Shemites into whose tents the Japhethtites would be "blessed" to reside. Notice that I did not suggest a resident of the Arabian Peninsula because, according to the same map, the Arabs are Hamites! Furthermore, a Vietnamese or Korean would be less boring than Christians who study scripture only to take the opportunity to extol their "Orthodox" approach to the Bible, or "Lutheran" approach, or "Baptist" approach, or "Methodist" approach, and so on. In turn, those same Christians use their approach to come up with a World Council of Churches that is ecumenical, unlike the Vatican they say, and yet it ends up building headquarters in Geneva, including staff emulating that of the United Nations, that would put to shame Solomon's temple and palace and all this is done, mind you, for God's great glory. The Protestant members, who form the majority, criticize the papal *bullae*, yet their statements function as their *bullae* or *encyclicals* giving their assessments of situations and even governments.[12]

Speaking of buildings and the like, just follow the *surreal* situation in which the entire world finds itself with the threat of a coronavirus pandemic. And yet, we USA—mostly Christian—citizens are spending so much time and money to cover newspaper articles and TV debates concerning statues. I am betting that an honest Vietnamese or Korean student of scripture would have pointed to Genesis 11:1-9 and asked, "Why in the world did you build those statues in the first place?" After all, as scripture has taught and even proven, one preserves "history" in writ, not in stone. And, this word "history" we are excited about to affirm our identity by over-extolling our

12 As a curious aside, Geneva is the seat of the Secretariat of the Ecumenical Patriarchate which is in Istanbul!

"fathers"—against the express teaching of Psalm 78—is not even found in scripture.[13] We Western Christians would never acquiesce—as a Vietnamese or Korean would—that statues are anti-scriptural, but would engage in the debate about them. Why? Because we have lived a contradiction all along. Instead of just penning Jeremiah's words (Do not trust in these deceptive words: "This is the temple of the Lord, the temple of the Lord, the temple of the Lord" – 7:4) at the entrance of a church, we have built an impressive statue of the prophet holding this text in stone, "for so we love to do" (Am 4:5).

The scriptural God is not the God of history, as Oscar Cullman wanted us to believe in his *Christ and Time: The Primitive Christian Conception of Time and History*, but the God of "life." It is high time that a Vietnamese would remind us that the contemporary pandemic put us all, animals as well as humans, in a situation similar to that of Noah and his three sons under "house arrest" in a finite ark floating at the mercy of the waves and, hopefully, at the mercy of God.

Today, we all are simply "human"—*'adamic*—despite our different colors and hues, floating on a finite planet under "house arrest"—pace Elon Musk and his spacecraft that was launched in the midst of the pandemic as an exciting Disneyland experience. If Musk is successful, then Mars will become another floating finite planet filled with humans, that is, another planet Earth. What a deal! Yet, we, especially in the West, are impressed because we have become quantitative: two and three are better than one.

I have an educated hunch that, had scripture been written in our century, the cunning authors would have told the story of the flood around two arks at the mercy of the same raging waters, one ark for the Terran humans and the other for the Martian or "Muskan" humans. The solution to the Covid-19 pandemic will not come out of contradictory press releases

---

13 In RSV, in Genesis 37:2 it is added and in 2 Chronicles 9:29 it is a mistranslation. The Greek noun *historia* occurs in the later Books of Maccabees (2 Macc 2:24, 32; 4 Macc 17:7) found only in the LXX.

doctored by their promoters, but out of a laboratory at the hand of an *'adamic* scientist working *à la* Marie Curie, "the only person uncorrupted by fame" in Einstein's words. Her work and personal dedication had nothing to do with her being Polish, or Russian, or French, or even being a woman. She was the *scientist* Marie Curie. The scientist who will eventually allow us to open the door of our ark imposed on us by Covid-19 will function as a scriptural "dove" as Marie Curie did. Still, just as with scripture, there is no assurance whatsoever that we shall learn our lesson. Most probably we shall erect a statue of that scientist in each country! Scripture has been around for almost twenty-three centuries and not only have we not listened to it, but more often than not we have abused it by misinterpreting it for our own interest: power, wealth, racism, and subjugation of entire populations as in the Americas and Africa, even using those whom we have enslaved to build statues of their enslavers. And in order to appease the Almighty, we build statues of his "saints" and then praise the human architect's art. We have learned well, not from scripture that forbids any kind of statue or image, but from Ancient Greece. Then, to cover our betrayal of the Lord's and Paul's command not to imitate the nations or Gentiles (Mt 5:47; 1 Cor 5:1; 6:1-8), we published studies praising the "symphony" between Christ and Caesar and even the "symphony" between Athens and Jerusalem.

Lately I learned that Christianity is a fusion between the "inner wisdom" of the faith—whatever that means—and the "outer wisdom" of the Greeks and Romans. I have been studying the letters of Paul for over sixty years and I remember having read in 1 Corinthians chapters 1 and 2 that Paul's view is, "If Ancient Greek thought is wisdom, then God's thought is folly." I also recall Paul's Lord, Jesus Christ, saying: "I thank thee, Father, Lord of heaven and earth, that thou hast hidden these things from the wise and understanding and revealed them to babes; yea, Father, for such was thy gracious will." (Mt 11:25-26; Lk 10:21) If by symphony my Orthodox co-religionaries mean that the patriarchs, bishops, and their clergy copied, if not took over, the Byzantine imperial garb, then yes, I see it. Then they legitimize their decision by looking for scriptural tidbits to be said aloud while donning each item of the vestments. However, when the good Lord in his justice decided to "punish" me for my being hard on my brethren the Orthodox, he made it so that, upon retirement from teaching in New York State, I would move to a warmer climate in the Carolinas. I never fathomed his intention until I went with friends to two mega-churches, one Baptist and the other Methodist, on a regular Sunday service. In my wildest dreams I would never have imagined that I would be attending, down to the vestments and the movements, a pageantry that would eclipse both a high church Anglican service and an Orthodox hierarchical liturgy.

My proposition is straightforward and simple, beginning with my co-religionaries and co-citizens, the North American Orthodox, who have spent and still spend millions, if not billions, of dollars on their stone churches and expensive iconography paid to the human hands—quite often flown in from Greece, Russia, Romania, and the middle East, and fed and roomed while here—that etched it. Mind you that these same expensive buildings and iconography need "retouching" at some point or another. Some of us, who converted from a Reformation background into Orthodoxy, even pride ourselves in pushing for the institution of tithing on the basis that it is scriptural, as though the scriptural criticism of buildings is unscriptural. The answer in this case would be: but this is the "Holy Tradition" of Greco-Roman architecture via the medium of the Greco-Roman Byzantium that was guided by the "symphony" between the rule of Caesar and the rule of Christ or, as earlier mentioned, the "symphony" between the "inner" and "outer" wisdoms. I am asking—challenging—them to set aside 0.01% of their yearly budgets and earmark it for the following project.

Find individuals from Southeast Asia or, closer, from the Native American tribes, who have no connection whatsoever with Christianity and are decided not to have any desire to "convert"—I can already hear the gasping of my readers, especially those committed to Christian Orthodox missionary work who need to raise money for the glory of Orthodoxy via that medium[14]—and offer them a full scholarship to cover their following expenses:

1. Thoroughly learning scriptural consonantal Hebrew[15] and some of its cognate Semitic languages for the sake of comparison and more clarity, but treating the Old Testament as an already "closed book," i.e., standing on its own. This would be along the lines of the work of the late Mitchell Dahood who insisted on the primacy of the consonantal Hebrew text of the Old Testament over not only the LXX and the Vulgate, but also the vocalized Masoretic text, a product that started as late as the seventh century A.D. The importance, if not necessity, of learning consonantal scriptural Hebrew is due not only to the content of its literature that influenced the content, imagery, and phraseology of the Old Testament, but also because it is strictly a literary consonantal language, just as Ugaritic is. None of us, including Mitchell Dahood, has ever met someone speaking Ugaritic.
2. Reading "theological" books is strictly forbidden.

14 Lately I learned that the Orthodox Christian Mission Center, which has been supporting missionary work in Africa, recently sent a missionary couple—husband and wife—to Sweden of all places! Be advised Lutheran Swedes, we Orthodox are bringing to you the Light of the real—understand American Orthodox—Christ!

15 Jerome did it in the fourth century, so why not they?

3. Reading only literature dealing with Ancient Near East, Ancient Greek, Ancient Roman socio-polities.
4. Upon mastering scriptural Hebrew, dedicating their life to sharing with us what they are convinced scripture is "saying."
5. Since they will be receiving a teacher's salary to support their livelihoods they could use the time to teach others who would be interested in learning the same and who would help them, the teachers, by testing their findings through questions for clarification.
6. Publishing the result of their, comparatively speaking, much less biased research since there would be nothing "in it for them," that is, their so-called "faith" or "calling" or "church." To make sure that the bias be kept to a minimum, the authors would not be allowed to refer to other so-called "scholarly" work whether in the main text or in footnotes.[16] They would be required to convince, to the best of their abilities, their "lay" readers and only secondarily the so-called European (Japhethite) and "White" American (neo-Japhethite) "scholars." It is high time that at least some of us would hear, as exactly as possible, what the original addressees "heard." Whether we shall hear the words *in order to do them* (Deuteronomy passim) or not, this is up to us. In this regard I heard once the following anecdote. In a Presbyterian church the tradition is that the presbyters have a say in the

16 Those who quote others are just trying to impress their readers by filling in extra lines and, more importantly, are risking to end up under Ezekiel's verdict: "they and their fathers have transgressed against me to this very day." (Ezek 2:3) Those of my readers who can afford the time may read Ezekiel 20 where the generations are depicted as repeating the *same* sin which is (mis)interpreting God's message.

> choice of the pastor and monitor what he teaches. On the first Sunday of his assignment a pastor preached a moving sermon that kept the entire congregation reeling. The subject was brotherly love. The presbyters congratulated the pastor as well as themselves on their choice. The following Sunday the pastor repeated verbatim the same sermon. The stunned community looked for an explanation: perhaps it is his way of stressing the importance of the matter. The third Sunday, the same scenario. The presbytery met with the pastor and complained since the church was "paying" him to preach. His reply was: "Oh yes, I have a set of sermons on different topics up my sleeve, however, I shall move on when you have implemented the requirements of my first sermon!"

A similar project would entail learning the Greek of the New Testament literature with the same aims.

A few years after the North American Orthodox, whether individually or communally, have committed to these projects, it would then be time to invite the other "Christians" and, for that matter, interested "non-Christians" to commit to the same projects. Hopefully, these projects would help put on the market an echo of scripture "as it is (was) written" rather than a "venerable" *translation* intended to become part of a "holy" tradition, whether Orthodox or otherwise (Roman Catholic, Anglican, Lutheran, and the like). It is my conviction that this is the only way one can give a chance to scripture "that is already written once and for all" to challenge the listeners as it was intended to do from the beginning. Scripture is a parody of human power and wisdom, and yet "scholars" made of it a source of infinite human wisdom and power and promise for success in order to sell their ideas and books to the rest of us whose egos feel ingratiated, just as Eve was by the serpent (*naḥaš*;

bad omen), the apparently seemingly "wisest" among the "living creatures of the field" (Genesis 3). Paul gave his unequivocal verdict on that serpent in his Corinthian correspondence (But I am afraid that as the serpent deceived Eve by his cunning, your thoughts will be led astray from a sincere and pure devotion to Christ; 2 Cor 11:3) where he castigated Ancient Greek "wisdom" as "folly" (1 Cor 1-2). Yet scholars still refuse to comprehend that scripture is a satire against their "educated" efforts to present that same scripture as a "font of wisdom," in spite of Ecclesiastes and Genesis 11:1-9 where we are told that God forcibly "scattered" the humans who refused to "spread," as he had planned for them, and congregated in one place with the intent of showing him they could reach up to him through their own efforts. If this is not already a caricature of ecumenical councils, church conferences, and national as well as international Christian assemblies, then what is? What can one really expect from a scholarship that translates (and thus understands and preaches) the original "serve (*'abad*) the earth and keep it" (Gen 2:15) into "till—and thus manipulate—the earth and keep at it." What can one really hope from a scholarship that translates (and thus understands and preaches) the original "Blessed is the man who 'spells out consonantally' (*hagah*; spell out, utter) the divine law" (Ps 1:2) and thus mumbles it from memory, into "Blessed is the man who meditates upon (and thus professes his own thoughts about) the divine law."

It is no wonder that Protestant preachers love lengthy sermons to convey to their congregants their "mental manipulations" of the scriptural reading of the day which they had chosen and not assigned to them as is the norm in the traditional churches. They choose a "text for the day" that allows them to say something about a topic that has been lately brewing in their mind and thus they plan God's agenda for him. On the other hand, the Orthodox love to "meditate," that is ponder their own thoughts. Moses met the Lord on a bare mountain where he was handed the divine decrees without footnotes, comments, debates or Q and A sessions. Orthodox monastics filled an entire mountain in Northern Greece with handmade buildings to encounter the same God. They even built a monastery on Mount Sinai itself that is officially named "Sacred Monastery of the God-Trodden Mount Sinai" to honor that same God who not only appeared on a bare mountain but also destroyed by decree the temple Solomon built *supposedly* in his honor.

Is there an assuredness that such scholars dedicated to conveying to the rest of us what the original text *already said* and—only in this sense—is saying will succeed in their efforts? No, since they will surely disagree with one another. However, the larger their number, the greater our hope and even our assuredness that, whenever they agree, we are on a much surer ground since their plan and aim is not to defend an age-long "eternal" truth, but, as in science, to look for what is already there waiting for us to discover. So, in a way, they will be discoverers of the truth of the matter of a text already closed rather than defenders of an unchanging truth to which they would be clinging as followers of a "sacred tradition" or a "school of thought" do and thus bend the data their way in order *not to disappoint themselves.*

In this regard I should like to end with this well-known anecdote: God will have different enclosed areas in heaven and St Peter, the doorkeeper, will invite those of us who get there into their specific area so that each one of us will realize that, indeed, heaven is only for those of one's own kind. However, as I have kept reminding my frustrated students, the trick is first to get in there and, according to the already sealed scripture, those who do get in will do so by having done the will of that God that is inscribed in scriptural Hebrew rendered also in scriptural Greek, and not by following some kind of "doctrine" glued together by human "luminaries."

It is in the name and by the authority of a human made doctrine that we relegate the "living"[17] scriptural God to the status of idol, which we then suffocate with our fumes of "theological" laudatory terms as well as with incense, while mistreating our peers:

> Hear the word of the Lord, you rulers of Sodom! Give ear to the teaching of our God, you people of Gomorrah! What to me is the multitude of your sacrifices? says the Lord; I have had enough of burnt offerings of rams and the fat of fed beasts; I do not delight in the blood of bulls, or of lambs, or of he-goats. When you come to appear before me, who requires of you this trampling of my courts? Bring no more vain offerings; incense is an abomination to me. New moon and sabbath and the calling of assemblies -- I cannot endure iniquity and solemn assembly. Your new moons and your appointed feasts my soul hates; they have become a burden to me, I am weary of bearing them. When you spread forth your hands, I will hide my eyes from you; even though you make many prayers, I will not listen; your hands are full of blood. Wash yourselves; make yourselves clean; remove the evil of your doings from before my eyes; cease to do evil, learn to do good; seek justice, correct oppression; defend the fatherless, plead for the widow. (Is 1:10-17)

I should like here to share with my readers three examples of behavior perpetrated in our own times in the West that prides itself on being beyond the Age of Medieval Church Inquisition and of allowing academic freedom. From these cases my readers will gather that, in fact, so-called academic freedom is controlled by either "the doctrine" or—which is worse—"the scholarly consensus." The latter is more insidious since, in science, it is the truth of the matter, and not consensus, that counts. In the scientific realm, jury verdicts and supreme court decisions are as much mirages as political leaders' pronouncements. Plato hampered rather than promoted scientific advancement, and yet the appeal of his unproven

---

17 In the original Hebrew in Ezekiel 5:11; 14:16, 18, 20; 16:48; 16:17, 19; 18:3; 20:3, 31, 33; 33:11, 27; 34:8; 35:6, 11: "I am (the) living (one)" that is usually rendered in translations "As I live" which is ludicrous according to me.

axioms that persists are as misleading as the serpent of the garden in Genesis 3.

I shall start with the example that is least in malignity since it did not affect the person and livelihood of the scriptural scholar. All the critics of Mitchell Dahood's "Commentary on Psalms" who, by and large, do not even have the mastery of Ugaritic he has, spend their energy critiquing him on the basis of a few samples they pick here and there and miss his most important argument, namely, that we are bound by the scriptural Hebrew "consonantal" text and not the much later—actually later than the LXX manuscripts of the fourth and fifth centuries—Masoretic "vocalized" text. I remind my readers that old manuscripts were written without separation between the individual words as we have them today. So, the assigned reader in the early synagogues and churches had to prepare ahead of time by parsing the text. Such an endeavor would not be possible unless the reader knew very well the original language and its rules. Still, reading a Greek manuscript is by far easier than reading a Semitic manuscript since Greek uses vowels as well as consonants as alphabetic letters, whereas Semitic languages have only consonants as alphabetic letters. Imagine trying to figure out whether WNT NT is "I went into" or "I want not." The solution lies in the context of the entire sentence. Consequently, Dahood's most important input is found in his extensive "The Grammar of the Psalter" that he detailed over eighty-seven pages—a small book—at the end of the third volume of his commentary. His critics fall under the critique of Michael V. Fox, Halls-Bascom Professor Emeritus in the Department of Hebrew and Semitic Studies at the University of Wisconsin-Madison. A former seminarian of mine relayed to me this story while he was doing his PhD studies:

> In our text courses with Dr Fox (we only had text courses with him), we all sat in a circle around a conference table. Our task was to read the verse aloud in Hebrew, translate the verse, and justify our translation. The courses were in a three-year cycle: Ezekiel, Isaiah, Wisdom Lit (Proverbs, Qohelet, Job), repeat. My

> first year was Wisdom Lit, known for its challenging vocabulary. When it came around to my turn, I read, translated, and justified.
>
> He backed up, "Wait! Why did you translate that word like that?"
>
> "That's what I found in BDB (Brown-Drivers-Briggs)."
>
> "Well, are they right?"
>
> Dr Fox forced us to examine and understand the context clearly. If BDB offered a definition that didn't fit the context, we had to know. Moreover, we had to generalize what the word meant from its other occurrences in the Bible. If BDB generalized a definition that didn't work in other contexts, we had to know. So "looking up" a word in the dictionary didn't mean reading the first line and gleaning the definition, it meant researching the rest of the lemma to look critically at how BDB came to that definition.

Granted one cannot start hearing a given text without a premise, however—and against the new fad of "reader response criticism" that became a basis of entitlement for each and every one without any real possibility of check—one is to assess the *validity* of one's premise in the "matter" (*dabar*) of the text one is hearing. One such premise, which is unacceptable by and to any "theology," is that it is the *same* scriptural Hebrew word *'elohim* that refers to either God or gods, with no ifs, ors, ands or buts.[18] Another example is how Israelis, including Arab Israelis who, given the circumstances, are bound by the modern Hebrew spoken in Israel, have to go around the same pronunciation of two words that are totally different in script even in modern Hebrew: *'et* עֵת (time, moment) and *'et* אֵת (with). Due to the fact that Israeli Hebrew was conceived by European Jews who are not able to correctly pronounce the ע pronouncing it instead as an א, the speaker has to undergo the following

18 I am always stunned by the double standard of many, mainly European Christian, theologians who insist on using the Hebrew *Adonay* instead of "the Lord" in their writings and at conferences out of deference toward—or to cajole—their contemporary Jews. It is amazing that they do not do the same when referring to the Hebrew *Elohim*. In acting the way they do, they are no better than the Witnesses of Jehovah who really believe that *Jehovah*—and in this pronunciation—is actually the factual "name" of the scriptural God in the same way as Paul or Nadim is my actual name. In both instances, the proponents have their own agenda.

circumvolution in communication and add "with a ע, pronounced ayin," or "with an א, pronounced aleph." The first and only time I heard that was when I was visiting Israel and riding with a Palestinian in his car while he was on the phone. Now the Arab Palestinian could well differentiate between the two pronunciations in Arabic but, because he was speaking modern Hebrew, he was bound to follow "the rules" though it sounded totally ludicrous to me.

The second, more serious example, is the case of Thomas Thompson. Although a doctoral student with an exceptional record, he was time and again ostracized for his views at both Roman Catholic and Protestant institutions of higher learning, in the United States as well as in Europe, and was barred from positions at universities. Of note is the rejection of his doctoral dissertation at the University of Tübingen, Germany because it contravened the "doctrine" of the church and he was accused of "biblical minimalism."[19] For many years he had to continue his research and publications as an independent scholar while earning his living as a high-school teacher, janitor, and house painter. Ultimately, he found a haven in academia in Denmark through Niels Peter Lemche whom he befriended at a conference in 1990. He landed a professorial position at the University of Copenhagen until his retirement. He still lives in Denmark and is a naturalized Danish citizen. One would think we are still living under the "Holy Inquisition" for the defense of the "faith"—a euphemism for "our doctrine." Mind you, Thompson was ostracized by Roman Catholics and Protestants alike, and even by Israelis during his one-year stay in Jerusalem.

The third example is the case of the Irish Dominican biblical scholar Thomas L. Brodie. Upon publication in 2012 of his latest book *Beyond the Quest for the Historical Jesus: Memoir of a Discovery*, in which he relates how he came about discovering the non-historicity of the Jesus of the Gospels, he was removed from his teaching position at the Dominican Biblical Institute in

19 Another "ism" tag coined by the "scholarly" intelligentsia.

Limerick which he helped set up and where he had taught many generations of seminarians and scholars. Then he was indicted by a committee of scholars of the Dominican Order most probably on a doctrinal, rather than scholarly, basis as is usually the case in "ecclesiastical" tribunals.

In all three cases, the "judgment" was emitted on the authority of consensus which amounts to the classic "Everybody knows that," "It is well known that," "It is evident that," or, in the aphoristic words of Thomas Thompson himself, "When everyone is agreed on something, it is probably wrong" and "in our fields, if all are in agreement, it signifies that no one is trying to falsify the theory: an essential step in any scientific argument."[20]

To end on a positive note, the good news for my proposed and hoped for Korean, Vietnamese, and Native American scholars, is that they would not have to worry about academic positions and judgmental "Christian scholarly consensus"[21] and thus would hopefully act as "slaves of the scriptural God" who set them free from the oppression of "institutions" that pay lip service to academic freedom. Those committed scholars will not have even an "alma mater" to which they will have to commit in word and in (monetary) deed in order to perpetuate it as an institution "where moth and rust consume and where thieves break in and steal" (Mt 6:19), but rather will commit themselves to serve the scriptural God who resides in a place "where neither moth nor rust consumes and where thieves do not break in and steal." (v.20)

---

20 Greg Doudna, "Is Josephus's John the Baptist Passage a Chronologically Dislocated Story of the Death of Hyrcanus II? in *Biblical Narratives, Archaeology and Historicity: Essays In Honour of Thomas L. Thompson,* 2019, p.119 fn.

21 Pun intended since the tradition in the West is that any scholarly consensus regarding the Bible and Christian doctrine is under the aegis of Christian "luminaries."

About the Author

The V. Rev. Dr. Paul Nadim Tarazi has been teaching Scripture for fifty years. His teaching ministry has included a full-time professorship at St Vladimir's Orthodox Theological Seminary in Crestwood, New York, as well as adjunct positions at Holy Cross Greek Orthodox School of Theology in Brookline, Massachusetts, and the St. John of Damascus Institute of Theology in Balamand, Lebanon. His work covers the full range of scriptural studies in Old and New Testaments, Biblical Hebrew and Greek, Academic Arabic, and Homiletics. He has been a guest lecturer at numerous universities and institutions in the United States and Canada, as well as Australia, Chile, Estonia, Finland, Greece, Israel, Jordan, Palestine, Romania, Serbia, and Syria, and has represented the Antiochian Orthodox Church at various ecumenical gatherings.

Fr. Paul is the author of a three-volume Introduction to the Old Testament, a four-volume Introduction to the New Testament, Galatians: A Commentary, I Thessalonians: A Commentary, Land and Covenant and The Rise of Scripture. His work in the Chrysostom Bible series includes Genesis: A Commentary, Philippians: A Commentary, Romans: A Commentary, Colossians & Philemon: A Commentary, 1 Corinthians: A Commentary, 2 Corinthians: A Commentary, Ezekiel: A Commentary, Joshua: A Commentary, Isaiah: A Commentary, Jeremiah: A Commentary, Hebrews: A Commentary, The Pastorals: A Commentary and Ephesians & 2 Thessalonians: A Commentary. His Audio Bible Commentaries on the books of the Old and New Testament are available online through the Orthodox Center for the Advancement of Biblical Studies (OCABS).

Fr. Paul was born in Jaffa, Palestine, moved to Cairo, Egypt and then to Beirut, Lebanon, where he studied at the Christian Brothers French School prior to attending the Jesuit University

School of Medicine in Beirut. He pursued theological studies at the Orthodox Theological Institute in Bucharest, Romania where he received his Th.D. degree in New Testament in 1975. He was ordained to the holy priesthood in the United States in 1976 and served as pastor of parishes in Connecticut and New York. He currently lives in St. Paul, Minnesota.

CPSIA information can be obtained
at www.ICGtesting.com
Printed in the USA
BVHW051558170223
658736BV00021B/1294/J